THE RESTORATION THEATRE

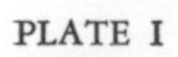
PLATE I

BETTERTON AND MRS. BARRY IN HAMLET
The Garrick Club

[*front*

THE RESTORATION THEATRE

By

MONTAGUE SUMMERS

Editor of The Nonesuch *Dryden*, *Congreve*, *Wycherley*, etc.

HUMANITIES PRESS

New York

1964

First published 1934 by
Routledge & Kegan Paul Ltd.

Reprinted 1964 by
HUMANITIES PRESS, INC.
303 Park Avenue South
New York 10, N. Y.

Library of Congress Catalog Card No. 64-14679

Printed in U.S.A. by
NOBLE OFFSET PRINTERS, INC.
NEW YORK 3, N. Y.

TO

SIR JOHN COLLINGS SQUIRE

CONTENTS

LIST OF ILLUSTRATIONS

INTRODUCTION

The following seven chapters, although comprising a detached study and entirely complete in themselves, may also be taken as the first Part or instalment of an extensive work upon the Restoration Stage, 1660–1700, which with many intervals and lengthy interruptions has engaged me during the last forty years.

In 1893, when I was first beginning my collections, the Restoration dramatists were very generally ignored, and even among professed scholars the period excited but puisne and lukewarm interest, an indifference, indeed, which it would scarcely be too much to say often amounted to positive aversion.

There were, it is true, some notable exceptions. Sir Edmund Gosse gave us many brilliant sympathetic studies of Congreve, Otway, and others, which in these days of the arid pedantry of the costive colon and comma school are a delight and a refreshment most welcome to read. Mr. G. Thorn-Drury, K.C., was known for his intensive study of Restoration poets, his acute scholarship, the treasures of his fine library. Mr. R. W. Lowe had written a monograph on Thomas Betterton, which—minor faults though it may have and inaccuracies—is alive with true enthusiasm and remains a piece of very real value and solid worth.

In 1911, during which year I was paying frequent visits to Stratford-upon-Avon, that ripe scholar and great Elizabethan, Arthur Henry Bullen, often used to discuss with me my note-books and outlined chapters for a History of the Restoration Drama, a book he was generously anxious should be issued by his own Press. However, I was diffident. I felt that my work was not as yet sufficiently shaped, that more research was necessary before I could put it into its ultimate and acceptable form. Bullen was reluctant to agree, but when I suggested that I should meanwhile edit for him some of the more neglected Restoration dramatists he at once gladly entered into the ancillary scheme. There had been reprints of Etherege by Nimmo in 1888, and of Vanbrugh by Lawrence and Bullen himself in 1893, but it was felt that neither Verity who undertook Etherege, nor W. C. Ward who was responsible for Vanbrugh, had quite that knowledge of the Restoration theatre which is the only outcome of long and concentrated study in difficult places, but which is none the less an essential equipment for the editor of Restoration plays.

In passing, I would pay a meed of tribute to the Mermaid Series, particularly to the Mermaid Series of the older days, when such men as Havelock Ellis, John Addington Symonds, Edmund Gosse, Arthur Symons were writing the Introductions to that array of volumes clothed in familiar green or brown, a series for which we must always be grateful, and which even if it were but for these masterly essays and for long association will always have a warm corner in our hearts. Although unexpurgated, the texts of the Mermaid were modernized for general reading, and the stage-directions adopted were those which had unfortunately been tinkered at and rewritten.

F. C. Brown's *Elkanah Settle His Life and Works,* published in December, 1910, is a painstaking but singularly frigid and jejune thesis. It is a work, so to speak, of surface dimensions. There is no background such as is essential in the study of Settle, who so continually clashed and re-clashed with his contemporaries, as he was jostled from political pillar to poetical post. In form this monograph smacks over much of the spirit or rather lack of spirit we too justly associate with such German studies as Edmund Plückhahn's *Die Bearbeitung ausländischer Stoffe im englischen Drama am Ende des* 17. *Jahrhunderts dargelegt an Sir Charles Sedley's : The Mulberry Garden und Bellamira or The Mistriss,* 1904; or Otto Auer's *Ueber einige Dramen Nathaniel Lee's mit besonderer Berücksichtigung seiner Beziehungen zum französischen heroisch-galanten Roman,* of the same year; or Walter Geiersbach's *Nathaniel Lee's Zeittragödien und ihre Vorläufer im Drama Englands,* 1907; laborious, comatose, and arid dissertations. A recent publication, *English Restoration Drama,* by Martin Ellehauge, Copenhagen, 1933, proves entirely valueless. The writer does not seem to be barely acquainted with those authorities who have dealt with the theatre of Charles II.

Bullen drew up with me a long programme of Restoration playwrights, bonny Mrs. Behn, Sedley, Shadwell, Congreve, Wycherley, Otway, Dryden, and many more. That Aphra Behn should come first both my old friend and myself were agreed, but whilst the six volumes comprising her works were in preparation I published with The Shakespeare Head Press Buckingham's *The Rehearsal,* a play which we both had so often laughed over and enjoyed. This appeared in 1914.

Mrs. Behn was well on her way. Ample notes were accumulating for Sedley and Shadwell. Unhappily the outbreak of that world catastrophe, the Great War, wrecked our plans. Mrs. Behn was published in 1915, but in 1920, when we were about to resume our dramatists Arthur Henry Bullen died.

In 1921 and 1922 I published two volumes of Restoration

Plays with Jonathan Cape, and incontinently there were signs of a great awakening of interest in the Restoration theatre. I remember well that when I sent him a volume of Restoration Plays, before which I had had the honour of placing his name, Edmund Gosse wrote to me: "You have opened the doors of the Restoration theatre, and the crowds are already beginning to press in," on which I can but comment that though the compliment be perhaps the praise of a too generous friendship, the truth of the presage is certainly approved.

In 1919 was founded the Phoenix Society for the adequate presentation of the plays of the older dramatists. In May, 1916, the Stage Society had revived Congreve's *The Double-Dealer,* a production which so far as existing circumstances would permit was given on the lines of the original presentation more than two and a quarter centuries before. The conventional nineteenth century mode of playing "old comedy"—the "School for Scandal way" as it was called—was entirely abandoned, and this revival together with the subsequent productions of *Love for Love, The Way of the World,* and Vanbrugh's *The Provok'd Wife,* culminated in the formation of The Phoenix. During my connection with The Phoenix we produced three plays by Dryden, two plays by Congreve, and a play apiece by Wycherley, Otway, and Buckingham. It is, of course, common knowledge how great an impetus these performances gave to the study of Restoration drama, and how they bore rich fruit in the many revivals which have proved so successful in the popular theatre.

Those were busy years of hard practical work, but in 1923 I edited Congreve for the Nonesuch Press, and this was followed in 1924 by Wycherley, in 1926 by Otway, in 1932 by Dryden's Dramatic Works for the same house, a tale of seventeen volumes. In 1927 I published a five volume edition of Shadwell's Complete Works with the Fortune Press, for which House in 1928 I also edited the important *Roscius Anglicanus* of Betterton's old prompter, John Downes.

These editorial labours of necessity seriously interrupted any concentration upon my *History of the Restoration Stage,* although they were indeed very largely auxiliary and supplementary to this study. As was inevitable, once the Restoration dramatists had attracted attention there began a steady flow of books dealing with the theatre of Charles II under various aspects. These, not to be too particular, are perhaps best summed up in Martial's line,

Sunt bona, sunt quaedam mediocria, sunt mala plura.

It is significant indeed to remark upon the number of cheap editions and cheaper studies of Congreve which have appeared since October, 1923. *Imita bene*! One cannot help feeling, however, that in view of the biography of Sir Edmund Gosse such a work as Mr. D. Crane Taylor's *William Congreve,* 1931, is entirely superfluous, and worse than superfluous, an opinion which apparently the reviewers fully shared. It is difficult again to see how the publication of such a rehash as *Brawny Wycherley,* 1930, by Willard Connely is to be justified from any point of view. The conveyances of Mr. Connely are ample—and unacknowledged. Mr. Connely advances one new theory (originally, I believe, suggested by Mr. G. Thorn-Drury) that Wycherley visited Spain; "the rest of the book," I quote from *The Times Literary Supplement,* 29th May, 1930, "is merely what the French call *vulgarisation.* Not only is there no new insight into the man, his work, or his time, but the whole of the old material which is used is served up so as to make it repulsive where it does not dull through familiarity."

As I am often asked if I purpose to edit any other of the Restoration dramatists it may not be impertinent to state that I have for some years been engaged—but slowly, I fear—upon editions of Southerne and Ravenscroft. Southerne I undertook at the express desire of Sir Edmund Gosse, and I feel it a pious duty to offer my work to the Memory of that greatest of critics and kindest of friends. One comedy of Ravenscroft's I have already printed—a dozen years ago now. I have also in the press two of Elkanah Settle's most representative tragedies.

But how much remains to be done! Nat Lee, I am glad to say, is safe in the hands of my friend Miss Maclean. Crowne, D'Urfey, Banks, Mountford, Sir Robert Howard, Davenant (here is a fine field), Colley Cibber, George Powell, Wilson; the ladies, Mrs. Manley, the philosophical Mrs. Trotter, and the fat Mrs. Pix, all need attention. Invaluable also would be a series of reprints of such plays as *The Villain, The Fatal Jealousie, The Reformation, The Revenge, The Slighted Maid, Flora's Vagaries, The Lover's Luck,* and a score beside, collected after the manner of old Dodsley, to make an incomparable *corpus* of Restoration drama.

Something of this kind were far more acceptable, far more useful than yet another derivative Congreve, yet another anæmically second-hand Otway!

It is not without purpose and design then that I have thought it better that the first part of my work to be published should be that section dealing with what may be termed the physical conditions of the Restoration theatre, the practical machinery of that stage for which the dramatists under Charles II and his brother were writing their plays.

Without some knowledge, some visualization of Restoration stage conditions the reader of a play by Dryden, Congreve, Otway, or any contemporary, must often find himself hopelessly puzzled and at sea, whilst a piece of stagecraft which is in itself singularly delicate and adroit will appear consumedly clumsy and awkwardly contrived. Unless he is familiar with his theatre the editor of a Restoration dramatist cannot but trip, blunder badly, and come to grief.

Actually this is what has happened. Passing over such deplorable ineptitudes as the identification of the sculptures representing Dorset Garden in the first quarto, 1673, of Settle's *The Empress of Morocco,* as illustrations of Lincoln's Inn Fields in 1675, an absurdity which occurs in a recent reprint (1926) of the *Works of Rochester—and others,* we find an editor who sets out to be far more serious writing of a " carpenter's scene " with " a painted back cloth set immediately within the proscenium " in 1668, and hence inserting in a comedy stage-directions corresponsive with his own misconception and mistakes.

We are the less surprised, then, in such a book as *The Private Life of Mrs. Siddons* (1933) by Naomi Royde-Smith to meet with a good many gross blunders. For example, the account of the eighteenth-century alteration of Southerne's *The Fatal Marriage; or, The Innocent Adultery* is both confusing and confused. We are told (p. 113) that " The scene is '*A Street*', in a town (on the sea-board of Bohemia for all we know), in any case, a cosmopolitan sort of place ". This is curious in view of the fact that it is distinctly stated the Scene of Southerne's tragedy is laid at Brussels. In Mrs. Inchbald's edition, 1808, *The British Theatre,* vol. vii, p. 6, after the *Dramatis Personae* of *Isabella* we find: SCENE—*Brussels.* In a few of the very late reprints such as John Cumberland's *Isabella; or, The Fatal Marriage,* 1825, the locality *Brussels* is omitted after the list of characters, but Miss Royde-Smith is at some pains to inform us that she has followed the original text—she speaks (p. 112) of " the musty pages of a seventeenth century prompt-book "—and there are moreover allusions to Brussels in the course of the play itself, in scenes which remain even after adaptation. I will quote from the late acting copy. Act III, Scene 3, Villeroy at his marriage receives a letter announcing that his brother has been taken ill whilst journeying to assist at the nuptials:

> Suddenly taken, on the road to Brussels,
> To do us honour.

Again, Act IV, Scene 1, *The Street,* when Biron and Belford have just arrived, the former says to his fellow-traveller: "We are got home at last . . . what I can command in Brussels, you shall find your own."

On pp. 121–2 of Miss Naomi Royde-Smith's book we have: "The curtain falls. When it rises once more our mind's eye shows us one of those small inset almost secret pictures the imagination of William Poel has reset for us when reviving plays of this or a slightly earlier period.

"Southerne's own stage direction runs:—

"*Scene drawn, shews Biron asleep on a Couch. Isabella comes in to him.*

"Even a reading of this scene from the yellowed pages of the little volume in which it is printed, with the long ſ and the plentiful besprinkling of capital letters of the seventeenth century is enough to conjure up the dim-lit stage, the heavy looping of curtains, the little inset space holding the couch and its sleeper and the chair into which Isabella is presently to fall . . ." All of which fine description is, I fear, just nonsense. Presumably Miss Royde-Smith refers to the first edition of *The Fatal Marriage,* 1694 (advertised as published, *London Gazette,* 19th–22nd March, 1693–4), as "the little volume", which seems a highly misleading description of a quarto play. And how petty are "the yellowed pages", "the long ſ", and "the plentiful besprinkling of capital letters"! However the main point is that the curtain did not fall, and that *Scene drawn* does not imply "one of those small inset almost secret pictures". Miss Royde-Smith would have been well advised to have studied the engraving of this actual scene in Tonson's edition of *The Fatal Marriage,* 12mo, 1735. The fact is the lady knows nothing of the staging of plays in either the seventeenth or eighteenth centuries, which seems something of a handicap for anyone who essays to write about Mrs. Siddons.

We learn (p. 111) that when Mrs. Siddons appeared as Isabella at Drury Lane in October, 1782, "Sheridan . . . followed up the shortened tragedy with William Whitehead's farce *A Trip to Scarborough.*" This sounds odd as *A Trip to Scarborough* is usually considered to be by Sheridan. Probably the farce intended is William Whitehead's *A Trip to Scotland,* first produced at Drury Lane on 6th January, 1770, as an after-piece to a performance of *The Fair Penitent.*

On p. 27 Miss Royde-Smith tells us she rejected *Rolla* and *Pizarro* "plays in which Kemble's part predominated". I do not know that Kemble had much to do with *Rolla.* In Reynold's operatic drama in three acts *The Virgin of the Sun,* founded on

Kotzebue's *Rolla* with some suggestion from Marmontel, and produced at Covent Garden, 31st January, 1812, Young acted Rolla. There is a *Rolla; or, The Peruvian Hero* by Monk Lewis, 8vo, 1799, and a *Rolla*; *or, The Virgin of the Sun* by Benjamin Thompson, 8vo, 1801 (included in the *German Theatre,* vol. iv), both from Kotzebue, but neither of these dramas was performed. There are also unacted versions, *The Virgin of the Sun,* from Kotzebue by Anna Plumptre, 8vo, 1799, and by James Lawrence, 8vo, 1799. Benjamin Thompson's *Pizarro; or, The Death of Rolla,* from the German of Augustus von Kotzebue, 1800 (*German Theatre,* vol. iv) was also unacted.

Perhaps Miss Royde-Smith became a little weary "when almost a hundred volumes had been searched" (p. 44). On p. 69 she speaks of "Perdita" Johnson, probably meaning Perdita Robinson. On p. 73 we learn that Mrs. Siddons "was allotted the part of Lady Anne when Garrick gave *Richard III* for his own farewell performance". Actually, of course, the farewell performance of Garrick was as Don Felix in Mrs. Centlivre's *The Wonder, A Woman keeps a Secret* at Drury Lane, on 10th June, 1776. Mrs. Yates was his Violante. The play bill "The Last Time of the Company's performing this Season" is extant and has been reproduced. Mrs. Siddons is *not* in the cast. Garrick had performed *Richard III* for the last time on the preceding 5th June, when Mrs. Siddons was the Lady Anne. But Richard III was not his farewell performance, and it is well known that for his last appearance the great actor deliberately chose a favourite rôle in a favourite comedy, lest upon such an occasion one of his great tragic parts should overtax his emotions and his strength.

On p. 26 we hear of "the musical comedy of *Inkle and Yarico* (in which the part of a little black savage called Wowski was played by Mr. Martyn)". *Inkle and Yarico* by George Colman the younger was produced at the Haymarket on 4th August, 1787. Wowski was one of the favourite rôles of that fair singer Mrs. Martyr (not Mr. Martyn), who also excelled as Flora in *Hob in the Well.* The portrait of Mrs. Martyr shows her as a most strikingly beautiful woman.

These inaccuracies evince the necessity for a writer to gain a clear grasp of theatrical detail. But Miss Naomi Royde-Smith does not forget to tell us of the Blessed John Kemble, of the pilgrimages to the Martyr's shrine, of the Relic of his Holy Hand venerated in the Church of S. Francis Xavier at Hereford. She quotes (pp. 58–62) a perfectly delightful ballad, wherefore much may be forgiven her.

An altogether more flagrant and reprehensible case occurs in

On Dramatic Method, "being the Clark lectures for 1930 by Harley Granville-Barker," London, 1931. His fourth chapter, pp. 113–155, Mr. Granville-Barker devotes to "Wycherley and Dryden". He soon makes it apparent that he knows much more about the Restoration stage than any of the stupid fellows who were writing their comedies and tragedies under Charles II and his immediate successors. In fact their technique is deplorable. They are not skilled dramatists. I concede, they are not skilled dramatists as judged by the standard of stage conditions in the twentieth century, electrical lighting, revolving stages, and the rest. But I submit that in reference to their own stage they were indeed most adroit and adept. Mr. Granville-Barker will not have it so. The Restoration dramatists have no technique. The fact of the matter is that Mr. Granville-Barker has no knowledge of the Restoration theatre. And Chapter IV of *On Dramatic Method* is neither very intelligent nor very discerning. I might justly use harder words, for the Phoenix revival of *The Country-Wife* in 1924 amply demonstrated how finished was the technique, how admirable the stagecraft of William Wycherley, in whose dispraise Mr. Granville-Barker is particularly voluble and jocular. I allow that *Love in a Wood* is not so neatly cut in parts as the later comedy, but to separate a stage-direction, entirely appropriate, fitting, and practical in its own context, a busy crowded scene, and misinterpreting it, to ridicule the dramatist's phrase, seems disingenuous, trivial, and altogether unfair.

Is it too much to hope that this present study may prevent a repetition of that sort of thing? Perhaps I am over sanguine. I do not for a moment wish to seem to pretend that I have elucidated all the points in Restoration production, that I have cleared up every crux. There are several stage-directions which appear to me very ambiguous. I have met with none which read sheer nonsense. Another factor in the case which must not be left out of consideration is that often the quartos are carelessly printed, and in some instances the proofs cannot have been corrected by the writers, nor indeed by any save a hackney hand. What this implies in the printing of a play perhaps only an editor of long standing knows.

Chapter VII of the present work gives some very particular attention to Costume in the Restoration Theatre. Here I have tried to show that the dresses worn upon the stage of Charles II, if mayhap incongruous, bizarre, and fantastical, were at any rate elaborate and effective. It is, I think, often believed that the actors and actresses of Betterton's day paid no heed at all to their costumes, and it is not impertinent to insist that such was very far from being the case. Even the minor dramatists are quite precise in their directions. Thus Thomas Southland, who was almost certainly the author of *The Ungrateful Favourite,* quarto, 1664, unacted, has in his Prologue : " Enter a Drunkard, a Morice-dancer, a Buffoon, a Bawd, a Whore, and a She-Gypsie ; they dance an Antick. Which done, Enter *Tragedy* in state, in a Crimson Robe held up by two Roman Gladiators, a Crown upon her head, a Scepter in one hand, and a Ponyard in the other, at whose entrance the Dancers all start back." Richard Flecknoe, also, in his *Erminia ; or, The Chaste Lady,* quarto, 1661, and duodecimo, 1665, writes a very explicit note concerning the costumes of his tragi-comedy, which incidentally may never have been seen on the stage : " *The Habits, the ancient Military Attire, for the more Heroick Parts : for the rest, the* Toga, *or Civil Vest, wide sleev'd, and loosely flowing to the knees, silver'd Buskins, &c. far more graceful and becoming then* Querpo, *especially for* Cyrena *represented in mans Attire.*"

In an Appendix I have given Robert Gould's *The Play-House,* a piece of the last rarity, which in spite of its verjuice and venom cannot fail to be of interest and value to the student of the Restoration Theatre. This satire has not to my knowledge been reprinted since 1709, and for more than two centuries it would appear to be almost entirely neglected and unknown. I have furnished explanatory notes.

I add Chapter V of Sam Vincent's *The Young Gallant's Academy,* a book which is none other than Dekker's *The Gull's Horn Book* brought up to date (1674), more or less. The instructions to the young gallant " *how to behave himself in the* Play-house ", Dorset Garden, are a lively comment upon the manners of the day.

Since I was so intimately connected with the Phoenix Society for the Production of Old Plays, concerning whose activities there has been no inconsiderable amount of misunderstanding and misstatement, it was warmly represented to me that a clear and exact outline of the aims of the Society would prove useful, whilst a record of the revivals could not but supply the theatrical historian with necessary material otherwise not easy to collect. Accordingly I have written a short note upon The Phoenix with a full chronicle of the productions of the Society. This will, I think, answer the present purpose. The story in detail I am telling elsewhere.

In subsequent studies of the Restoration Theatre I design to devote one volume to the Actors and Actresses of the period. Another will deal with the minor dramatists, men of one or two plays. Another surveys politics and personalities in the theatre.

I also intend to issue a Bibliography of Restoration Plays from 1660–1700, which, compiled many years ago, I have but recently revised.

In the Introductions and Explanatory Notes to the seven dramatists whose works I have edited much has already necessarily been said concerning the technique of a Restoration play and the practical stagecraft both of the Theatre Royal and Dorset Garden.

In 1912 and 1913 Bullen published from the Shakespeare Head Press *The Elizabethan Playhouse and Other Studies* by Dr. W. J. Lawrence, two Series wherein several features of Restoration staging were incidentally discussed.

Professor G. C. D. Odell's *Shakespeare from Betterton to Irving*, 2 volumes, 1921, deals at considerable length with the Age of Betterton. Professor Odell is always interesting, suggestive, and for the most part candid in his argument and clear-cut in his conclusions. Once or twice at most have I found his purview a little confused (as it seemed to me) and lacking in precision,—especially perhaps is this the case in reference to the number, use, and position of the proscenium doors,—but even thus on those points where I am constrained to differ from him I have only done so after traversing the ground a second, and often a third time, with especial cogitation and care.

I must not omit to mention here two wholly admirable books of the very first importance, indispensable to any intelligent study of the Restoration stage, Sir Frederick Bridge's *Shakespearean Music in the Plays and Early Operas*, 1923, and Professor E. J. Dent's *The Foundations of English Opera*, 1928. It is almost impossible to speak too highly of these works.

Would there not be something lacking, too, if I did not honour the memory of old John Genest whose *Some Account of the English Stage* will assuredly never be superseded, and as yet has not even been approached?

With regard to the Illustrations, in the first place I have to offer my loyal duty and humble thanks to His Majesty the King for Gracious Permission to give from the Royal Collection at Hampton Court the triple portrait upon one canvas of John Lacy, the famous comedian, in three rôles.

I also have to thank the Warden and Fellows of All Souls College, Oxford, for permission to reproduce Sir Christopher Wren's sectional design for the second Theatre Royal, 1674; the Authorities of the Bodleian Library, Oxford, for permission to reproduce a page from the MS. prompt book of Settle's play *The Lady's Triumph*; the Authorities of the British Museum for affording facilities to photograph rare engravings; Mrs. Gabrielle

Enthoven, O.B.E., for allowing reproductions of engravings from her famous collection; the Committee of the Garrick Club for permission to reproduce the painting of Betterton and Mrs. Barry in the Closet Scene, *Hamlet*; Sir Barry Jackson for permission to reproduce a photograph of the Court Scene of *Marriage A-la-Mode,* as revived at the Birmingham Repertory Theatre in April, 1928; the Director and Authorities of the Victoria and Albert Museum, South Kensington, for permission to reproduce the miniature of Anne Quin, as also for permission to photograph two Sculptures from the exceptionally fine copy of Settle's *The Empress of Morocco,* 4to, 1673, in the Dyce Library; Kenneth W. Sanderson, Esq., for the generous loan of and permission to reproduce the scarce mezzotint of Mrs. Bracegirdle in his Collection; the President and Fellows of Sion College for permission to reproduce a page of the printed prompt-book in the Sion College Library of Shirley's *The Sisters,* 8vo, 1652–3, marked by Charles Booth, the prompter of the Theatre Royal, for a revival of 1668–1671; the Provost and Fellows of Worcester College, Oxford, for permission to reproduce the frontispiece of Duffett's farce, *The Empress of Morocco,* 4to, 1674, William Harris in the title-rôle, from the copy in the Library of Worcester College.

It is my pleasure to thank most gratefully for their particular kindnesses Mrs. Gabrielle Enthoven, Mr. Bache Matthews, and Sir Charles Oman, who went to no small trouble to afford me facilities and secure me permission to reproduce illustrations for this book.

As I have already said, from first to last I have been engaged upon the particular study of the Restoration period for no less than forty years, and whatever else I may have learned or may have missed in that time one lesson I have been most straitly taught, and this in the phrase of Herodotus is: *Τὰ καλὰ πάλαι εὕρηται.*

MONTAGUE SUMMERS.

THE RESTORATION THEATRE

CHAPTER I

ANNOUNCEMENTS AND ADVERTISEMENTS

THE INTRODUCTION

The Candles lighted, before the Curtain's drawn, Enter one of the Actors, another (suppos'd no Actor) calling after him.

1. Hark you, hark you, whither away so fast?
2. Why to the Theater, 'tis past three o' th Clock, and the Play's ready to begin.

Richard Flecknoe, *The Damoiselles A La Mode.*
A Comedy. London: Printed for the Author, 1667.

By the same aid, the Stage invites her friends,
And kindly tells the banquet she intends;
Thither from real life the many run,
With SIDDONS weep, or laugh with ABINGDON;
Pleas'd in fictitious joy or grief, to see
The mimic passion with their own agree;
To steal a few enchanted hours away
From care, and drop the curtain on the day.

CRABBE, *The Newspaper.*

However ingenious, elaborated, and enticing it has become in its latest developments there are perhaps few things more essentially conservative than the art of advertisement, whilst theatrical advertising is necessarily as old as the theatre itself. Thus in England during the Middle Ages the performances of miracle-plays were announced throughout the country-side by *vexillatores* or bearers of bannerols, who were often accompanied by a noise of minstrels. This was the case with the *Ludus Conventriae* and the Croxton Sacrament play; the Chester cycles were proclaimed up and down the streets by the Town Crier on 23rd April, S. George. Frequently these notices were delivered in good set form, and in order that they might be learned the more easily by the vexillator they were versified in galloping rhymes. So *The Castell of Perseverance,* which must be dated not later than the middle of the reign of Henry VI,[1] has a prologue, or rather a poetized circular to be published verbally by two advance-agents, and after a fanfare of trumpets to collect a crowd, the action was described, and know ye

> These parcellis in propyrtes we purpose us to playe,
> This day sevenenyt, be-fore you in syth,
> At N[2] on the grene, in ryall a-ray.
> Ye, haste you thanne thedyrward, syris, hendly in hyth,[3]
> All goode neyboris, ful specyaly we you pray,
> And loke that ye be there be-tyme, luffely and lyth,
> For we schul be onward be underne of the day.

If the performance was to conclude by nine o'clock, or well before noon, it must indeed have begun rathe and early.

It is remarkable that this form of advertising plays, the earliest method known in England, endured for several centuries and flourished long after the introduction of the written or printed playbill and placard. In Elizabethan days nothing more surely attracted the folk of a country town to gape and stare than the throb of the drum and the sound of the trumpet which heralded a procession of players through their midst, for as the manager of the touring company remarked to Dr. Primrose, "strollers always have more spectators without doors than within." Even in London at least as late as 1587 drums and trumpets were used to advertise performances, since William Rankins in his *A Mirrour of Monsters*[4] makes reference to this practice which, however, the puritans and civic authorities very soon prohibited and suppressed so far as their jurisdiction was empowered. In his *A Sermon Preached at Paules Crosse* on 24th August, 1578, John Stockwood[5] cries: "Wyll not a fylthye playe, wyth the blast of a Trumpette, sooner call thyther a thousande, than an houres tolling of a Bell, bring to the Sermon a hundred?" This, however, does not allude to a histrionic procession through the streets with blare of clarions, but rather to the custom of sounding from the door in the cockloft surmounting the topmost story of the theatre three trumpet-calls at set intervals as a final warning to belated or hesitant playgoers. The address, "Ad Lectorem" before Dekker's *Satiromastix,* 4to, 1602, commences: "In steed of the trumpets sounding thrice, before the play begin, it shall not be amisse (for him that will read)" to note certain errata in the printed text. At the beginning of *The Poetaster*, acted in 1601, "After the Second Sounding," Envy arises through a trap in the midst of the stage and delivers a bitter oration. As he concludes we have "The Third Sounding", and an "armed Prologue" rushes in setting his foot on the head of the monster who is disappearing down below. Many other examples might be cited. That the parade with drum and trumpets was not usual, or rather not permitted in London, is shown by the fact that as part of their outfit in February, 1600, Henslowe bought a drum and two trumpets for the Admiral's Men " when to go into the country ".[6] It will be readily remembered how Parolles averred Captain Dumain had " led the drum before the English tragedians ".[7]

Throughout the provinces the custom of the Thespian drummer parading the streets and bawling out the programme of the evening's entertainment at the local theatre or booth or barn with appropriate encomiums and *fioriture* persisted until the dawn of the nineteenth century, perhaps, in the case of certain strollers we might say even later.[8] Occasionally handbills were distributed, and if the company was sufficiently numerous two individuals were employed, one to row-didi-dow upon the drum, the other to proclaim the divertissement in no uncertain voice.[9] In *The Memoirs of the Countess of Derby* (1797)[10] it is related that in the case of actors on tour not many printed bills were available owing to the need of strictest economy, but to atone for this deficiency they were wont to distribute the few sheets that could be spared for each place " by beat of Drum, in order that their arrival and intentions may be known to every inhabitant. A Drum, on this account, always makes a part of the Property of a Country Company ". So in Hogarth's picture, " Strolling Actresses Dressing in a Barn," among the profusion of properties strawed all out of kelter everywhere can be discerned a trumpet and a mighty drum. The last vestiges of these histrionic processions may even yet be sometimes seen at fair time in villages and smaller market towns, when the travelling circus which has pitched its tents and wagons in the fields or on some open ground hard by parades its tinselled heroines and their liveried squires, its zanies and merry-andrews, its gaudy chariots and caparisoned horses, all its glitter and tawdriness, and thus seeks to ensure a full house to applaud the evening's mime and mummery.

It is common knowledge that in the Elizabethan theatres an hour or two before a performance a flag was hoisted to announce to the public that it was an acting-day. This flag, blazoned with its proper cognizance of a swan, is flying gaily in the famous sketch of the interior of the Swan Theatre,[11] which has very frequently been reproduced from the drawing after Johannes de Witt in Arend van Buchell's commonplace book (*c.* 1596). There are continual references to this custom, and Heywood in his *An Apology for Actors* (1612), mistranslates Ovid's " Tunc neque marmoreo pendebant vela theatro " (*De Arte Amandi*, i, 103) as:—

In those days from the marble house did waive
No sail, no silken flag, no ensign brave.

Ovid's *velum* is, of course, the awning stretched over the theatre as a protection from the sun, as Propertius similarly says: "Nec sinuosa cavo pendebant vela theatro." [12] Borchard Cnippingius [13] commenting upon this passage of Ovid has: "Vela in theatris umbram faciebant: quod primus omnium invenit Q. Catulus, quum Capitolium dedicaret. Mox Caesar totum forum Romanum intexit." There are also allusions to the circumstance that during Lent when acting surceased, or at such times as a visitation of the plague closed the theatres, the flag was no longer flown. Thus in Middleton's *A Mad World, my Masters* (1604–6), we have: "'Tis Lent in your cheeks; the flag is downe."

It is not generally realized that, in common with many another old tradition, the practice of thus hoisting a flag upon the playhouse roof was maintained in Restoration days, and in the bird's-eye view of the Dorset Garden Theatre as it appears in Lea and Glynn's undated "map of London, Westminster and Southwark" [14] the flag may be discerned at the northern end of the house, bravely unfurling to the breeze. The flag was hoisted for particular performances and shows at least as late as 1699,[15] but the practice appears to have been dying out at the end of the century, and it may, I think, be taken as certain that it was finally discarded just about that time the hour of the play grew later and from afternoon became evening. Yet to-day we have a close parallel. The globe that crowns the Coliseum music-hall in S. Martin's Lane nightly blazes (or used to blaze) a radiant ball of electric fire, a glowing landmark in the West End of London, serving the same purpose as the Bankside flags which notified the public across the river that it was an acting-day.

In France the *affiche* had been utilized as early as 1556,[16] and in England the playbill as a poster must have come into evidence but a little later, since on 23rd February, 1564, the puritanical Edmund Grindal, Bishop of London,[17] in a letter [18] to the Secretary of State, Sir William Cecil, remarks that he has of late noticed "these Histriones, common playours; who now daylye, butt speciallye on holydayes, sett vp bylles, whervnto the youthe resorteth excessively". In *Merry Tales, Wittie Questions and Quick Answeres* (1567), cxxxiii, a story is told of a cheat practised by one Qualitees, who cozened an audience by feigning a performance would be given, and who set up "vpon postes aboute London" bills for "an antycke plaie". In 1577 John Northbrooke, the minister of Henbury, near Bristol, published his fanatical *Treatise against Idlenes, Idle Pastimes, and Playes,* in the course of which he bitterly complains that in London the actors " vse to set vp their billes vpon postes certain dayes before, to admonishe the people to make their resort vnto their theatres, that they may thereby be the better furnished ". Rankins, whose *Mirrour of Monsters* (1587) has already been quoted, reprobates actors " sticking of their bills in London ". Another fanatic is even more irate, and in a letter (Harleian MS. 286, f. 102) addressed to Sir Francis Walsingham, loudly laments that " every day in the weake the players billes are sett up in sondry places of the cittie, some in the name of her Majesties menne, some of thc Earl of Leic^r, some the E. of Oxford, the Lo. Admyralles, and dyvers others: so that when the belles tole to the Lectorer, the trumpetts sound to the stages, whereat the wicked faction of Rome lawgheth for joy, while the godly weepe for sorrowe ". Marston in *The Scourge of Villainy* (1598) has " Go read each post, view what is play'd to-day ".

In the Induction to *A Warning for Faire Women,* 4to, 1599, Tragedy thus indignantly addresses History and Comedy:—

> Ile scourge and lash you both from off the stage,
> T'is you haue kept the Theatres so long,
> Painted in play-bils, upon euery poast,
> That I am scorned of the multitude
> My name prophande.

In *Bartholomew Fair,* first acted in 1614, Sharkwell and Filcher enter with bills of the puppet-play, and Cokes reads the bill aloud.

Again in *The Devil Is An Ass,* produced 1616 (printed in the Second Folio, 1631), I, vi, when Fitzdottrel asks Engine—

> art thou sure
> The play is play'd to-day?

the reply is:

> O here's the bill, Sir:
> I had forgot to give it you.

And we have a stage direction " Hee giues him the Play-bill ". Thus we see that not only were bills set up on posts in prominent places about the city and especially at the playhouse doors,[19] but copies were also made for distribution. On 30th October, 1587, as entered in the Stationers' Register, John Charlwood obtained a licence for " the onely ympryntinge of all manner of billes for players ", but none the less it seems that a number of bills were continually written out by hand, and most certainly in the country all of necessity were thus engrossed.

On 8th September, 1592, Dr. Some, Vice-Chancellor of Cambridge, addressed a complaint to the Privy Council, inasmuch as "certaine light persons, pretending themselves to be her Majesties Plaiers,[20] &c., did take boldness, not onely here to proclaime their Enterludes (by setting up of writings about our college gates) but also actually at Chesterton to play the same".[21] Although the playbill, particularly the written copy, must have been brief and confined to essentials, obviously the title of the piece would be shown in bolder letters than the rest, and it is no doubt to this circumstance that are due such inveigling titles as *Look About You*; *Come, See a Wonder*; *A Mad World, my Masters*; all catch-labels to attract attention and tickle curiosity. The very same device is common enough to-day when revues and lightest fare are given highly allusive and quarter-quibble names to wheedle and entice the vulgar. Later the bills inflated and grew bombastic, farced with flourishing and fustian detail, but this was not until the eighteenth century had dawned, and it would appear not unlikely that in the first place this infection of grandiloquence was caught by the regular houses from the booths and petty motions of Bartlemy Fair.

Flecknoe in his *Miscellania*, 1653 (pp. 141–2), has: "From thence passing on to Black-fryers, and seeing never a *Play-bil* on the Gate, no *Coaches* on the place, nor *Doorkeeper* at the *Play-house* door with his *Boxe* like a *Church-warden*, desiring you to remember the poor *Players*, I cannot but say for *Epilogue* to all the *Playes* were ever acted there:—

> *Poor House, that in dayes of our Grand-sires,*
> *Belongst unto the* Mendiant Fryers[22]:
> *And where so oft in our Fathers dayes*
> *We have seen so many of* Shakspears *Playes,*
> *So many of* Johnsons, Beaumonts, *&* Fletchers.

As we might suppose, when at the Restoration the theatres once more opened their doors with official approval and legislation, the custom of advertising upon the posts was resumed, no doubt with wider scope and in neater design. Yet the formula was simple enough as seems indicated by the Prologue to Tuke's *The Adventures of Five Hours,* produced at Lincoln's Inn Fields, when "*The Prologue Enters with a Play-Bill in his hand, and Reads,* This Day being the 15th of *December,*[23] shall be Acted a New Play, never Plai'd before, call'd *The Adventures of Five Hours*". This appears very scanty information, and obviously the name of the theatre must have been given, but be it noted presumably not the hour of commencement. The reason why this detail, the theatre, is here omitted is that the audience were already seated in the house and the prologue was just beginning, so to make an announcement of the place would have been truly superfluous. To the advertising by the display of a bill on posts in the street there are many references. Thus in *The Wild Gallant,* 4to, 1669, ii, Isabella with a sharp bob at Failer says to him: "Mr. *Failer,* what do you think this Fellow was saying of you? . . . That you were one of the errantest Cowards in Christendom, though you went for one of the Dear Hearts: that your name had been upon more posts than play-bills."

In *Sr Martin Mar-All,* produced at Lincoln's Inn Fields, Thursday, 15th August, 1667, Mrs. Millisent is about to go to the theatre when Sir Martin stupidly blurts out that the piece at the Duke's is a damn'd play and that at the King's e'en as bad, upon which Warner hurriedly intervenes with "There was an ill Play set up, Sir, on the Posts, but I can assure you the Bills are altered since you saw 'um, and now there are two admirable Comedies at both Houses". At the conclusion of *The Rehearsal,* produced at the Theatre Royal, 7th December, 1671 (4to, 1672), when Mr. Bayes in high dudgeon carries off his script crying "And so farewel to this Stage for ever, I gad", the Second Player calmly advises: "Come then, let's set up Bills for another Play: We shall lose nothing by this, I warrant you."[24] In William Chamberlayne's tragi-comedy *Wits Led by the Nose: or, A Poet's Revenge,* acted at the Theatre Royal in 1677,[25] the speaker of the prologue, supposed a country gentleman, comes on before the curtain by a proscenium door and reads a playbill attached to the door as if it were placarded upon a post in the street. He sees the name of the play, and remarks that it has never been acted before. On Monday, 24th March, 1662, Pepys notes: "I went to see if any play was acted, and I found none upon the post, it being Passion week." Thursday, 28th July, 1664, he has: "Dined, after 'Change, at home, and then abroad, and seeing 'The Bondman' upon the posts, . . . I went thither. Then I saw it acted. It is true, for want of practice, they had many of them forgot their parts a little; but Betterton and my poor Ianthe [26] outdo all the world."

Bills were also delivered at the houses of persons of quality and wealthy patrons of the theatre. Thus in Vanbrugh's *The Provok'd Wife* (the second version in which Sir John Brute masquerades not as a Parson but dons the petticoats of a fine lady), Act IV, the scene with the Justice, who inquires of the supposed Woman of Quality, how she passes her mornings, the answer is that after trailing out of bed about two in the afternoon,

"I sit—and yawn for my Breakfast—If it don't come presently I lie down on my Couch, to say my Prayers, while my Maid reads me the Play-Bills." It will be remembered that as late as 1838 when Mr. and Mrs. Curdle vouchsafed to become patrons of Miss Snevellici's bespeak at the Portsmouth Theatre, Mrs. Curdle gave many directions "relative to keeping the places for them, and dusting the seat, and sending two clean bills as soon as they came out".

In *The Library,* Fourth Series, vol. xi, No. 4, March, 1931 (pp. 499–502), Miss Boswell has described and reproduced a bill of *A King, and No King* to be given at the Theatre Royal, on Tuesday, 22nd February, 1687, "Begin[illegible] Exact[ly a]t Four of the Clock."

Dr. W. J. Lawrence in *The Elizabethan Playhouse* (Second Series), Appendix II (pp. 240–1), describes four play-bills discovered among the Verney Papers at Claydon House, comitatu Bucks, two of 1692 and two of 1694. These were the types of bills delivered at patron's house.

All five bills afford the most meagre information; the name of the piece to be acted, the theatre, and the date. The bill of *A King, and No King* is alone in stating the hour of the performance.

It may be noted in passing that Congreve in his Prologue spoken by Joe Haines to Powell's comedy *A Very Good Wife,* produced at Drury Lane in 1692–3, 4to, 1693, speaks of early arrivals in the pit:—

> Now ye, our City Friends, who hither come
> By three a Clock to make sure Elbow-room . . .
> Pray ye be kind, . . .

Early in 1672 a company of French actors paid a visit to London, and although their stay appears to have been short it aroused a good deal of jealousy and ill-feeling at the Duke's house and among Killigrew's company. The latter, indeed, were especially aggrieved. Owing to the disastrous fire of 25th January, 1672, they had been burned out of the Theatre Royal, Bridges Street, and in dire distress they were obliged to take refuge in the Lincoln's Inn Fields theatre which had just been vacated by their rivals. A foreign invasion to boot galled them to the uttermost. Moreover the French comedians were resorting to attractive novelties which drew packed houses. In Paris at this time each theatre used playbills of a different and distinctive colour, red bills being the especial prerogative of the Hôtel de Bourgogne.[27] Now London too saw coloured bills, not merely strangely fascinating by their freshness, but bills of far greater dimensions than the conservative English placards. Little wonder that Dryden writes bitterly in the Prologue which he furnished to Carlell's *Arviragus and Philicia,* revived at Lincoln's Inn Fields about Easter, 1672:—

With sickly Actors and an old House too,
We're match'd with glorious Theatres and new,
And with our Ale-house scenes and Cloaths bare worn
Can neither raise old Plays nor new adorn.
If all these Ills could not undo us quite,
A brisk *French* Troop is grown your dear delight;
Who with broad bloody Bills call you each day
To laugh [illegible] break your Buttons at their Play;
Or see some serious Piece, which we presume
Is fall'n from some incomparable plume . . .

The curious part is that the English managers and actors were not astute enough to take a hint, they neither made their native bills larger nor did they employ scarlet and vermilion. Indeed in the Epilogue to *The Temple of Love,* a Pastoral Opera by Motteux, Haymarket, 7th March, 1706, the beau, satirically girding at foreign attractions, advises:—

Set up some famous Singer of no Fame,
And, tho' she's Dutch, Italianize *her Name.*
What tho' the Singing or the Face affright,
Worse Syrens *get their Twenty Pounds a Night.*
Put out Red-Letter'd Bills, and raise your Price,
You'll Lure a select Audience in a trice.

The name of the author of the play did not find a place upon our English bills until the very end of the seventeenth century, and this innovation was due to circumstances that well might be termed accidental. Writing to Mrs. Steward on 4th March, 1699, Dryden says [28]: "This day was play'd a reviv'd comedy of Mr. Congreve's, call'd *The Double-Dealer,* which was never very takeing. In the play-bill was printed—'Written by Mr. Congreve; with severall expressions omitted.' What kind of expressions those were, you may casily ghcss, if you have seen the Monday's Gazette,[29] wherein is the King's order for the reformation of the stage: but the printing an author's name in a play-bill is a new manner of proceeding, at least in England." It was then, indirectly at least, a consequence of Collier's attack in 1698, *A Short View of the Immorality and Profaneness of the English Stage,* wherein *The Double-Dealer* was heavily abused (p. 64), that a dramatist's name in England first appeared upon the play-bills.

Another result of this ebullition of nasty puritanism was that, as Luttrell records, on Tuesday, 21st May, 1700, the Grand Jury of the City "presented to the court at the old Baily, that for any person to goe to play houses was a publick nusance: and that the putting up bills in and about this citty for playes was an encouragement to vice and prophanesse; and prayed that none be suffered for the future". A week or so after this protest, early in June, the Mayor and Aldermen published an Order forbidding play-house bills to be placarded in any part of the city or the liberties. In the Epilogue, spoken by Joe Haines, to Mrs. Centlivre's first play, *The Perjur'd Husband; or, The Adventures of Venice,* produced in the summer of 1700 at the Theatre Royal, Drury Lane, the following couplet occurs:—

> *Let Magistrates consider 'tis but fitting,*
> *That as they take down Bills, they'd put down Cheating.*

In William Burnaby's *The Ladies Visiting Day,* Lincoln's Inn Fields, December, 1700, Act I, Sir Thrifty Gripe the dour cit of "St. *Magnes* Parish" boasts: "I live soberly, and mind the Main Chance, I never spend a Penny but in Coffee; I sell by a Short Yard, and pull down the Play Bills, to shew my Aversion to the Wickedness that's practis'd there," in the theatres.

The inhibition was strict, and remained very sensibly in force for no brief period. Farquhar in his *Discourse upon Comedy,* published in *Love and Business,* 1702, has: "true downright sense was never more universal than at this very day; 'tis neither confin'd to one nation in the world, nor to one part of a city; . . . 'tis neither abdicated the Court with the late Reigns, nor expell'd the City with the Play-house bills." The following year, 1703, the proposals to refurnish Dorset Garden, now only used for very occasional performances, afforded the Grand Jury of Middlesex an opportunity to make a formal complaint, and request "The having some effectual course taken, if possible, to prevent the youth of this city from resorting to playhouses, which we rather mention because the playhouse bills are again posted up throughout the city in contempt of a former presentment and a positive order of the Lord Mayor and Court of Aldermen to the contrary, dated June, 1700; as also because we are informed that a playhouse within the liberties of this city, which has been of late disused and neglected, is at this time refitting in order to be used as formerly".[30] They suggest that the Queen be petitioned to prevent this.

Since the theatres could not announce their plays by bills upon the posts, although the aristocratic patrons might still be notified in the usual way, it was necessary that some other means must be found to reach the public, and the natural result of this sustained prohibition was that theatrical advertisements began to appear in the newspapers with far greater frequency. The brief old play-bill did not give any cast; not even the names of the principal actors were mentioned, with or without any indication of the rôles they sustained. At first the advertisements, the earliest of which had appeared just before 1700, were but a replica of the play-bill, but before long they developed; the names of the principal performers were printed, and then were added the characters these supported, the whole rounded with a favourite phrase "and all the other Parts to the best advantage"; finally a full cast, or practically a full cast, was supplied and the programme had come into existence. Thus the *Daily Courant,* 13th November, 1706, advertises: "At the Queen's Theatre in the Hay-Market, this present Wednesday, being the 13th of November, will be presented a Play, call'd The Spanish Fryar, or The Double Discovery. All the Parts being perform'd to the best Advantage.[31] Particularly the part of Torrismond by Mr. Betterton, Bertran by Mr. Mills, Lorenzo by Mr. Wilks, Raymond by Mr. Keen, Gomez by Mr. Norris, Father Dominick by Mr. Bullock, Leonora by Mrs. Barry, and Elvira by Mrs. Oldfield. And to-morrow will be presented a Comedy (never acted here before) call'd The Recruiting Officer. Most of the Parts being perform'd as they were originally. These Plays are sold by J. Knapton at the Crown in St. Paul's Church-Yard and B. Lintott next Mando's Coffee-House, Temple Bar."[32]

During the eighteenth century the orange-girls used to vend play-bills both outside and within the theatre, and when Foote, in 1748 at his "Diversions of the Morning" (Mr. Foote's giving Tea to his Friends), mimicked Peg Woffington "in the squeaking pipe" of "an orange woman to the Play-house", he shrilled: "Would you have some oranges?—have some orange-chips, ladies and gentlemen!—Would you have some nonpareils?—Would you have a bill of the play?" In Sam Vincent's *The Young Gallant's Academy, or, Directions how he should behave himself in all Places and Company,* published in the spring of 1674, a manual which is scarce other than Dekker's *The Gull's Hornbook* (1609) brought up to date, the fifth chapter, "*Instructions for a young Gallant how to behave himself in the Play-house,*" is especially interesting as having been almost entirely rewritten from Dekker's sixth chapter to bring it into accordance with the changed conditions of the theatre. Vincent directs his Gallant "to give a hum to the *China-Orange-wench,* and give her her own rate for her Oranges (for 'tis below a *Gentleman* to stand haggling like a *Citizens wife*) and then to present the fairest to the next Vizard-Mask". But not a word is said or suggested of the purchase of a play-bill. During the famous Play-house scene which opens the Fourth Act of Shadwell's *A True Widow,* produced at Dorset Garden in December, 1678, *Several young Coxcombs fool with the Orange-Women.* An Orange-Woman bawls: "Oranges; Will you have any Oranges?" but she does not cry Play-bills nor when the First Bully accosts her with: "What Play do they play? some confounded Play or other," does she proffer him a bill. It does not appear that in Restoration days bills were sold in this manner. None the less from time to time certain pieces were distributed or vended in and about the theatre.

In 1661 a French company came to London from Paris, and for a time occupied that very favourite old theatre the Phœnix (or Cockpit) in Drury Lane. It was only natural that since the King and all his courtiers had for so many years been imbued with French ideas, that there should be a regular Gallomania amongst fashionable folk and that everything French, or indeed Continental, should achieve a regular triumph in England. Thus on Thursday, 8th August, 1661, Pepys being in company with Monsieur Eschar "Met with Mr. Mage,[33] and discoursing of musique, Mons. Eschar spoke so much against the English and in praise of the French that made him mad, and so he went away".

On Friday, 30th August, 1661, Pepys took his wife "to Drury Lane to the French Comedy, which was so ill-done and the scenes and company and everything else so nasty and out of order and poor, that I was sick all the while in my mind to be there. . . . There being nothing pleasant but the foolery of the farce, we went home".

For all that it seems doubtful whether in truth the French comedians were not very much better than Pepys was inclined to allow. At any rate, they presented that very elaborate piece by Chapoton, *Le Mariage d'Orphée et d'Eurydice,* which had been originally produced in 1648,[34] and the fourth act of which has its scene laid in the realms of Dis.

There is extant a pamphlet of eighteen pages in English and French issued in 1661 by Robert Crofts of the Crown in Chancery Lane, "The Description of the Great Machines Of the Descent of Orpheus Into Hell. Presented by the French Comedians at the Cockpit in *Drury-lane.* The Argument Taken out of the Tenth and Eleavnth Books of *Ovid's* Metamorphosis," and this was undoubtedly sold in or about the theatre just as in the palmy days of the opera the libretti, with the Italian on one side and English on the other, were vended and hawked in and about Covent Garden. At the production of *The Indian Emperour,* the Theatre Royal *circa* Easter, 1665, Dryden caused a short handbill to be printed and distributed throughout the house showing the " Connection of the Indian Emperour to The Indian Queen " and explaining how the new play was the sequel to Sir Robert Howard's famous drama, in which he also had no small hand. This kind of broadside was most certainly an innovation, and it struck the audiences of the day as so remarkable, not to say even a little ridiculous, that when *The Rehearsal* was produced on 7th December, 1671, Buckingham with a sharp hit at Dryden's device, makes Bayes say to Johnson : " Besides, Sir, I have printed above a hundred sheets of papyr, to insinuate the Plot into the Boxes."

On Saturday, 19th October, 1667, was produced at the Theatre Royal Orrery's magnifical but lengthy tragedy *The Black Prince,* which the audience, although " mightily pleased, towards the end of the fifth act began to find a little too long ". And here, unfortunately, for the explaining of the plot Lord Delaware reads aloud a somewhat complicated and prolix letter, " a quarter of an hour long." Not a few began to laugh and ominous hisses were heard. Accordingly the letter was printed as a broadside " and so delivered to every body at their going in [to the Theatre], and some short reference made to it by Hart [who acted Lord Delaware] in the play, which do mighty well ", says Pepys four days later.

On 10th February, 1669, Mrs. Evelyn writing to a friend, Mr. Terryll in Ireland, tells him of various plays and mentions amongst others " One of my Lord of Newcastle's for which printed apologies are scattered in the Assembly by Briden's (Dryden's) order, either for himself who had some hand in it, or for the author most ; I think both had right to them ".

The play in question was no doubt *The Heiress,* produced at the Theatre Royal on Saturday, 30th January, 1669, which, according to Pepys, gossip at once attributed to the Duke of Newcastle. It appears that young Ned Kynaston " did act a part therein, in abuse to Sir Charles Sedley ", and this fine gentleman and fine blackguard promptly hired two or three hooligans who assaulted the actor and so beat and bruised him that he was obliged to keep his bed for several days.[35]

It was probably not many years after the Restoration that the custom arose of printing the prologues and epilogues of new plays (as well as other occasional addresses) as broadsides or leaflets, and these were sold about the streets and at the theatre doors. Fortunately a number have been preserved, and the Bindley collection,[36] now so largely represented in the Bodleian Library, is especially rich in these pieces.

It may be remarked that not infrequently the Prologues and

Epilogues as printed in these leaflets or broadsides, that is to say in their original state, differ very considerably from the same addresses as they appear in the first quartos of the plays when so published. Thus the Prologue and Epilogue written by Dryden for Mrs. Behn's *The Widdow Ranter,* a leaf of which only one examplar has been traced (Bodley, Ashmole G. 15), are not those printed with the quarto play, 1690.

These sheets were sold not in, but outside the theatres, and this serves to throw some light upon the fact that when the programme came into being, it also was vended outside the theatre, and it was not until comparatively lately that it was actually sold within the house. Perhaps it may be worth remark that in 1893, when the late Sir Henry Irving was acting the title-rôle in Tennyson's *Becket,* at the Lyceum Theatre, there were hawked in the vicinity of the house a number of cheap reprints of *Thomas À Beckett*: "An Historical Drama," by Douglas Jerrold, which was originally produced at the Surrey Theatre on 30th November, 1829.[37] These were disguised in a gay red wrapper upon which was printed in bold letters "Becket; Sir Henry Irving as Becket", in order that the unwary, many of whom fell into the trap, might be induced to suppose they were purchasing the book of Tennyson's drama.[38]

In the earlier theatre, indeed, books and brochures of all kinds were hawked among the audience, and W. Fennor, in his *Descriptions* (1616) writes: "I suppose this Pamphlet will hap into your hands before a Play begin, with the importunate clamour of 'Buy a new Booke!' by some needy companion that will be glad to furnish you with worke for a turned teaster." There was no such vending of printed ware in a Restoration theatre.

It has already been emphasized that until the eighteenth century the names of actors did not appear upon the bills, but when Malone stated as much he was contradicted by J. P. Collier, who asserted that this great scholar "was decidedly wrong . . . as is proved by the play-bill opposite (if genuine, which may be doubted), sold among the books of the late Mr. Bindley; it was subsequently separately printed."

This bill, however, has long since been shown to be spurious, although as there exists in the Harvard Theatrical Collection a quarto Type reproduction, not a facsimile, of which the paper has the watermark of 1818, and the reproduction was certainly made within a few years, the forgery is not the work of Collier himself, as otherwise might be suspected. The history of the fictitious play-bill has been dealt with so often and in such detail that it is hardly necessary to review the evidence against it here.[39]

Suffice to say that the bill was questioned as early as 1854, when a correspondent who signed himself "F. L." wrote to *Notes and Queries,* First Series, x, 99, to point out certain slips which indicated this could not be a genuine piece. The bill is fully dated. It was not customary to put the year on play-bills

BY HIS MAJESTY'S COMPANY OF

COMEDIANS,

AT THE

New Theatre in Drvry-Lane,

This Day, being Thvrsday, April
8th, 1663,

Will be acted a Comedy, called

THE HVMOVROVS LIEVTENANT.

The King - - - - - - -	Mr. WINTERSEL.
Demetrivs - - - - - - -	Mr. HART.
Selevers - - - - - - -	Mr. BVRT.
Leontivs - - - - - - -	Major MOHVN.
Lievtenant - - - - - -	Mr. CLVN.
Celiæ - - - - - - - -	Mrs. MARSHALL.

The Play will begin at Three o'clock exactly.

Boxes, 4s.—Pit, 2s. 6d.—Middle Gallery, 1s. 6d.—Upper Gallery, 1s.

until at least a century later. 8th April, 1663, fell on a Wednesday, and not a Thursday. The first Theatre Royal opened on Thursday, 7th May, 1663. The 8th April, 1663, fell not merely in Lent, but also in Passion Week, when all theatres were closed.[40] The term Drury Lane was not applied to the Theatre Royal, Bridges Street, until about 1690. Indeed on the title-page, 4to, 1704, of *Love the Leveller ; or, The Pretty Purchase* by G. B.

Gent., this play is said to have been acted at the Theatre Royal "in *Bridges-Street,* Covent Garden". Lacy,[41] and not Clun, was playing the rôle of the Lieutenant in *The Humorous Lieutenant.* The inevitable "Vivat Rex" is omitted from the bill. Nor is it topped by the Royal Arms. Thursday, the day of the week, is printed with the short *s*, and not the long.

The famous forged bill, in fine, is a maladroit concoction founded on a blunder made by old Downes in the *Roscius Anglicanus.*

Since the bill gave neither the author's name nor the names of the actors and there was no sort of programme, it may be asked how did the audience know by whom the play was written and who were sustaining the various characters. In the first place it must be borne in mind that the patrons of the theatre were comparatively speaking few in number, and that they circulated theatrical gossip and talk amongst themselves far more freely than is even the case to-day.

A theatre-goer would make it his business to pick up all kinds of stray news in the pit, he would spread it in the shops, through the coffee-houses, and among all his acquaintance, moreover it would often be conveyed as a theme of exceptional interest to all his friends in the country, less favoured than he in their remoteness from the Duke of York's and the Theatre Royal.

Farquhar in his *A Discourse upon Comedy* (1702) speaks of this kind of advertisement as the regular method of procedure. A young spark sets to work upon a play. "'Tis then whisper'd among his Friends at *Will's* and *Hippolito's* that Mr. *such-a-one* has writ a very pretty Comedy; and some of 'em, to encourage the young Author, equip him presently with *Prologue* and *Epilogue.*" Again and again do we find correspondents in London retailing the latest theatrical rumour as a special tit-bit in the mode. Thus when John Wilson's capital comedy *The Cheats* was produced at Vere Street, Abraham Hill writing to John Brooke on 28th March, 1663, tells him: "The new play called "The Cheats" has been attempted on the stage, but it is so scandalous that it is forbidden." The trouble was raised by the puritans on account of the character of Mr. Scruple, the Presbyterian minister, a figure too exact for the liking of his brethren. 22nd August, 1673, James Vernon, dispatching a letter from Court to Sir Joseph Williamson at Cologne, has much to say of "an Opera and great machines" preparing at the Duke's House. This was Shadwell's *Psyche.* 5th May, 1688, Lord Granville writing to Sir William Leveson mentions the production of Crowne's *Darius King of Persia,* the forthcoming production of *The Squire of Alsatia,* Mrs. Boutell's return to the stage, and the recent death of Sarah

PLATE II

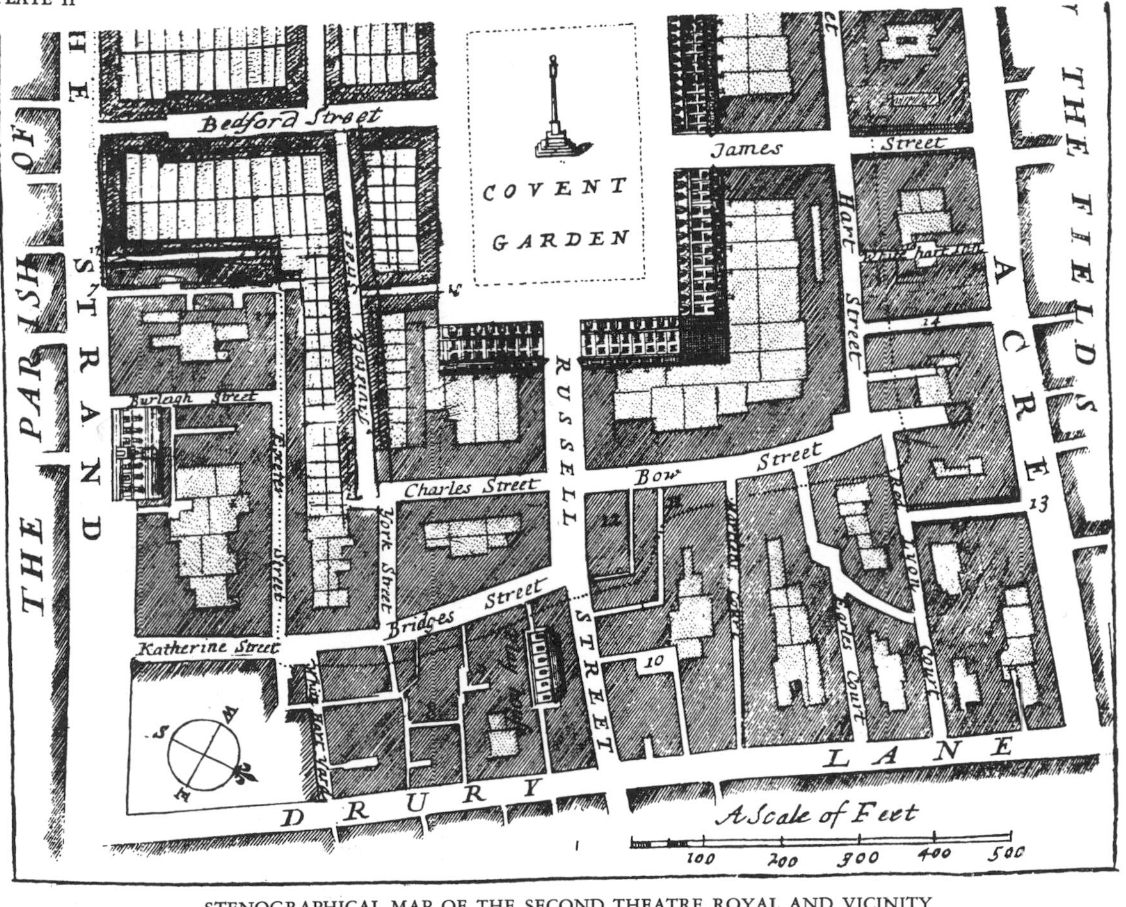

STENOGRAPHICAL MAP OF THE SECOND THEATRE ROYAL AND VICINITY
Strype's Stow, 1720

[*fac*

Cooke. Etherege at Ratisbon is well pleased to hear of the success of Sedley's *Bellamira ; or, The Mistress* (letter 23rd May–3rd June, 1687) ; he is continually referring to actors and actresses and quoting from plays ; he particularly asks for *The Squire of Alsatia* "when it is printed" (27th February–8th March, 1687–8) ; he gibes at the failure of D'Urfey's *A Fool's Preferment.* Dryden writing to Mrs. Steward, of Cotterstock, in Northamptonshire, mentions a revival of Congreve's *The Double-Dealer* (4th March, 1698–9), or again tells her of the production of Charles Hopkins' *Friendship Improv'd* (7th November, 1699), and relates the failures of John Dennis' *Iphigenia* and of Boyer's *Achilles, or Iphigenia in Aulis* (14th December, 1699).

Gossip round the town was assuredly no bad method of advertisement, and by ingenious exploiting of preliminary rumour a good deal of curiosity might be awakened and sustained. Thus the magnificent production of Shadwell's opera *Psyche,* 27th February, 1674–5, was heralded by many weeks of careful rumour and cleverly-bruited talk so that the theatrical world was all agog with excitement and anticipation. And then, as Downes says, "the long-expected Opera of *Psyche* came forth in all her ornaments."

On Thursday, 10th December, 1663, Pepys calling at Wotton the shoemaker's, hears "That Harris is come to the Duke's house again ; and of a rare play to be acted this week of Sir William Davenant's : the story of Henry the Eighth with all his wives".

Naturally enough, such gossip must have been often very loose and inaccurate, and so on Tuesday, 15th September, 1668, we find that Pepys actually ascribes Flecknoe's *Damoiselles A La Mode,* to Dryden, a passage which has occasioned considerable discussion, although when one appreciates the conditions of a Restoration Theatre, it should not thus mislead. "By water to the King's Playhouse, to see a new play, acted but yesterday, a translation out of French by Dryden, called 'The Ladies a La Mode', so mean a thing as, when they come to say it would be acted again to-morrow, both he that said it, Beeson, and the pit fell a-laughing, there being this day not a quarter of the pit full."

Incidentally we may hence note this second way in which the public were informed of performances at the Theatre, the next day's piece was given out by an actor at the end of each performance, a traditional method which survived until well within the nineteenth century. On 24th October, 1842, at Drury Lane Macready produced *King John,* one of the most expensive and elaborate of all his great Shakespearean revivals. It was received with unbounded favour, and *The Times,* 25th October, thus concluded a most laudatory notice: "King John is a 'hit'. Macready announced it for repetition twice a week amid vociferous applause, and the principal actors were called for." The dramatic critic of *The Illustrated London News* dealing with the revival of *Love for Love* at Drury Lane on Saturday, 19th November, 1842, having praised the excellence of the acting, adds: "The get-up of the comedy was admirable . . . It was announced for repetition amidst general applause." Although the earlier evidence regarding this practice is scanty, we know that it originated in pre-Restoration days, as in the first folio Beaumont and Fletcher, 1647, among the numerous copies of verses prefixed to this collection the last in order, entitled *The Stationer* and signed H. Moseley, commences:—

> As after th' *Epilogue* there comes some one
> To tell *Spectators* what shall next be shown;
> So here, am I; but though I've toyld and vext,
> 'Cannot devise what to present 'ye next.

In the contemporary French theatre the functionary to whose duty it fell thus to announce the play for the morrow was known as the *Orator*.

On Saturday, 12th January, 1668, Pepys hears a budget of theatrical news from Mrs. Knepp and amongst the rest "Of a play shortly coming upon the stage, of Sir Charles Sidly's, which, she thinks, will be called 'The Wandering Ladys', a comedy that, she thinks, will be most pleasant". The reference here is, of course, to Sedley's dull play *The Mulberry-Garden,* which was produced at the Theatre Royal on Monday, 18th May, 1668. It is evident that when a new piece by a reputed wit was on the way, it was harbingered by much eulogy and commendation which filled the theatre just as well as a column of advertisements.

Indeed, at the first performance of *The Mulberry-Garden* Pepys particularly notices the crowded house attracted by the reputation of the author of a comedy "so long expected". Precisely the same thing happened when Etherege's second comedy *She wou'd if she cou'd,* was produced at Lincoln's Inn Fields on Thursday, 6th February, 1668, when so great was the crush even an hour and a half before the play began that at least a thousand were turned back as the pit was already packed to suffocation.

It was then, chiefly by oral communication and by the gossip of friends, that a playgoer in Restoration days informed himself of forthcoming plays and of their authors, although, as we have seen, even in the case of an ardent theatre lover such as Pepys who had a wide and close theatrical acquaintance, the information thus conveyed was not always extremely accurate.

The famous forged bill says: "*The Play will begin at Three o'clock exactly,*" and this seems to be based upon the title-pages of Davenant's Operas *The Cruelty of the Spaniards* and *Sir Francis Drake,* both of which were advertised as "Represented daily at the *Cockpit* in *Drury-Lane,* At Three after noone punctually".

This was in 1658, but half-past three seems to have been the regular time for the commencement of the theatre throughout the reign of Charles II. In the original Prologue to *The Wild Gallant,* produced at Vere Street, 5th February, 1663, two Astrologers are introduced. "*The Prologue is presented to them*" as having been sent by the poet, who

> "*from this Scheme, drawn for the hour and day,*
> *Bid me inquire the fortune of his Play.*"

The first Astrologer reads: "A figure of the heavenly Bodies in their several Apartments, Feb. the 5th, half an hour after three after Noon, from whence you are to judge the success of a new Play called *the Wild Gallant.*" Cibber in his *Apology,* chapter v, says that "*Kynaston* at that time was so beautiful a Youth that the Ladies of Quality prided themselves in taking him with them in their Coaches to *Hyde-Park* in his Theatrical Habit, after the Play; which in those Days they might have sufficient time to do, because Plays then were us'd to begin at four a-Clock". The reference is presumably to the first decade after the Restoration, but I doubt whether Cibber's remark as to the time of commencement can be too precisely pressed as of evidential value for any precise date. Sparkish in *The Country-Wife,* produced in January, 1674–5, hurries off to dine early that he may not miss seeing the new play on the first day, and it would not appear to commence after half-past three. Lionel in Sedley's *Bellamira; or, The Mistress,* produced at Drury Lane, 12th May, 1687, II, i, declares: "I am tir'd with these daily Beauties of the Town, whom we see Painted and Patch'd in the Afternoon at the Play house, in the Evening at the Park, and at Night in the Drawing room." Towards the end of the seventeenth century the hour of performance was inclined to get somewhat later, and in 1695 it appears to have been four o'clock. The Epilogue, spoken by Mrs. Bracegirdle, as Angelica in boy's attire, to Lord Lansdowne's *The She-Gallants,* acted at Lincoln's Inn Fields in the winter of 1695, concludes:—

> "On Pain of being posted to your Sorrow,
> Fail not at Four, to meet me here To-morrow.'

Lord Foppington, in Vanbrugh's *The Relapse; or, Virtue in Danger,* produced at Drury Lane on Saturday, 21st November, 1696, when giving an account of his day informs the company that after his dinner at Locket's "I go to the Play; where, till Nine a-Clock, I entertain myself with looking upon the Company; and usually dispose of one Hour more in leading them out".

In Settle's opera *The World in the Moon,* produced at Dorset Garden, May, 1697, Act I, the following dialogue occurs between Stanmore and Wildblood:—

Stan. O fye *Frank,* almost Seven a Clock: The Play's half done by this time.

Wild. Time enough for the last Act. Thou know'st I never take a turn to a Play, but either just pop in my Head before the Curtain rises, or before it drops again . . .

Stan. But why are you so unkind to the Play-houses, especially at this Low-water time with them, to take a turn (as you call it) before the Curtain rises?

Wild. Out of pure Charity, *Ned.* I gallop round the Pit, hear the last Musick, pick up a Mask, and carry her off before the Play; and so save the poor Whore her Half Crown.

Stan. But why can't you sit out the Play?

Wild. Oh Intolerable! . . .

Stan. But why do you tell me you never stay out a Play, when you know I have seen you perking behind the Scenes, from the first Musick to the last Candle, to a clear Stage; nay, and to a clear Dressing-room, the very last Man bourn [*sic*].

Wild. Behind the Scenes! Ay, there the Case is altered. There *Ned*, I have nothing to say to the Play, but the Players—Oh! I could dance Attendance, and dangle at the Train of a High Feather, and a Stage Princess (especially that *Phœnix* amongst 'em under the reputation of a Virginity) as contentedly and with as much mortal Resignation for three whole Hours together, as I could lye a whole Night by her.

(The allusion to the *Phœnix*, Mrs. Bracegirdle, will not escape notice.)

A bill of *The Relapse,* "At the Theatre Royal in Drury Lane this present Tuesday being the 18th day of May," 1703, announces "To begin exactly at half an hour after Five". An advertisement of *The Confederacy* "the sixth day of November, 1705", has "beginning exactly at Five of the Clock". The Fourth Canto of Garth's *Dispensary,* 4to, 1699, commences:—

Not far from that most famous Theater,
Where wandering Punks each Night at five repair;
When purple Emperors in Buskins tread,
And rule imaginary Worlds for Bread. . . .

In "The Trial of Cuckolds" which is printed with Tom Brown's *Dialogues of the Dead* (1702), the shades of the cornuted beaux chatter together and their spokesman, my Lord Flippant's Ghost, proceeds to describe the details of his day on earth in explanation of the fact that his wife has so thoroughly horned him: "Whilst I was at *Will's* coffee house, fastened in controversy or poetick rhapsodies, though I had neither religion nor learning, she was sure of me till play-time, and then too; for at five, 'Come, *Dick*,' says I (to a brother of the orange and cravat string), 'd—— me, let us to the play.'" The Epilogue to Farquhar's *The Recruiting Officer,* which was produced at Drury Lanc in April, 1706, smartly commences: "All Ladies and Gentlemen, that are willing to see the Comedy call'd the *Recruiting Officer,* let them repair to morrow night by six a Clock, to the Sign of the *Theatre Royal* in *Drury Lane*, and they shall be kindly entertain'd."

In London six o'clock seems to have remained the general time for many years. Thus on Thursday, 24th February, 1737, when *The Mourning Bride* was given at Drury Lane for the benefit of Mrs. Porter, who played Zara, the performance was announced "to begin exactly at Six o'clock". On 6th November, 1740, *The Recruiting Officer* was revived at Covent Garden: "The Part of Sylvia by Miss Woffington (being the first time of her performing on that stage) . . . to begin exactly at Six o'clock." On 28th September, *Romeo and Juliet* was acted at Covent Garden. "The part of Juliet to be performed by Mrs. Cibber . . . to begin exactly at six o'clock."

It may be remarked that the circumstance of performances being given at the public theatres in the afternoons was particularly convenient inasmuch as it allowed plays to be acted at night before the King, in "the theatre in the Great Hall".

It has not, I think, been remarked by any stage historian that although (as we have seen) performances in the public theatres under the Restoration commenced at half-past three, and even at the end of the seventeenth century rarely seem to have begun later than four o'clock, there are continual references in prologue and epilogue to "Night", and on the face of it, it might well seem as if plays were being acted at the public theatres in the evening, which emphatically was not the case. Thus, in the prologue, spoken by Joe Haines, to Lee's *The Tragedy of Nero, Emperour of Rome,* produced at the Theatre Royal in May, 1674, we have:—

A bloody fatal Play you'l see to night,
I vow to Gad, 'thas put me in a fright.

The prologue, spoken by Mrs. Roche, to *Gloriana; or, the Court of Augustus Caesar,* Theatre Royal, January, 1674–5, gave the actress these opening lines:—

He whose attempt is shown this Night to please,
Beheld me entring and my arm did seize,
Cry'd, Madam, stay, stay but one minute more;
But I your Servant left him at the door.
How dear, and yet how dreadfull is the Night,
That makes a Poet, or undoes him quite?
Such is the Night when a kind-hearted Maid
Becomes a Sacrifice to Bridal-bed.

In the epilogue to the same tragedy Joe Haines said:—

They told me at t'other House y'had left us quite,
And I was going to hang my self out-right,
But for the hopes of pleasing you to Night.

The epilogue, spoken by Crosby, to *The Counterfeit Bridegroom; or, The Defeated Widow,* a vacation play, acted at Dorset Garden in the summer of 1677, commences:—

Knowing too well, Gallants, your natural spight
We bar your censuring priviledg to Night.

Abundance of further evidence might be cited.[42] The point is a small one, but none the less it is interesting to observe that performances which actually took place in the afternoon by some conventional phrase were indifferently spoken of as being at night.[43]

It must be remembered that in the leisurely days of the Restoration the playgoers not only arrived at the theatre long before the actual time of commencement of the performance, but they also lingered long in the house after the Epilogue had been spoken, criticizing the drama and passing the news of the day. It is true that in modern London and other cities vast queues will assemble and persons will await their turn to be admitted for hour after hour with patience seemingly inexhaustible. But in the days of King Charles the doors opened early, and the audience expected to enter, not to be detained in the street without. On the occasion of a new piece it would, of course, prove necessary to attend right early if a good place, or indeed any seat at all, were to be secured. It appears that about noon was the regular time for admitting to the house. Of the first performance of Etherege's *She wou'd if she cou'd,* Thursday, 6th February, 1667–8, Pepys writes: "At noon home to dinner, and my wife being gone before, I to the Duke of York's playhouse; where a new play of Etherige's, called 'She Would if she Could'; and though I was there by two-o-clock, there was 1000 people put back that could not have room in the pit: and I at last, because my wife was there, made shift to get into the 18d box, and there saw; but Lord! how full was the house." Again on Monday, 18th May, 1668, Pepys notes: "To my tailor's, and there did find Mercer come with Mrs. Horsfield and Gayet according to my desire, and there I took them up, it being almost twelve o'clock or a little more, and carried them to the King's playhouse, where the doors were not then open; but presently they did open; and we in, and find many people already come in, by private ways, into the pit, it being the first day of Sir Charles Sidly's new play, so long expected, 'Thc Mullberry Guarden,' of whom, being so reputed a wit, all the world do expect great matter."

Significant are the following lines in the Prologue to Settle's *Ibrahim The Illustrious Bassa,* Duke's Theatre, March, 1676:—

> *'Tis true, when any Favourites Plays appear,*
> *Then Kindness and Good-nature brings you here:*
> *And to secure the Censures of the Town,*
> *The Pit is fill'd with Friends in the Fore-noon;*
> *And those five long expecting hours you stay,*
> *Are spent in making Proselytes to th' Play.*

Probably it will seem curious to us to-day that the theatre-going public should have been content to tolerate such inconveniences, but these long waits were by no means so irksome as might appear, for the pit and boxes were notorious rendezvous, centres of intrigue, of bustle, of movement and life. It was in the pit men met their friends; it was from the pit they ogled the fair and frail ladies in the boxes, as when the dashing young William Wycherley, who had attracted the wanton ardour of the Duchess of Cleveland, boldly made assignation with that lovely courtezan and asked: "Will your Ladyship be at the Play to-night?" with the result that "She was that Night in the first Row of the King's Box in Drury Lane, and Mr. *Wycherley* in the Pit under her, where he entertained her during the whole play".[44] There are indeed numberless references to the thousand and one businesses of venery and every kind of pleasure which occupied those who were waiting for the play to commence, and, one might add, engaged them whilst the play was in progress.

My Lady Flippant, agog for matrimony, in *Love in a Wood* (acted in 1671) frequents the play-houses as one of the most notorious "Publick Marts where Widows and Mayds are expos'd", and she further informs us that if a fine lady can but keep her coach she has scarce need of a lodging, " for her Visits she receives them in the Play-house." Frank Townly in *The London Cuckolds* (acted in 1681) meets Arabella at the theatre, notes " her rallery with the Sparks ", is asked by her for a new song he is humming and so presents her with the book in which he had written it, which she will only take on condition he will accept it back again next time they meet in the Pit. Sir Courtly Nice is to meet a fine lady, with whom he is afterwards to sup, about five o'clock in the King's box. Tom Brown, describing *The Play-House,*[45] says: " 'Tis frequented by Persons of all Degrees and Qualities whatsoever, that have a deal of idle Time lying upon their Hands, and can't tell how to employ it worse. Here *Lords* come to laugh, and to be laughed at for being there and seeing their Qualities ridiculed by every Triobolary Poet. Knights come thither to learn the amorous Smirk, the *Alamode* Grin, the antick Bow, the newest fashioned Cringe, and how to adust their Phiz, to make themselves as ridiculous by Art as they are by Nature.

" Hither come the Country Gentlemen to shew their Shapes, and trouble the Pit with their Impertinence about Hawking, Hunting, and their handsom Wives, and their Housewifery.

". . . Here the Ladies come to shew their Cloaths, which are often the only things to be admired in or about 'em."

It appears that individuals seldom, if ever, took umbrage at the loss of time which must have been involved in playgoing, and there are few expressions of resentment or vexation. There is indeed a grumble in a Satire printed with the motto *Quem Natura neget dabit Indignatio Uersum*[46] in *Poems on State-Affairs,* vol. iii, 1704 (and also to be found MS. Harl. 7317, folio 6*b*). The writer who is bitterly attacking Otway, when presented by a bookseller with *Venice Preserv'd,* cries out:—

> Was't not enough that at his tedious Play
> I lavish'd half a Crown, and half a Day;
> But must I find, patch'd up at ev'ry Wall,
> Such stuff that none can bear, who starves not at *Whitehall?*

The puritans, of course, were acid when they spoke of hours wasted at the theatre, but generally the conditions were freely accepted if not in truth exploited and enjoyed. If one had business, or had not eaten, it was possible to hire somebody to retain a place. Thus at the production of Shadwell's *The Sullen Lovers,* Saturday, 2nd May, 1668, Pepys dined and " thence to the Duke of York's playhouse, at a little past twelve, to get a good place in the pit, against the new play, and there setting a poor man to keep my place, I out, and spent an hour at Martin's, my bookseller's, and so back again, where I find the house quite full. But I had my place ". Upon the first day (Monday, 18th May, 1668) of *The Mulberry-Garden,* Pepys came to the Theatre Royal about twelve o'clock, and " I having sat here awhile, and eat nothing to-day, did slip out, getting a boy to keep my place; and to the Rose Tavern, and there got half a breast of mutton, off of the spit, and dined all alone. And so to the play again." The custom of sending footmen to retain places, a proceeding which had become quite general by the end of the seventeenth century and which was long to endure, was introduced by the French troupe who visited England in the spring of 1672. This novelty, soon to be adopted in London, is jeered by Dryden in the prologue written for a revival of Carlell's *Arviragus and Philicia* by the King's players. The Theatre Royal in Bridges Street having been burned to the ground the homeless actors were forced to instal themselves as tenants of the small theatre in Lincoln's Inn Fields, which had just been abandoned by their rivals for the golden glories of Dorset Garden. Dryden makes piteous reference in his prologue to their misfortunes, a sorry plight not alleviated by the advent of the French company which has become the delight of the Town and draws packed audiences :—

> And therefore, *Messieurs,* if you'l do us grace,
> Send Lacquies early to preserve your Place.
> We dare not on your Priviledge intrench . . .

The obvious point of the couplet consists in quoting the substance of a notice that was prominent upon the French play-bills. The footmen, however, soon proved no small evil, as when they retired to give up the various seats they had been retaining they congregated in the passages and on the staircases of the theatre and here they proceeded to quarrel and ramp outrageously. To this circumstance Dryden makes allusion in the Epilogue spoken at the Theatre Royal on 16th November, 1682, the Union of the two Companies :—

> Then for your Laqueys, and your Train beside,
> (By whate'er Name or Title dignify'd,)
> They roar so loud, you'd think behind the Stairs,
> *Tom Dove,*[47] and all the Brotherhood of Bears:
> They're grown a Nuisance, beyond all Disasters;
> We've none so great but their unpaying Masters.
> We beg you, Sirs, to beg your Men that they
> Would please to give you leave to hear the Play.

The stairs leading to the three tiers may be clearly seen in the Wren design for the second Theatre Royal. Towards the end of the seventeenth century the footmen were admitted gratis into the Upper Gallery at the beginning of the fifth act. Southerne's comedy *The Wives' Excuse; or, Cuckolds make Themselves*, Drury Lane, December, 1691, opens with the ante-chamber of a fashionable music-meeting. A number of footmen are in attendance and the first flunkey cries: "A Pox on these music-meetings; there's no fifth act here, a free cost, as we have at the play-houses, to make gentlemen of us, and keep us out of harm's way."

NOTES TO CHAPTER I

[1] *English Miracle Plays, Moralities, and Interludes.* Edited by A. W. Pollard. 4th ed., 1904, p. 197. For the text see the *Macro Plays,* E.E.T.S., Extra series, XCI, p. 81.

[2] *Nomen*; the name of the town or village where the performance was to be given was here inserted.

[3] The quatrain which is found in Petronius (Tertium edidit Buecheler, Berolini, 1895, p. 17, xxiii), chanted by the "cinaedus, homo omnium insulsissimus" may possibly be an excerpt from a song inviting to a lewd entertainment of a semi-musical and dramatic nature, verses of the kind some comedian of a travelling troupe would declaim publicly to draw an audience:—

> huc huc cito conucnite nunc, spatalocinaedi,
> pede tendite, cursum addite, conuolate planta,
> femoreque facili, clune agili et manu procaces,
> molles, ueteres, Deliaci manu recisi.

For "ueteres" Buecheler conjectures "ueneres". Arnobius, *Aduersus Gentes,* ii, 42, writing "de lasciuia mimorum" has: "Ut symphoniacas agerent et fistulatorias artes, cantionibus ut praeirent obscoenis numerositer, et scabillorum concrepationibus sonoris, quibus animarum alia lasciuiens multitudo incompositos corporum dissolueretur in motus, et ad ultimum clunibus et coxendicibus subleuatis lumborum crispitudine fluctuaret." I omit a few phrases from a long passage.

[4] *A Mirrour of Magistrates: Wherein is plainely described the manifold vices and spotted enormities, that are caused by the infectious sight of Playes, with the description of the subtile slights of Sathan making them his instruments.* 1587. John Field in his *A godly exhortation by occasion of the late iudgment of God, shewed at Parris-garden, the thirteenth day of Ianuarie* . . . (1583) speaks of no "Theater that can be found empty. Those flagges of defiance against God, and trumpets that are blown to gather together such company, will sooner preuail to fil those places, then the preaching of the holy worde of God . . . to fill Churches".

[5] Stockwood was Master of Tonbridge Grammar School.

[6] *Henslowe Papers,* 1907, i, 118.

[7] *All's Well that Ends Well,* iv, 3.

[8] In the Midlands early in the twentieth century there were still strollers who visited the smaller towns and in a caravan theatre gave performances of old Stock drama. I have been told that *Pizarro* was among their repertory. Their arrival was advertised by a procession or parade, sans drum or trumpet however, and much shorn of ancient glories. In *The Show Boat,* a heterogeneous piece given at Drury Lane, which enjoyed much popularity in London, 1927–8, a morning parade of this kind was introduced in the First Act. The scene was laid in America about 1850.

[9] Dr. W. J. Lawrence, "The Origin of the Theatre Programme," *The Elizabethan Playhouse,* Second Series (1913), p. 59, n. 1, says: "The drummer and crier (two

individuals working together) were institutions in Paris early in the seventeenth century. Cf. Eugène Rigal, *Le Théâtre Français avant lâ Période Classique,* p. 197, note 5."

[10] Elizabeth Farren (1759–1829). She married the Earl of Derby in 1797.

[11] It may also be remarked that a man is depicted sounding the trumpet from the garret door.

[12] V, i, 15. Recensuit Lucianus Mueller, Lipsiae, 1894.

[13] Editio, Amstedolami, "Prostant apud Wacsbergios, Boom, & Goethals," 1702. Vol. i, p. 519.

[14] Maps of London, Gough Collection, vol. xxi, Bodleian Library.

[15] See the advertisement cited in W. G. Bell's *Fleet Street in Seven Centuries,* p. 336.

[16] Eugène Rigal, op. cit., p. 197, n. 2. Apud Lawrence, *Elizabethan Playhouse,* ii, p. 60.

[17] Afterwards Archbishop of York, and thence translated to Canterbury, 1576.

[18] Lansdowne MS. 7, f. 141. See also Styrpe's *Life of Grindall* (1821), p. 122, and Grindal, *Remains* (1843), 269; T. Wright, *Queen Elizabeth and her Times,* 2 vols (1838), i, 166; and Collier, *English Dramatic Poetry* (1879), i, 181–2.

[19] In *Histriomastix* (*circa* 1599) Gulch remarks of a poet: "It is as dangerous to read his name at a play-door, as a printed bill on a plague door." Cf. Flecknoe, *Epigrams Of All Sorts,* 1670, p. 70, *On a bungling Dramatick Poet* :—

> We are as feard as of the plague, and more,
> When we but see thy Bills upon the Door.

[20] Camden, *Annals,* says that the plague was raging in London in the autumn of 1592; the theatres were closed, and this would account for the tour of the Queen's Players.

[21] Collier, op. cit. (ed. 1879), i, p. 281.

[22] Originally the Priory buildings had consisted mainly of a great Dominican Church 220 feet long and 66 feet broad with a cloister on the south side forming a square of 110 feet, and a small cloister again to the south of this. At the dissolution the property passed into the possession of the Crown.

[23] But under Thursday, 8th January, 1662–3, both Evelyn and Pepys have entries in their respective Diaries to note that they were present on that day at the first performance of Tuke's play. This evidence is decisive. No doubt the 15th December of the Prologue, a date perhaps originally intended for the *première* remained unaltered by accident.

[24] The Third Quarto, 1675, reads: "*Enter* Players. 1. *Play.* Come then, let's set up Bills for another Play. 2. *Play.* I, i: we shall lose nothing by this I warrant you."

[25] Langbaine, *English Dramatick Poets* (1691), p. 57, says that *Wits led by the Nose* appeared "upon the Stage in 1678". But the piece is in *The Term Catalogues,* Michaelmas (26th November), 1677, "Acted at the Theatre Royal."

[26] A name given by Pepys to Mrs. Betterton owing to her fine performance of that rôle in *The Siege of Rhodes.*

[27] V. Fournel, *Curiosités Théâtrales* (1878), p. 126.

[28] Malone, *Prose Works of John Dryden* (1800), vol. i, part ii, pp. 80–1.

[29] The *London Gazette,* No. 3474, Monday, 27th February, 1698–9, contains the Order to which allusion is made. It states that the Master of the Revels has represented that "the Actors do often neglect to leave out such profane and indecent expressions as he has thought proper to be omitted". They are charged to be more careful in this respect "as you shall answer it at your utmost peril".

[30] Fitzgerald, *New History of the English Stage,* i, 315.

[31] It may be noted that Betterton and Mrs. Barry were playing the rôles they had originally created six and twenty years before, at Dorset Garden, in March, 1679–1680.

[32] Advertisements of theatrical performances now begin to grow numerous and full. Thus The *Daily Courant,* Saturday, 28th December, 1706, No. 1468, announces *The Recruiting Officer* at the Queen's Theatre in the Hay-Market with Keen as Ballance; Mills, Worthy; Wilks, Plume; Cibber, Brazen; Fairbank, Kite; Bullock, Bullock; Norris, Pearmain; Kent, Apple-tree; Mrs. Oldfield, Silvia; Mrs. Porter, Melinda; and Mrs. Bicknel, Rose. On the following Monday, 30th December, at the same theatre *The Rival Queens* is announced with Verbruggen,

Alexander; Booth, Clytus; Bowman, Hephestion; Husband, Cassander; Mrs. Bracegirdle, Statira; Mrs. Barry, Roxana; and Mrs. Porter, Parisatis. The following day, Tuesday, 31st December, *The Silent Woman* is advertised at the same theatre: Betterton, Morose; Wilks, Truewit; Booth, Dauphinie Eugène; Mills, Clerimont; Cibber, Sir John Daw; Bullock, La Fool; Fairbank, Captain Otter; Norris, Cutbeard; Mrs. Oldfield, the Silent Woman.

On Monday, 30th May, 1709, the *Daily Courant* has five advertisements of performances at Drury Lane. On Thursday, 2nd June, Betterton acted Thersites in *Troilus and Cressida*. On Friday, 3rd June, *Hamlet* was given "For the Benefit of Mr. Cave Underhill the old Comedian". Wilks is announced as Hamlet; Keen, the King; Cross, Polonius; Powell, Laertes; Mills, Horatio; Booth, the Ghost; Underhill, First Grave-Digger; Bickerstaffe, Marcellus; Cibber, Osric; Mrs. Knight, the Queen; Mrs. Bradshaw, Ophelia. "Being the last time of Acting this Season. With a new Prologue and Epilogue."

The tendency of these advertisements is to become more and more detailed.

[33] Henry Madge, who in 1674 was one of the King's four and twenty fiddlers.

[34] It was revived at Paris in 1662.

[35] Mr. V. de Sola Pinto in his *Sir Charles Sedley,* 1927, p. 112, apparently approves of this choice ruffianism which he finds "not without humour".

[36] James Bindley, 1737–1818, First Commissioner in the Stamp Office; the friend of Malone. His library was sold 1818–1821.

[37] S. Thomas à Becket was played by Rumball; Henry II, Dibdin Pitt; Walter de Mapes, Williams; Lucia, Miss Vincent; the nun Idonea, Mrs. Egerton.

[38] When Sir Henry Irving learned of this practice he was greatly annoyed, but it proved exceedingly difficult, if not impossible, to check the peddling of false ware.

[39] See Percy Fitzgerald, "The Playbill: Its Growth and Evolution," *Gentleman's Magazine,* June, 1900, p. 352. (Mr. Fitzgerald had seemingly accepted the bill as genuine in his *New History of the English Stage,* 1882, vol. i, pp. 87–8.) Also W. J. Lawrence, *The Elizabethan Playhouse* (Second Series), 1913, pp. 74–8; and Montague Summers, *Roscius Anglicanus,* 1928, pp. 102–4.

[40] Cf. Pepys, Monday, 24th March, 1662: "I went to see if any play was acted, and I found none upon the post, it being Passion Week."

[41] This was by the King's particular command. See Pepys, Friday, 8th May, 1663.

[42] See for example the Epilogue to Tate's *Brutus of Alba,* D. G., 1678; Prologue to Banks' *The Destruction of Troy,* D. G., 1678; Epilogue to Crowne's *Ambitious Statesman,* T. R., 1679; Epilogue to Lee's *Massacre of Paris,* T. R., 1689; Epilogue to Southerne's *Sir Anthony Love,* T. R., 1690; Epilogue to Mountfort's *Greenwich-Park,* T. R., 1691; Prologue to Southerne's *The Wives' Excuse,* T. R., 1691; *cum multis aliis.*

[43] Performances in the Hall Theatre, Whitehall, were given at night.

[44] Dennis, *Original Letters,* 1731, pp. 215–18.

[45] *Amusements Serious and Comical Calculated for the Meridian of London.* Amusement IV. *The Play-House.* I quote from the edition of 1720, *The Works of Mr. Thomas Brown,* vol. iii, pp. 37–43.

[46] *Si natura neget, facit indignatio uersum.* Juvenal, i, 79.

[47] To Tom Dove, who was a bear of great renown, there are many allusions e.g. *Proteus Redivivus,* 1675 (p. 109): "He leads them by the Nose (as the *Bear-heard* does *Tom Dove* up and down the Town)." Mrs. Behn's *The Town-Fop; or, Sir Timothy Tawdrey,* produced at Dorset Garden, September, 1676, i, 2, where Sir Timothy cries: "Oh, *Ned,* I'm glad thou'rt come—never was *Tom Dove* baited as I have been." In Southerne's *The Maid's Last Prayer; or, Any, rather than Fail,* Drury Lane, January, 1692–3, ii, 2, Granger on receiving an invitation to dinner exclaims: "Zounds! a man had as good be ty'd to a stake, and baited like *Tom Dove* on *Easter Monday,* as be the necessary appurtenance of a great man's table."

Chapter II

SYSTEMS OF ADMISSION

Now up wi' Boots, and have at all!
Ev'n you whom we Town-Gallants call;
Who with your round Feathers make a great show;
We mean you did wear such three years agoe;
Come then, and stand fair, that now we may hit ye,
Because ev'n like Turks without any pity,
You visit our Plays, and merit the Stocks
For paying Half-Crowns of Brass to our Box.
Nay, often you swear, when places are shewn ye,
That your hearing is thick,
And so, by a Love-trick,
You pass through our Scenes up to the Balcone.

And some (a duce take 'em!) pretend
They come but to speak with a friend;
Then wickedly rob us of a whole Play
By stealing five times an Act in a day.
O little England! *speak, is it not pity,*
That Gallants ev'n here, and in thy chief City,
Should under great Perukes have heads so small,
As they must steal wit, or have none at all?
Others are bolder and never cry, shall I?
For they make our Guards quail,
And 'twixt Curtain and Rail,
Oft Combing their hair, they walk in Fop-Ally.

Gallants relent and eke repent,
For your so foul, nay, bad intent
Of paying us Brass instead of true Coyne;
And, for amends we only enjoyn,
That ev'ry Man, to declare conscience in ye,
Shall whisper a Friend, and borrow a Guinny;
Which in our Box you may carelessly throw,
And pay him who lends it to morrow to mow.
And now to conclude, 'tis fit to acquaint ye
That though this Epilogue
Does not flatter and cogg
Yet a new Ballad may pass for a dainty.

The Epilogue. In a Ballad, sung by Two.
D'Avenant, *The Man's the Master,* 4to, 1669.

Upon entering the theatre it must be borne in mind that although we are apt to speak and to think of the Restoration theatre as the establishment of the picture-frame stage, and in one sense no doubt this is true enough, the principles upon which the architects of the buildings worked and the methods they employed for their auditoriums were entirely different from the conditions that now prevail. The actual stage will be more particularly described a little later. The floor of the house was entirely devoted to the pit. This rose in a gradual slope towards the first tier, so that persons seated in the last benches were actually on a higher level than those whose station was in the front rows. In *A Tale of A Tub,* 1704, Swift remarks: " in the Contrivance and Structure of our Modern Theatres . . . the Pit is sunk below the Stage . . . the Boxes are built round, and raised to a level with the Scene." [1] This circumstance makes clear a passage in a letter of Congreve, who on 26th March, 1701, writes to Joseph Keally, of Dublin, an account of a performance of *The Judgment of Paris* at Dorset Garden, and says: " The boxes and pit were all thrown into one; so that all sat in common; and the whole was crammed with beauties and beaux, not one scrub being admitted." The stage, which ran out beyond the proscenium arch far into the pit, was in front convex, in correspondence with the concentric semicircles of the seats on the ground floor. A French traveller, Balthasar de Monconys, describing a visit paid to the Theatre Royal in Bridges Street on Friday, 22nd May, 1663, that is to say only a fortnight after the opening of the new house, writes as follows: " L'apresdinée nous fusmes chez le Milord de S. Alban, & de là à la Comedie dans la loge du Roy. Le Théâtre est le plus propre & le plus beau que j'aye iamais veu, tout tapissé par le bas de bayette verte; aussi bien que toutes les loges qui en sont tapissées avec des bandes de cuir doré. Tous les bancs du parterre où toutes les personnes de condition se mettent aussi, sont rangez en amphitheatre, les vns plus hauts que les autres. Les changemens de Theatre & les machines sont fort ingenieusement inuentées & executées." [2] Another French traveller, Samuel de Sorbière, a friend of Monconys, who visited England independently in the same year, 1663, and who published at Paris in 1664 his *Relation d'vn Voyage en Angleterre,* describes the theatre as follows: " La Comedie est bien plus diuertissante, & plus commode aux entretiens. Les meilleures places sont celles du parterre, où les hommes & les femmes sont assis pesle-mesle, chacun auec ceux de sa bande. Le theatre est fort beau, couuert d'vn tapis verd,[3] & la scene y est toute libre, auec beaucoup de chāgemens, & des perspectiues. La symphonie y fait atendre agreablement l'ouuerture du theatre, & on y va volontiers de bonne heure pour l'escouter. Les acteurs & les actrices y sont admirables."[4] Thirty-five years later yet another French observer, Misson, in his *Memoires et Observations Faites par un Voyageur en Angleterre*, The Hague, 1698, describes the pit of the second Theatre Royal as "an Amphitheater fill'd with Benches without Backboards, and adorn'd and cover'd with green Cloth. Men of Quality, particularly the younger Sort, some Ladies of Reputation and Vertue, and abundance of Damsels that hunt for Prey, sit all together in this Place, Higgledy-piggledy, chatter, toy, play, hear, hear not. Farther up, against the Wall, under the first Gallery, and just opposite to the Stage, rises another Amphitheater, which is taken up by Persons of the best Quality, among whom are generally very few Men. The Galleries, whereof there are only two Rows, are fill'd with none but ordinary People, particularly the Upper one".[5] Accordingly we see that the benches in the pit were gradually ascending so that the last row was only a very few feet under the ledge of the boxes. To-day this is the case in the old Theatre Royal, Bristol, and a person standing in the pit can with perfect ease converse with one seated in the front row of the circle, the Restoration boxes. Again, the pit benches were arranged in concentric semicircles; they were without backs; and they were covered with green cloth. With reference to the latter detail it may be remarked that Dryden in the Prologue to *Cleomenes, The Spartan Heroe,* produced at Drury Lane in April, 1692, speaks of the rowdy fellows who frequent the pit:—

> *Who, to save Coach-hire, trudge along the Street,*
> *Then print our Matted Seats with dirty Feet;*
> *Who, while we speak, make Love to Orange-Wenches,*
> *And between Acts stand strutting on the Benches:*
> *Where got a Cock-horse, making vile Grimaces,*
> *They to the Boxes show their Booby Faces.*[6]

If the benches had been furnished with backs it would have been difficult for these merry andrews to have stood strutting on the seats during the acts, and it would be quite impossible to get astride them and sit staring up and glouting at the boxes. Thus in the Prologue to a revival of Cartwright's *The Ordinary* we have:—

> But to the young brisk men who think it fit, }
> To spend no Afternoon but in the Pit, }
> Whether we will or no we must submit. }
> Some come with lusty *Burgundy* half-drunk,
> T'eat *China* Oranges, make love to Punk;

And briskly mount a bench when th' Act is done,
And comb their much-lov'd Periwigs to the tune,
And can sit out a Play of three hours long,
Minding no part of it but the Dance and Song.[7]

Again, in his prologue "*for the Women, When they Acted at the Old* Theatre *in* Lincoln's Inn Fields", that is to say at some date between Monday, 26th February, 1671–2, and midsummer, 1673, Dryden writes:—

Here's good Accommodation in the Pit;
The Grave demurely in the midst may sit,
And so the hot *Burgundian* [8] on the Side
Ply Vizard Masque, and o're the Benches stride.

In Wycherley's *The Gentleman Dancing Master,* Act II, Hippolita rallies Gerrard: "This is one of your confident Tricks too, as I have been told, you'll be acquainted with a Woman in the time you can help her over a Bench in the Play-house."

The first tier of the house was divided into boxes and here was the Royal box exactly opposite the stage. When the King or any other great personage did not happen to be present, even this box, like the rest, was let off in separate seats to ordinary spectators, and there are many references which show that as this was the most prominent, and presumably the most comfortable place in the theatre, so it was the most coveted especially by those who came to be seen as well as to see. Over the King's Box, which was surmounted by a richly carved and gilded figure of Apollo,[9] were appropriately blazoned the Royal Arms.

In 1669 Prince Cosimo III of Tuscany, who was to succeed his father as Grand-Duke in the following year, visited England, and there is recorded by Count Lorenzo Magalotti who was of his suite a minute and detailed description of his Travels [10] which are extremely interesting and valuable. On 25th April the Prince went "towards evening to the King's Theatre, to hear the comedy, in his majesty's box. This theatre is nearly of a circular form, surrounded, in the inside, by boxes separated from each other, and divided into several rows of seats, for the greater accommodation of the ladies and gentlemen, who, in conformity with the freedom of the country, sit together indiscriminately; a large space being left on the ground-floor for the rest of the audience. The scenery is very light, capable of a great many changes, and embellished with beautiful landscapes. Before the comedy begins, that the audience may not be tired with waiting, the most delightful symphonies are played; on which account many persons come early to enjoy this agreeable amusement".

On the 3rd May following "In the afternoon, his highness left home earlier than usual to make visits, that he might be at the King's Theatre in time for the comedy, and a ballet set on foot and got up in honour of his highness by my Lord Stafford, uncle of the Duke of Norfolk.

"On arriving at the theatre, which was sufficiently lighted on the stage and on the walls to enable the spectators to see the scenes and the performances, his highness seated himself in a front box, when, besides enjoying the pleasure of the spectacle, he passed the evening in conversation with the Venetian ambassador, the Duke of Norfolk, Lord Stafford, and other noblemen.

"To the story of Psyche,[11] the daughter of Apollo, which abounded with beautiful incidents, all of them adapted to the performers and calculated to express the force of love, was joined a well-arranged ballet, regulated by the sound of various instruments, with new and fanciful dances after the English manner, in which different actions were counterfeited, the performers passing gracefully from one to another, so to render intelligible, by their movements, the acts they were representing.

"This spectacle was highly agreeable to his highness from its novelty and ingenuity; and all parts of it were likewise equally praised by the ladies and gentlemen, who crowded in great numbers to the theatre, to fill the boxes, with which it is entirely surrounded, and the pit, and to enjoy the performance, which was protracted to a late hour of the night. At the end of it, his highness returned home, and dismissing his attendants, retired to his apartments, and supped in private."

It has already been noted that de Monconys when he visited the Theatre Royal had a place "dans la loge du Roy". In Etherege's *The Man of Mode; or, Sir Fopling Flutter,* produced at Dorset Garden in March, 1675–6, Dorimant when told of a fine young gentlewoman newly come to Town cries: "This fine Woman, I'le lay my life, is some awkward ill fashion'd Country Toad, who not having above Four Dozen of black hairs on her head, has adorn'd her baldness with a large white Fruz, that she may look sparkishly in the Fore Front of the Kings Box, at an old Play." In Mrs. Behn's novel *The Court of the King of Bantam,* the incidents of which take place at Christmas, 1683, Mr. Wou'd-be King has a seat in the Royal box at Dorset Garden where *The London Cuckolds* is being played. Hither Sir Philip conducts Lucy, and leaves the lady with Mr. King, who is her admirer. In Tom Brown's *Letters from the Dead to the Living* we have one from Julian "late Secretary to the Muses" to William Peer, of Lincoln's Inn Fields play-house, wherein, recalling how in his lampoons whilst he lived characters about Town were shown in no very enviable light, he particularizes that " the antiquated Coquet was told of her age and ugliness, tho' her vanity plac'd her in the first row in the King's box at the play-house ". With regard to the anecdote of Wycherley and the Duchess of Cleveland to which reference has already been made it may be presumed that the lady did not on this occasion occupy her place in the front row of the King's box at Drury Lane in privilege of her connection with royalty, but merely as any other person of quality or fashion who might have taken a similar position in the house.

John Dennis, in his comedy *A Plot, and no Plot,* Drury Lane, 8th May, 1697, has a bit of business with the boxes which if when new, or rather unusual, might have been mildly effective in a music-hall way, has been reiterated *ad nauseam* since. Act II opens in the Play-house. The curtain is down, and on the apron "*Frowzy, Friskit, and Brush, appear at the Curtain*", entering through a Proscenium Door. *One from the Side Box.* Look yonder is *Frowzy,* arriv'd piping hot from Flanders. *Another from the other Side Box. Frowzy,* upon my life! Was there ever such an impudent Bawd! Presently *Sylvia appears in the Side Box.* (Bullock acted Sue Frowzy, the bawd.)

Elkanah Settle's *The City-Ramble, or A Play-House Wedding,* produced at Drury Lane 17th August, 1711, which is founded on *The Knight of the Burning Pestle,* attempts a similar novelty. When the play commences the Common-Council-man (Johnson), his Wife (Mrs. Knight), and their daughter Jenny (Miss Sherburne) are seated as spectators in the Middle Gallery side box over one of the proscenium doors. An actor enters to deliver the Prologue, but he is interrupted and then follows a discussion between him and the Common-Council-man. The latter with his Wife presently descend on to the stage. Miss Jenny, whose lover is one of the actors, slips down after them, whilst a friendly actress masked and borrowing her scarf takes her place. The husband and wife appear below upon the stage and are handed into a stage-box by the actor speaking the Prologue. The play within the play commences, and during the intervals the Common-Council-man and his good spouse discuss the action. In Act IV " *Enter* Jenny *dress'd up as a Shepherdess, and her Lover as a Swain, call'd* Damon *and* Phyllis ". "Look, Fubby, look," cries the Common-Council-man ; then gazing up at the box, he exclaims, " Nay were not the Chicken safe in yonder Coop I should swear 'twas she." At the end of Act IV Darby and Joan decide to take a short Trip behind the Scenes during the Musick Time, and as Act V commences, representing a Grove, they enter from the back scenes attended by a Player. Damon and Phyllis occupy the boards and in jest the Common Council-man joins their hands with his blessing. He then retires with his wife to their stage-box only to discover at the end (after the inset play is over) that he has actually given his consent to his daughter's marriage with an actor, and that the knot has been tied.

This practice of letting out the single seats in boxes to separate individuals remained in voguc almost until the present day. In fact it persists even now in minor theatres and smaller music-halls in the provinces, and I believe in London itself it is not altogether unknown in some Surrey-side houses. Forty years ago Mr. Lowe spoke of "the stage-boxes of the Brittania Theatre, where, for eighteen pence, you may have your single seat, among a miscellaneous company".[12] No doubt a considerable party together or several persons of importance would bespeak the whole of one box so that they might be comparatively private and undisturbed. Among the Exchequer Documents are various bills against Nell Gwyn for side-boxes at the Duke's Theatre, to which she never went alone but often with as many as four people for all of whom she paid. Thus, in September to December, 1674, she saw *The Tempest* four times, *Macbeth* once, *Hamlet* once, and, in June, 1675, *King Lear* once. There are Treasury Orders for payment to her.[13]

The tier above the boxes, a portion of which at any rate was similarly divided into boxes, was known as the "middle gallery", and constituted the most popular part of the house, as we shall see in greater detail when we describe the audiences of the day. Higher still was ranged the third tier, the "upper gallery" which was the cheapest part of the theatre.

The witty Epilogue, spoken by Estcourt, who had played Captain Hearty, a Sea Officer, to Mrs. Centlivre's *The Basset Table,* produced at Drury Lane in November, 1705, has these opening lines:—

This goodly Fabrick to a gazing Tarr,
Seems Fore and Aft, a Three Deckt-Man of War:
Abaft, the Hold's the Pit, from thence look up;
Aloft! that's Swabber's Nest, that's the Main-Top.
Side Boxes mann'd with Beau, and modish Rake,
Are like the Fore-castle and Quarter-Deck.
Those dark disguised, advent'rous black-nos'd few,
May pass for Gunners, or a Fire-Ship's Crew.
Some come like Privateers a Prize to seize,
And catch the French *within the Narrow Seas.*
The Orange-Ladies, Virgins of Renown,
Are Powder-Monkies running up and down.

The " black-nos'd few " are, of course, the Vizor-Masks, the train of Venus who plied the theatre as their particular province. Nor must the punning allusion to the Fire-Ship be unnoticed. A Fire-Ship was a cant word for a whore, as in *Love in a Wood* (4to, 1672), II, i, when Sir Simon meeting My Lady Flippant who is masked in S. James' Park at night, cries : " Are you not a Fireship ? a Punk, Madam ? " In Swift's *Polite Conversation,* ii (1738), we have : *Neverout.* Well, but, sir *John,* are you acquainted with any of our fine ladies yet ? *Sir John* : No ; damn your fire-ships, I have a wife of my own.

There are, as might be expected, continual references to the prices charged for seats in the various parts of the theatre, and the rate remained unaltered for a very long time. The admission to the boxes was four shillings ; to the pit, half a crown ; to the middle gallery, eighteen pence ; and to the upper gallery, one shilling. It would appear that these prices held good almost until the end of the eighteenth century.

Incidentally it should be remarked that the charges for admission to the Nursery differed from those of the ordinary theatres. On Monday, 24th February, 1667–8, Pepys pays two shillings at the Nursery, but he does not say in which particular part he was seated, and further details are wanting, save that we may reasonably infer a cheaper rate.

With regard to the regular houses a few allusions to the charge of four shillings, the price of admission to the boxes, may serve for very many. In Dryden's Epilogue (*Intended to have been Spoken to the PLAY before it was forbidden last Summer*) to *The Duke of Guise,* which was to have been produced in July, 1682, but was banned and postponed until the following November, the poet having commented on the rowdiness of the pit, especially at political plays, when swords were not infrequently drawn and lives endangered, continues :—

> This makes our Boxes full ; for men of Sense
> Pay their four Shillings in their own defence :
> That safe behind the Ladies they may stay ;
> Peep o'er the Fan, and Judg, the bloudy Fray.

In Shadwell's *The Sullen Lovers,* produced at Lincoln's Inn Fields on Saturday, 2nd May, 1668, Lady Vaine endeavouring to persuade Emilia to accompany her to the theatre, promises " A Rare Play, with a Jigg in't, would do your heart good to see it ; but if there were nothing else in't, you might have your four shillings out in Thunder and Lightning ". In his prologue to *The Bath ; or, The Western Lass,* which Whincop says was produced in 1697, but as it was advertised for publication in the *Post Boy,* 22nd July, 1701, may more probably be assigned to this year, D'Urfey says:—

> *I'm told that Beaus with Perukes cover'd o're,*
> *Make such strange shift to save poor shillings four,*
> *They'll in Side-Box three Acts for nothing sit,*
> *At last sneak down for Six-pence to the Pit.*

Since the pit was that part of the theatre most favoured by the regular playgoers, the gallants [14] and the critics, there are numberless references to the half-crown which was the rate of admission. On Wednesday, 1st January, 1667–8, Pepys going to the Duke of York's Theatre to see *Sr Martin Mar-all* soberly reflects: "Here a mighty company of citizens, 'prentices, and others; and it makes me observe that when I begun first to be able to bestow a play on myself, I do not remember that I saw so many by half of the ordinary 'prentices and mean people in the pit at 2s. 6d. a-piece as now: I going for several years no higher than the 12d. and then the 18d. places, though I strained hard to go in then when I did: so much the vanity and prodigality of the age is to be observed in this particular." The Epilogue to John Corye's comedy *The Generous Enemies; or, the Ridiculous Lovers,* produced at the Theatre Royal in 1671, gave Mrs. Boutell these lines:—

> Though there I see—Propitious Angels sit
> (*points at the Boxes*)
> Still there's a Nest of Devils in the Pit,
> By whom our Plays, like Children, just alive,
> Pinch'd by the Fairies, never after thrive:
> 'Tis but your Half-crown, Sirs: that won't undo.

In the Epilogue to *The Dutch Lover,* produced at Dorset Garden in February, 1673, Mrs. Behn protests:—

> *She never gull'd you Gallants of the Town*
> *Of Sum above four Shillings, or half a Crown.*

The Prologue to *The Young King; or, The Mistake,* a rococo but excellent play by Mrs. Behn, which was produced at the Duke's Theatre in the summer of 1679, has a vigorous allusion to a brawl in the pit (Tartarus) of the theatre, a scuffle much talked of at the time since Churchill, afterwards Duke of Marlborough, had been challenged and wounded by Otway the poet.[15]

> *But never yet Rencounter cou'd compare*
> *To our late vigorous* Tartarian *War:*
> *Cudgel the Weapon was, the Pit the Field;*
> *Fierce was the Hero, and too brave to yield.*

But stoutest Hearts must bow; and being well can'd,
He crys, Hold, hold, you have the Victory gain'd.
All laughing call—
Turn out the Rascal, the eternal Blockhead;
—Zounds, crys Tartarian, *I am out of Pocket:*
Half Crown my Play, Sixpence my Orange cost;
Equip me that, do you the Conquest boast.
For which to be at ease a Gathering's made,
And out they turn the Brother of the Blade.

The Epilogue to Crowne's tragedy, *Thyestes,* produced at the Theatre Royal early in 1681, an address which reflects the storms and political disorders of the time, thus concludes:—

But pray let Poets live, for they no ways
Offend you with damn'd Plots, but in their Plays,
And ask but half a Crown for holding forth,
And that's as much as any lye is worth.

City Politiques, a comedy by the same author, which—the days being dangerous—was for some six months prohibited because of its just censure of the Whigs, was at length permitted, and produced either late in December, 1682, or early in the following January.[16] The Prologue, spoken by Smith, scarifies rogues and traitors and ends with the following couplet:—

Heaven knows what sums the Cause has cost this Town!
Here you may see it all for half a Crown.

There are many exact allusions. Sam Vincent, from whom we have quoted, warns his Proud, Huffing, Self-conceited, Foppish and Lascivious Young Gallant to run on tick at the ordinary, "that he may keep half a Crown in his Pocket to sit in the Pit in the Play-house" (pp. 80–1). For "He much frequents the two Theatres: picks up a Miss, and pinches her fingers", plying her pretty hotly, "and if he cannot prevail with her for —— and he finds her honest, then he cries, *Damye for a precise whore, What make you in the Pit here? the Twelve-penny Gallery end Foot-boys are good enough for you*: and so leaves attacquing her. And if he lights of no other game, when the Play is done, if you mark his rising, 'tis with a kind of walking Epilogue; mounts the Stage from the Pit, and walks to and fro the Stage, and amongst the Scenes to see if his Suite may pass for currant" (pp. 78–9).

Ours is a Common Play: and you pay down
A common Harlots price—just half a Crown,

said Joseph Williams in the prologue written by Dryden for Harris' tragi-comedy *The Mistakes; or, The False Report* produced at Drury Lane late in 1690. This couplet is not unlike the lines in the epilogue to Settle's *The Empress of Morocco,* produced at Dorset Garden 3rd July, 1673:—

> *Nay, now you've Cast it off, yet do not Frown:*
> *Though like the refuge of a* Miss *o' th' Town,*
> *It is turn'd Common, Yours for half a Crown.*

On Friday, 29th November, 1661, Pepys notes: "Thence Sir W. Pen and I to the Theatre, but it was so full that we could hardly get any room so he went into one of the boxes, and I into the 18d. places, and there saw 'Love at First Sight',[17] a play of Mr. Killigrew's, and the first time that it hath been acted since before the troubles." In *The Sullen Lovers* Sir Positive has challenged two clerks to fight, and he expounds the reason to Stanford: "Why, look you Sir, for him to sit in the Eighteen pence Gallery, pray mark me, and rail at my Play alowd the first day, and did all that lay in his power to damn it." The Clerk gently protests: "'Tis true, I sate in the Eighteen Pence Gallery, but I was so far from Railling against your Play, that I cry'd it up as high as I could." "How high did you cry it up?" asks the author. "Why, as high as the upper Gallery, I am sure of that." Sir Positive returns: "Why do you say, you did not Raile? Did not I sit just under you in the Pit." Upon this the clerk's friend exclaims, "Lord! Who would expect to see a poet in the Pit at his own Play." In Wycherley's *The Country-Wife,* produced at the Theatre Royal, January, 1674–5, Horner banters Pinchwife: "I saw you yesterday in the eighteen penny place with a pretty Country-wench." The Honourable John Stafford in his Epilogue to Southerne's *The Disappointment; or, The Mother in Fashion,* produced at Drury Lane in the spring of 1684, fervently exclaims:—

> Let all the Boxes, *Phoebus,* find thy grace,
> And ah! preserve thy eighteen penny place!

The Upper Gallery, the shilling gallery, was a humble if lofty position. It is generally referred to with sarcasm or banter. Thus, Dryden in his Prologue to Tate's *The Loyal General,* produced at Dorset Garden in the winter of 1679, advises the rowdy pit:—

> Remove your Benches, you apostate Pit,
> And take Above, twelve penny-worth of Wit.

"*The Upper-tire of pop-gun wit*" Sir Harry Sheeres dubbed the upper gallery in his Prologue to Dryden's *Don Sebastian,* an address which was prohibited and not spoken. Dryden also jeers this part of the house in the Epilogue to John Banks' tragedy *The Unhappy Favourite, or, The Earl of Essex,* produced at Drury Lane in 1681, since the couplet

> *Confess the truth, which of you has not laid*
> *Four Farthings out to buy the* Hatfield *Maid?*

is marked as to be addressed "To the Upper Gallery".[18]

The *Hatfield Maid* was a broadside "Of a Strange and Wonderful Apparition" which was seen on 27th January, 1681, by Elizabeth Freeman, of Bishops-Hatfield, Herts. This vision—a Woman all in White—was recognized as the mother of Monmouth, Lucy Walters, who came to announce that her son was truly legitimate and heir to the throne with a heap of other treason and Whiggish propaganda.

> *Hatfield* Maids,
> Dreams, Whimsies, and the strange affrights
> Of Enthusiastic Bethlemites,

sings D'Urfey in his *Butler's Ghost,* 1682, Canto ii, p. 124.

In the ballad-prologue sung by Leveridge before *The Island Princess,* "Made into an Opera," by Motteux, Drury Lane, January, 1699, there are allusions to both the middle and the upper gallery:—

> *Ye Gallery haunters, who Love to Lie Snug,*
> *And munch Apples or Cakes while some Neighbour you hug,*
> *Ye loftier Genteels, who above us all sit,*
> *And look down with Contempt on the Mob in the Pit!*

In the Epilogue to Manning's *The Generous Choice,* Lincoln's Inn Fields, February, 1700, Miss Porter said:—

> *He challenges by Crowds*
> *Brush'd Beavers, Nat'ral Bobs, and Velvet Hoods*
> *And all behind the Scenes, and all above the Clouds.*

In the 4to, 1700, a footnote on *Clouds* runs: "Alluding to the Upper Gallery above the Ceiling."

The Prologue to William Philips' *The Revengeful Queen,* Drury Lane, 1698, sums up in a couplet the progress of the theatre cyprian:—

> *Just so the Nymph, no more by Honor aw'd,*
> *She turns Pit-Whore, then Gallery, then Bawd.*

In the Prologue, spoken by Doggett, to William Burnaby's *Love Betray'd; Or, The Agreable Disapointment,* Lincoln's Inn Fields, February, 1703, the following lines occur:—

We have our Judges too—such as they are ;
Some Frown ! some Swell ! some Nod too ! and some Hear !
Tho' they can't See— [The Upper Gallery.

The Earl of Clarendon in his *Dialogue Concerning Education* (written before 1674), reproves the extravagance of a plain citizen who would often spend " a shilling to see a Play when he had not got 'em so much that Day to support his Wife and Children ". Yet this long remained the cheapest part of the theatre, and although at Oxford Anthony à Wood may have contrived on occasion to see plays for sixpence there was no such rate in a London house.

Peter, Martin, and Jack, Swift's three brothers of *A Tale of a Tub* (1704),[19] when they were all three out of fashion and had not as yet adopted the modish *shoulder-knots,* soon discovered their Want by sad Experience, meeting in their walks with forty Mortifications and Indignities. " If they went to the *Play-house,* the Door-keeper showed them into the Twelvepeny Gallery."

Upon certain special occasions the prices were raised ; thus at the first performance of new plays they were doubled, a pre-Restoration practice to which there is not infrequent allusion, as in the First Act of Shackerley Marmion's *A Fine Companion,* 4to, 1633, I, v, the young gallant Spruse says : " a new Play, and a Gentleman in a new suit, claime the same priviledge, at their first presentment their estimation is double." On Monday, 16th December, 1661, Pepys notes : " After dinner to the Opera, where there was a new play (' Cutter of Coleman Street '), made in the year 1658, with reflections much upon the late times ; and it being the first time the pay was doubled, and so to save money, my wife and I went up into the gallery, and there sat and saw very well ; and a very good play it is." The doubled prices upon the first day were intended to compensate the company for the writing cost of the new piece.

Prices were also advanced, not only doubled, but sometimes even trebled at every performance of a new opera, since by these enhanced rates the management endeavoured to reimburse themselves for the outlay upon musicians, machines, dresses, scenery, and singers. In 1674, probably on 30th April, was given at Dorset Garden Shadwell's operatic version of *The Tempest,* altered little more than half a dozen years previously by Davenant and Dryden, and this proved one of the most popular, as it was one of the most splendid, spectacles known to the London stage. The Opera was mounted with immense preparation and at vast expense, circumstances repeatedly emphasized in the prologue and epilogue. The latter address says :—

Witt is a Mistress you have long enjoy'd,
Her beauty's not impair'd but you are cloy'd!
And Since 'tis not Witt's fault that you decay,
You, for your want of appetite must pay.
You to provoke your selves must keep her fine,
And she must now at double charges shine.

The advanced prices are thus alluded to by Dryden in the earlier version of his prologue to Charles Davenant's opera, *Circe,* produced at Dorset Garden in March, 1676–7:—

The Brothers of the Trade,
Who, scattering your Infection through the Pit,
With aking Hearts and empty Purses sit,
To take your dear five Shillings worth of Wit.

The epilogue of Shadwell's *Psyche,* Dorset Garden, 27th February, 1674–5, half apologizes for the magnificence of opera:—

But Oh a long farewell to all this sort
Of Plays, which this vast Town can not support.
If you could be content th' Expense to bear,
We would improve and treat you better ev'ry year.

In the Prologue, (spoken by Joe Haines,) to his burlesque, *Psyche Debauch'd,* which was given at the Theatre Royal in the spring of 1675, Duffett, with a dry bob at the increased prices for *Psyche,* Shadwell's opera at Dorset Garden, says:—

Let 'em restore your Treble prices too,
To see how strangely still they bubble you,
It makes me blush; and that I seldom do. . . .
But Oh! a long Farewell to all this sort,
Which Musick, Scenes, nor Preface can support
Yet you admire it, make 'em thankful for't:
Alass their Charge was great, and you must pay't. . . .
Show some of your good Natures here kind Sirs;
If our Conceit less proud or gay appears,
She's less expensive, and more brisk than theirs.

But the Prologues at the Duke's Theatre too were sometimes not sparing in their reflections upon the public taste for spectacle and show. Thus the Prologue to *Tunbridge-Wells,* Dorset Garden, February–March, 1678, caustically tells the audience:—

And that each act may rise to your desire
Devils and Witches must each Scene inspire,
Wit rowls in Waves, and showers down in Fire . . .
Your souls (we know) are seated in your Eies,
An Actress in a Cloud's a strange surprize,
And you ne're paid trebble prizes to be wise.

From the agreement which was entered into by Davenant with his actors on 5th November, 1660, we are able to glean some information concerning the methods of admission to the Duke's Theatre at that time. The " General Receipte of the Theatre " was to be by " ballatine,[20] or tickets sealed for all doores and boxes ", although with regard to the latter part of the house the system does not seem to have been strictly maintained. The manager appointed three persons who were to receive the money for these tickets in a room adjoining the theatre, which might be said to correspond with a box-office. The actors, for their part, had the right to appoint their own under-agents to keep a check upon the proceedings of the managerial nominees. It is worth noting that the well-known old exterior view of Wren's Drury Lane, which opened 26th March, 1674, shows that there are three doors giving admittance into the house. From the view from the river of the front of the Duke's Theatre, Dorset Garden, a drawing [21] which was taken shortly before its demolition in 1709, it would appear that there was in this building only one large public entrance standing behind a double arch. With regard to the Theatre Royal, presumably the system of admission there in force differed little, if at all, from Davenant's practice, but there is no precise evidence concerning this detail. W. Fennor in his *Compters Commonwealth,* published in 1617, remarks: " Each man sate down without respecting of persons, for he that first comes is first seated, like those that come to see plays." [22] Nor had there been any change in this respect under Charles II. Seats were neither numbered nor reserved. Actually the tickets technically known as " sealed tickets ", introduced by Davenant at the Duke's Theatre in 1661, were discs of brass or some other metal, of the roundness and about the size of a shilling. Such a ticket for the Duke's Theatre, Dorset Garden, Upper Gallery, 1671, is shown in an engraving (Plate 206) by Robert Wilkinson in his *Londina Illustrata.* On one side is stamped the monogram of the house surmounted by a coronet, on the reverse " VPPER GALLERIE 1671 ". There is no indication of a seat number.

It is perhaps not impertinent to mention that these metal tickets persisted until well within the nineteenth century, and that printed tickets originated from the need for something more distinctive to mark special and extraordinary occasions, such as an actor's benefit. We find indeed that printed tickets were used for galas and similar celebrations as early as the beginning of the eighteenth century since there is extant a notice referring to a concert of music (about 1702) which runs: " The boxes will be opened into the pit, into which none will be admitted without printed tickets."[23] Both authors and actors were in the habit of soliciting their patrons' favour by personal application and by letter, and to present or enclose a printed ticket would, of course, be greatly preferable to tendering the usual brass check. Sometimes, too, the printed ticket would be very ornate and remarkable. Such a one is the well-known specimen which is engraved with a scene from Congreve's *The Old Batchelour* drawn by Hogarth for the benefit of his friend the facetious Joe Miller at Drury Lane in 1717. Yet even the printed tickets did not reserve a seat, and indeed this comfortable custom of collocation did not prevail until the nineteenth century itself.

In the fifth chapter of Vincent's *Young Gallant's Academy*, 1674, the following instructions are given for the buck to enter the playhouse: "Therefore, I say, let our Gallant (having paid his *half Crown*, and given the Door-keeper his *Ticket*) presently advance himself into the middle of the *Pit*." The furiously fanatical Prologue to Crowne's tragedy *Thyestes*, Theatre Royal early in 1681, concludes with these lines:—

We like the Pope regard not much your praise,
He Tickets sells for Heaven, and we for Plays;
All but to make advantage of the Keys;
Pay for your Tickets, and go where you please.

In Farquhar's *The Recruiting Officer*, Drury Lane, April, 1706, IV, i, Plume promises Rose "I'll buy you a furbeloe scarf, and give you a ticket to see a play". "A play!" cries her brother, "Wauns, Ruose, take the ticket, and let's see the show." In *Three Hours after Marriage*, Pope, Gay, and Arbuthnot, 1717, Act I, Phoebe Clinket consoles her overworked Abigail with "But have Patience: I will remember the three Gallery-Tickets I promis'd thee at my New Tragedy". In *The Conscious Lovers*, Drury Lane, 7th November, 1722, ii, 2, Bevil inquires of Indiana: "Pray how did you like the Opera last night?" Upon which the lady replies: "First give me leave to thank you for my tickets."

Although of a far later date it may not be entirely out of place here to mention "bones", that is to say theatre checks made of bone instead of metal. Towards the end of the eighteenth century the custom arose of allowing the leading members of a company a certain number of passes to the boxes and gallery for the use of their friends. These were the "bones", bone checks stamped with the name of the actor or actress, and also with the number of persons to be admitted. Naturally the more important members of a cast would enjoy the right to give free entry to more individuals than a player of less distinction could thus admit.

Not the least curious custom which obtained in the Restoration theatre, a practice which obviously lent itself to much chousing and trickery, was the regulation that any person who made the excuse he wished to speak with one of the audience and did not intend to stay, or who undertook not to remain longer than one act, was entitled to enter the theatre without payment. Thus on Tuesday, 7th January, 1667–8, Pepys promised to meet his wife, Mercer, and Willet at the Nursery, " But the house did not act to-day ; and so I was at a loss for them, and therefore to the other two playhouses into the pit, to gaze up and down, to look for them, and there did by this means, for nothing, see an act in 'The Schoole of Compliments' at the Duke of York's house, and 'Henry The Fourth' at the King's house ; but, not finding them, nor liking either of the plays, I took my coach again, and home."

In Etherege's *She wou'd if she cou'd* (Lincoln's Inn Fields, February, 1667–8), i, 2, Gatty describes the fops who run and ramble here, and there, and everywhere, " From one Play-house, to the other Play-house, and if they like neither the Play nor the Women, they seldom stay any longer than the combing of their Perriwigs, or a whisper or two with a Friend ; and then they cock their Caps, and out they strut again." As might have been expected, this extraordinary privilege of seeing one act of a piece without paying was heartily abused and led to some pretty ingenious napping and bluff. Thus it was possible for an unscrupulous person who wished to see some new play to take an early opportunity of attending for the whole of the first act, then to leave the theatre ; and on the next afternoon to be in good time for the second act, and so during successive days to see a several act in like manner, and eventually he would have been present throughout the whole piece for nothing. This kind of shift became so impudent and so notorious that Davenant in the ballad-epilogue (sung by Harris and Samuel Sandford) to his comedy *The Man's the Master,* produced at Lincoln's Inn Fields, 26th March, 1668, took occasion soundly to rattle the offenders for this and other malpractices.

And some (a duce take 'em !) pretend
They come but to speak with a friend ;
Then wickedly rob us of a whole Play
By stealing five times an Act in a day.

In spite of so public a jobation the custom continued, and in Lacy's posthumous comedy *Sir Hercules Buffoon ; or the Poetical*

Squire, produced at Dorset Garden and printed quarto, 1684, I, i, Laton says: "that's wit to see Plays for nothing, one Act in the Pit, another in a Box, and a third in the Gallery, that's wit. And lastly, to cheat your Hackney Coachman, Link Boy, and your Whore, and give 'em nothing: O that's mighty wit!" James Wright, also in the prologue to *The Female Vertuoso's,* produced at Dorset Garden in 1693, refers to the nuisance of the "One-acters", and again in Farquhar's *The Beaux Stratagem,* produced at the Haymarket, 8th March, 1707, Archer and Aimwell calling to memory the days in London when their fortunes were at the lowest ebb relate how they were often "oblig'd to sneak into the side-Box, and between both Houses steal two Acts of a Play, and because we han't Money to see the other three,[24] we come away discontented, and damn the whole five".

In *The Beau Defeated* by Mrs. Pix, Lincoln's Inn Fields, February, 1700, the rich Lady Landsworth is testing young Clerimont. She gave a rendezvous in the play-house, and when Mrs. Betty asks whether she intended seriously to keep it, "Yes indeed," she replies, "last Night; and to try his Generosity, when the Door-keeper came into the side Box for Money, I seem'd in a great fright, and said, I had left my Purse at home, he immediately offer'd me a Guinea, which tho' I accepted, by the melancholy Air of his Face, I guess'd it had not a Twin Brother."

Farquhar again, in his *Discourse upon Comedy* (1702), pleasantly writes of "a sort of Gentlemen . . . who . . . make a shift to spend a handsom Patrimony of two or three Thousand Pound, by soaking in the Tavern all Night, lolling A-bed all the Morning, and sauntering away all the Evening between the two Play-houses with their Hands in their Pockets; you shall have a Gentleman of this size, upon his knowledge of *Covent-Garden* and a knack of witticising in his Cups, set up immediately for a Playwright. But besides the Gentleman's Wit and Experience, here is another Motive: There are a parcel of saucy, impudent Fellows about the Play-house call'd Doorkeepers, that can't let a Gentleman see a Play in Peace, without jogging, and nudging him every Minute. *Sir, will you please to pay?—Sir, the Act's done, will you please to pay, Sir?* I have broke their Heads all round two or three times, yet the Puppies will still be troublesom. Before gad, I'll be plagued with 'em no longer; I'll e'en write a Play my self; by which means my Character of Wit shall be establish'd, I shall enjoy the Freedom of the House."

Here we have another point of considerable interest, that is to say the free list. All authors who had written plays, whether these were successful or not, and all poets who had contributed prologues or epilogues enjoyed the right of free admission to the theatre. Mr. Lowe was inclined to believe that any poet who had printed his works shared this privilege, but although this was very probably the case one should perhaps hesitate before asserting it too definitely. There are many allusions to this circumstance, as for example the following lines which occur in *A Satyr upon the Poets, being a Translation out of the 7th Satyr of Juvenal* [25] :

> But on your Ruin stubbornly pursue,
> Herd with the hungry little chiming Crew,
> Obtain the empty Title of a Wit,
> And be a free-cost Noisy in the Pit:
> Print your dull Poems, and before 'em place
> A Crown of Laurel and a meager Face.

Oldham in his *Satyr* which brings in " *The Person of* Spencer . . . *Dissuading the Author from the Study of* Poetry " [26] has :—

> But who would now write Hackney to a Stage,
> That's only thought the Nuisance of the Age?
> Go after this, and beat thy wretched Brains,
> And toil to bring in thankless Ideot means:
> Turn o'er dull *Horace,* and the Classick Fools,
> To poach for Sense, and hunt for idle Rules:
> Be free of Tickets, and the Play-Houses,
> To make some tawdry Act'ress there thy Prize,
> And spend thy third Days gains 'twixt her clapp'd Thighs.

When Congreve entrusted the manuscript of *The Old Batchelour* to Mainwaring and Moyle, it was almost immediately submitted by them to Southerne, who forthwith brought it to the notice of Dryden himself. The two elder dramatists were so loud in their praises of the new writer's work, that not only was the play accepted for production at Drury Lane, but by an unusual privilege a considerable time before the actual performance of his first comedy Congreve was accorded the right of a free entrance to the theatre.

An abuse, which from various references seems to have been far from infrequent in the Restoration theatre was that men of quality and fashion were permitted to run on tick for plays. This, of course, entailed a certain amount of personal credit with the door-keepers, and no doubt in most cases those who became thus liable eventually had to pay pretty dearly for their obligations to these gentry, whose honesty, as we shall see later on, was anything but above suspicion. On Monday, 30th December, 1667, Pepys went with Sir Philip Carteret to the Theatre Royal to see Shirley's tragedy, *Love's Cruelty,* and he remarks: "I could not but observe that Sir Philip Carteret would fain have given me my going into a play; but yet, when he come to the door, he had no money to pay for himself, I having refused to accept of it for myself, but was fain; and I perceive he is known there, and do run upon the score for plays, which is a shame." Presumably this practice persisted until well within the eighteenth century, for in some verses signed F. P., prefixed to Henry Higden's *The Wary Widdow; or, Sir Noisy Parrat,* quarto, 1693, there is an allusion to impecunious gallants who at the "*Playhouse judge on tick*".

No more vivid picture of a Restoration theatre is given than by that most accurate observer of contemporary life and manners, Thomas Shadwell, the fourth act of whose comedy *A True Widow,* produced at Dorset Garden in December, 1678, has as its scene the Play-house. The act commences with a number of the characters "coming into the Play-house, seating themselves". We see all the bustle and business of the pit. The audience chatter of indifferent things, they discuss the author and the play; the orange-women cry their wares; a bevy of fair cyprians appear and the coxcombs begin to buzz about 'em. One man settles himself to stare at the ladies; another is only concerned with his clothes and his cravat; a third proposes to send for a pack of cards and play at Lang-trilloo in the box. All is movement and stir. Then we have:—

Enter several Ladies, and several Men.

Door-keep. Pray, Sir, pay me, my Masters will make me pay it.
3 *Man.* Impudent Rascal! Do you ask me for Money? Take that, Sirrah.
2 *Door-keep.* Will you pay me, Sir?
4 *Man.* No; I don't intend to stay.
2 *Door-keep.* So you say every day and see two or three Acts for nothing.
4 *Man.* I'll break your Head, you Rascal.
1 *Door-keep.* Pray, Sir, pay me.
3 *Man.* Set it down, I have no Silver about me, or bid my Man pay you.
Theodosia. What, do Gentlemen run on tick for Plays?
Carlos. As familiarly as with their Taylors.
3 *Door-keep.* Pox on you, Sirrah! go, and bid 'em begin quickly.
[Ex. *Door-keeper.*

"As infamous a Fellow as ever broke the Head of a Box-Keeper," says Sir Friendly Moral in Cibber's *The Lady's Last Stake* (Haymarket, 1707), and no doubt it sometimes went hard with the door-keeper, but it was a case of diamond cut diamond

ANNE BRACEGIRDLE AS SEMERNIA
Gabrielle Enthoven Collection

[*face p.* 48

since from the earliest years of the theatre these sharp blades were notorious for thimblerigging and palmer's play. Adepts in every sleight and chouse again and again do they come under the lash of the satirist. Thus in a tractate, bearing the date 24th January, 1643, entitled *The Actor's Remonstrance, or Complaint, for the Silencing of their Profession, and Banishment from their several Playhouses,* it is fleeringly said: "Nay, our verie doore keepers, men and women, most grievously complain that by this cessation they are robbed of the privilege of stealing from us with licence; they cannot now seem to scratch their heads where they itch not, and drop shillings and half crown pieces in at their collars."

As we may well suppose, the Restoration door-keeper was fully versed in all the cunning of his predecessors. On Monday, 24th February, 1667–8, Pepys having taken his wife and Deb Willet, the maid, to the Nursery where they saw *The Spanish Tragedy,* complains: "I was prettily served this day at the Playhouse door where, giving six shillings into the fellows hand for us three, the fellow by legerdemain did convey one away, and with so much grace faced me down that I did give him but five, that, though I knew the contrary, yet I was overpowered by his so grave and serious demanding the other shilling, that I could not deny him, but was forced by myself to give it him."

So far from their peculations being checked as time went on, the doorkeepers, either because the superintendence was lax and corrupt or else because their devices grew more daring and dexterous, profited exceedingly and often accumulated no inconsiderable fortunes. Davies in his *Dramatic Miscellanies* [27] relates a striking instance of this. "In a letter to Lord Berkley, Buckingham [the author of *The Rehearsal*] desired him to tell a certain lady, that he had resolved to swear by no other than Joe Ash; "and, if that," said his grace, "be a sin, it is as odd an one as ever she heard of." Joe Ash was, it seems, a box-keeper at Drury-lane play-house. How this man could merit this distinction I know not, unless he lent the duke money to supply his necessities, which were often very urgent. Box-keepers, whatever they may be now, by the managers keeping an eye over their conduct, were formerly richer than their masters. A remarkable instance of it I heard many years since. Colley Cibber had, in a prologue, or some part of a play, given such offence to a certain great man in power, that the play-house, by order of the lord-chamberlain, was shut up for some time, Cibber was arrested, and damages laid at ten thousand pounds. Of this misfortune Booth and Wilks were talking very seriously, at the play-house, in the presence of a Mr. King, the box-keeper; who asked if he could be of any service, by offering to bail

Cibber.—"Why, you blockhead," says Wilks, "it is for ten thousand pounds."—"I should be very sorry," said the box-keeper, "if I could not be answerable for twice that sum." The managers stared at each other; and Booth said, with some emotion, to Wilks, "What have you and I been doing, Bob, all this time? A box-keeper can buy us both!"

Dr. W. J. Lawrence thus briefly sums up a few important points: "There had been a custom in Caroline days of collecting money in the boxes after the performance had commenced; and this the gallants of old Rowley's court—who were never very flush of cash and sometimes did their playgoing on tick—insisted on being revived. Davenant and Killigrew, the two rival managers, weakly complied; and the duty of collecting fell upon the boxkeepers, who, from all accounts, seldom resisted the temptation to feather their own nests. The result was that towards the end of the century the office of 'the numberer' was instituted with a view to keeping a tally upon the box-keepers. During the performance the numberer occupied an elevated stage box on middle gallery level, and busied himself counting the people who came from time to time into the front and side boxes. In 1742 Garrick made innovation at old Drury by insisting upon checks being taken for the boxes as for the other parts; but, such is the force of custom, the numberer went on numbering till the close of the century. Even in Restoration days apart from the exclusion of the boxes from the check system, the vicious old ways still struggled for existence."

Truly, for not only fraud but force also was employed to gain admittance to the play in the days of Charles II. As early as 7th December, 1663, the King issued an order dealing with this: "Whereas We are informed that diverse persons doe rudely presse and with evill Language and Blows force theire wayes into the two Theatres at the times of theire publique Representations and Acting without paying the prizes established, to the greate disturbance of Our Servants lycenced by Our Authority . . . Our Will and pleasure therefore is . . . that no person of what Quality soever presume rudely or by force to come into either of the two theatres till the Playes are quite finished . . . notwithstanding theire pretended priviledge by custome of forceing theire Entrance at the fourth or fifth Acts without Payment." So little attention was paid to this Ordinance that in February, 1665, another edict was promulgated to the effect that since "Divers persons refused to pay at the first door of the said Theatre [Royal] thereby obliging the door-keepers to send after, solicit, and importune them for their entrance money . . . Our will and pleasure is that all persons coming to the said Theatre shall, at the first door, pay their entrance money (to be restored to them again in case they return the same way before the end of the Act) requiring the guards attending there, and all whom it may concern, to see that obedience be given hereunto . . ."

It should be remarked that shortly after the Restoration officers were appointed to preserve order in the case of quarrels among the audience in the theatres, and in days when every gentleman wore a sword which leaped from its scabbard at the slightest provocation, such a precaution was entirely necessary. In August, 1660, there had been something like a riot at the Cockpit in Drury Lane owing to certain soldiers forcing their way into the house, so that the Duke of Albemarle issued a strict proclamation to the military forbidding any such procedure. In November of the same year the King gave John Rogers authority to provide men to guard "the publique playhouses and showes from all molestation". Upon the opening of Davenant's Theatre in Lincoln's Inn Fields, and the Theatre Royal in Bridges Street, a regular military guard was assigned to each house, and throughout the performances sentries stood at the front of the buildings. The view of the second Theatre Royal, designed by Wren, which opened in 1674, shows two niches, one on either side of the centre door, and these are duly occupied by two musketeers under arms. It may be noted that in later days when the King attended the theatre the presence of yeomen from the Tower in their old-time costume of Henry VIII added to the picturesqueness of the scene.

Even the order of 1665 was so slightingly regarded that it became necessary for the King to issue on the 23rd July, 1670, a more imperative proclamation. The former injunctions were straitly reiterated. Moreover, nobody "by any pretended usage of an entrance at the fifth act" was to be permitted to force his way into the house. Any person deliberately offending in this manner was to be arrested by the guards in attendance at the theatre, and if the officers failed promptly to do their duty they were to lose a day's pay. On 6th November, 1672, yet another warrant was issued. This, however, only concerns the temporary Theatre Royal, as the Lincoln's Inn Fields Theatre was styled, whilst the King's servants were acting there. Yet a new but important detail is emphasized, "that no attendants of the nobility or gentry take a place in the house without paying." Eventually on the 2nd February, 1673–4, a proclamation was issued from Whitehall. It repeats and rehearses in the weightiest terms the provisions of former enactments; the regulations concerning payment are to be enforced, since it is laid down

" That no Person of What Quality soever, do presume to come into either of the said Theatres [called the Theatre Royal in Bridges-street, and the Dukes Theatre in Dorset-Garden] before and during the time of Acting, and until the Plays are quite finished, without paying the Price established for the respective Places" ; and it proceeds to command " (to avoid future Fraud) That none hereafter Shall enter the *Pit, First,* or *Upper Gallery,* without delivering to the respective Door-keeper the Ticket or Tickets which they received for their Money paid at the first Door". Nobody is allowed to stand or sit on the Stage, or to come " within any part of the scenes". With a few variants this order was reissued, under William and Mary, on 14th November, 1689. And yet for all this continual and recapitulated legislation there were only too many such as Major Rakish in Cibber's *Womans Wit; or, The Lady in Fashion,* produced at Drury Lane in the winter of 1699, who when asked how he managed his pleasures boasted that he " got up, and din'd with *Sir Bartholomew Bumper,* drank my two Bottles and Half with him by Five o'Clock—then call'd in at the Play (Impudence my Ticket) pick'd up a Parson's Wife, gave her the Remains of an old Clap, and so pawn'd her at *Philip's* for three Pints of Spirit of Clary."

NOTES TO CHAPTER II

[1] 1704, Introduction, p. 40. The " Scene " is of course the " Stage ".

[2] *Journal des Voyages de Monsieur de Monconys,* Lyon, 1666, Seconde Partie, pp. 25–6.

[3] It should be remarked that *theatre* here means *stage,* and in the English translation of de Sorbière *A Voyage to England,* 1709, this is correctly rendered (p. 69): " the Stage is very handsome, being covered with Green Cloth." The " Green Cloth " is the " Tragic Carpet ", for which see later.

[4] *Voyage en Angleterre,* Paris, 1664, pp. 166–7.

[5] I quote from the English translation of 1719 by Ozell, pp. 217–220, under *Plays.* In the original French edition, 1698, the account will be found under *Comédie,* pp. 63–5. " La Parterre est en Amphithéatre & rempli de bancs sans dossiers, garnis & couverts d'une étofe verte."

[6] *Dryden The Dramatic Works,* edited by Montague Summers ; vol. vi, p. 330. Odell, *Shakespeare from Betterton to Irving,* vol. i, pp. 125–6, misunderstanding the references of Monconys and de Sorbière, has been led into error, and hence is bound frankly to acknowledge that as regards the Prologue to *Cleomenes,* " What he means by ' matted ', I confess I do not know."

[7] *A Collection of Poems,* . . . London, Printed for Tho. Collins, 1673, p. 164.

[8] So in Wycherley's *Love in a Wood,* v, 1, during her night ramble in S. James' Park Lady Flippant cries : " The Park affords not so much as a Satyr for me (and that's strange) no Burgundy Man, or drunken Scourer will reel my way."

[9] For references to which see Dryden (Crowne and Shadwell) *Notes and Observations On The Empress of Morocco. Or, Some few Erratas* . . . 4to, 1674, p. 59.

[10] *Travels of Cosmo the Third Grand Duke of Tuscany, Through England* (1669). " Translated from the Italian Manuscript [of Count Lorenzo Magalotti] in the

Laurentian Library at Florence." London, 1821, pp. 190–1 and pp. 347–8. Flecknoe in his *Epigrams Of All Sorts,* 1670, has two poems, pp. 18–19, "*To his Highness* Cosmo, *Prince of* Tuscany, *On his Travels*" and "*To the same, On his coming into* England".

[11] Heywood's *Loves Mistris.* On Saturday, 15th August, 1668, Pepys went "to the King's playhouse, and there saw 'Love's Mistresse" revived, the thing pretty good, but full of variety of divertisement".

[12] *Thomas Betterton,* 1891, p. 32. See Pepys, 19th October, 1667, for the custom of letting off single seats in the upper boxes.

[13] *Third Report of the Historical MSS. Commission* (Appendix, p. 266).

[14] Ned Ward in *The London Spy,* October, 1699, part xii, p. 6, says that when entering a crowded tavern "we were forc'd to Struggle as hard for an Admittance, as a couple of be-lated *Beaus* do to squeeze into the Pit, when the Girl is to Sing a New Bawdy Song, or *Dogget* in *Love for Love* is to Play *Son Benjamin*".

[15] For a full account of this see *The Works of Thomas Otway,* edited by Montague Summers, Nonesuch Press, 1926, vol. i, Introduction, pp. lxix–lxxi.

[16] *City Politiques* was licensed 15th June, 1682. On 26th June it was prohibited by a particular order of the Lord Chamberlain. Leave to produce this play was not given until the following 18th December.

[17] *The Princess : Or Love at first Sight,* with separate title-page, 1663, in the folio *Comedies and Tragedies,* "Written by Thomas Killigrew," 1664.

[18] I quote from the text of the quarto play, 1682. The Epilogue is reprinted in *Miscellany Poems,* 1684, where this couplet is marked "*Looking above*", p. 294.

[19] *A Tale Of A Tub,* 1704, p. 64. Swift had already spoken of "the middle Region" of the Play-house, and "highest of all . . . a fourth Place, called *the Twelve-peny Gallery*", Introduction, p. 41.

[20] In a letter from Sir H. Wotton to Sir Edmund Bacon (Wotton, ii, 13), the writer tells his correspondent: "On Sunday last at night, and no longer, some sixteen apprentices (of what sort you shall guess by the rest of the story) having secretly learnt a new play without book *The Hog hath lost his Pearl,* took up the White-Fryers for their theatre: and having invited thither (as it should seem) rather their mistresses than their masters; who were all to enter *per bullettini* for a note of distinction from ordinary comedians, towards the end of the play the sheriffs (who by chance had heard of it) came in (as they say) and carried some six or seven of them to perform the last act at Bridewel; the rest are fled." The reason for this raid was that Sir John Swinnerton, the Lord Mayor, was intended by the Hog, and there was also in the play some reflection on Lord Salisbury, the late Lord Treasurer. This was probably softened when the piece came to be printed, quarto, 1614, "Divers times Publikely acted, by certaine London Prentices." The author is Robert Tailor. The date of the performance which Wotton describes was the first Sunday in Lent, 21st February, 1613.

[21] An engraving 6 × 8, was published by J. Nichols and Co., 1st July, 1814.

[22] Quoted by Collier, *English Dramatic Poetry,* ed. 1879, vol. iii, p. 145.

[23] Percy Fitzgerald, *A New History of the English Stage,* 1882, vol. i, p. 228.

[24] Ned Ward, *The London Spy,* February, 1700, The Second Volume, part iv, second edition, p. 14, relates how when the Spy was sauntering in Grays Inn Walks, presently "the *Bellfa's* . . . began to flow as fast into the Walks, as Whores into the eighteen-penny Gallery at the third Act".

[25] Poems on Affairs of State, vol. ii, 1703, p. 139.

[26] *The Works of Mr. John Oldham,* The Seventh Edition, Corrected, 1710, p. 303.

[27] 1784, vol. iii, pp. 307–8.

CHAPTER III

THE AUDIENCE, PLEASED AND DISPLEASED; ORANGE-WENCHES AND VIZARD MASKS

What pleasure is it to give you delight,
When most of you are fit to Judge and write:
Here none t'appear fantastick take great pains,
Or under huge white Perr'wigs have no brains;
No blustring *Bullyes* come in here half drunk,
For *Chyna* Oranges and love to Punck;
To fly at Vizard Masks talk Nonsence loud,
And with their noise out-vye Bear-baiting Croud.
  Poets should be above such Judges rais'd,
To be condemn'd by such is to be prais'd.

Prologue at Oxford. *A Collection of Poems Written upon several Occasions By several Persons.* London, Printed fr *Tho. Collins.* 1673.

Seeing that the tradition of the theatre is so conservative it must be remarked as significant that one common practice of pre-Restoration times disappeared under Charles II, to wit the presence of members of the audience upon the stage. I say advisedly that this custom was in abeyance " under Charles II ", since, as will be shown, but half a dozen years after his death it had already been revived and very soon then became thoroughly established. It is safe to conclude that it was the King's own influence and desire which suppressed this nuisance, and the novelty of scenery in the public theatres afforded a first-rate opportunity for the discouragement and discontinuance of so improper an intrusion. Writing in 1664 Sorbière particularly noted that in London the stages of the theatres were not occupied by spectators, " la scene y est toute libre ",[1] and when Vincent issued his alteration of *The Gull's Hornbook* as the *Young Gallant's Academy* in 1674 all mention of sitting on the stage is omitted, thus Dekker's " For do but cast up a reckoning, what large comings-in are pursed up by sitting on the stage " becomes " let him but consider what large comings-in are pursed up sitting in the *Pit* ". Pepys certainly has no mention of the stage being encumbered with any of the audience, and although it would appear from the edict of February, 1673–4 that something of the kind was attempted any such essay was immediately frustrated and forbidden. Gallants crowded behind the scenes and in the tiring-rooms, where Pepys as the friend of Henry Harris of the Duke's House and Mrs. Mary Knepp of the Theatre Royal was a frequent visitor. On Thursday, 7th May, 1668, being at the back in the Theatre Royal when the play was just finished, he " did see Beck Marshall come dressed, off of the stage, and looks mighty fine, and pretty, and noble: and also Nell, in her boy's clothes, mighty pretty. But, Lord! their confidence! and how many men do hover about them as soon as they come off the stage, and how confident they are in their talk! "

In Shadwell's *A True Widow* the performance of the play (within the play) is interrupted, and Carlos says: " Boy, Go find the Company; I have prepar'd an Entertainment upon the Stage; we'll have an Entry, a Song, or some Musick; there is no loss of the Play." Thereupon " *The Scene changes to the Stage and Scenes* " and a number of the characters enter behind the Scenes, where also Mr. Lump, a puritanical citizen, " a mortal Enemy to Wit " finds his way. He has not been in the front of the house, and since his entrance at the back causes no great surprise nor remark among the company, it would appear that practically any person might find admittance to so general a place of rendezvous. Private rooms are also mentioned, as the coxcomb Selfish having been a little too familiar with Mrs. Gartrude, enters bawling out to Bellamour: " I have enjoy'd the prettiest Creature, just now, in a Room behind the Scenes."

It was behind the Scenes that Sir Gilbert Gerrard was wont to linger amid the throng of fops and witlings for his fair inamorata, Lady Slingsby, a circumstance alluded to in *A Satyr on Both Whigs and Tories* (1682–3, unprinted MS.):—

Thou Thing made up of Buttons, Coach, and Show,
The Beasts that draw thee have more sense than thou.
Yet still thou mightst have fool'd behind the Scenes,
Have Comb'd thy Wig and set thy Cravat Strings,
Made love to *Slingsby* when she played the Queen,
The Coxcomb in the Croud had passed unseen.

In the Epilogue to *The Gentleman Dancing-Master* produced at Dorset Garden in March, 1672, spoken by the actress who played Flirt, the following invitation is given:—

You good men o' th' Exchange, *on whom alone*
We must depend, when Sparks to Sea are gone;
Into the Pit already you are come,
'Tis but a step more to our Tyring-room

Where none of us but will be wondrous sweet
Upon an able Lover of Lumber-*street:*
You we had rather see between our Scenes,
Than spend-thrift Fop with better Cloaths and meens.

The hint was meant seriously enough, as also were the concluding lines of the prologue, spoken by Hart, to *The Country-Wife*, produced at the Theatre Royal in January, 1674–5:—

We set no Guards upon our Tyring-Room,
But when with flying Colours, there you come,
We patiently you see, give up to you
Our Poets, Virgins, nay, our Matrons too.

In *The Plain-Dealer,* produced at Drury Lane in the winter of 1676, Mrs. Hoyden is said to be "As familiar a Duck As an Actress in the Tyring-room", and Manly jeers the fop Novel as "the refuse of the Play house tiring-rooms". Dryden in his Prologue, spoken by Hart, to *Marriage A-la-Mode*, produced by the King's Company at their temporary house, Lincoln's Inn Fields, about Easter, 1672, has:—

'Twas a sad sight, before they went from home,
To see our Warriors in red Waistcoats come,
With hair tuck't up into our tyring Room.
But 'twas more sad, to hear their last adieu.
The women sob'd, and swore they would be true,
And so they were as long as ere they cou'd;
But powerful Guinny cannot be withstood:
And they were made of Play-house Flesh & blood.

Again, in the epilogue "To The King And Queen, At The Opening Of Their Theatre Upon The Union Of The Two Companies In 1682" he scommatically pleads with the gallants:

We beg you, last, our Scene-room to forbear
And leave our Goods and Chattels to our Care.
Alas, our Women are but washy Toys,
And wholly taken up in Stage Employs:
Poor willing Tits they are: but yet I doubt
This double Duty soon will wear them out.

The earliest allusion to the Green Room of a theatre occurs in Shadwell's *A True Widow,* produced at Dorset Garden in December, 1678; 4to, 1679; Act IV, where when Lady Busy is pressing Gartrude upon Stanmore the gentleman refuses: "No, Madam; *Selfish,* this Evening, in a green Room, behind the Scenes, was before-hand with me; she ne'r tells of that." A little earlier at the play-house when the company are at the back of the stage Selfish ecstatically exclaims: "Ah *Bellamore !*

I am the happiest Man, I think, that ever the Sun shin'd on: I have enjoy'd the prettiest Creature, just now, in a Room behind the Scenes." In Cibber's *Love makes a Man; or, The Fop's Fortune,* produced at Drury Lane in the winter of 1700; 4to, 1701; (p. 44), Clodio says: "I do know *London* pretty well, and the Side-box, Sir, and behind the Scenes, ay, and the Green Room, and all the Girls and Women-Actresses there." The Green Room is so called because originally painted, or hung with, green.[2]

Quotations might be multiplied to show how the men about town crowded behind the scenes and in the tiring-room, but as yet their intrusion upon the stage in full view of the audience, although as we gather from the royal edicts, attempted, had been successfully checked.

With regard to this custom in France Claude Perrault in his translation *Les Dix Livres d'Architecture de Vitruve,* folio, 1673, has a note as follows upon Book V, chapter 6[3]: "l'Orchestre parmy les Grecs auroit esté une partie de la Scene. Mais aux Theatres des Romains aucuns des Acteurs ne descendoit dans l'Orchestre, qui estoit occupée par les sieges des Senateurs: Ce que nous imitons dans nos Comedies, dans lesquelles les gens de grande qualité se placent quelquefois sur le Theatre, & occupent une partie de la place qui est destinée aux Acteurs."

The recidivation of the old abuse in England commenced about 1690, and before many years had passed the stage was as thickly thronged as ever it had been when Blackfriars had its "private stages audience, the twelve-penny stool gentlemen". Both actors and dramatists had no liking for the practice, and in D'Urfey's *The Marriage-Hater Match'd,* produced at Drury Lane in January, 1692, Lady Subtle says of Lord Brainless: "'Dslife, there's no avoiding him, he will visit every body, nor is every House sufficient, but like a Fly he'll be buzzing in every Corner on't." "Just as he uses the Play-house," Berenice rejoins, "from the Box, whip he's in the Pit, from the Pit, hop he's in the Gallery, from thence, hey pass between the Scenes in a moment, when I have seen him spoil many a Comedy, by baulking the Actors entrance, for when I have eagerly expected some Buffoon to divert, the first nauseous appearance has been my Lord."[4] Charles Gildon's letter farced with many a compliment which was prefixed to the play when published, 4to, 1692, has one particularly pertinent and interesting passage which shows that to the actors the presence of some portion of the audience on the stage was—as may very well be believed—a nuisance and a balk. "If there be any fault in this play," writes the panegyrizing Gildon, "'tis that which few are guilty of; that is, there are too many good Characters, too full of Humour, a very pardonable failing, which only proceeds from Variety, the life of Pleasure and Wit, tho' the Stage's being throng'd with Spectators, did not a little contribute to the imperfect Acting of it, which accidental Misfortunes concurring with the Endeavours of an opposite Faction, must needs have damn'd it, had it not by the Force and Vigour of its own Worth rais'd itself the second day with the general Applause of all that saw it." [5] The Prologue to *The Fairy Queen,* produced at Dorset Garden in April, 1692, emphatically protests against a malpractice which so seriously incommoded the theatre :—

> *But that this Play may in its Pomp appear;*
> *Pray let our Stage from thronging* Beaux *be clear.*
> *For what e're cost we're at, what e're we do,*
> *In Scenes, Dress, Dances; yet there's many a* Beau,
> *Will think himself a much more taking show.*
> *How often have you curs'd these new* Beau-skreens,
> *That stand betwixt the Audience and the Scenes?*
> *I asked one of 'em t'other day*—Pray, Sir,
> Why d'ye the Stage before the Box prefer?
> *He answer'd*—Oh! There I Ogle the whole Theatre,
> My Wig—my Shape, my Leg, I there display,
> They speak much finer Things than I can say.
> *These are the Reasons why they croud the Stage;*
> *And make the disappointed Audience rage.*

In the Prologue to Wright's *The Female Vertuoso's,* produced at Dorset Garden in April, 1693, it is pointedly said that once the Stage had been "kept free from *Beaux* and Bullies". The Prologue spoken by Mrs. Verbruggen on the Third Day of Vanbrugh's *The Relapse; or, Virtue in Danger,* which was produced at Drury Lane, Saturday, 21st November, 1696, has many allusions to beaux invading the boards of the theatre.

> *Before the Play's half ended, I'll engage*
> *To shew you* Beaux, *come crowding on the Stage, . . .*
> *How have I shook, and trembling stood with awe,*
> *When here, behind the Scenes, I've seen 'em draw*
> *—A Comb, that dead-doing Weapon to the Heart,*
> *And turn each powder'd Hair into a Dart.*
> *When I have seen 'em sally on the Stage,*
> *Drest to the War, and ready to engage.*

The famous epilogue to Thomas Scott's tragedy, *The Unhappy Kindness; or, A Fruitless Revenge,* acted at Drury Lane in 1697, an address "*written by Mr.* Brown, *and spoke by* Jo. Haines, *in the Habit of an Horse-Officer, mounted on an Ass*", commences :—

> You have seen (before now) since this *shape-shewing* age,
> *More asses* than *mine,* on a *beau crowded* stage.

Motteux in his epilogue to *The Innocent Mistress,* a comedy by Mrs. Pix, produced at Lincoln's Inn Fields in 1697, echoes the same phrase:—

> *Then all thus stor'd, tho Money's scarce this Age,*
> *We need not fear t'have a* Beau-crowded *Stage.*

Again in Motteux' *Love's a Jest,* acted at Lincoln's Inn Fields in 1696, iv, 1, Airy remarks: "I can easily believe you've been . . . Side-boxing at the Play-house, Acting in the Pit, nay on the Stage too." In Shadwell's *Bury-Fair,* produced at the Theatre Royal in the spring of 1689, iii, 1, Wildish declares he will haunt Gertrude everywhere. "What," she cries, ". . . will you Dress at me? and tye Cravats at me?" . . . "Even so," he replies, "and stare, and goggle at you; and never have my Eyes off you, while I Side-box you in the Play-house." "What, where the Beaux draw up three Ranks deep every day?" "Yes." But as yet there is no mention of beaux on the stage itself.

So in Vanbrugh's *Æsop,* Part II, 4to, 1697, the following dialogue takes place between the Young, Gay, Airy Beau and Æsop:—

Æs. Pray what may be your Name?
B. *Empty.*
Æs. Where do you live?
B. In the Side-Box.
Æs. What do you do there?
B. I Ogle the Ladies.
Æs. To what purpose?
B. To no purpose.
Æs. Why then do you do it?
B. Because they like it, and I like it.

The author of *A Comparison between the Two Stages* (1702) remarking upon the popularity of Farquhar's *The Constant Couple,* produced at Drury Lane in November, 1699, makes Sullen say: "At that Play, I have seen the Pit, Box, and Stage so crowded—."[6] "Oh 'tis an unspeakable Pleasure to be in the Side-box or crowd to the Stage, and be distinguish'd by the Beaus of Quality," says Sir William Mode in Mrs. Centlivre's *The Beau's Duel; or, A Soldier for the Ladies* (Act II) produced at Lincoln's Inn Fields in the summer of 1702. There was further legislation, and on 17th January, 1704, Queen Anne was "pleased to issue her royal commands for the better regulation of the Theatres", and one clause of the edict strictly enjoins "that no person of what quality soever presume to go behind the scenes, or come upon the stage, either before or during the acting of any play". This prohibition seems to have checked the malpractice for a year or two at least, and in *Farewel Folly* by Motteux, Drury Lane, January, 1704–5, it is said "now no body comes behind the Scenes", but very shortly afterwards things were as bad as ever, and upon certain extraordinary occasions when spectators were excluded from the stage actually an apologetic and even pleading tone was adopted in the announcements. Thus at the first performance of Cibber's *She wou'd, and She wou'd not; or, the Kind Impostor* at Drury Lane, 26th November, 1702, the bill has: "And it is humbly desir'd, that no Gentleman may interrupt the Action by standing on the Stage the First Day." Some similar phrase is of constant occurrence in the bills, and there is an appeal to authority, for the Drury Lane advertisements in *The Spectator*, 1711–12, frequently conclude: "By her Majesty's Command no Persons are to be admitted behind the Scenes." When Betterton's famous benefit took place at Drury Lane on 7th April, 1709, and *Love for Love* was given "By the desire of several Persons of Quality" the boxes, pit, and stage were laid together, and no person admitted save by ticket, "the lowest at half-a-guinea a ticket." Steele, who has described the occasion in the first number of *The Tatler,* remarks: "There has not been known so great a Concourse of Persons of Distinction; the Stage it self was covered with Gentlemen and Ladies, and when the Curtain was drawn, there appeared also a very splendid Audience."

It is plain that even in Elizabethan days the stool-holders could not have sat about promiscuously but must have been confined to a certain prescribed area, and so soon as the usage of spectators on the stage was established and maintained in the eighteenth century definite provision perforce had to be made so this portion of the audience occupied benches arranged at the sides of the stage from the orchestra half-way to the back scene. These pews were corralled with balustrades, or, as appears from Hogarth's painting (1728), of *The Beggar's Opera*, by a railing, heavily hung with scalloped, fringed, and tasselled drapery. Even if such spectators were quiet and orderly their presence so close to the performers and their numbers must have been extremely discomposing, although apparently in course of time the inconvenience was simply tolerated and endured, but when, as often, the fine gentlemen who coveted these prominent places floundered in flush from the tavern after the play had well begun the noise and nuisance must have been truly insufferable. Yet such Bacchic interruptions were far from infrequent, and in an anonymous comedy *Sir Giddy Whim, or, The Lucky Amour*, 4to, 1703, the Alderman says to Captain Smart: "You get your first load of Claret by Seven—then to the Play-house, where you reel about the Stage, disturb the Actors, and expose your self to all the World at once." Moreover we hear of other spectators packing the wings and presenting a formidable obstruction to the players about to make an appearance upon the scene, "beaux and no beaux," says Tate Wilkinson,[7] "crowding the only entrance." He describes "Mrs. Cibber prostrating herself on an old couch, covered with black cloth as the tomb of the Capulets, with at least (on a great benefit night) two hundred persons behind her . . . Mr. Quin, aged sixty-five, with the heavy dress of Falstaff . . . was several minutes before he could pass through the numbers that wedged and hemmed him in". The anonymous author of *An Apology for the Life of Mr. T[heophilus] C[ibber]*, 1740, speaks of the "Nusance of having crouds" of strangers "behind our Scenes", and pertinently inquires: "Will a *dozen Crowns* compensate the Affront given to a whole Audience of a hundred or a hundred and fifty Pounds?"

To what an excess the abuse was carried may be judged by the dialogue between Æsop and the Fine Gentleman in Garrick's Dramatic Satire *Lethe,* produced at Drury Lane, 15th April, 1740. Having had some account of modish amusements Æsop asks: "How do you spend your Evenings, then?" "I dress in the Evening," replies the Fine Gentleman, "and go generally behind the Scenes of both Play-houses; not, you may imagine, to be diverted with the Play, but to intrigue and show myself—I stand upon the Stage, talk loud, and stare about—which confounds the Actors and disturbs the Audience; upon which the Galleries, who hate the Appearance of one of us, begin to *hiss* and cry *off, off*, while I undaunted, stamp my Foot so—loll with my Shoulder thus—take Snuff with my Right-hand, and smile scornfully—thus—This exasperates the Savages, and they attack us with Vollies of suck'd Oranges and half-eaten Pippins." "And you retire?" "Without doubt, if I am sober—for Orange will stain silk, and an Apple may disfigure a Feature."

It was not, indeed, until 1763 that Garrick finally succeeded in banishing spectators from the stage, and even perhaps he would not then have achieved his end had not the pantomimes with their elaborate scenery and machines paved the way, as upon the occasions of gorgeous spectacle which necessitated the whole retinue of the theatre, carpenters, scene-shifters, mechanicians, and the rest, in busy action, it was clearly impossible to accommodate any persons upon their arena. Even harlequin John Rich "kept his holy rites and mysteries of serpents, lions, and druids, &c. sacred from the inspection of all curious prying inspectors". The public in fine preferred their beloved pantomimes before the vicious privilege of encumbering the stage. When we consider how firmly fixed was the tradition, and how tenaciously the gallants, among the chief supporters of the theatre, clung to this custom, scotched often but ever ready to revive, we must at least honour and applaud King Charles II for his so firm determination that the abuse should not be tolerated during his day in his own or his brother's theatre.

There is, unfortunately, no scientific method of determining the capacity of any of the Restoration houses. The Duke's Theatre, Dorset Garden, which is said to have been designed by Sir Christopher Wren, and opened on 9th November, 1671, was constructed with the most sumptuous magnificence, and the cost which in a petition of Charles Davenant, Charles Killigrew, and Christopher Rich, dated 1709, is said to have been about £5,000, later investigations based upon a statement of Thomas Cross, treasurer of the theatre, show actually to have been as much as £9,000. The dimensions of the building as reckoned from Ogilby and Morgan's large scale-map of 1677, were: length over all, 140 feet; width, 57 feet. The stage of Dorset Garden had considerably more depth than the stage of the Theatre Royal, and hence perhaps it may be safe to assume that their several auditoriums were in ratio. Houses built in tennis courts must have been of indifferent seating capacity, and therefore the Theatre Royal in Vere Street, which occupied Gibbons' Tennis Court, and the Duke's Play-house in Lincoln's Inn Fields, which building was a conversion of Lisle's Tennis Court, were both inconvenient and sadly restricted in this respect. Cibber refers to the Lincoln's Inn Fields house as "small, and poorly fitted up, within the Walls of a Tennis *Quaree* Court, which is of the lesser sort".[8] Julian Marshall in his *Annals of Tennis* speaks of that kind of tennis court "which was called *Le Quarré*, or the Square",[9] and says that the usual length of such a Square was 100 feet. It has been computed that the first Duke's Playhouse, fronting Portugal Street, was some 75 feet in length and about 30 feet wide. In 1695 Betterton at the head of the seceders from Drury Lane reopened the Lincoln's Inn Theatre, which from the time the King's Company used it as their temporary home from February, 1672, until 1674, had reverted to its former estate of a tennis court. The extremely indifferent seating capacity of this theatre was one reason why "a new Project was form'd of building them a stately Theatre in the *Hay-Market* by Sir *John Vanbrugh*".

The dimensions of the first Theatre Royal, Bridges Street, have been computed at 112 feet in length by 58 or 59 feet in width. When the second Theatre Royal was planned the company determined to erect a scene-room in Vinegar Yard to the rear of the house, and this addition was 58 feet by 28 feet. Accordingly the width of the second theatre was the same, but the total length was increased to 140 feet. The price of the first Theatre Royal had been £2,400, and the second house cost "neere Two Thousand pounds more than when it was first built".

François Brunet in his unpublished *Voyage en Angleterre, 1676*,[10] has an interesting description of a visit to the Dorset Garden theatre. With his friends he went to see "la Comedie de la trouppe de Mr Le Duc Dyorcq ou nous n'entendismes que baragouines. Les habits des Comediens Sont a la françoise, La magnificence n'est pas plus grande que celles des troupes qui vont dans nos Provinces, Le lieu ou l'on joue est incomparablement plus beau et plus propre que ceux de nos Comediens, on est assis dans le parterre qui est en Amphitheatre ou l'on entend jamais de bruit, il n y a que Sept Loges qui peuvent contenir chacun Vingt personnes. Il y a pareil nombre au dessus et un paradis plus haut.

"On donne en tout temps quatre Chelins qui valent 54 sols pour chaque place des Premiers loges deux Chelins pour le parterre, et un Chelin et demy pour les secondes loges, Le paradis est pour les lacquais qui entrent gratuitement.

"L'On joue Les françois dans la plus part des Comedies qui sont faites pour Se mocquer de nos moeurs. La Composition en est bonne, et ils pretendent que leur poesie surpasse la nôtre à cause de la liberté de l'expression ils n'obseruent la regle des vingt quatre heures ny les autres qui nous contraignent dans les ouvrages du theatre françois. nous n'y demeurasmes que jusquà la fin du second acte parce que nous n'y entendions rien. nous y vismes de tres belles personnes qui ne nous empescherent pas de nous en aller."

Brunet is certainly in error when he gives "deux Chelins" as the price of admission to the pit; and the price for the upper gallery "paradis" was one shilling, the footmen only being allowed in free at the end of the fourth act. It is quite easily understood how he might have mistaken or have been misinformed upon these petty details. Brunet's manuscript has been discussed in an article entitled "A Restoration Theatre" in *The Tribune*, 6th August, 1906, by Dr. W. J. Lawrence, who in a private letter to myself adds: "I estimated that Dorset Garden held about 1,000 spectators, allowing 140 for the boxes, 140 for the middle gallery, 170 for the upper gallery, and 550 for the pit. Also that a full house at the prices given by Brunet would have amounted to some £93 10*s*. But as Drury Lane held £30 more than this, I apparently erred on the modest side. I made no calculation re the side boxes (which Brunet ignores) and these at front box prices would add another £20, and bring the Dorset Garden seating capacity up to perhaps 1,200."

In *The Theatrical Inquisitor and Monthly Mirror* of July, 1816, was printed a document stated (and no doubt with truth) to be a list of takings at the Theatre Royal for a performance of Dryden's *All For Love* on Wednesday, 12th December, 1677, when it must be borne in mind this great tragedy was entirely new. The list is as follows:—

		£	*s.*	*d.*
The King's box				
Mr. Hayle's box		3	0	0
Mr. Mohun's boxes		1	12	0
Mr. Yeate's boxes		0	12	0
James's boxes		2	0	0
14 Mr. Kent's pit 10 Mr. Britain's pit	117	14	12	0
30 Mr. Bray's gallery 18 Mr. Johnson's gallery	63	4	14	6
Mr. Thomson's gallery		1	13	0
		£28	4	6
House rent		5	14	0
Music				

From this it would appear that the tale of persons who paid for admittance to the theatre was 249. No doubt there were many more present who either by practice or by privilege had entered free. But the total of the receipts leaves only a clear £22 10*s*. to meet the actors' salaries and general expenses.

The list of takings at Lee's *The Rival Queens; or, The Death of Alexander the Great* on Wednesday, 26th December, following at the same house was:—

		£	*s.*	*d.*
The King's box		1	10	0
Mr. Hayle's boxes		2	16	0
Mr. Mohun's boxes		3	16	0
Mr. Yeate's boxes		1	15	6
James's boxes		2	4	0
34 Mr. Kent's pit, 112 16 Mr. Britain's pit, 79	191	23	17	6

		£	s.	d.
30 Mr. Bray's gallery, 100 / 40 Mr. Johnson's gallery, 44	144 . .	10	16	0
Upper Gallery, 119		5	19	0
Mrs. Kempton			5	0
		£52	19	0
House rent		5	14	0
Music				

It is probably superfluous to remark that Mr. Hayle, Mr. Mohun, Mr. Yeate were the respective box-keepers. Mohun was probably a son of the great actor.

The figures, especially those for *All for Love,* appear surprisingly low, particularly when we consider that these two plays were among the great successes of their day, tragedies written by two of the most applauded poets. D'Urfey's phrase is hardly an exaggeration when in the epilogue to *The Fool Turn'd Critick* (acted at the Theatre Royal in the winter of 1676), an address afterwards used by the same author as the Prologue to his *The Injured Princess,* he speaks of the Nonconformist preacher who

> melts in durance half his Grease away,
> To get, like us, poor thirteen Pounds a day.

Samuel Chappuzeau in his *Europe Vivante,* licensed September, 1666, published Geneva, 1667, in speaking of the London theatres says: " quoy qu'on ioue tous les jours, que ces maisons ne desemplissent jamais et que cent carrosses en barricadent les avenues." Yet on Friday, 26th February, 1668–9, Pepys notes: " I went with my wife and girls to the King's playhouse, to shew them that, and there saw ' The Faithfull Shepherdesse '. But Lord! what an empty house, there not being, as I could tell the people, so many as to make up above £10 in the whole house! The being of a new play at the other house, I suppose, being the cause." The previous day had been the première of Shadwell's *The Royal Shepherdesse* at Lincoln's Inn Fields. On Saturday, 29th August, 1668, Pepys " carried Harris to his playhouse, where, though four-o'-clock, so few people there at ' The Impertinents ' as I went out; and do believe they did not act, though there was my Lord Arlington and his company there ". Occasionally a notice is to be found that however small the audience the company will act and not dismiss. Thus at Lincoln's Inn Fields on 9th May, 1704, was given *Don John; or, The Libertine Destroyed,* " to begin exactly at ½ past 5, and not to dismiss, tho' the audience should be small." On the following 9th August at the same house *Don Quixote* (probably Part II) was produced with *The Cheats of Scapin* as an afterpiece, and intending playgoers were assured "Note; we shall not dismiss let the audience be what it will; and begin punctually at half past six at the furthest". During the darkest days of the Theatre Royal—in February, 1681, James Gray, the treasurer of that house, explained that the company "did heretofore sometimes desist from acting of plays" since the receipts were too small, "and that they have for the same reason dismissed the Audience and returned their respective moneys." Another treasurer, William Murray, recorded the sums they had taken on three particularly bad days: "11th May, 1681, £3 14*s*. 6*d*.; 30th May, 1681, £3 2*s*.; 18th June, 1681, £3 13*s*."

Ten pounds was, of course, under normal conditions, as Pepys notes, an exceptionally bad house, but the author of *The Laureat* (1740), an attack upon Colley Cibber, says that even the great Betterton himself more than once had played "to an audience of twenty pounds or under". Cibber in his *Apology* (1740), chapter xii, remarks: "We have seen within these two Years even *Farinelli* singing to an Audience of five and thirty Pounds." Davies in his *Life of Garrick* speaks of one melancholy occasion in 1763 at Drury Lane when although both Garrick and Mrs. Cibber were in the cast the house only held £3 15*s*. 6*d*. Possibly Benjamin Victor, in his *History of the Theatres of London and Dublin* (1761, iii, 95) was correct when he estimated that the receipts for a performance at a Restoration theatre "seldom exceeded seventy Pounds". It may be remembered that when Isaac Fuller the scene painter brought an action against the Theatre Royal in 1669–1670 he deposed that the Company had acted Dryden's *Tyrannick Love* "about 14 days together, and received all that while about 100 ll per diem, Whereas at other plays they are not wont usually to receive above 40 or 50 ll per diem And that their said House all the said 14 days was very full".[11]

One of the remarkable successes of the period was *The Squire of Alsatia,* produced at Drury Lane in May, 1688. It "had an uninterrupted run of 13 days together", which was quite exceptional, and in his Dedication of the quarto, 1688, to the Earl of Dorset, Shadwell writes that "*no Comedy, for these many Years . . . fill'd the Theatre so long together: And I had the great Honour to find so many Friends, that the House was never so full since it was built, as upon the Third day of this Play: and vast numbers went away that could not be admitted*". Downes in his remarks upon this comedy has: "*Note.* The Poet receiv'd for his Third day in the House in Drury-Lane at single Prices 130£.

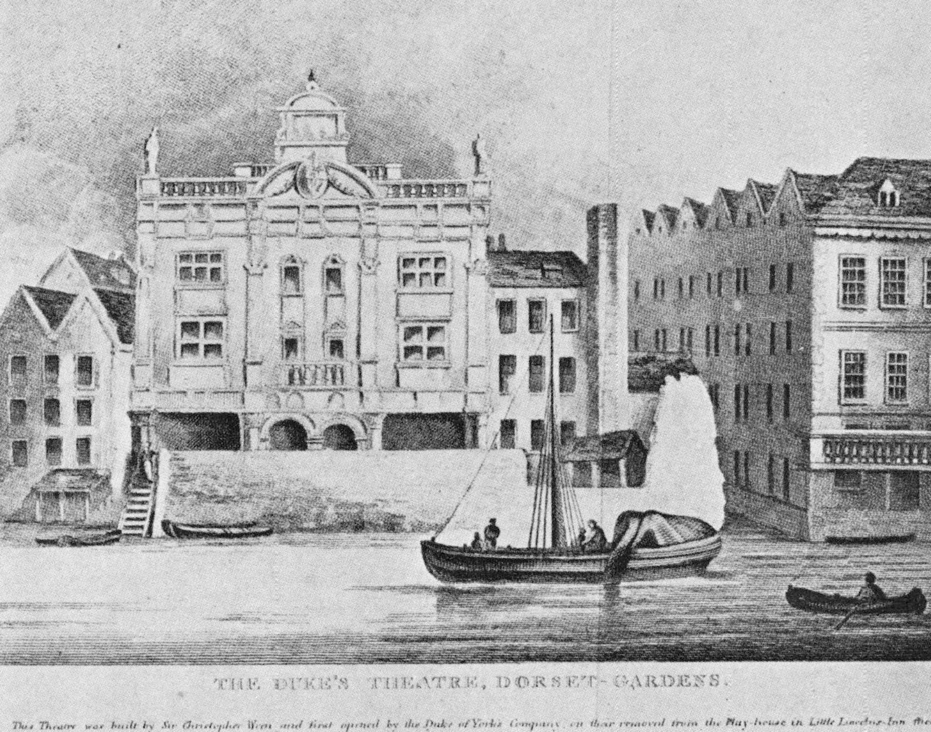

THE DUKE'S THEATRE: THE RIVER FRONT

Gabrielle Enthoven Collection

which is the greatest receipt they ever had at that house at single prices."

The estimates of Sir Henry Herbert in his petition to the Earls of Clarendon and Manchester, as dated 11th July, 1662, are not to be relied upon, and such a detail as the following is probably much exaggerated: "That Sir William Dauenant drawes 10 shares of 15 shares, which is valued at 200*l*. per week, cleer profitt, one week with another, as credibly informed." [12]

It has already been pointed out that a number of individuals among the audience were "dead-heads", be it permitted to use that popular but expressive term, and as is the nature of the beast these so far from showing their appreciation of the courtesy extended them were irrepressibly noisy and intolerant. Certainly it is somewhat surprising to find François Brunet in his *Voyage d'Angleterre,* 1676, writing of the Duke's House: "Le lieu ou l'on joue est incomparablement plus beau et plus propre que ceux de nos Comediens, on est assis dans le parterre qui est en Amphitheatre ou l'on entend jamais de bruit."

The critics and the gallants crowded the pit, which was more often than not the sphere of rowdiest licence and quarrels that led to brawls and duelling. The more respectable part of the audience favoured the boxes, as Dryden pointedly remarks in the Epilogue to *The Duke of Guise,* printed as a broadsheet, 1682, and "*Intended to have been Spoken to the* PLAY *before it was forbidden last Summer*".[13] Referring to the rowdyism and fights in the pit, the poet says:—

> This makes our Boxes full; for men of Sense
> Pay their four Shillings in their own defence:
> That safe behind the Ladies they may stay;
> Peep o'er the Fan, and Judg, the bloudy Fray.

Incidentally it may be remarked that stalls in the theatre were not introduced until the eighteen-forties.

The middle gallery—"the masqued Middle-Gallery" Jevon calls it in his bantering Epistle prefixed to *The Devil of A Wife,* 4to, 1686—may not untruly be termed the popular part of the house and was noisy enough in all conscience, whilst the upper gallery was so little esteemed that references to its exalted denizens are slighting and comparatively few. Ladies of easy virtue crowded the theatre as their own happy hunting-ground; and the orange wenches bawled their wares incessantly up and down the house.

Pepys often refers to the noise and chatter of the pit, and it seems extraordinary to us that nobody should have complained or protested against the interruptions of his neighbours. There is a vivid passage in his entry under Monday, 18th February, 1666–7, which however well known must be quoted yet once again: "To the King's house, to 'The Mayd's Tragedy'; but vexed all the while with two talking ladies and Sir Charles Sedley; yet pleased to hear their discourse, he being a stranger. And one of the ladies would, and did sit with her mask on, all the play, and, being exceeding witty as ever I heard woman, did talk most pleasantly with him; but was, I believe, a virtuous woman, and of quality. He would fain know who she was, but she would not tell; yet did give him many pleasant hints of her knowledge of him, by that means setting his brains at work to find out who she was, and did give him leave to find out all means who she was, but pulling off her mask. He was mighty witty, and she also making sport with him very inoffensively, that a more pleasant rencontre I never heard. But by that means lost the pleasure of the play wholly, to which now and then Sir Charles Sedley's exceptions against both words and pronouncing were very pretty." In Betterton's *The Amorous Widow; or, The Wanton Wife,* produced at Lincoln's Inn Fields about 1670, ii, Brittle complains: "my House is grown as common as the Exchange, or Playhouses, where all sorts of Company meet to laugh and talk Bawdy." And a little later his wife informs him that she and her cousin are going "to see a Play at the Duke's House, where we shall have such Sport . . .'Tis the pleasant'st Thing in the whole World to see a Flock of wild Gallants fluttering about two or three Ladies in Vizard Masks, and then they talk to 'em so wantonly, and so loud, that they put the very Players out of countenance—'Tis a better Entertainment, than any Part of the Play can be". It would seem that the frequenters of the pit had not the least consideration for the actors, or indeed for the rest of the audience, and in Thomas Jordan's *A Royal Arbor of Loyal Poesie,* as early as 23rd June, 1660, we have: "*A Speech by way of Epilogue to those that would rise out of the Pit at the* Red Bull *in the last Scene, and disturb the Conclusion, by going on the Stage.*"

A "Prologue Against the Disturbers of the Pit" which will be found in the Third Edition (so-called) of Curll's *The Works of The Right Honourable the Earls of Rochester and Roscommon,* 1709,[14] gives a vivid picture of the noisy nuisances that pestered a Restoration theatre.

> Laughers, Buffoons, with an unthinking Croud
> Of gaudy Fools, impertinent and loud,
> Insult in ev'ry Corner. Want of Sense,
> Conform'd with an outlandish Impudence,

Among the rude Disturbers of the Pit,
Have introduc'd ill Breeding and false Wit.
To boast their Lewdness here young Scowrers meet,
And all the vile Companions of the Street,
Keep a perpetual Brawling at the Door,
Who beat the Bawd last Night? who bilkt the Whore?
They snarl, but neither fight, nor pay a Farthing;
A Play-House is become a meer Bear-Garden,
Where ev'ry one with Insolence enjoys
His Liberty and Property of Noise . . .
While ev'ry little Thing perks up so soon,
That at Fourteen it hectors up and down,
With the best Cheats, and the worst Whores in Town;
Swears at a Play, who should be whipt at School,
The Foplings must in Time grow up to Rule.

It were easy, but superfluous, to accumulate quotations from plays, prologues, epilogues, satires, and lampoons describing the noise and nonsense of the pit. Some few passages showing their manners may serve for very many. When Lee's *Sophonisba* was played at Oxford the speaker of the Epilogue expresses the delight of the company to act in so famed a seat of learning:—

Free from the partial censure of the Town,
Where senseless Faction runs the Poet down;
Where flutt'ring Hectors on the Vizard fall,
One half o' th' Play they spend in Noise and Brawl,
Sleep out the rest then wake and damn it all.

Shadwell, that close observer of contemporary life, describes the hopeful youth who "at Sixteen forsooth, set up for Men of the Town. Such as come Drunk and Screaming into a Play-house, and stand upon the Benches, and toss their full Periwigs and empty Heads, and with their shrill unbroken Pipes, cry, *Dam-me, this is a Damn'd Play; Prithee let's to a Whore, Jack*" (*The Virtuoso,* Dorset Garden, May, 1676, i, 1). Old Mr. Snarl too, in the same comedy has a fling at the young men of the Age, "vitious, illiterate, foolish Fellows, good for nothing but to roar and to make a noise in a Play-house. To be very brisk with pert Whores in Vizards, who, though never so ill-bred, are most commonly too hard for them at their own weapon, *Repartee*—And when Whores are not there, they play Monkey-tricks with one another, while all sober men laugh at them." In Vincent's *Young Gallant's Academy,* 1674, Chapter v, "*Instructions for a young Gallant how to behave himself in the* Play-house", the modish gentleman is told: "It shall Crown you with rich Commendation to laugh aloud in the midst of the most serious and sudden Scene of the terriblest Tragedy, and to let the *Clapper* (your

Tongue) be tossed so high, that all the House may *ring* of it: for by Talking and laughing, you heap *Pelion* upon *Ossa,* Glory upon Glory: as first, all the eyes in the Galleries will leave walking after the Players, and only follow you." In the Epilogue to *The Fatal Jealousie,* Dorset Garden, 1672, Harris said:—

> *we'd have you know,*
> *We wish we'd none but true brisk wit to show,*
> *We silence wish that Men might hear a Play,*
> *And wish that Vizard Mask would keep away:*
> *But we as well might wish we were those Kings*
> *We sometimes Act, as hope to see these things.*

Dryden commenced his Epilogue "To The King And Queen, At The Opening Of Their Theatre Upon the Union Of The Two Companies In 1682" thus:—

> New Ministers, when first they get in place,
> Must have a care to please; and that's our Case:
> Some Laws for public Welfare we design,
> If you, the Power Supream, will please to join.
> There are a sort of Pratlers in the Pit,
> Who either have, or who pretend to Wit;
> These noisy Sirs so loud their Parts rehearse,
> That oft the Play is silenc'd by the Farce:
> Let such be dumb. . . .

But that is just what they would not. As Sir Anthony says in Southerne's comedy *Sir Anthony Love; or, The Rambling Lady,* Drury Lane, winter of 1690, the young fellows "go to Taverns to swallow a drunkenness; and then to a Play, to talk over their liquor".

Sedley in the Prologue to *Antony and Cleopatra,* Dorset Garden, February, 1677, speaks of the bawling fops in the audience whom he might imitate:—

> *And tear applause from evry Fool in Town;*
> *Make Love to Vizards in a Wit-like Noise,*
> *Dull in his Sense, yet aiery in his Voice,*
> *Catch at each Line that grates, and keep the good*
> *With his damn'd Noise from being understood.*

The Prologue to *Bellamira; or, The Mistress,* produced at the Theatre Royal in 1687, commences:—

> *Is it not strange to see in such an Age*
> *The Pulpit get the better of the Stage?*
> *Not through Rebellion as in former days,*
> *But Zeal for Sermons and neglect for Plays.*
> *Here's as good Ogling yet, and fewer spies.*

For Godly Parents watch with whites of Eyes.
Here gallants do but pay us for your Room,
Bring if you please, your own brisk wit from home.
Proclaim your drunken fray's three benches round
What Claps y'have met with, and what punks are found
Who are the Bully-rocks: and who gives ground.
We take all in good part, and never rage:
Tho the shrill Pit be louder than the Stage.
There you must sit demure, without a word:
Nor Perruque comb'd, nor Pocket tortoise stir'd
Here you may give the Lye, or draw your Sword.
Be low'd and senseless, huff, dumbfound, and roar;
Till all the Lady's and some gallants scowre.

In the Epilogue, spoke by Jevon, to Ravenscroft's *Dame Dobson,* Dorset Garden, 1683, the following lines occur:—

And Criticks *here with the same spirit stickle*
For Liberty, *as* Whiggs *in* Conventicle.
'Gainst Sheriffs *and* Poets *equally you Baul,*
You Riot in a Play-House, *they't* Guild-Hall.
But Noise, you see, and Faction often fails.

In the Epilogue, spoken by Mrs. Mary Lee, to Otway's farce *The Cheats of Scapin* which followed as an afterpiece *Titus and Berenice,* produced at Dorset Garden in the winter of 1676 or in January, 1676–7, this lady thus addressed the audience:—

How happy were we, when in humble guise
You came with honest Hearts and harmless Eyes:
Sate without Noise and Tumult in the Pit:
Oh what a pretious Jewel then was Wit . . .
Time was ye were as meek as now y'are proud,
Did not in curst Cabals of Criticks croud,
Nor thought it witty to be very loud.

In the Prologue, "Spoken by a Woman" and "Written by a Person of Quality" to *The Debauchee: or, The Credulous Cuckold,* Dorset Garden, January, 1677, some very trenchant lines are directed to the pittites:—

You'd be so welcome here, would you but sit
Like Cyphers, as you are, and grace the Pit,
Well drest, well bred, we'd never look for Wit.
But you come bawling in with broken French,
Roaring out Oaths aloud, from Bench to Bench,
And bellowing Bawdy to the Orange-wench;
Quarrel with Masques, and to be brisk, and free,
You sell 'em Bargains for a Repartee,
And then cry, Damn 'em Whores, who ere they be.
For shame from these Barbarities remove . . .

Sir Car Scroop in the Prologue to Lee's *The Rival Queens, or the Death of Alexander the Great,* Drury Lane, March, 1676–7, wrote:—

> *As for you, Sparks, that hither come each day,*
> *To act your own and not to mind our Play;*
> *Rehearse your usual Follies to the Pit,*
> *And with loud Nonsense drown the Stages Wit;*
> *Talk of your Clothes, your last Debauches tell,*
> *And witty Bargains to each other sell;*
> *Glout on the silly She, who for your sake*
> *Can Vanity and Noise for Love mistake;* . . .

"To sell witty Bargains" or "selling Bargains" was an ancient and impudent vulgarity which still persists. The gentlemen who favoured this elegant amusement having led their interlocutor to ask some innocent question suddenly replied "with frequent applications to him to salute that part which is generally introduced into all controversies that arise among the lower orders of the English gentry at horse-races, cock-matches, and other public places. Allusions to this part are likewise often made for the sake of the jest. And here, I believe, the wit is generally misunderstood. In reality, it lies in desiring another to kiss your a— for having just before threatened to kick his; for I have observed very accurately that no one ever desires you to kick that which belongs to himself, nor offers to kiss this part in another".[15] In Shadwell's *The Virtuoso,* Sir Samuel Hearty who "by the help of humorous, nonsensical By-Words, takes himself to be a Wit" is extremely given to this sort of pleasantry, a trait Dryden did not forget to mention in *Mac Flecknoe:*

> Where sold he Bargains, Whip-stick, kiss my Arse,
> Promis'd a Play and dwindled to a Farce?

In the Duke of Buckingham's *The Rehearsal,* Act V, Bayes represents an eclipse by bringing on to the stage the Earth, the Sun, and the Moon with song and dance. As he explains to Johnson, "that there may be something in't too of a Joque, I bring 'em in all singing, and make the Moon sell the Earth a bargain." Accordingly Luna and the Earth appear to the old country tune of Tom Tyler. The Earth sings:—

> What means *Luna* in a veil?
> *Luna.* *Luna* means to shew her tail.

"There's the bargain," bawls Bayes.

Dryden in his prologue [16] to *The Prophetess, or, The History of Dioclesian* produced at Dorset Garden in 1690, has a flirt at the gallants who are away taking part in the campaign in Ireland, and addressing the ladies, says:—

> With your Propitious Presence grace our Play,
> And with a Sigh their Empty Seats survey;
> Then think, on that bare Bench my servant sate,
> I see him Ogle still, and hear him Chat;
> Selling facetious Bargains, and propounding
> That witty Recreation, called Dum-founding.

Dumbfounding was a silly and rude form of practical joke. *The Dictionary of the Canting Crew* (*c.* 1699) has: "*Dum-found,* to beat soundly. *I dumfounded the Sawcy Rascal,* I bang'd his Back tightly." In Shadwell's *A True Widow,* produced at Dorset Garden in December, 1678, during the play-house scene, Act IV, Prig shows himself an adept in this tomfoolery. He whispers: "You shall see what tricks I'll play; faith! I love to be merry." [*Raps people on the Backs, and Twirls their Hats, and then looks demurely, as if he did not do it.* But a little later: "*Prig strikes a Bully over the Back, he takes it to be another, and strikes him. They fight.*" A general *mêlée* ensues. In Otway's *The Souldiers Fortune,* Dorset Garden, 1680, ii, when Sir David appears, and Beaugard says: "Surely he does not see us yet," Fourbin impudently replies, "See you, Sir, why he has but one eye, and we are on his blind side; I'll dumb-found him." He then strikes him smartly across the shoulders.

At the music-meeting in Southerne's *The Maid's Last Prayer; or, Any, Rather than Fail* (1693, iv, we have: "1 *Bully.* Pox o' this scraping, and tooting: shall we eclipse, *Tom,* and make it a rantrum? 2 *Bully.* No, no, we'll dumbfound the baronet. (*They dumfound him on each side as he turns.*) *Sir Symphony.* Who's that? What do you mean? (*Turning quick, one hits him in the eye.*)—This is not to be borne: is't you, take that, sir." In the Epilogue "spoken by Mrs. *Barry,* made by a Person of Quality" to Mrs. Behn's *The False Count,* Dorset Garden, 1682, the pit are told:—

> *Thus in true hate of Sense, and Wit's despite,*
> *Bantring and Shamming is your dear delight.*
> *Thus among all the Folly's here abounding,*
> *None took like the new Ape-trick of Dumfounding*
> *If to make people laugh the business be,*
> *You Sparks better Comedians are than we;*
> *You ev'ry day out-fool ev'n* Nokes *and* Lee.
> *They're forc'd to stop, and their own Farces quit,*
> *T'admire the Merry-Andrews of the Pit.*

The Prologue "spoken in Lent" to Ravenscroft's *Titus Andronicus; or, The Rape of Lavinia,* 4to, 1687, but produced at the Theatre Royal some seven or eight years before (" about the time of the *Popish-plot* ", says Langbaine), advises the gallants :—

> *Leave all your Jests of Bant'ring and Dum-founding*
> *Leave sharping for your selves and pay your Guinny*
> *For Procuration there to honest* Jenny.

Jenny Cromwell was a famous bawd of the day to whom there is an allusion in the Epilogue, spoken by Joe Haines, to Lee's *Gloriana,* Drury Lane, January, 1675–6 :—

> *We'll deal with you, Gallants, in your own way,*
> *And treat you like those Punks that love for pay;*
> Cartwright *and I, dress'd like two thundring Whores,*
> *With Rods will stand behind the Play-house Doors,*
> *And firk ye up each Day to Pleasures duly,*
> *As* Jenny Cromwell *does, or* Betty Buly.

Betty Buly is mentioned with other *ruffiane* of contemporary notoriety in the burlesque epilogue to Duffett's farce *The Empress of Morocco,* given at the Theatre Royal in the winter of 1673.[17]

According to Dryden, those of the audience who wished to see the play and hear as best they could chose the centre of the pit. In his Prologue written " *for the Women, When they Acted at the Old* Theatre *in* Lincoln's Inn Fields ", that is to say during the temporary occupation (from February, 1672, to March, 1674) of this house by Killigrew's company, he has, as we may remind ourselves, although the lines have been previously quoted :—

> Here's good Accommodation in the Pit
> The Grave demurely in the midst may sit,
> And so the hot *Burgundian* on the Side,
> Ply Vizard Masque, and o'er the Benches stride.

Naturally the foremost seats nearest the stage would be the most favoured part for those who came to be seen rather than to see. It is true that Pepys on Thursday, 6th February, 1668, at the first performance of *She wou'd if she cou'd* notes " among the rest, here was the Duke of Buckingham to-day openly sat in the pit ; and there I found him with my Lord Buckhurst, and Sidly, and Etherige, the poet," but this was a particular occasion. In his Epilogue " *Spoken at the opening of the New House,* 26th March, 1674 " Dryden has :—

> But you, loud Sirs, who thro' your Curls look big,
> Criticks in plume and white Vallancy Wig,
> Who lolling on our foremost Benches sit,
> And still charge first (the true forlorn of Wit) . . .

So may Fop corner full of Noise remain,
And drive far off the dull, attentive Train; . . .
So may not *France* your Warlike Hands recal,
But leave you by each other's Swords to fall,
As you come here to ruffle Vizard Punk,
When sober rail, and roar when you are drunk.

As one may suppose critics such as these paid little attention to the plays acted upon the stage before them, and the dramatists often gird at the idle foplings, who to save themselves the trouble of thinking, damned tragedy and comedy galore. A Prologue [18] which appeared for the first time in *Covent Garden Drollery,* 1672, very neatly but not without a strain of serious castigation rallies this portion of the audience:—

He who comes hither with design to kiss,
And with a bum revers'd, to whisper Miss,
To comb a Perriwig, or to shew gay cloathes,
Or to vent Antique nonscence with new oathes,
Our Poet welcomes as the Muses friend;
For hee'l by irony each Play commend.
Next these we welcome such as briskly dine,
At *Locket's,* at *Iiffords,* or with *Shataline.*
Swell'd with Pottage, and the *Burgundian* Grape,
They hither come to take a kindly nap.
In these our Poet don't conceive much harm;
For they pay well, and keep our benches warm.
And though scarce half awake, some Playes they dam,
They do't by Wholesail; not by Ounce, and Dram.

The Epilogue to *Love's a Jest,* by Motteux, Lincoln's Inn Fields, autumn of 1696, commences:—

Mr. Underhil. *Now for the Epilogue.*
Mr. Bowen. *There's none I think!*
Mr. Underhil. *Let down the Curtain then and let's go drink.*

Enter Mr. Mynns, *one of the Gypsies.*

Gypsie. *Hold!*
I must here tell Fortunes e're you stir . . .
First Criticks, here in pain you'll always sit,
And swear, all's as Damn'd stuff, as tho by you *'twere writ,*
You'll strive not *to be pleas'd, and while we're playing*
Asses will chat, or hiss instead of Braying.
Poor Masks, who lay out half Crown to get Cully,
You'll often sit alone damn'd Melancholy . . .
You, Rakish Sparks, shall jogg from House to House,
Look big, Shift Boxes, and not pay a Souse.

Certainly the audiences were always ready enough to express very emphatically their likes and their dislikes, particularly the latter. Even the presence of the King in the royal box was no curb upon the denizens of the pit when they wished to give vent to their feelings with very audible sibilations. At the first performance of Orrery's heroic tragedy *The Black Prince* at the King's house on Saturday, 19th October, 1667, the people already a little weary of the long stately drama took occasion to jeer at the letter read in the fifth act. Indeed they deemed it "so unnecessary that they frequently begun to laugh, and to hiss twenty times, that, had it not been for the King's being there, they had certainly hissed it off the stage". Mrs. Pepys was scandalized at such behaviour in the presence of the King.

When honest John Downes had a mind to quit his prompting and come out on the open boards they gave him the rôle of Haly in *The Siege of Rhodes*. On Tuesday, 2nd July, 1661, the King, the Duke of York, and a splendid show of the nobility thronged the house. But "*the sight of that* August *presence*" spoiled him for an actor. He trembled and tottered, could not remember his lines, and "was so much out that he was hissed off the stage".[19]

When D'Urfey's *The Banditti, or a Ladies Distress,* given at Drury Lane in February, 1686, was damned, the author dedicated the printed quarto, 1686 (Licensed 1st March, 1685–6) in a strain of completest irony to "The Extreme Witty and Judicious Gentleman, Sir Critick Cat-call", whose "prejudice took vent even before the Play began; the Actors were Disturb'd, and cou'd not perform, particularly in the Second Act: After which the Scenes were all promiscuously decry'd both good and bad, the Songs and Musick hoop'd and whistl'd at, thô they have since been Sung in several other Plays with generall Applause, which I think sufficiently discovers the ungenerous Malice and poor Partiality that was us'd". The same poet's *A Fool's Preferment; or, The Three Dukes of Dunstable* produced at Dorset Garden early in 1688 proved a sad failure, and Sir George Etherege writing from Ratisbon when the quarto was sent him is ill-natured enough to say "I rejoiced to hear that it was so solemnly interred to the tune of catcalls".

Complaints of the harshness and caprice of the audiences are common. Thus Henry Higden, whose comedy *The Wary Widdow; or, Sir Noisy Parrat*[20] was exploded when produced at Drury Lane in March, 1693, in the course of his Dedication to the Earl of Dorset shows himself extremely mortified by the severity of those in the house who "with a barbarous variety of Noise and Tumult" so interrupted the acting of his play "that many of the well meaning Spectatours (for I am sure it had very few Hearers) must conclude it a very criminall performance".

Mrs. Behn frequently expresses her warm indignation at the unjust and silly attacks which were made on her comedies, and she freely exposes the factions that were eager to damn her scenes. The old weary cry was raised. In her address to the Reader prefacing that capital play *Sir Patient Fancy,* Dorset Garden, late in 1677 or early 1678; 4to, 1678; she administers a deserved jobation to those who protested "*That it was Baudy*", and when the same peevish cavilling was heard on the occasion of the production of *The Luckey Chance; or, An Alderman's Bargain* (Drury Lane, December, 1686, or January, 1686–7) she defends herself at greater length and with the utmost vivacity, shrewdly remarking of the brisk critics and rival poets "nothing makes them so thorough-stitcht an Enemy as a full Third Day".[21]

It was the custom when the play was over for all who would be thought judges of literature and the theatre to assemble in force at Will's Coffee House and hold a solemn inquest upon the piece. This famous resort which had its name from Will Unwin who kept it was No. 1 Bow Street, Covent Garden, on the west side corner of Russell Street. The wits' room was upstairs on the first floor. Mrs. Behn tells us with reference to *The Luckey Chance* "that a Wit of the Town, a Friend of Mine at *Wills* Coffee House, the first Night of the Play, cry'd it down as much as in him lay, who before had read it and assured me he never saw a prettier Comedy. So complaisant one pestilent Wit will be to another, and in the full Cry make his Noise too". [22]

The hub of all the turmoil and clamour, the wit and the obscenity that passed for wit in the Restoration Theatre, was Fop corner, a portion of the house nearest the stage, a hornet's nest of malice and scandal where the fair-pated beaux and snarling critics clustered and buzzed and stung. The Prologue, spoken by Hart, to Dryden's *Marriage A-La-Mode,* produced at Lincoln's Inn about Easter, 1672; 4to, 1673; commences:—

Lord how reform'd, and quiet are we grown,
Since all our Braves, and all our Wits are gone,
Fop-corner now is free from Civil War:
White-Wig and Vizard make no longer jar.

In Shadwell's *A True Widow,* the play-house, Act IV, when the Curtain-time is played all take their places. "*Selfish and Young Maggot go to sit down.*" Young Maggot cries: "Don't come to us; let you Wits sit together," to which Prig returns: "These Fellows will be witty, and trouble us; go to your Brother Wits, and make a noise among your selves, Brother Wits. [*They go on the other side.*" The Epilogue, spoken by

Mrs. Butler, to Mrs. Behn's *The City Heiress,* produced at Dorset Garden, 15th May, 1682, rallies the ladies:—

> *You break into our Quarters for Provision;*
> *Invade Fop-Corner with your glaring Beauties,*
> *And 'tice our Loyal Subjects from their Duties.*

In Radcliffe's *The Ramble* [23] the man about town is satirically described:—

> Then it began to visit Playes,
> And on the Women it wou'd gaze,
> And looked like Love in a Maze
> Or a Wood.
> Into Fop-corner you wou'd get,
> And use a strange obstreperous Wit,
> Not any quiet to the Pit
> Allowing.

The famous play-house scene, to which frequent allusion has been made, and whence many illustrations have been drawn, in Shadwell's *A True Widow,* Dorset Garden, December, 1678, culminates in a general fracas. Prig has been briskly engaged in his usual game of dumfounding. "*Prig strikes a Bully over the Back, he takes it to be another, and strikes him. They fight.*" 1 *Man.* Zounds you Rogue! Do you play your tricks with me? 2 *Man.* Have at you, Dog. "*Bellamore, Stanmore, Carlos beat the Bullies out of the House; the Actors run off; Ladies run out shrieking.*" Presently when the disorder is a little quieted one of the actors returns to announce: "Sir, We cannot go on with our Play, one of our young Women being frighted with the Swords, is fallen into a Fit, and carried home sick."

Such brawls, which sometimes terminated fatally, were matters of frequent occurrence in the pit of a Restoration Theatre. In a letter, dated 23rd June, 1679, from John Verney in London to Sir Richard Verney, of Claydon House, *comitatu* Bucks, mention is made of an event which was causing great talk: "Churchill, for beating an orange wench in the Duke's playhouse, was challenged by Capt. Otway (the poet), and were both wounded, but Churchill most. The relation being told the King by Sir John Holmes, as Churchill thought to his prejudice, he challenged Holmes, who fighting disarmed him, Churchill." This is the occasion referred to by Mrs. Behn in the Prologue to *The Young King; or, The Mistake,* which was produced at the Duke's Theatre in the summer of 1679:—

> *They're sparks who are of Noise and Nonsense full,*
> *At fifteen witty, and at twenty dull;*

That in the Pit can huff, and talk hard Words,
And briskly draw Bamboo instead of Swords:
But never yet Rencounter cou'd compare
To our late vigorous Tartarian *War:*
Cudgel the Weapon was, the Pit the Field;
Fierce was the Hero, and too brave to yield.
But stoutest Hearts must bow; and being well can'd,
He crys, Hold, hold, you have the Victory gain'd.
All laughing call—
Turn out the Rascal, the eternal Blockhead;
—Zounds, crys Tartarian, *I am out of Pocket:*
Half Crown my Play, Sixpence my Orange cost;
Equip me that, do you the Conquest boast.
For which to be at ease a Gathering's made,
And out they turn the Brother of the Blade.

"*I am out of Pocket*" is a sharp bob at the notorious stinginess of Churchill, and the whole episode is treated with much point and wit.[24] Dryden in the Prologue to *The Spanish Fryar,* Dorset Garden, March, 1680, has:—

Scowring the Watch grows out of fashion wit,
Now we set up for Tilting in the Pit,
Where 'tis agreed by Bullies, chicken-hearted,
To fright the Ladies first, and then be parted.[25]

Nahum Tate in his *Poems,* second edition, 1684,[26] has some satirical verses "*The Battle of the* B—ds *in the Theatre Royal,* December *the 3d* 1680" which commence—

Give ore ye Tilters of the Pit, give ore,
Frighten the Boxes and your selves no more:
Two Amazons of Scandalous renown,
Have with dire Combats made the Field their own.
Their fray on no slight Ground (like yours) was made,
But for precedence in their famous Trade; . . .

An account of the caning of Sir George Hewitt in the pit of the Theatre Royal by Ravenscroft the dramatist on Monday, 2nd July, 1673, and the various quarrels and ill consequences which resulted are presented to us very vividly in a letter, 4th July, 1673, addressed by Henry Ball to Sir Joseph Williamson, who was then one of the English plenipotentiaries at the Cologne Congress. "The quarrell on Monday att the King's Theatre was occasioned thus: one Mr. Ravenscroft having half a yeare since received an affront from Sir George Hewitt in the play-house, and having ever since studyed retalliation, came that day to the play, where finding him there, beate him with his cane and so went away; presently after which my Lord Buck-hurst and Capt. Bulkley going out with intentions to the other play-house, were followed by chance by Coll. Strode, so that all three being at the doore and Mr. Ravenscroft and company going by, and my Lord by chance blaming the action, Mr. Ravenscroft presently fell to words, and then they all drew. My Lord was hurt in the body, Capt. Bulkley in the necke, and the Collonell in his hand and eare, but all their hurts are now cured." Three days later Ball informs his patron: "His Ma^{ty} has sent his order to the Earle Marshall to seize Sir George Hewitt for sending a challenge to Ravenscroft, and to take the three brothers of them into custody for falling upon my Lord Buckhurst and his company, resolveing if possible to prevent those ill consequences which such disorders will produce." On 11th July in another letter Ball has a further item of news to give: "This quarrell between Sir George Hewitt and Mr. Ravenscroft is not yet composed, nor the latter rendered themselves, his Majesty having commanded the Mareshall to make them peremptorily quitt his kingdomes if they come not in and be punished, which makes the Inns of Court men rayle horridly at the actions of the Court, and draw themselves into partyes to affront the courtiers any where, so that it's feared that foolish quarrell may have too ill consequences." [27]

But there were even more serious frays than these. In his review of *Macbeth* [28] Langbaine writes: "At the Acting of this Tragedy, on the Stage, I saw a real one acted in the Pit; I mean the Death of Mr. *Scroop,* who received his death's wound from the late Sir *Thomas Armstrong,* and died presently after he was remov'd to a House opposite to the Theatre, in *Dorset-Garden.*" This happened on Saturday, 28th August, 1675. In February, 1679, a hot dispute between some gentlemen who cried out against "the Duchess of *Portsmouth* and other persons of honour" in the pit at the Duke's Theatre led to so general a disturbance that acting was temporarily prohibited. *The Impartial Protestant Mercury* for 2nd May, 1682, notes that on the previous 27th April, "Mr. *Ch*[*arles*] *De*[*ering*] son to Sr. *Edward D.*, and Mr. *V*[*aughan*], quarrelled in the *Duke's* Playhouse, and presently mounted the stage and fought, and Mr. *D.* was dangerously wounded, and Mr. *V.* secured lest it should prove mortal." A news-letter of some seven or eight years later mentions a scuffle in the pit between Captain Leinster and another, when swords were quickly drawn on all sides. The *Post-Boy*, 22nd–25th June, 1695, notes that "on *Saturday* last words arose between Mr. *Cary* and Mr. *Young* in the Playhouse, about a Gentlewoman, and the next morning they fought a duel in *Hide* Park, when they were both wounded: the former died in the evening at the *Star Inn* in the *Strand.*"

It were as needless as it were easy to multiply examples of this fatal turbulence and riot. The actors themselves were quick " to lugg out the porker ", as the cant phrase went. On Wednesday, 14th November, 1666, Mrs. Knepp gossiping with Pepys told him " how Smith, of the Duke's house, hath killed a man upon a quarrel in play ". According to Tony Aston " fiery *Jack* " Verbruggen's " Sword was drawn on the least Occasion ". William Mountford was assassinated in the street on Friday, 9th December, 1692, and it is disputed whether he had time to draw his sword or no. On the night of Monday, 18th May, 1696, young Hildebrand Horden, one of the most handsome actors of his time, " was kill'd at the Bar of the *Rose-Tavern* in a frivolous, rash, accidental Quarrel." *The London New-Letter,* 20th May, 1696, has: " On *Monday* Capt. *Burges* . . . kill'd Mr. *Harding* a Comedian in a Quarrel at the *Rose* Tavern in *Hatton* [should be *Covent*] *Garden,* and is taken into custody." It is announced on Tuesday, 30th November, 1697, that Captain Burgess " who killed Mr. *Horden* the player, has obtained his majesties pardon ". William Bowen, Chetwood tells us, " was fiery to a Fault, and passionate to his Prejudice, which drew on his own Death, by the unwilling Hands of Mr. *Quin,*" in 1718. It appears that Quin had said Ben Johnson was a better actor of Jacomo in *The Libertine* than Bowen, and accordingly the latter in a fury got his critic alone in a tavern, and " pressed so furiously upon him, that he receiv'd the Wound which occasion'd his Death three Days after. However, when the Loss of Blood had weakened his Rage, he confess'd his own Folly and Madness had justly drawn on his own Misfortune; and, at the Tryal, Mr. *Quin* was honourably acquitted ". Actually the coroner's inquest found *se defendendo,* whilst the Old Bailey jury returned a nominal verdict of manslaughter. Another time Quin gave offence to an actor named Williams, who waited for him under the Covent Garden piazza, and assaulted him with drawn sword. Quin was obliged to retaliate, and in the scuffle that ensued Williams was killed. Upon being brought to trial Quin was wholly cleared and acquitted. These and many other like incidents show the fevered atmosphere of the theatre. Both before and behind the scenes blades leaped from their scabbards at the slightest occasion; a fancied affront, too sharp a word, too true a jest, and satisfaction was demanded upon the spot. Nor, may we remark, was this punctilio of English growth: Carranza's rules flourished mightily on the continent. Well might the Council of Trent enact the severest penalties against " the detestable custom of duelling which the Devil had originated ".

As we have seen, Churchill was challenged by Otway for

beating an orange-girl at Dorset Garden, and no doubt this bully richly deserved a swingeing himself, although with their pert clack and incessant bawling of their wares it may well be supposed that the wenches added their quota to the noise.

In *Collin's Walk Through London and Westminster* [29] the country visitor to the metropolis is taken to the play. Here he saw many strange sights unknown to rustic eyes :—

> The Beau that rambles from the Boxes
> To the middle Gallery where the Pox is ;
> The Cully too that makes a show
> With Punk in the side Box below,
> From whence his Heart e're she can ask it
> Leaps into th' Orange-Wenches Basket ;
> There Pants, and Praises the damn'd Features
> Of that most Impudent of Creatures.

D'Urfey adds a gloss : " The Character of an Impudent Play-House Orange Wench, being there every day acted, I think needs no further Comment."

The chief orange-woman, Mrs. Mary Meggs, known as Orange Moll, was a famous figure in the theatre. She was a widow, and resided in the parish of S. Paul, Covent Garden. On 10th February, 1662–3, the authorities of the Theatre Royal, Bridges Street, that is to say Sir Robert Howard, Killigrew, and other sharers, granted her on payment of £100 " full, free, & sole liberty, licence, power, & authority to vend, utter, & sell oranges, Lemons, fruit, sweetmeats, & all manner of fruiterers & Confectioners wares & commodities " throughout the house with the exception of the Upper Gallery. This licence ran for thirty-nine years, and she paid six shillings and eightpence a day for the privilege.[30]

A news-letter, 27th January, 1671–2, describing the fatal fire which burned down the Theatre Royal says : " 20,000*l.* damage. The fire began under the stairs where Orange Moll keeps her fruit." [31] Pepys has several references to the lady. On Wednesday, 29th August, 1666, he " found Sir W. Pen talking to Orange Moll, of the King's house, who, to our great comfort, told us that they begun to act on the 18th of this month ". On Thursday, 22nd August, 1667, he saw *The Indian Emperour,* and " Knipp sent by Moll to desire to speak to me after the play ". " She outdoes a playhouse orange-woman for the politick management of a bawdy intrigue," pertinently remarks a character in *Tunbridge-Wells.* On Monday, 26th August, 1667, Pepys saw *The Surprisal* at the Theatre Royal, and " there Sir W. Pen and I had a great detail of discourse with Moll ", who retailed scandals concerning

Nell Gwyn. When Pepys was at *Henry IV* on Saturday, 2nd November, 1667, " it was observable, how a gentleman of good habit, sitting just before us, eating of some fruit in the midst of the play, did drop down as dead, being choked ; but with much ado Orange Moll did thrust her finger down his throat, and brought him to life again." On Monday, 30th December, 1667, when Pepys was with Sir Philip Carteret at *Love's Cruelty,* " in the first act Orange Moll come to me, with one of our porters by my house, to tell me that Mrs. Pierce and Knipp did dine at my house to-day, and that I was desired to come home." Mrs. Meggs, as was no doubt necessary in her position, had a sharp and bitter tongue, but it was unfortunate that she let it loose upon Rebecca Marshall for this great tragedienne proved quite capable of looking after herself, and on 5th November, 1669, the Lord Chamberlain at her instance issued " A Warrt to App Mary Meggs for abuseing Mrs Rebecca Marshall one of his Mates Comoedians to ye disturbance of his Mates Actors and Comitting other Misdemeanours ".

From time to time there were complaints on the part of the Theatre that Orange Moll was not only in arrears with her daily fees but that she was denying many of her liabilities. She asserted that she had been thrust out of the theatre by force and violence, and refused entry for at least six weeks to her great detriment. At the Union the amalgamated Company " put in a person of their own to sell Fruit and Sweetmeats and kept the Defendant out until about the beginning of October ", 1683. This was the subject of a suit in Chancery in 1684, but in 1690 there was fresh trouble. However, before matters could be adjusted Mary Meggs died on 21st January, 1691.[32]

Her executor was Philip Griffin, the actor, to whom by her will, dated 24th April, 1682, she left her fruit-vending licence, which had considerably increased in value. A portrait of himself, found in her house, was claimed by Griffin. She also left her brother, a naval man, three houses of no small value ; one of which was let at £50 a year.

Although perhaps not quite so disturbing a feature of the theatre in the eighteenth century as in Restoration days the damsels, their baskets " laden with Pippins and Hesperian Fruit ", nevertheless remained quite sufficiently in evidence. In a pamphlet of 1768, *The Conduct of the Four Managers of Covent-Garden Theatre* by " A Frequenter of that Theatre ", these gentlemen are roundly accused of gross profiteering, especially by exploiting to its full—the doors opening early and the play commencing late—" the benefit accruing to you from selling tea, coffee, and fruit, by means of the eight bawling women who constantly attend at each of your houses, often to the great incommoding of the audience."

In Vincent's *Young Gallant's Academy,* 1674, chapter v, the young gallant is instructed to advance to the middle of the pit, to bow to the company, and pulling out his comb settle his flaxen wig. "The next step is to give a hum to the *China-Orange-wench,* and to give her her own rate for her Oranges (for 'tis below a *Gentleman* to stand haggling like a *Citizens wife*) and then to present the fairest to the next Vizard-mask." Indeed the wenches might pretty smartly resent any cheapening of their ware, and it was ill work for a man to fall foul of them. Their honesty was not above suspicion as Pepys found when he was at the Duke's House to see *The Tempest* on Monday, 11th May, 1668. He writes, "The orange-woman did come in the pit and challenge me for twelve oranges, which she delivered by my order at a late play, at night, to give to some ladies in a box, which was wholly untrue, but yet she swore it to be true. But, however, I did deny it, and did not pay her; but, for quiet, did buy 4*s.* worth of oranges of her, at 6*d.* a-piece."

In Shadwell's *A True Widow,* the play-house scene, Act IV, "*Several young Coxcombs fool with the Orange-Women,*" who begin their lusty cry "Oranges; Will you have any Oranges?" Samuel Butler in his "Character of A Jugler" remarks that when trading grows scant these fellows join up with puppet-shows or some other mountebanks, "and admit the Cut-Purse and Ballad-Singer to trade under them, as Orange-Women do at a Playhouse," which is a dry bob at the ill repute of these wenches. Again in his *Panegyric on Sir John Denham* he has the following couplet:—

> Nor furiously laid orange-wench a-board
> For asking what in fruit and love you'd scored.

In the First Act of James Howard's *The English Mounsieur,* 4to, 1674, but acted at the Theatre Royal a decade before, Mr. Vaine cries: "I can't imagine how I first came to be of this humour, unless 'twere hearing the orange-wenches talk of ladies and their gallants. So I began to think I had no way of being in the fashion, but bragging of mistresses."

The following lines occur in the Prologue [33] to *A Commonwealth of Women,* produced at the Theatre Royal in August, 1685, an address spoken by "Mr. *Haynes,* Habited like a WHIG, Captain of the Scyth-men in the *West,* a Scythe in his Hand":

> *Critticks, like Flyes, have several Species.*
> *There's one that just has paid his grutch'd half-Crown,*
> *Cries, Rot the Play, Pox on't, let's cry it down.*

The censuring Spark wou'd fain seem Great and Witty,
Yet whispers Politicks with Orange Betty;
She cracks his Philberds, whilst he, in her Ear,
Is Fighting o're again the Western War,
Bragging what numbers his sole Arm has kill'd,
Tho' the vain Fop perhaps was ne're i' th' Field.

The topical allusions are, of course, to the rout of the rebels at Sedgemoor, 6th July, 1685.

In his Preface to *The Banditti; or, A Ladies Distress,* 4to, 1686, the same dramatist complaining of the failure of his play writes: "In former times, a play of humour, or with a good plot could certainly please; but now a Poet must find out a third way, and adapt his scenes and story to the Genius of the Critic, if he'd have it pass; he'll have nothing to do with your dull *Spanish* Plot, for whilst he's rallying with the orange-wench, the business of the Act gets quite out of his Head, and then 'tis 'Damme, what stuff's this?' he sees neither head nor tail to't." In the Prologue to *Cleomenes, The Spartan Heroe,* Drury Lane, April, 1692, Dryden complains of the "Bear Garden" fellows in the pit, "*Who, while we Speak, make Love to Orange-Wenches.*" In the Prologue to *A Fool's Preferment,* Dorset Garden, early in 1688, we have:—

The Noble Peer may to the Play repair,
Court the pert Damsel with her China *Ware,*
Nay, Marry her, if he please, no one will care.

Again in the Prologue to *Don Quixote,* Part I, produced at Dorset Garden in the spring of 1694, D'Urfey protesting that his comedy is free from satire, writes:—

The Orange-Miss, that now cajoles the Duke,
May sell her rotten Ware without Rebuke.

Even more notorious and more numerous than the orange-girls were the vizard-masks who swarmed in both play-houses. Indeed throughout the literature of the Restoration there is no commoner term for a whore than "vizard-mask" or "mask", especially for a *bona roba* who plies her recognized province, the theatre. Masks were used by ladies as early as the reign of Elizabeth, and at the return of King Charles II they became very general. On Friday, 12th June, 1663, Pepys being at a performance of *The Committee* at the Theatre Royal saw Lord Fauconberg and his wife Lady Mary Cromwell "who looks as well as I have known her, and well clad; but when the House began to fill she put on her vizard and so kept it on all the play; which of late is become a great fashion among the ladies, which hides their whole face. So to the Exchange, to buy things with my wife; among others, a vizard for herself".

It may, perhaps, not be altogether impertinent to remark that the vizard or mask entirely covered the whole face, and that it was generally of black velvet. The domino or half-mask was of later invention. In the second picture of Hogarth's *The Harlot's Progress* a mask is seen lying upon the dressing-table, and in the fifth plate of *Marriage A La Mode* the lady's mask has been thrown upon the floor with her hoop and the remainder of her discarded attire. My Lady Squeamish in Otway's *Friendship in Fashion,* Dorset Garden, April, 1678, sends her maid to fetch "a Mask with an Amber-Bead". At a masquerade or court ball the dresses and masks might be more remarkable. In Dryden's *The Assignation; or, Love in a Nunnery,* Lincoln's Inn Fields, winter of 1672, Lucretia at an entertainment in masquerade given by the Duke of Mantua wore "a loose long Robe, streak'd black and white, girt with a large Silver Ribband, and the Vizor was a *Moor's* Face".

To give examples of the term "Mask" or "vizard-mask" as equivalent to a cyprian of the theatre would be to quote from well-nigh every prologue and epilogue of Dryden and the contemporary dramatists. The term was also often used generally to denote a lady of pleasure. In Nevil Payne's comedy *The Morning Ramble; or The Town-Humours,* Dorset Garden, November, 1672, among the characters are Three Vizard-Masks, that is three prostitutes. In the Prologue (spoken by Mohun who acted Abdelmelech) to the Second Part of *The Conquest of Granada,* Theatre Royal, 1670–1, there is a famous passage:—

> *But, as when Vizard Masque appears in Pit,*
> *Straight, every Man who thinks himself a Wit*
> *Perks up; and, managing his Comb, with grace,*
> *With his white Wigg setts off his Nut-brown Face:*
> *That done, bears up to th' prize, and views each Limb*
> *To know her by her Rigging and her Trimm:*
> *Then, the whole noise of Fopps to wagers go,*
> Pox on her, *'t must be she; and* Damm'ee *no.*

That the banter between these masks and the gallants was not over delicate may very well be believed. Shadwell has etched us in *A True Widow,* Act IV, a vivid esquisse. The scene is the Duke's play-house.

Stanmore. I cannot find my Mistress; but I'll divert my self with a Vizard in the mean time.

1 *Man.* What, not a word? all over in disguise: Silence for your Folly, and a Vizard for your ill Face.

2 *Man to a Vizard.* Gad! some Whore, I warrant you, or Chamber-maid, in her Lady's old Cloaths.

[*He sits down, and lolls in the Orange-wench's Lap.*

3 *Man.* She must be a Woman of quality; she has right Point.

4 *Man.* Faith! she earns all the Cloaths on her Back by lying on 't; some Punk lately turn'd out of Keeping, her Livery not quite worn out.

Isabella. I deserve this by coming in a Masque; and if I should now discover my self, 'twould make a Quarrel.

In Ravenscroft's *The London Cuckolds,* Dorset Garden, winter of 1681, when Ramble returns to Townly the lost tablets this latter declares "the Woman I gave it to, is the person of all the World I most fancy". "Was she very handsome?" asks his friend. "I know not the Charms of her Face, 'tis her Wit I admire," Townly returns. Ramble retorts: "Has it been then a Night Intrigue, and carried on in the dark?" "No," Townly explains, "I have seen her often in a Vizard at Plays, she has a delicate shape, and a pretty, pretty hand . . . she was Roguish but not Impudent, Witty but not Rampant; without doubt she has a husband that is proud of her, and takes delight to hear her talk, for I observ'd a kind of City-elder always sit a little distant from her, who listen'd to her rallery with the Sparks, and seem'd pleas'd in his countenance, when she was smart in her Repartees upon the little Cockerils of the Pit, that came flirting at her with her sparring blows."

Cibber in his *Apology*[34] recalling the good old days writes: "I remember the Ladies were then observ'd, to be decently afraid of venturing bare-fac'd to a new Comedy, 'till they had been assur'd they might do it, without the Risque of an Insult to their Modesty; or, if their Curiosity were too strong, for their Patience, they took care, at least, to save Appearances, and rarely came upon the first Days of Acting, but in Masks (then daily worn, and admitted, in the Pit, the Side-Boxes, and Gallery) which Custom, however, had so many ill Consequences attending it, that it has been abolish'd these many years."

When Lucinda and Pindress her woman in Farquhar's *Love and a Bottle,* Drury Lane, 1699, are walking in Lincoln's Inn Fields early one fine summer morning they converse thus:—

Lucinda. The Walks fill apace; the Enemy approaches, we must set out our false colours.

[*Put on their Masks.*

Pindress. We Masks are the purest Privateers! Madam, how would you like to cruise about a little?

Lucinda. Well enough, had we no Enemies but our Fops and Cits: But I dread these blustring Men of War, the Officers, who after a Broad-side of Damme's and Sinkme's, are for boarding all Masks they meet as lawful Prize.

Pindress. In Truth, Madam, and the most of them are lawful Prize, for they generally have *French* Ware under Hatches.

Lucinda. Oh hideous! O'my Conscience, Girl, thou'rt quite spoil'd. An Actress upon the Stage would blush at such Expressions.

Pindress. Ay, Madam, and your Ladyship would seem to blush in the Box, when the Redness of your Face proceeded from nothing but the Constraint of holding your Laughter. Didn't you chide me for not putting a stronger Lace in your Stays, when you had broke one as strong as a hempen Cord with containing a violent Tehee at a smutty Jest in the last Play?

Whilst the more prosperous bona-robas favoured the pit, the poorer fireships mustered in the middle gallery, and in the upper gallery were to be found the bulkers. Not that the boxes also were not obliged by the presence of the daughters of Venus, for in Dryden's *The Kind Keeper,* Dorset Garden, March, 1678, Father Aldo when assigning their several provinces to his *clientèle* and composing matters between Mrs. Termagant and Mrs. Hackney, addressing the latter directs: "At the Play-houses, she shall ply the *Boxes,* because she has the better Face; and you shall have the *Pit,* because you can prattle best out of a *Vizor Mask.*" As may be supposed the galleries were often a scene of vulgarity and disorder. In the Prologue to an Opera by Motteux, *The Island Princess, or the Generous Portuguese,* produced at Drury Lane in the winter of 1698, there is an allusion to the common amours which were carried on in this part of the house.

Ye gallery-haunters, who love to lie snug,
And munch apples or cakes, whilst some neighbour you hug.

When Pinchwife brought his wife to London and he took her to the play they had their seats in the eighteen-penny Place, that is the middle gallery, in order to escape the ogling and staring of the gallants in the pit. But Mrs. Pinchwife protested: "We sat amongst ugly People: He wou'd not let me come near the Gentry, who sat under us, so that I cou'd not see'em. He told me, none but naughty Women sat there, whom they tous'd and mous'd: But I wou'd have ventur'd, for all that."

Dryden thus concludes the Prologue [35] to Southerne's comedy, *The Disappointment; or, The Mother in Fashion,* Theatre Royal, spring of 1684:—

Last, some there are, who take their first Degrees
Of Lewdness, in our Middle Galleries:
The Doughty BULLIES enter Bloody Drunk,
Invade and grubble one another's PUNK:

ANNE QUIN

A miniature (centre) with talc overlays, Victoria and Albert Museum

[*face p.* 88

They Caterwaul and make a dismal Rout,
Call SONS of WHORES, and strike, but ne're lugg-out:
Thus, while for *Paultry Punk* they roar and stickle,
They make it *Bawdier* than a CONVENTICLE.

In the same poet's Epilogue upon the Union of the two Companies, delivered on 16th November, 1682, he writes:—

But stay; methinks some Vizard Mask I see
Cast out her Lure from the mid Gallery:
About her all the fluttering Sparks are rang'd;
The Noise continues, though the Scene is chang'd:
Now growling, sputt'ring, wauling, such a clutter,
'Tis just like Puss defendant in a Gutter;
Fine Love, no doubt; but ere two days are o'er ye,
The Surgeon will be told a woful story.
Let Vizard Mask her naked Face expose,
On pain of being thought to want a Nose.

Complaint is made in the Epilogue [36] to *Sir Courtly Nice; or, It Cannot Be* produced at the Theatre Royal, 4th May, 1685; 4to, 1685; of the turmoil:—

Our Gallerys too were finely us'd of late,
Where roosting Masques sat cackling for a Mate;
They came not to see Plays, but act their own,
And had throng'd Audiences when we had none.
Our Plays it was impossible to hear,
The honest Country-men were forc't to swear;
Confound you, give your bawdy prating o're,
Or, Zounds, I'll fling you i' the Pitt, you bawling Whore.

In the Prologue [37] to *A Commonwealth of Women,* acted in August, 1685, D'Urfey sharply enough snibs the beau-critics:—

Another to compleat his daily task,
Fluster'd with Claret, seizes on a Mask,
Hisses the Play, steals off with Punk i' th' dark,
He Damns the Poet, but she Claps the Spark.

In *The Fire-Ships,* a satire, 4to, 1691, we have the following mordant lines:—

Permit me now *Dear Strephon,* to relate,
The Tricks and Wiles of Whores of *Second Rate,*
The *Play-house Punks,* who in a loose Undress,
Each Night receive some *Cullies* soft Address;
Reduc'd perhaps to the last poor *half Crown,*
A tawdry *Gown* and *Petticoat* put on,
Go to the House, where they demurely sit
Angling for *Bubbles,* in the noisy *Pit*:

Not *Turks* by *Turbants, Spaniards* by their *Hats,*
Nor *Quakers* by Diminutive *Cravets*
Are better known, than is the *Tawdry Crack*
By Vizor-Mask, and Rigging on her Back.
The *Play-house* is their place of Traffick, where
Nightly they sit, to sell their *Rotten Ware* :
Tho' done in silence and without a Cryer,
Yet he that bids the most, is still the Buyer ;
For while he nibbles at her *Am'rous Trap,*
She gets the *Mony,* but he gets the *Clap.*
Intrencht in *Vizor Mask* they Giggling sit,
And throw designing Looks about the *Pit,*
Neglecting wholly what the Actors say,
'Tis their least business there to see the *Play.*

Yet sometimes these ladies set up for critics, and Congreve in the Epilogue, spoken by Mrs. Mountford, to *The Double-Dealer,* Drury Lane, November, 1693, notes :—

The Visor-Masks, that are in Pit and Gallery,
Approve, or Damn, the Repartee and Rallery.

The Prologue to Otway's *The Atheist,* Dorset Garden, September, 1683, with a bob at the overworked rhymes that were made to do their duty again and again in these addresses, thus jeers the poet :—

With Wit *and* Pit *he keeps a hideous Pother ;*
Sure to be damn'd by One, for want of T'other :
But if, by Chance, he gets the French *Word* Raillery,
Lord, how he fegues the Vizor-Masques with Gallery !

During the violent reaction against the stage in the closing years of the seventeenth century, that puritan ebullition of which Collier's *Short View Of The Immorality, and Profaneness Of The English Stage,* 1698, was the opportunity if not the occasion, amongst other edicts of Queen Anne " for the better regulation of the Theatres " an Order of 17th January, 1704, forbade and straitly banned for the future any use of vizard masks by the audiences in either house. This particular decree, to which attention has been already drawn, was published in the *Daily Courant* for 24th January, 1704, and after the usual preamble continues ". . . and being further desirous to reform all other indecencies and abuses of the stage, which have occasioned great disorders and justly give offence Our Will and Pleasure therefore is, and We do hereby strictly command, that no person of what quality soever presume to go behind the scenes, or come upon the stage, either before or during the acting of any play, that no woman be allowed or presume to wear a vizard mask in either of the Theatres, and that no persons come into either House without paying the price established for their respective places . . . Given at Our Court of S. James' the 17th day of January in the 2nd Year of Our Reign ".

Other clauses might be—and actually were—violated, but it appears that the prohibition of vizards in the theatre was strictly enforced. The threnody of the mask was sung by the tuneful John Bowman who, when for his wife's benefit on 1st June, 1704, *Love for Love* was given at Lincoln's Inn Fields, delighted the thronging boxes and pit with a *bonne bouche* "The Misses' Lamentation for want of their Vizard Masks at the Playhouse ".

As may be supposed, little is said by the poets of the Upper Gallery, and that little is generally contemptuous enough. Pepys in his early days was occasionally content with this humble if high placed sphere. On Monday, 16th December, 1661, at the first performance of Cowley's *Cutter of Coleman Street,* "the pay was doubled, and so to save money, my wife and I went up into the gallery, and there sat and saw very well." Dryden has a flick at the shilling seats now and again, as when in his prologue to Tate's *The Loyal General,* Dorset Garden, winter of 1679, he advises :—

> Remove your Benches, you apostate Pit,
> And take Above, twelve penny-worth of Wit,

and in one epilogue, spoken to Banks' *The Unhappy Favourite ; or, The Earl of Essex,* at Drury Lane in 1681, he jeers them in some stinging couplets [38] addressed, so the direction expressly runs, "*To the upper Gallery.*"

About 1697–8 Christopher Rich because, as Cibber tells us, "he imagined the People of Quality had preferr'd the Actors of the other House, to those of his own," hit upon a most unhappy expedient. "To ballance this misfortune he was resolv'd, at least, to be well with their Domesticks, and therefore cunningly open'd the upper Gallery to them *gratis* : For before this time no Footman was ever admitted, or had presum'd to come into it, till after the fourth Act was ended : This additional Privilege (the greatest Plague that ever Play-house had to complain of) he conceiv'd would not only incline them, to give us a good Word, in the respective Families they belong'd to, but would naturally incite them, to come all Hands aloft, in the Crack of our Applauses : And indeed it so far succeeded, that it often thunder'd from the full Gallery above, while our thin Pit, and Boxes below, were in the utmost Serenity. This riotous Privilege, so craftily given, and which from Custom, was at last ripen'd into Right, became the most disgraceful Nusance that ever depreciated the

Theatre. How often have the most polite Audiences, in the most affecting Scenes of the best Plays, been disturb'd and insulted, by the Noise and Clamour of these savage Spectators?" [39] Early in 1737 this custom was abolished but the lackies were greatly incensed and on the 5th May whilst *The Provok'd Husband* was being played at Drury Lane for the benefit of Macklin and Mrs. Furnival, in spite of the presence of the Prince and Princess of Wales in the house, a mob of some three hundred armed with offensive weapons broke into the theatre, molesting and wounding several of the audience. Colonel De Veily who was present, after a vain attempt to read the Riot Act, caused the ringleaders to be seized and some thirty were sent to Newgate. Fleetwood, the manager, received a letter which demanded that the footmen should be admitted into the gallery as before, and if the claim were refused it was threatened that the play-house should be burned to the ground. However, a strong guard of fifty soldiers was set, and as these were much in evidence for two or three weeks no further attempt was made on the part of the footmen, and before long a greater decorum prevailed in the gallery.

The denizens of this lofty region might be, and often proved, a nuisance in the theatre, but the time was yet in the future when they were to become a power, the gods whom the actors sought to please and who from their high position bestowed unbounded applause upon the heroes and heartily hissed the villains of the play.

NOTES TO CHAPTER III

[1] *Voyage en Angleterre,* p. 167.

[2] In *The Female Wits: Or, The Triumvirate of Poets At Rehearsal,* 4to, 1704, but produced about 1697, Act II, Praiseall says to the actresses: "I'll treat you all in the Green Room with Chocolate"; (p. 18).

[3] *Les Dix Livres . . . de Vitruve,* p. 161.

[4] 4to, 1692, Act II, Scene 1, p. 14.

[5] Ibid., "A Letter to Mr. *D'Urfey* Occasioned by his Play Called the Marriage-Hater Match'd," signed Charles Gildon; the concluding paragraph.

[6] *A Comparison . . .* p. 55. It may be remarked that this work has been frequently, but incorrectly, attributed to Gildon.

[7] Tate Wilkinson.

[8] *Apology,* 1740, p. 179.

[9] *The Annals of Tennis,* 1878, p. 35. See also pp. 84–6.

[10] British Museum, Add. MS. 35, 177.

[11] L. Hotson, *The Commonwealth and Restoration Stage,* p. 252, quoting from the papers of the Chancery Suit.

[12] Malone, *Variorum Shakespeare,* 1821, iii, p. 265.

[13] *Dryden The Dramatic Works,* ed. Montague Summers, v, pp. 291–2.

[14] Part i, p. 123.

[15] *Tom Jones,* book vi, chapter 9.

[16] This was not printed with the play, 4to, 1690, having been prohibited for political reasons. It first appears in *Poems on Affairs of State,* part iii, 1698, pp. 223–5. See *Dryden The Dramatic Works,* edited by Montague Summers, 1931, i, Introduction, pp. cxxii–cxxiii.

[17] For Mrs. Buly, who dwelt in Durham Yard, and was a figure of note in her day see the notes upon Duffett's farce *The Empress of Morocco* in my edition of Settle's tragedy *The Empress of Morocco.*

[18] There is no indication to which play this was originally spoken. It was reprinted as the second prologue to *The Amorous Old-woman,* 4to, 1674, a comedy ascribed to Duffett; it was repeated later as the prologue to D'Urfey's *The Fool Turn'd Critick,* produced at the Theatre Royal in November, 1676; 4to, 1678; and it was yet again printed as the prologue to Orrery's *Mr. Anthony,* 4to, 1690, a comedy which had been produced at the Duke's House in 1671.

[19] Downes, *Roscius Anglicanus,* edited by Montague Summers, p. 34, and note, p. 212. See also Pepys, 2nd July, 1661.

[20] 4to, 1693.

[21] *The Works of Aphra Behn,* edited by Montague Summers, 1915, vol. iv, p. 7, and vol. iii, p. 185.

[22] Ibid., iii, p. 187.

[23] An Anti-Heroick Poem; 1682, p. 99.

[24] *The Works of Thomas Otway,* edited by Montague Summers, 1926, vol. i, Introduction, pp. lxix–lxxi.

[25] *Dryden The Dramatic Works,* ed. Montague Summers, 1932, v, p. 124, and note, p. 442.

[26] Tate, *Poems,* 1684, pp. 153–4.

[27] *Letters addressed from London to Sir Joseph Williamson . . . at . . . Cologne in the Years* 1673 *and* 1674, ed. by W. D. Christie, Camden Society, 1874, vol. i, pp. 87, 94, 100.

[28] *English Dramatick Poets,* Oxford, 1691, p. 460.

[29] 1690. Canto iv, pp. 144–5; and note, p. 207.

[30] Hotson, op. cit., pp. 291–2.

[31] *The Works of William Wycherley,* edited by Montague Summers, 1924, i, Introduction, p. 39.

[32] There is possibly some truth (as regards Mrs. Meggs) in the following: "Every body in the City knows that *Moll Meggs* and my Lord *S-nd-rl-and* were admitted into the Popish Chappel at *White-hall* on the same day." *The Late Converts Exposed,* 4to, 1690, Part the Second, p. 28.

[33] Broadside, 1685. "This may be Printed. *Aug.* 20, 1685. *R. L. S.*"

[34] First ed., 1740, p. 155.

[35] Broadside, *London, Printed for E. Lucy,* MDclxxxiv. Bodley; Shelfmark, Ashmole, G 15, cxlvi.

[36] I quote from the epilogue as given in the 4to, 1685. The text of the epilogue to *Sir Courtly Nice,* as published in a broadside (*Printed for* Tho. Benskin) offers several variants. See my *Restoration Comedies,* 1921, pp. 370–2 for both epilogues, and notes pp. 399–400.

[37] Broadside, 1685. See supra, n. 31.

[38] Which have been previously quoted, see p. 40.

[39] First edition, 1740, p. 135.

Chapter IV

THE CURTAIN; THE PROLOGUE; CHANGES OF SCENE

Florimel. Now not one word or step farther, but take your Leave in dumb shew, and be gone.
Celadon. Oh! [*Bowing and affecting a Sigh.*
Flor. Oh Impertinent!

> *So have I seen, in Tragick Scenes, a Lover,*
> *With dying Eyes his parting Pains discover,*
> *While the soft Nymph looks back to view him far,*
> *And speaks her Anguish with her Handkercher:*
> *Agen they turn, still ogling as before,*
> *Till each gets backward to the distant Door:*
> *Then, when the last, last Look their Grief betrays,*
> *The Act is ended, and the Musick plays.*

[Exeunt, mimicking this.

The End of the Third Act.

Colley Cibber, *The Comical Lovers. A Comedy.* 4to (1707), p. 42.

To a modern spectator, and indeed to a modern actor, perhaps the most striking and most prominent structural difference between the interior of a Restoration play-house and a theatre of to-day would be that in the former the stage advanced very considerably beyond the proscenium arch and formed what is technically known as an "apron". In Wren's sectional design for the second Theatre Royal, Bridge's Street, which opened on 26th March, 1674, the apron can be clearly seen extending beyond the proscenium arch into the body of the auditorium, and this apron is some 17 feet deep. Some twenty years ago, in the library of All Souls, Oxford, Mr. Hamilton Bell discovered a number of designs for theatres by Wren, and of these one so closely agrees in measurement with the dimensions of Killigrew's first theatre in Bridges Street, 112 feet in length, that we may certainly take it we have here Wren's design for the second Theatre Royal which was built on the same site. Writing in *The Architectural Record,* April, 1913, Mr. Bell says that the design "scales 112 to 113 feet in length outside; the stage, with its tiring-rooms occupies 64 feet with a 3 feet space for the

PLATE VIII

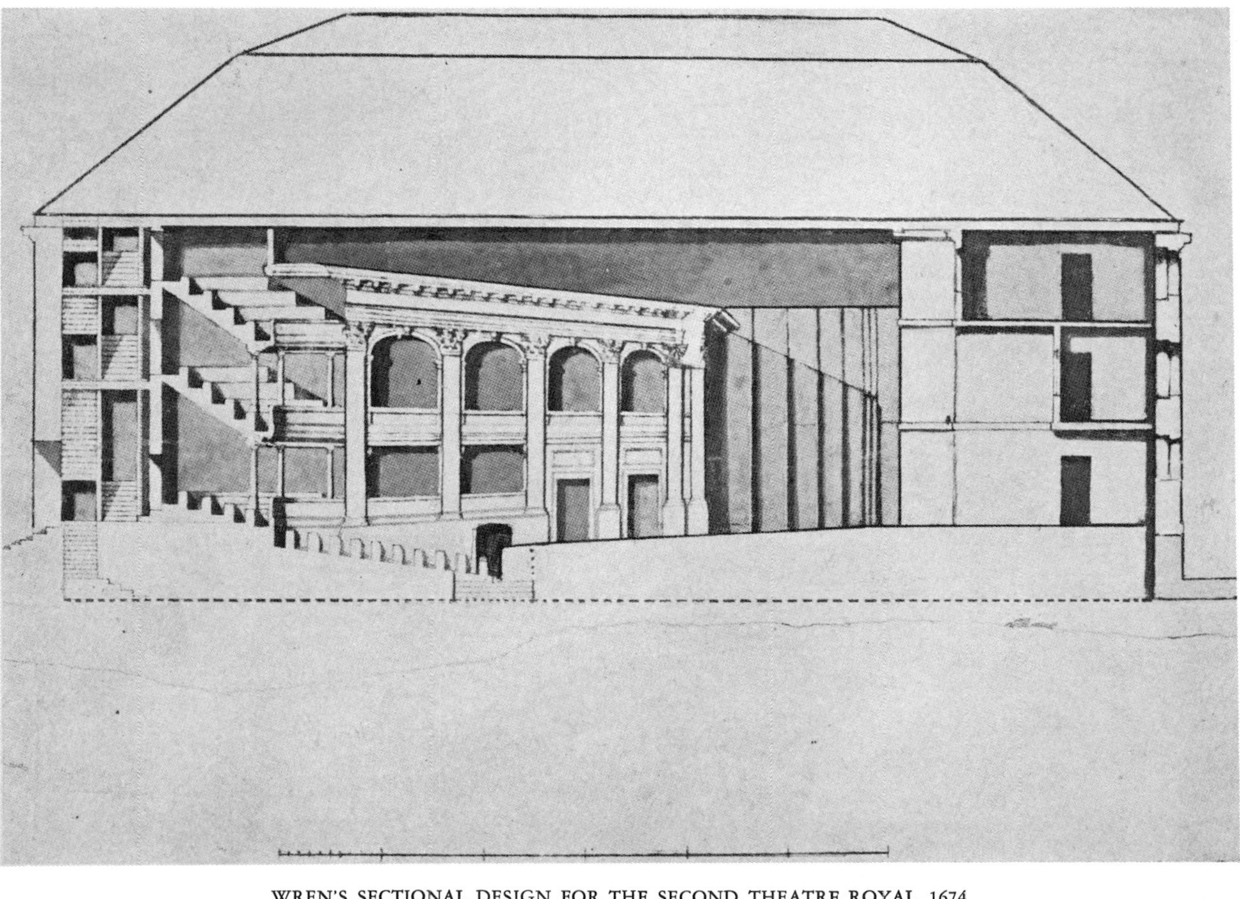

WREN'S SECTIONAL DESIGN FOR THE SECOND THEATRE ROYAL, 1674

Library of the All Souls College, Oxford

[*face p.* 94

orchestra in front again; leaving 56 feet for the salle and 8 feet for the lobbies, staircases, etc. The stage projects into the pit 17 feet in the form of an apron. . . . The fronts of the galleries are curved in plan, and the top [upper] gallery runs up through the cornice, to afford sight lines from the rear seats. . . . There are ten rows of seats in the pit, and four in each of the galleries." It should be remarked that the stage is built as on a slight incline, very gently sloping towards the pit so that actually the back wall is on a higher level than the front of the apron. In the Wren drawing the dotted line near the front of the stage (running from top to bottom) is an architectural indication that the front of the stage was convex, in correspondence with the concentric semicircles of the seating in the pit. The proscenium, then, so far from being a frame, as it were, beyond which nothing in the picture can advance, in the Restoration theatre may be better conceived of as an arch which separated the stage into two halves, or at least into two portions of fairly equal dimensions, of which that part projecting beyond the proscenium was from the acting point of view by far the most important and the most generally employed.

It may indeed be said that the Elizabethan "platform stage" and the new "picture stage" overlapped, and this fusion or compagination lasted for more than two centuries, since the strict practice of regarding the proscenium as a frame within which the picture is set did not prevail until some sixty years ago. There was no sudden and abrupt transition from the "platform stage" to the "picture stage" with the introduction of scenery in the public theatre, but rather a gradual remoulding and adaptation, a process of long time during which much that was Pre-Restoration persisted and was blended with the new. Even to-day how far the complete abscission of the apron is an advantage remains a very open question. With an apron there vanishes, of course, the theory which is known as the theory of the Fourth Wall, and probably this is no great loss. The suggestion is that the spectators are looking into an actual room from which the fourth wall has been taken away or become invisible, so that the three sides are displayed in all the stark realism of life. It is to be presumed that this imagination can only be exercised in the case of entirely modern plays and of plays moreover whose scenes are domestic, or at any rate very limited, interiors. It is not possible even in theory to remove a Fourth Wall from a street or from Hyde Park, Hampstead Heath, the gardens of the Tuileries, the High Street, Oxford, or the Giudecca at Venice. And even in the case of the strictly domestic interior I conceive the whole theory collapses at the outset. The scene may be laid in an ordinary middle-class home or even in the apartment of impecunious and indigent persons. Upon the very rising of the curtain we see that the room is far larger and far more spacious than any such room could be in real life. A narrow parlour assumes the proportions of a vast and lofty hall, and actuality is dissipated. There are many other points which might be pressed to show the absurdity of the ultra-realism of the Fourth Wall problems, but it were impertinent to labour these details here. We should only arrive at the impasse which has in fact been reached by Evreinov and Pirandello. What is essentially required by the spectator of a play is an ounce of imagination.

Dr. Lawrence writes that " The Apron, so long a characteristic of our theatre, was apparently born of the physical imitations of the Duke's Theatre in Lincolns Inn Fields. In a long, narrow house, where many of the audience were situated remote from the players it was necessary that the stage should jut out as far as possible, so that the players might come well to the front to make themselves heard. At a slightly later date a similar apron had to be introduced into the Italian opera houses for an almost identical reason ".[1] In the twelfth chapter of his *Apology*,[2] which was published in April, 1740, Cibber describes at length the alteration made in Drury Lane Theatre by Christopher Rich about 1696, with the view of enlarging the pit. " It must be observ'd then, that the Area, or Platform of the old Stage, projected about four Foot forwarder, in a Semi-oval Figure, parallel to the Benches of the Pit ; and that the former, lower Doors of Entrance for the Actors, were brought down between the two foremost (and then only) Pilasters ; in the Place of which Doors, now the two Stage-Boxes are fixt. That where the Doors of Entrance now are, there formerly stood two additional Side-Wings, in front to a ful Set of Scenes, which had then almost a double Effect, in their Loftiness, and Magnificence.

" By this original Form, the usual Station of the Actors, in almost every Scene, was advanc'd at least ten Foot nearer to the Audience, than they now can be ; because, not only from the Stage's being shorten'd, in front, but likewise from the additional Interposition of those Stage-Boxes, the Actors (in respect to the Spectators, that fill them) are kept so much more backward from the main Audience, than they us'd to be : But when the Actors were in Possession of that forwarder Space, to advance upon, the Voice was then more in the Centre of the House, so that the most distant Ear had scarce the least Doubt, or Difficulty in hearing what fell from the weakest Utterance : All Objects were thus drawn nearer to the Sense ; every painted Scene was stronger; every Grand Scene and Dance more extended; every rich, or fine-coloured Habit had a more lively Lustre: Nor was the minutest Motion of a Feature (properly changing with the Passion, or Humour it suited) ever lost, as they frequently must be in the Obscurity of too great a Distance: And how valuable an Advantage the Facility of hearing distinctly, is to every well-acted Scene, every common Spectator is a Judge."

It should be remarked that the greater part of the action took place upon the apron and there are continually to be noted stage directions which bid a character to "*come forward*", especially if any person has been "*discovered*" by the rising of the curtain or the drawing of a scene, that is to say the opening of a pair of flats. Although early, it may not be too premature perhaps to say a few words here with regard to one of the most wonted and most useful devices employed for scene-shifting in the theatre of Charles II, a convention without the full and practical understanding of which it is impossible either to appreciate or to judge the dramatic technique of any Restoration play. Incidentally it may be noted that again and again the playwrights of the period have been sharply enough criticized in modern essays and articles as awkward, maladroit, incompetent, bad craftsmen, and, whatever may be their literary flavour, mere bunglers without dexterity at their own business, only because our later writers are themselves either ignorant of or else have not clearly borne in mind the usage, management, and journey-working, especially in this particular, of the stage for which the pieces in question were written, adapted, and designed.[3]

As will be shown in some detail the curtain in the Restoration theatre rose after the delivery of the Prologue and (save in a few rare instances duly to be noted) did not fall until the Epilogue had been spoken. The end of each Act was indicated by a clear stage. How then, it will be asked, were changes of scene effected? Simply by the drawing together of two portions of a flat. These flats were of three kinds: the usual shutters which met in the centre, or which ran across the stage; the "relieves", or scenes in relief, moulded scenes; and the cut scenes where some part was cut out to show a distant prospect or perspective extending behind. The "relieves" were an heritage from the old masque. Thus in Jonson's *Masque of Hymen,* 1606, two great statues "feigned of gold" bore up the clouds "which were of relievo, embossed, and tralucent as naturals : to these a cortine of painted clouds joined which reached to the utmost roof of the hall"; in Daniel's *Tethys' Festival, or the Queenes Wake,* performed at Whitehall on 5th June, 1610: "Betweene the two pillers on eyther side were great ornaments of relieuo, the Basement were two huge Whales of siluer"; and in Campions' *The Lords Maske*, 1613, "*there appeared a Wood in perspectiue, the inner most part being of releaue, or whole round, the rest painted.*"[4]

It was perhaps the transparencies of the masques which suggested cut scenes. Thus in Jonson's *Oberon, the Fairy Prince*, produced 1st January, 1611, "the whole scene opened, and within was discovered the frontispiece of a bright and glorious palace, whose gates and walls were transparent." Transparencies were, of course, themselves utilized on the Restoration Stage, as in the last act of *The Fairy-Queen*, Dorset Garden, April, 1692, when there was discovered (by flats drawn off) "*a transparent Prospect of a Chinese Garden*". The burning of Troy in Settle's *The Siege of Troy* was exhibited "*by Illuminations and transparent Paintings seen scatter'd thro' the Scenes*".[5] As an example of a Restoration cut scene we may take Orrery's *Guzman*, folio, 1693,[6] p. 37: "*The Scene a Garden.* [The Garden in *Tryphon* as a Back Scene." This is in contradistinction to the many flat scenes in *Guzman*; "*The Scene the* Piazzo. [The New Flat Scene" (p. 23); "Act IV. *The New Flat Scene*" (p. 27); "*The New Flat Scene*" (p. 34); "*The Scene the Piazzo.* [The New Flat Scene"; and others. Woods and groves naturally suggested themselves as cut scenes, and it is pretty clear that of this kind was "*The Grove*" of Mrs. Behn's *The Dutch Lover*, Dorset Garden, February, 1673, i, 3; whilst Scene 2, Act III of the same play is "*A flat Grove*". In *The Widdow Ranter* by the same lady, Drury Lane, November, 1689 (a posthumous production), v, 3, "*A thick Wood*" certainly indicates a cut scene.

The two flats were often drawn off, parting in the centre, merely to commence another scene in a different setting. Since this was the normal practice it is seldom indicated in the printed quartos, yet it is occasionally marked. One example will stand for many, and we may take the Third Act of Mrs. Behn's *Sir Patient Fancy*, Dorset Garden, January, 1678. The last scene of Act II is a Chamber in Sir Patient's house. "Act III, Scene 1. *Scene draws off to a room in Sir* Patient Fancy's *house, and discovers Lady* Knowell" and other characters "*Men and Women, as going to dance*". Scene 2, the flats draw over and show a room in Lady Knowell's house. Scene 3 opens to "*A Garden*". Scene 4, the Garden "*Draws off, and discovers L.* Fancy *in her Night-gown, in a Chamber as by the dark*". Scene 5, *Changes again to a Garden*, by drawing over; Scene 6, *Draws off to Lady* Fancy's *Anti-Chamber*; Scene 7, *Changes to Lady* Fancy's *Bed-chamber, discovers her as before*; Lodwick *as just risen in Disorder from the Bed*," a full set with a four-poster bed on the stage; at the conclusion "*The*

Scene draws over Sir Patient *and Lady: draws again and discovers* Scene VIII. *The Garden,* Wittmore, Fanny, *and* Isabella". Lodwick and Maundy enter; Wittmore and Lodwick quarrel; they draw; "They fight out, Isabella, Fanny, *and* Maundy run off. Scene IX, *Changes to the long Street, a Pageant of an Elephant coming from the farther end with Sir* Credulous *on it*."

If a scene was unchanged between two Acts it was often the wont to note: *Scene continues*. Thus in D'Urfey's *Don Quixote*, Part I, Dorset Garden, May, 1694, Act I, Scene 2, is "*An Inn*". "Act II, Scene 1, *Continues*." Act III, Scene 2, "*Mountains and Rocks at the end of the Deep Grove*." In this scene Don Quixote releases Gines de Passamonte and the other galley-slaves who thank him for the courtesy by running to a heap of stones, and when "Don Quixote sets upon 'em"; they *knock both him and* Sancho *down, and beat 'em*. The rascals rub off, but the Don and Sancho are left lying on the stage during the *entr'acte*. Act IV, Scene 1, "*The Mountain of* Sierra Morena *continues*. Don Quixote *and* Sancho *appear lying along on the Ground*," and forthwith begin to lament their bruises and thumps.

Occasionally a dramatist utilized the drawing apart of two flats in order to exhibit a "situation" or a spectacular inner scene. Thus in Crowne's *Juliana, Or The Princess of Poland*, Lincoln's Inn Fields, July, 1671, Ossolinsky demands where is the Cardinal. "He lies so near," replies the Officer, "Torches may show him you. *The Scene is drawn, the* Cardinal presented dead *in a Grotto, a Gentleman waiting by him*." In Dryden and Lee's *Oedipus*, Dorset Garden, December, 1678, Act II, Scene 1, is "*An open Gallery. A Royal Bed-Chamber being suppos'd behind. The Time Night. Thunder, &c*". Haemon, Aleander, Pyacmon enter and discuss the Prodigies, "The perfect Figures of a Man and Woman" which have appeared in the blazing sky. With thunder "*The Scene draws and discovers the Prodigies*". Later "*The Cloud draws that veil'd the heads of the Figures in the Skie*". Act III, Scene 1, of the same tragedy is "*A dark Grove*", the mystic wood of the Furies. Various rites are performed towards the end of which Oedipus and Theban nobles enter. At the conclusion of the scene all exeunt save *Oedipus solus* and the scene is now in the palace. The palace flats had drawn together shutting out the grove, and leaving Oedipus *in situ* on the stage yet in another place. In Act V we have the exterior of the palace. Towards the end when Haemon exclaims:—

> But see! the furious mad *Jocasta*'s here,

"*Scene Draws, and discovers* Jocasta *held by her Women, and stabb'd in many places of her bosom, . . . her children slain upon the Bed*."

In other words a door was supposed to be opened and to exhibit an inner room, the queen's bedchamber.

This is not dissimilar to the climax of the *Agamemnon* when, as John Addington Symonds writes; " Horror huddles upon horror, as the spectacle of slaughter is itself revealed—the King's corpse smoking in the silver bath, Cassandra motionless in death beside him. Above them stands Clytemnestra, shouldering her murderous axe, . . . glorying in her deed . . . Some such spectacle as this was revealed to the Athenians by the rolling back of the eccyclema at the end of the *Agamemnon*." [7]

Spectacular effects were exhibited in Lee's *Mithridates, King of Pontus,* Drury Lane, January, 1678, III, 2, the Palace-Garden, and when Pharnaces cries: " But see, *Ziphares* comes," " *The Scene being drawn, represents* Ziphares'*s Triumph; which is a Street full of Pageants, crouded with People who from the Windows fling down Garlands* . . ." In the same author's *Lucius Junius Brutus,* Dorset Garden, December, 1680, Act III, 1, " *The Scene draws, showing the Sacrifice; one burning, and another crucify'd.*"

As has just been noted in *Oedipus* the drawing of the two flats apart represented in Act V the opening of the palace doors, and very frequently this convention was employed to indicate that a door—it might be the door of a room or the gate of a castle—was thus thrown open.

A striking example is to be found in Mrs. Trotter's *The Fatal Friendship,* produced at Lincoln's Inn Fields in 1698. Castalio is in durance when Gramont visits him. " *Cas*[*talio*] *goes within the Scene,* Gra. *Advances, a Scene shuts representing the outside of the Castle. Manet* Gramont."

Very often some command is given to open the door, or a character knocks as the cue for the drawing of the flats. Thus in Dryden's *The Rival Ladies,* Theatre Royal, April–May, 1664, Act the Fifth, " *Enter a* Pyrat, *and the* Captain. The Scene lying in a Carrack." After some dialogue the Captain says: " Don *Rod'rick's* Door opens, I'l speak to him. [*The Scene draws and discovers the* Captains *Cabin*; Rodorick *on a Bed, and two* Servants *by him.*]" In Otway's *The Souldiers Fortune,* Dorset Garden, 1st March, 1680, V, Sir Davy cries: " Break down that door, I'l have that Door broke open; break down that door, I say. [*Knocking within*" and " *Scene draws, and discovers* Beaugard *and Lady* Dunce". Again in Crowne's *Sir Courtly Nice; or, It Cannot Be,* Drury Lane, 4th May, 1685, Act I, Leonora says: " Open the Door. *The Scene is drawn, and a Company of Crooked, Wither'd Ill-look'd Fellows are at Breakfast, and Aunt with them.*" " How now?" cries the Aunt, " who open'd the door without my Leave?" In Act V of the same play Violente directs:

"Open the Door." "*The Scene is drawn, and* Farewel, Leonora, *a Parson,* Crack, Testimony *appear.*" In Dilke's *The City Lady; or, Folly Reclaim'd,* Lincoln's Inn Fields, January, 1697, III, 1, Lady Grumble bids: "Here, will some of you open those folding Doors there?" "Scene opens."

In Drake's *The Sham-Lawyer; or, The Lucky Extravagant,* printed 4to, 1697, "As it was Damnably Acted at the Theatre-Royal In *Drury-Lane,*" on 31st May, 1697, Homily has brought old Serjeant Wrangle to visit Spade the sexton who is supposed to be dying. Homily invites: "Will you walk in, Sir? This is the Door of the Chamber where he lies." Then "[Homily *knocks; the Scene opens, and presents an Alcove Room,* Spade *lying as in Bed,* Careless *and others standing about the Bed, a Table, with Pen, Ink and Paper, a Candle, Porringer of Blood, Glasses, Pots, and other Apothecaries Utensils scatter'd about it*]". At the end of Act I of this play we have: "*Exeunt Ambo.* Act II, Scene, *Wrangle's* House. Scene *Opens, and discovers* Wrangle *sitting at a Table, with Money, Jewels, and Writings before him; an Egg roasting at a Candle, and* Famine *his Man tending it.*"

There occur in Betterton's elaborate opera *The Prophetess; or, The History of Dioclesian,* Dorset Garden, April–May, 1690, a number of extremely significant and interesting stage directions, of which one or two at least require some brief, but especial notice. At the commencement of Act III, 2, we find: *A Curtain falls representing the entrance into the inner parts of a Magnificent Pallace. A noble Arch; behind it two Embroider'd Curtains, part of the first ty'd up on either side, the farther Curtain hanging down. Figures of Diana on each side of the Arch standing on large Pedestalls.* (The *two Embroider'd Curtains* are paintings on the scene.) Act IV, Scene 1, is "Scene *the Great Curtain*". At the end of the scene Drusilla "*waves her Wand thrice. Soft Musick is heard. Then the Curtain rises, and shews a stately Tomb . . .*"

The conclusion that these curtains, first seen on the London stage in 1690, were "drops" is unavoidable. "Drops" were used in the French theatre at least as early as 1664, and probably rather before that date. But it must be emphasized that "drops" were never employed by Inigo Jones in the Caroline Masques, nor throughout the whole reign of Charles II, and to talk of "drops" before 1690 is wholly erroneous. When these "drops" known as "curtains" were first introduced they were only utilized as something quite extraordinary, a device wholly belonging to opera rather than to the regular stage.

It is true that we have a puzzling use of the term "curtain" in Powell's *The Cornish Comedy,* produced at Dorset Garden in June, 1696. In this play Act IV, Scene 1, "*Curtain draws, discovers* Swash *and* Sharper *at Cribbidge . . . News Papers on the Table.*" At *Exeunt* (4to, 1696, p. 28) we have "*Enter* Froth, *running*". Scene 2, "*Curtain drawn, discovers* Margaret *sitting at a Table; two Waiting-Maids behind the Chair. Bags, Deeds, and Bonds on the Table.* Shuffle *at the other end with Pen, Ink, and Paper. Enter* Freeman, Busy, *standing at the entrance of the Stage,*" the proscenium door. Powell was just then experimenting with opera, his *Brutus of Alba; or, Augusta's Triumph* followed at the same house in September, scarce three months later, and either through carelessness or as a novelty he introduced an operatic convention into a regular comedy.

Rehearsal plays such as Buckingham's *The Rehearsal,* and *The Female Wits* of a quarter of a century later, often had scenes proper to the action before the curtain. These were exceptional. In Southerne's comedy *The Wives Excuse,* Drury Lane, December, 1691, we have: "Act I, Scene 1. *The outward Room to the Musick-Meeting. Several Footmen at Hazard, some rising from Play.*" At the end of the scene, "*Exeunt Omnes. The Curtain drawn up shews the Company at the Musick-Meeting.*" At the finish of this scene we have: "Scene. *Changes to the Street.* [*Several Link-Boys, and Footmen.*] Two street-flats closed over, and the link-boys, footmen entered. At the commencement of Act II the street-flats opened for "Act II, Scene 1. Witwou'd *at a Table, with* Betty, *and a Footman waiting*".

The question rises, was the first scene played on the apron before the curtain? Tables and chairs could easily have been placed in position before the audience assembled, but it would have been absurd for the footmen to have entered and engaged at cards. It appears as if "*curtain*" here must mean "drop-scene" representing the exterior of the music-room, an ante-chamber or hall.

It must be noticed that all these uses of "*curtain*" both as a technical term and in practice are to be dated about 1690. The innovation in regular plays did not please and was soon discarded, although owing to the necessity of the case it was allowed in operas. For example in Settle's *The Virgin Prophetess; or, The Fate of Troy,* an extremely spectacular opera produced at the Theatre Royal, 15th May, 1701, the *curtain* or drop-scene is very much in evidence. There is a similar employment of the curtain in a later play, Mrs. Manley's *Lucius, The First Christian King of Britain,* given at Drury Lane on 11th May, 1717.

In the Restoration period proper things were somewhat differently managed. Thus in Mrs. Behn's *Abdelazer; or, The Moor's Revenge,* produced at Dorset Garden in the autumn of 1676, Act II, Scene 1, is "*A Chamber of State*"; Scene 2, "*A*

Banqueting Hall. A Banquet, under a Canopy the King, Leonora, Florella, *Ladies waiting*; Philip, Mendozo, Alonzo, Ordonio, Antonio, Sebastian, *Lords and Attendants: As soon as the Scene draws off, they all rise, and come forward.*" That is the flats upon which was painted the Chamber of State drew off, one on either side, discovering the Banqueting Hall with the characters who then advanced on to the apron.

In Otway's *The Souldiers Fortune,* to which comedy reference has already been made, Act V, we have a scene in the house of Sir Davy Dunce. Sir Jolly is with Beaugard and Lady Dunce. They are interrupted by Sir Davy who presently goes out. Then "*The Scene shuts, and Sir* Jolly *comes forward*". Various characters enter and converse with Sir Jolly. Next the "*Scene changes to Sir* Jollies, *A Banquet. Enter Sir* Jolly, Beaugard, *and Lady* Dunce". They are interrupted at their collation by the Constable and Watch, who have been informed that a man was murdered in the house. Sir Jolly hurries Beaugard and Lady Dunce into a recess, crying "get ye away both into the Alcove there". Whereupon "*Enter* Constable, Watch *and Sir* Davy. *Scene shuts. Sir* Jolly *comes forward*". Southerne's comedy *The Wives Excuse; or, Cuckolds make Themselves,* produced at Drury Lane in December, 1691, commences: "Act I, Scene 1, Scene *the outward Room to the Music-Meeting. Several footmen at hazard, some rising from play.*" There is a long conversation between these footmen and then we have the amusing airs of two pages who enter. At last this is interrupted by voices within, and the attendants hurry out to get the coaches to the door. "*Exeunt omnes. The curtain drawn up, shows the company at the music-meeting; after an* Italian *song,* Lovemore, Wellville, Wilding, Courtall, Springame, Friendall, Sightly, Witwoud, Fanny, *advance to the front of the stage.*" An interesting succession of scenes occurs in Act III of Dilke's *The Lover's Luck,* Lincoln's Inn Fields, November, 1695. Act II is the Alderman's house. At the end of the Act flats drew over for "Act III. Scene Covent-Garden". There is some dialogue between Eager and Sapless, who go off to the Tavern. "*Exeunt.* Scene *changes to a Room in . . . the* Alderman'*s House.*" After a while: "Scene *opens, and discovers Sir* Nich. Purflew, Alderman, Breviat, *and* Goosandel *rising from a Table with Bottles and Glasses; they come forward and the Scene closes.*" After some dialogue: "*Exeunt.* Scene *opens to Collonel* Bellair'*s Chamber, and discovers* Bellair *upon a Couch in a Melancholy Posture; he rises and comes forward.*" At the close of this scene the Act ends. There is no *Exeunt,* since the flats drew over for "Act IV. Scene Covent-Garden". Mrs. Centlivre's first play *The Perjur'd Husband; or, The*

Adventures of Venice, produced at Drury Lane in September, 1700, commences: "Act I, Scene 1, *The Curtains fly up and discover a Mask in* Pizalto's *House.* Pizalto, Lady Pizalta, Lucy; Ludovico *talking to Lady* Pizalta; Bassino *and* Aurelia *talking together*; Florella *and other Maskers. A* Spanish *Entry. While the Dance is performing, enter* Armando *and gives* Bassino *two Letters, which he opens and reads. Lady* Pizalta *and* Lucy *advance to the Front of the Stage.*" In Vanbrugh's *The Confederacy,* produced at the Haymarket on 30th October, 1705, Act V, the Scene is laid in Gripe's house. After some dialogue between Brass, Flippanta, and others, "Scene *Opens.* Araminta, Corinna, Gripe, *and* Moneytrap *at a Tea-table, very gay and laughing.* Clarissa *comes in to 'em.*" Presently Mr. Clip the goldsmith is announced, and enters having business with Gripe. "*Clip.* If you please to let me speak with you in the next room, I have something to say to you. *Gripe.* Ay, with all my Heart. Shut the Door after us. (*They come forward, and the Scene shuts behind them.*) Well, any News?" From this point to the end of the play the action takes place *forward,* that is to say upon the apron, and eleven characters, practically the whole cast are concerned in the dénouement of the intrigue. Many other examples indeed might easily be quoted to demonstrate that the apron was the chief vantage-ground of the actors.

Occasionally some ingenuity was employed by the dramatist to bring his characters well forward. In the Dryden-Davenant version of *The Tempest,* Lincoln's Inn Fields, November, 1667, the young Duke of Mantua has been wounded. "Hippolito *discovered on a Couch,* Dorinda *by him.*

Dor. How do you find your self?
Hip. I'm somewhat cold; can you not draw me nearer
To the Sun, I am too weak to walk?
Dor. My Love, I'le try.
[*She draws the chair nearer to the Audience.*"

This bit of business was retained by Shadwell in his operatic version of *The Tempest.* The necessity for it arose from the fact that Hippolito was lying on a Couch or Chair and if the spectators were to hear clearly it was essential that he should be brought as near to them as possible, particularly as he is supposed to speak in the feeble faltering voice of sickness. So in Dryden's *Love Triumphant, or, Nature will Prevail,* Drury Lane, late winter of 1693, Act II opens with a dialogue between Alphonso and Victoria. The stage direction is: "*The Scene is a Bed-Chamber, a Couch prepar'd, and set so near the Pit that the Audience may hear.* Alphonso *enters with a Book in his hand, and*

PLATE IX

THE EMPRESS OF MOROCCO: ACT I: SCENE I, 4to, 1673

[*face p.* 104

sits; reads to himself a little while; Enter Victoria, *and sits by him, then speaks.*"

Before dealing with other details it may be convenient in the first place to say a few words about the proscenium and the use of the curtain. With regard to the proscenium at the second Theatre Royal we have no details, and unfortunately no drawing of this interior has come down to us. We are, however, justified in thinking that it was much less elaborate, simpler in design, and less ornate than the lavishly decorated and gilded proscenium of Dorset Garden, of which we fortunately have a beautiful engraving by W. Dolle. In fact Dryden's Prologue [8] at the opening of the second Theatre Royal commences by something like an apology for their æsthetic simplicity:—

> A Plain built House, after so long a stay,
> Will send you half unsatisfi'd away;
> When, fall'n from your expected Pomp, you find
> A bare convenience only is designed.
> You, who each Day can Theatres behold,
> Like *Nero*'s Palace, shining all with Gold,
> Our mean ungilded Stage will scorn, we fear,
> And for the homely Room, disdain the Chear.

This obviously alludes to the mass of superb baroque, carven and aureate, that adorned the interior of Dorset Garden, which the decorator had moreover furnished with pictures and busts of the great English dramatists, a circumstance Dryden uses for a neat point in his Epilogue upon the same occasion:—

> Though in their House the Poets Heads appear,
> We hope we may presume their Wits are here.

In the Dryden, Crowne, and Shadwell *Notes and Observations on the Empress of Morocco,* 1674, p. 59, the gloss upon the last line of Settle's tragedy runs: "*An Age in Empyre's but an houre in love.* How an age in Empyre is but an houre in love, I cannot understand, and if he can make me, I will conclude him to be as great as Apollo, as he stands over the Kings Boxe, which seems to be made for Mr. *Settles* statue amongst the poets heads."

In 1690, when Dorset Garden after the Union of the two companies had been (save for an occasional spectacular production or the performance of an Opera) some eight years well nigh deserted, Tom D'Urfey in his burlesque poem *Collin's Walk Through London and Westminster,* Canto iv, Wednesday's Walk, makes the doughty Major carry Master Collin to Dorset Garden, where—

He saw each Box with Beauty crown'd,
And Pictures deck the Structure round;
Ben, Shakespear, and the learned Rout,
With Noses some, and some without.

In *The London Spy,* May, 1699, Part vii,[9] the Spy and his companion take oars and land at Salisbury Court, "where a Stately Edifice (the Front supported by Lofty Columes) presented to our view. I enquired of my Friend what Magnanimous Don *Cressus* resided in this noble and delightful Mansion? Who told me No-body, as he knew on, except Rats and Mice; and perhaps an Old Superanuated *Jack-Pudding* to look after it, and to take Care that no decay'd Lover of the Drama, should get in and steal away the Poets Pictures, and sell 'em to some Upholsters for *Roman Emperours,* I suppose there being little else to lose, except Scenes, Machines, or some such Jimcracks. For this, says he, is one of the Theatres, but now wholly abandon'd by the Players; and 'tis thought will in a little time be pull'd down."

Drury Lane then also boasted a similarly appropriate decoration to which reference is made by Dennis in the Prologue to his comedy, *Gibraltar; or, The Spanish Adventure,* produced at that house on 16th February, 1705. This address concludes:—

And Poets treat you at their own Expence;
Who proud of Inborn-worth, despising show,
And writing like the best of that Majestick Row } *The Picture of the Poets.*
Shall to themselves their charming beauties owe.

Every play in the Restoration theatre, and for many a long year after, was introduced by a Prologue and concluded with an Epilogue. It were superfluous to insist upon the quality of these lively addresses, which in the hands of so great a poet as Dryden have added not a little to English literature. Intensely topical and intensely vital, they are indeed a mine of information, not merely with regard to things theatrical but also as indicative of popular feeling and the political currents of the day. In fact it is no exaggeration to say that we have here a body of historical documents, and so fresh and fadeless is their wit that, as has been proved to be the case, when spoken at performances to-day even a modern audience has been convulsed by their liveliness and humour. Those who were present on the occasion of the revival of Dryden's *Marriage A-la-Mode* for two performances in February, 1920, will not easily forget the laughter and cheers which greeted the delivery of the brilliant Epilogue[10] which is attached to that comedy. It is inevitable that some points must be lost, but if after the passage of 250 years they can yet thus delight an audience, in their own time they must indeed have been irresistibly piquant. John Dryden was acknowledged by all as supreme master of this species of composition, but this is not to say that other pens also were unable to produce some exceptionally good work, and we have addresses of this kind by Otway, Lee, Duke, Lord Falkland, Crowne, Mrs. Behn, Congreve, and many others which are extremely happy. Of Dryden, Malone judges: "Nothing, perhaps, more strongly shows the great fertility of his mind, than his having written near one hundred Prologues and Epilogues, for the most part of extraordinary excellence; having never been assisted by a friend with this kind of decoration to any of his own plays, except in two instances; and having supplied the contemporary dramatists with above forty pieces, of this difficult species of composition."[11] In a note (first published in 1751), on Pope's lines on Southerne's birthday, 1742:—

> May Tom, whom heaven sent down to raise
> The price of Prologues and of Plays . . .

Dr. Warburton relates that Dryden originally asked a fee of four guineas for a Prologue or an Epilogue, but being requested by Southerne to furnish one for a new play he required six guineas; "Not, young man, out of disrespect to you, but the players have had my goods too cheap." This story, Warburton says, was told by Southerne to him and Pope, nearly at the same time.[12] It may be remarked that in some versions of the tale the sums are said to have been five and ten guineas. So they appear in the life of Southerne which was published by Shiels and Theophilus Cibber: whilst Dr. Johnson, I know not upon what authority, mentions that the original price was two guineas and that this was raised to three.

It may be noted that very often the same Prologue was used for more than one play, and that sometimes without much idea of fitness or congruity. Thus the address which was printed in *Covent Garden Drollery*, 1672, as the "*Prologue to the Double Marriage*", and which commences—

> Gallants you have so long bin absent hence,
> That you have almost cool'd your diligence

was printed as the Epilogue to Mrs. Behn's *The Widdow Ranter*, 4to, 1690, and as the Prologue to her *Abdelazer; or the Moor's Revenge* when this tragedy was reprinted in 1690. The first quarto of *Abdelazer* is without a Prologue. Actually Dryden wrote both a Prologue and an Epilogue for *The Widdow Ranter*, but for some reason these were not printed with the play, and only exist on a separate leaf.[13] It may be remarked that although

Downes mentions that Fletcher's tragedy *The Double Marriage* was revived at Drury Lane after the union in 1682, and we know that it was played at Whitehall, on 6th February, 1688, there does not appear to have been traced any exact record of performances prior to 1672. In *Covent Garden Drollery* again there is printed, without any indication for what play it was originally intended, a Prologue commencing:—

> He who comes hither with design to hiss,
> And with a bum revers'd, to whisper Miss, . . .

and with trifling variations it is printed before Duffett's *The Amorous Old-woman; or, 'Tis Well if it Take,* quarto, 1674, as "a second Prologue intended but not spoken". It also appeared as the Prologue to D'Urfey's *The Fool Turn'd Critick,* quarto, 1678, and yet again with some alterations it seems to have served as the Prologue to Lord Orrery's *Mr. Anthony,* a play printed quarto, 1690, but probably produced twenty years before. An Epilogue to be found in the same collection of 1672, with the opening lines:—

> Our next new Play, if this Mode hold in vogue,
> Shall be half Prologue, and half Epilogue,

although assigned to no definite play, ten years later was printed as the Epilogue to D'Urfey's *The Injured Princess; or, The Fatal Wager,* quarto, 1682, a position which it singularly ill fits. A line in this Epilogue runs "This Play was writ nine years agoe", a circumstance which has led R. S. Forsythe souse into one of his many egregious blunders that mar his jejune *A Study of the Plays of Thomas D'Urfey,* Cleaveland, 1916.[14] This same Epilogue, in part, was attached to Orrery's *Mr. Anthony,* 4to, 1690. From these examples, and many others might be cited, it will be seen how frequently such addresses were sadly overworked, and how after an interval of some few years, if they were deemed to have been forgotten, they were ruthlessly resurrected.

Since the Prologue was spoken after the music had played we should perhaps first devote a brief consideration to the orchestra. The overture was divided into three parts, known as First, Second, and Third Music. The Third Music was also known as "the Curtain-tune" or "the Curtain-Time", since it was the Prelude to the drawing of the Curtain. Thus in the play-house scene, Act IV, of Shadwell's *A True Widow,* we have: "*They play the Curtain-time, then take their places*" whereupon Carlos remarks: "Now they'll begin," and almost immediately the piece commences. Matthew Locke's instrumental music to Shadwell's operatic *The Tempest* (produced April, 1674) was printed in 1675 in "The English Opera; or the Vocal Musick in Psyche . . . To which is adjoyned the Instrumental Musick in the Tempest". Mr. W. Barclay Squire writes: "Locke's music is very valuable. It consists of First and Second Music (played while the audience was assembling), Curtain Tune (or Overture), four Act Tunes and a Conclusion. The First Music comprises an Introduction, Galliard, and Gavotte; the Second Music a Saraband and 'Lilk' (a term which is defined in no dictionary); the Curtain Tune evidently attempts to depict the storm with which the play opens; the First Act Tune is a Rustic Air; the Second a Minuet; the Third a Corant; the Fourth a Martial Jig, and the Conclusion (probably played as the audience were dispersing) a Canon, 4 in 2." [15] It may be noted that although the term "Curtain-Time" (or "Curtain-Tune") did not endure longer than the beginning of the eighteenth century, the terms First, Second, and Third Music remained in vogue for at least a hundred years later. Thus in a pamphlet by Theophilus Cibber which is quoted by Percy Fitzgerald,[16] and which may be dated about 1740, an individual is mentioned who "often, as he loved music (or pretended a taste for it), would take a place in the pit, to hear the First and Second Music (which latter used to be some select piece), but prudently retired, taking his money again at the door before the third Music, and by that means often kept out a spectator who would have been glad to have enjoyed the whole entertainment, though he paid for it".

In some lines written by John O'Keeffe to Wilde, the Covent Garden prompter, about 1798 we have:—

> Thro' dressing rooms is heard the warning call,
> "First music, gentlemen; first music, ladies";
> "Third music!" that's the notice to appal.[17]

Whalley in his edition of Ben Jonson, seven volumes, 1756, has a note upon *After the second sounding* at the commencement of *Every Man out of his Humour*: "These several *Soundings* are in the modern theatre, termed first, second, and third music." [18]

In the Pre-Restoration play-house the music room—the prototype of which was plainly the music gallery of the old banqueting halls—was the curtained upper room on the first story of the tiring house, which if necessary could also be utilized as an acting-place. After the Restoration, Killigrew's first house, the Theatre in Gibbons' Tennis Court, Vere Street, was from first to last a platform-stage theatre, and here also the musicians occupied an elevated position. This we know from an allusion in the Prologue to Wilson's *The Cheats*, a comedy produced at Vere Street in March, 1663:—

> We've no sententious Sir, no grave Sir *Pol,*
> No little pug nor devil—bless us all!
> No tedious sieges to the Musick-Room,
> Nor frisks abroad! No,—our scene's all at home!

These lines with their references to *Volpone* and *The Devil is an Ass* echo a passage from an elegy by Jasper Mayne in *Jonsonus Virbius,* 1638, where Mayne [19] compliments Jonson for his classical preservation of the unities, and writes:—

> Thine were *land-Tragedies,* no Prince was found
> To swim a whole *Scœne* out, then o th' *Stage* drown'd;
> Pitch't fields, as *Red-Bull* wars, still felt thy doome,
> Thou laidst no sieges to the *Musique-Roome.*

That is to say Jonson avoided all the extravagances which were so common, especially in plays of the type popular at the Red Bull such as Heywood's *The Four Prentices of London. With the Conquest of Jerusalem* and Kirke's *The Seven Champions of Christendom,* and also he never introduced in his dramas robustious scenes of towns besieged with scaling ladders, bombast episodes such as are shown in *Tamburlaine,*[20] *I King Henry VI,*[21] and other Histories.

When Pepys on Friday, 8th May, 1663, paid a visit to the Theatre Royal, Bridges Street, "being the second day of its being opened," he judged that "The house is made with extraordinary good contrivance, and yet hath some faults, as the narrowness of the passages in and out of the pitt, and the distance from the stage to the boxes, which I am confident cannot hear; but for all other things, it is well, only, above all, the musique being below, and most of it sounding under the very stage, there is no hearing of the bases at all, nor very well of the trebles, which sure must be mended". Killigrew's innovation, although in fact he placed the musicians in the very place they occupy to-day, was not a success. The music room was certainly restored to the upper regions, an alteration probably made during the spring of 1666 when the theatre was being extended, and, in part at least, re-built. On Monday, 19th March, 1666, Pepys notes that after dinner he walked with Sir John Minnes "to the King's play-house, all in dirt, they being altering of the stage to make it wider. But God knows when they will begin to act again; but my business here was to see the inside of the stage and all the tiring-rooms and machines; and, indeed, it was a sight worth seeing." At the commencement of Act IV of *The*

Chances, as altered by the Duke of Buckingham, and thus produced at the Theatre Royal in 1666–7, the 2nd Constantia enters with her Mother. The good lady being weary and dry enters a convenient tavern and presently "*Mother looks out at the Window*" to call her daughter with "Come up, *Cons,* the Fiddlers are here". Shortly after we have the stage-direction *Musick plays above.* In a ballad, quoted by Mr. Percy Fitzgerald,[22] *On the Unhappy Conflagration of the Theatre Royal, January* 25, 1672, there are some lines which show that the music room had been raised aloft, and was then almost directly under the roof of the theatre:—

> But on a sudden a *Fierce Fire* 'gan rage,
> In several scenes, and overspread the stage.
> The *Horrors* waiting on the dismal sight
> Soon taught *th' players to th' life to act a Fright.*
> The *Boxes* where *splendours* us'd to surprise
> From constellations of *bright ladies'* eyes,
> A different blazing lustre now is found
> And the music-room with whistle flames doth sound.
> Then catching hold o' th' roof it does display,
> Consuming fiery trophies every way.

In the first Duke's House, Lincoln's Inn Fields, the music-room was aloft, and on Thursday, 7th November, 1667, when Pepys went to the first performance of Dryden and Davenant's alteration of *The Tempest,* he found the house so "mighty full", that he was "forced to sit in the side belcone over against the musique-room at the Dukes House". Again on Wednesday, 12th May, 1669, he notes: "After dinner my wife and I to the Duke of York's Playhouse, and there, in the side balcony, over against the musick, did hear, but not see, a new play, the first day acted, 'The Roman Virgin,' an old play,[23] and but ordinary, I thought; but the trouble of my eyes with the light of the candles did almost kill me." This entry shows that he was well within the glare of the coronas or chandeliers of lighted candles which hung fairly low over the stage.

Of the music room at Dorset Garden there is extant an actual drawing in five of the copperplates which illustrated the first quarto of *The Empress of Morocco,* 1673. Here between the two figures, Thalia and Melpomene, over the proscenium arch we have a curtained window with leaded sashes opening inwards. Smaller windows, able to be closed, with curtains, are placed in the curves to the right and left of the statues of the two dramatic Muses. The ledge beneath the centre window is occupied with the heraldic emblems of the patron of the theatre, the Duke of York. These have as their supporters two cherubs, all proper; but on the ledges beneath the two side windows are painted, to the right a drum and a trumpet, to the left a violin and a music score, decorations eminently suitable to the orchestral loft.

Incidentally it may be remarked that the kind of half-roof which can be discerned slightly projecting inwards from under the proscenium arch, and which soffit was doubtless intended to serve as a sounding-board is obviously the shadow, cover, or heavens (three synonyms) of the Elizabethan public play-house.

With regard to the little curtained windows, often technically known as the " garret windows ", one on either side, it should be noted that on occasion they were made use of by the actors if so required. In *All Mistaken; or, The Mad Couple* [24] by the Hon. James Howard, acted at the Theatre Royal, and seen by Pepys on Friday, 20th September, 1667, Philidor plays a trick on the six Ladies :—

> They came just now into my chamber,
> One by one, hoping to have found me alone,
> To have preach'd matrimony to me; but
> To my blest deliverance, no sooner
> One was there, but another came; so I
> Persuaded them one by one, to slip up
> Into a garret: so still as one knock'd
> At the door, the t'other ascended; there
> Have I secur'd them with this key.

Mirida enters, and he tells her :—

> I have great care upon me; I
> Must provide Meat for half-a-dozen ladies,
> That shou'd have been my spouses. Look up yonder;
> In that very garret . . .
>
> *Mir.* . . . . Prythee let's
> Go under the window and call to them.
>
> *Phil.* Come away, you shall hear what vollies we shall
> Have from the castle . . .
>
> [*Women look out.*
>
> *1st Lady.* Rogue!
> *2nd Lady.* Rascal!
> *3rd Lady.* Villain!
> *4th Lady.* Dog!
> *5th Lady.* Slave!
> *6th Lady.* Hell-hound!
>
> *Phil.* Methinks you represent the hemisphere,
> Because you are enthron'd so high; your eyes
> Appear like stars to us poor mortals here
> Below.

It is plain from this last speech and indeed from the tenor of the whole scene that the ladies are occupying a very lofty position, the garret, and not merely a proscenium balcony.

The Prologue to *The Virtuous Wife; or, Good Luck at Last,* a comedy by D'Urfey, produced at Dorset Garden, 1679, is spoken by Mrs. Barry. It must be borne in mind that the curtain is down, and the actress is well forward on the apron as she addresses the house. She tells them that candidly she is not over pleased with her rôle, Olivia,

> *For* Vnderhil, Jevan, Currier, Tony Lee,
> Nokes, *all have better characters than me.*[25]

[Lee *peeps out of a little window over the Stage.*

Lee. What Mrs. *Barrer!* Hah—What's that you say?
Have I a better Character in th' Play?— . . .
This is a Plot, a trick—'twixt you and *Nokes*—

[Nokes *peeps out of a little window the other side of the Stage.*

Nokes. How me? And what of me, peart brother Tony?

They banter, and Mrs. Barry cries:—

> Come, come—be friends, I'll Act—for once I'll trye.

Lee. Why then all's well again.
[*Shuts one Window.*

Nokes. And so say I—
[*Shuts t'other Window.*

It was from one of these little windows that Sir David Dunce looked out in Act IV of Otway's *The Souldiers Fortune,* produced at Dorset Garden early in 1680. The scene is the middle of Sir David's house and he has just gone to his closet " in the Garret ". A moment or two later he calls from the garret, and the stage direction is " *Sir Davy appears at a Window above* ". In the last act of Mrs. Behn's *The Roundheads; or, The Good Old Cause,* produced at Dorset Garden late in 1681, or possibly in January of the following year, when the fanatics are all in hiding, among the first to make himself scarce is Fleetwood; and presently, the scene being laid in a street we have the direction " Fleetwood *peeping out of a Garret-Window* " to see if the coast is clear. This was one of the little windows of the proscenium arch.

On particular occasions, when an Opera was to be given, and the number of violins was increased from twelve to twenty-four, the musicians generally sat at the front of the stage, but it must be emphasized that this was an unusual position. And so Shadwell's operatic version of *The Tempest* has before Act I a very long and elaborately detailed description of the special arrangement this most spectacular production entailed. "*The front of the Stage is open'd, and the Band of 24 Violins, with the Harpsicals and Theorbo's which accompany the Voices, are plac'd between the Pit and the Stage. While the Overture is playing, the Curtain rises, and discovers a new Frontispiece, join'd to the great Pilasters, on each side of the Stage.*" This frontispiece or temporary proscenium is directly derived from the masque, and its original may be found in Italy. A similar arrangement is described in Dryden and Grabu's opera *Albion and Albanius,* produced on Saturday, 6th June, 1685, at Dorset Garden. "The Frontispiece. *The Curtain rises, and a new Frontispiece is seen, joyn'd to the great Pylasters which are on each side of the stage.*"

It may perhaps seem that a proscenium loft was not a very convenient place for the musicians, but actually such is far from the case. Their duties almost wholly consisted of playing the Preludes and the tunes between the Acts. As we shall see a little later, when any incidental song or dance was introduced into a play the musicians came on to the stage itself. It is interesting to note that Alessandro Guidotti in the elaborate introduction to his *Anima e Corpo,* given in 1600, and set to music by Emilio del Cavaliere, remarks: "Gli stromenti, perchè non sian veduti, si debbano suonare dietro le tele della scena, e da persone che vadino secondando chi canta, e senza diminuzioni, e pieno."

There are some interesting and valuable indications concerning the musicians in the prompt copy of Shirley's *The Sisters,* which was prepared by Charles Booth, the book-keeper of Killigrew's company. The book is the printed octavo, with date 1652, of Shirley's *The Sisters,* contained in the collection "Six New Plays" with general title-page 1653. This copy is now preserved at Sion College, London.[26] The date of the revival can be narrowed down to one possible period. It must have taken place between 1668 and 1671. In the margin of the book eighteen lines before the end of the first act the prompter has written "Act Ready", and at the last line he has made a manuscript note "Ring". Act II has "Act Ready" twenty-nine lines before the end of the Act, and at the last line "Ring". Act III has "Ring" at the end. Act IV has "Act Ready" twenty-three lines before the conclusion, and "Ring" at the last couplet of the scene. Act V has "Ring", but no "Act Ready". Here the word "Act" is used not in its modern sense the act of a play, but as the interval which occurs between two acts, and also for the music which is played between those acts. "Act Ready" refers then to the preliminary warning of the musicians for the inter-act music, and may be paralleled with the Elizabethan

" Whilst the Act plays ", as in Marston's *Parasitaster,* Act V, to which is prefixed the Stage-direction "Whilst the Act is a-playing, Hercules and Tiberio enter. . . ." The direction " Ring " is undoubtedly the signal for the musicians to commence.[27] Curiously enough, it has crept into at least two printed plays. The conclusion of the First Act of Sedley's *The Mulberry-Garden,* produced at the Theatre Royal, Monday, 18th May, 1668 (4to. 1668), stands thus :—

> *Alth.* Farewel, *Diana,* and be sure you do
> Nothing unworthy of your Love and Vow.
> *Exeunt* Diana *and* Althea *severally.* Ring.

At the commencement of Mountford's farce *The Life and Death of Doctor Faustus,* 4to, 1697, but produced a decade or more before, we have : " Act I, Scene 1, *Dr.* Faustus *seated in his Chair, and reading in his Study. Good and bad Angel ready.*" After a few lines : " Mephostopholis *under the Stage,*" where he is shortly required to speak, and " *A good and bad Angel fly down* ". Presently is the stage direction : " [*Ring. Good and bad Angel descends.*"

In Rochester's alteration of *Valentinian,* quarto, 1685, Act III, Scene 3, at the entry of Lycias there is a marginal note " *A Ring !* " It is perhaps worth while pointing out that here the prompter's direction does not refer to the call for the music, but to a ring, a jewel which Lycias is to present to Lucina as from her husband to bid her come to court, and the marginal note was made by the prompter to remind him that the actor who played Lycias should be duly provided with the property required. In *A Lampoon on the* Greenwich *Strowlers* by Joseph Haines, the comedian, first printed in *Covent Garden Drollery,* 1672, we have the couplet :—

> And therefore because for fear she'd be lack'd,
> I ordered the Drummer to beat a long Act.

The drummer united in his one person the complete orchestra of the strolling players, and Haines, who had taken the leading lady aside for certain purposes of gallantry, desires him to make the music during the interval (i.e. the Act) as long as possible.

It has been said that when the musicians were required to accompany a song or a dance during a play they were introduced on to the stage. Towards the end of the Third Act of the Hon. James Howard's *All Mistaken ; or, The Mad Couple,* Theatre Royal, 1667, the Six Ladies rush out and bind Philidor and Mirida, leaving them until a boy who is passing gets a shilling to set them free. Philidor departs, and the act ends. *Enter* Fiddler.

Mir. A fiddle! nay, then I am made again;
I'd have a dance, if I had nothing but my
Smock on. Fiddler, strike up, and play my jig,
Call'd, *I care not a pin for any man.*
Fid. Indeed, I can't stay: I am going to
Play to some gentlemen.
Mir. Nay, thou shalt stay
But a little.
Fid. Give me half-a-crown then.
Mir. I have no money about me. But here, take
My handkerchief. [*Dance and Exit.*

Obviously the Fiddler appears only to afford Nell Gwyn, who created Mirida, the occasion to dance her famous jig, which when she gave it to round off an Epilogue had saved many a poor play, as the Duke of Buckingham avers in the Epilogue to his alteration of *The Chances,* when he declares:—

the author dreads the strut and mien
Of new-prais'd poets, having often seen
Some of his fellows, who have writ before,
When *Nell* has danc'd her jig, steal to the door,
Hear the pit clap, and with conceit of that
Swell, and believe themselves the Lord knows what.

But frequently an entrance of fiddlers was effected with a certain amount of ingenuity so that they became characters in the piece and took part in the action. Thus in Etherege's *The Comical Revenge; or, Love in a Tub* produced at Lincoln's Inn Fields in March, 1664, when Sir Frederick Frollick goes at night to serenade Mrs. Rich, the scene is laid in Covent Garden, and we have, Act III, Scene 2, "*Enter Sir* Frederick Frollick, *with Fidlers before him,* and *six or eight Link-boys, dancing and singing.*" He gains admittance to the house, and then calls in his friends, "*Enter the Fidlers, and a Masque of the Link-boys, who are Dancing-masters, disguis'd for the Frollick.*" Sir Frederick in fact is seldom without a noise of fiddlers at his heels. The stage direction which opens Scene 7 of the Fourth Act is: "*Sir* Frederick *is brought in upon a Bier, with a mourning Cloth over him, attended by a Gentleman in a mourning Cloak: Four Fidlers carry the Corps, with their Instruments tuck'd under their Cloaks.*" In the preceding scene Dufoy, whilst under the influence of a little opium, is clapped into his Tub by the Coachman and another servant, what time Betty and Lettice prepare to jeer the hapless French valet. Betty summons a fiddler: "Is the Fidler at hand that us'd to ply at the blind Ale-house?" "He's ready," answers the Coachman. "*Enter a Fidler.*" *Betty.* Well, let's hear now what a horrible

PLATE X

THE COMICAL REVENGE: ACT IV: SCENE 6
Collection of the Author

noise you can make to wake this Gentleman. "[*Fidler plays a Tune . . .* Dufoy *begins to wake*." This is the episode which gives the comedy its name, and it has been depicted by Du Guernier in his frontispiece to the 1715, 12mo, of the play, a plate reproduced in some subsequent eighteenth century editions, when the characters are seen mocking Dufoy fast in his tub, and the crowd is making merry music on his fiddle.

In Dryden's *An Evenings Love; or, The Mock-Astrologer,* produced at the Theatre Royal on 12th June, 1668, Act II, Wildblood and Bellamy resolve to serenade their mistresses. Accordingly, "*Enter Musicians with disguises; and some in their hands*." Wildblood introduces them with: "You know the men, if their Masquing habits were off; they are the Musick of our Embassadors Retinue." A song is sung; the ladies appear in the balcony, signify their thanks, and retire. Then "*Musick and Guittars tuning on the other side of the Stage*". Don Lopez and Don Melchior appear with servants and musicians. In a few moments the rivals, Spaniards and English, fight, and the attendants and musicians on both sides join in the general scuffle. In Wycherley's *The Gentleman Dancing-Master,* produced at Dorset Garden in March, 1672, towards the end of Act V, when Hippolita has just been married to Mr. Gerrard, we have: "*Enter two* Blacks, *and the* Spaniard *follow'd by* Prue, Martin, *and five other Gentlemen like Fiddlers*." "How now," asks the Don, "who sent for you, Friends?" Martin replies: "We Fiddlers, Sir, often come unsent for." "They are Gentlemen Fiddlers, forsooth," mutters Monsieur. Again, in Etherege's *The Man of Mode; or, Sir Fopling Flutter,* produced at Dorset Garden, 11th March, 1676, Act IV, "*The Scene opens with the Fiddles playing a Country Dance*." Later the gentlemen call for a bottle, and sing a bacchic, for which Sir Fopling summons the fiddlers back on to the stage with a "Hey! Musick!" After the song he suggests: "Hark you *Medley,* let you and I take the Fiddles and go waken *Dorimant*." The next scene is the lodging of Dorimant, who is just taking leave of Bellinda, when her departure is hastened by the sound of "*Fiddles without*". It may be noted that if the musicians were not to appear the stage directions are always careful to note the fact.

Dryden's *Love Triumphant,* Drury Lane, winter of 1693, has Act III, Scene 1, *The Scene* Victoria'*s Chamber. Enter* Alphonso, *with Musick. A Song is Sung: When it is beginning,* Victoria *Enters*. After the song "*Exeunt Musitians*" from the stage. At Dalinda's wedding, "*The Dance is first, then the Song, the last Words of which are Sung while the Company is going out, and the Musick Plays before Them*."

During the first Act of Dryden's *The Kind Keeper; or, Mr. Limberham,* Dorset Garden, March, 1678, we have "*Musick at the Balcony over head; Mrs.* Tricksy *and* Judith *appear*". Woodall exclaims: "Hark! there's Musick above!" and a Song follows. The singer was placed in a proscenium balcony.

In Mrs. Behn's *The Town-Fopp; or, Sir Timothy Tawdry,* Dorset Garden, autumn or winter, 1676, III, 3, Sir Timothy designs to serenade Bellmour and Diana. The scene is a street; "*Enter Sir* Timothy, Sham, *and* Sharp, *with Fidlers and Boy,*" who presently sings the aubade "*The happy Minute's come, the Nymph is laid*". *The City Heiress; or, Sir Timothy Treat-All,* Dorset Garden, Easter, 1682, presents a lively episode in Act III: "*Enter Musick playing, Sir* Anthony Meriwill *dancing with a Lady in his Hand, Sir* Charles *with Lady* Galliard, *several other Women and Men.* Sir *Anth.* [*singing*] Philander *was a jolly swain.*" *The Luckey Chance; or, An Alderman's Bargain* opens with "The Street, at break of Day". In a few moments, "*Enter Mr.* Gingle, *and several with Musick . . . They play and sing. Enter* Phillis *in the Balcony, throws 'em Money.*" "Fie, Mrs. *Phillis,* do you take us for Fiddlers that play for Hire?" expostulates Gingle. "She sends it only to drink her Health," answers the maid. "Come, Lads, let's to the Tavern then." "*Ex. Musick.*" In Act II, 2, at the wedding, "*Enter Fiddles playing, Mr.* Bearjest *and* Diana *dancing*; Bridwel, Noisy, *&c.*"

There are many songs and dances in the three parts of D'Urfy's *Don Quixote.* Part III was produced during the winter of 1695, presumably at Dorset Garden. In Act II, Scene 2, we have the marriage of Camacho and Quitteria. "*A noise of Pipes and Rural Instruments are heard within.*" After which: "*Enter, first, Musick playing; then* Camacho *led like a Bridegroom between two Maids; ajter him,* Quitteria *like a Bride, led between two Men: After them, Shepherds, Shepherdesses, Dancers and Singers, Men and Women.*" There is some dialogue and "*follows an Entertainment of Musick and Dancing*". In the next act also, at the marriage of Mary the Buxom the music is first heard within, and afterwards the fiddlers come on to the stage.

The Prologue was delivered before the curtain was drawn, the speaker entering on to the apron through one of the proscenium doors. There are many examples of a direction for the drawing of the curtain after the Prologue. Settle's *Cambyses, King of Persia,* Lincoln's Inn Fields, January, 1670–1, immediately after the Prologue, begins thus: "Actus primus. Scena prima. Scene, a Pavillion Royal. *The Curtain drawn, is represented* Cambyses *seated on a Throne; attended by* Otanes, Darius, Artaban, Prexaspes, *Guards, Slaves, and Attendance; with the*

Princess Mandana *and Ladies.* Cambyses *descends from the Throne.*"

Nevil Payne's *The Fatal Jealousie,* Dorset Garden, 1672, after the Prologue, spoken by Smith, opens: "Act the First. Scene the First. *The Curtain drawn Discovers* Don Antonio *and* Cælia *in Morning-Gowns. Chamber and Bed.*" Don Antonio was played by Smith, Cælia by Mrs. Shadwell. The same author's tragedy *The Siege of Constantinople,* Dorset Garden, 1674, commences: "Act I. *The Curtain drawn discovers the Emperor,* Thomazo, Theophilus, *and* Dorello, *on one side of a Table, the Cardinal, Chancellor, and* Justiniano *on the other, as at Councel; they arise and* Exeunt, *all with great reverence to the Emperor, except* Thomazo and Dorello, *who stay with him.*" D'Urfey's *Don Quixote,* Part I, Dorset Garden, May, 1694, opens thus: "Act I, Scene 1. *A Champian, with a Windmill at distance. The Curtain drawn,* Don Quixote *is Seen . . . upon his Horse* Rosinante; *and* Sancho *by him upon* Dapple *his Ass.*"

In Crowne's *The Destruction of Jerusalem,* I, produced at Drury Lane, January, 1677; quarto, 1677; there is printed after the Prologue the song of the Levites, "*on the opening of the Scene.*" Then, "Act I, Scene 1. *The curtain drawn, the brazen gates of the Temple appear; music is heard within.*" Tate's *Brutus of Alba,* Dorset Garden, summer of 1678, commences: "Act the First. *The Curtain drawn, discovers the Queen,* Amarante, Brutus, Soziman, *and Attendants.* Banks' *The Destruction of Troy,* Dorset Garden, late autumn of 1678, has: "Actus Primus, Scena Prima. *The Curtain being drawn up, discovers* Agamemnon, Achilles, Menelaus, Ulysses, Patroclus, Diomedes, *and* Ajax, *in Council.*" Rochester's *Valentinian,* 4to, 1685, is equipped with no less than three Prologues. "Prologue Spoken By Mrs. Cook The First Day. Written by *Mrs. Behn*"; "Prologue Intended For *Valentinian,* To be spoken by *Mrs. Barry*"; "Prologue to *Valentinian.* Spoken by Mrs. *Cook* the second Day." Then: "Act I, Scen. 1. *The Curtain flies up with the Musick of* Trumpets *and* Kettle-Drums; *and discovers the* Emperor *passing through to the Garden, Attended with a great Court.*"

The Prologue to D'Urfey's alteration of Fletcher's *The Noble Gentleman* which he named *A Fool's Preferment; or, The Three Dukes of Dunstable,* produced with poor success at Dorset Garden early in 1688, was spoken by Jevon. After this the opening stage direction is: "Act I, Scene 1, *A Garden, discovering* Lyonel *crown'd with Flowers, and Antickly drest, sitting on a Green Bank.*" Obviously the curtain drew, when Jevon had retired through a proscenium door, and discovered the garden. The Prologue to the same author's *The Marriage-Hater Match'd,*

Theatre Royal late winter of 1691, was spoken by Mountford, who acted Sir Philip Freewit, and Mrs. Bracegirdle who acted Phoebe, disguised in boy's clothes as Lovewell. "Prologue. *Mr. Monford* Enters, meets *Mrs. Bracegirdle* dressed in Boy's Cloaths, who seemingly Endeavours to go back, but he taking hold of her, Speaks:—

Monf. Nay, Madam, there's no turning back alone;
Now you are Enter'd, faith you must go on;
And speak the *Prologue,* you for those are Fam'd.

The Prologue ends: "— *and so let's off.* Exeunt." Then commences: "Act I, Scene 1, *Enter* Sir Philip *and* Lovewell." Clearly after the Prologue Mountford and Mrs. Bracegirdle retired, the curtain was drawn, and they again entered to begin the first scene.

The Prologue to Dryden's *Love Triumphant,* Drury Lane, winter of 1693, was spoken by Betterton, who played Alphonso. After the Prologue: "Act I, Scene 1. *At the Drawing up of the Curtain,* Veramond, *King of* Arragon, *appears:* Ximena *the Queen by him*: Victoria *their eldest Daughter on the Right Hand; and* Celidea *their younger Daughter on the left: Courtiers stand attending in File on each side of the Stage. The Men on the one hand, the Ladies on the other. Amongst The Men, Don* Lopez; *amongst the Women,* Dalinda *his Daughter. The Scene is suppos'd a Presence-Chamber.*" Alphonso enters in triumph thirty-one lines later.

The Prologue to *The Innocent Mistress,* a comedy by Mrs. Mary Pix, produced at Lincoln's Inn Fields in 1697, was spoken by Verbruggen, who acted Sir Francis Wildlove. Act I opens: "Sir Francis Wildlove in his Chamber Dressing with Searchwell his man." Searchwell was played by Knap.

Thoms Dilke in the Dedication to his comedy, *The City Lady; or, Folly Reclaim'd,* 4to, 1697, complains that the ill-success of his play was largely due "to the tedious waiting to have the Curtain drawn after the Prologue was spoke". Farquhar, in his *Discourse upon Comedy,* 1702, writes: "Here is a new play; the house is throng'd, the Prologue's spoken and the Curtain drawn represents you the scene of *Grand Cairo.*"

It was very rarely that the Prologue was delivered after the Curtain was drawn, and indeed only two instances seem recorded, altogether exceptional occasions. The one is when Killigrew's company opened temporarily at Lincoln's Inn Field with *Wit without Money,* and Dryden furnished the Prologue which is printed in *Covent Garden Drollery,* and also in *Westminster Drollery,* the Second Part, 1672. In the British Museum is a MS.[28] of this Prologue: "The Prologue of a Play entitled Witt without

Money—Spoken at the Dukes old Theatre (after the Kings was burnt) by the Kings players, Feb. 26, 1671. The Curtaine being drawne up all the Actors were discover'd on the stage in Melancholick postures, & Moone advancing before the rest speaks as follows, addressing himself chiefly to ye King then p^r^sent."

The second—first in point of time—is the Prologue to Dryden and Sir Robert Howard's *The Indian Queen,* produced at the Theatre Royal in January, 1663–4. "Prologue. As the Musick plays a soft Air, the Curtain rises softly, and discovers an *Indian* Boy and Girl sleeping under two Plantain-Trees; and when the Curtain is almost up, the Musick turns into a Tune expressing an Alarm, at which the Boy wakes and speaks." There is no stage direction at the commencement of the play beyond "Act I. Scene 1. *Enter* Ynca, Orazia, Montezuma, Acasis, *Prisoners, with* Peruvians", but I think we may fairly surmise that the curtain was not dropped, but that the Indian landscape with the "two Plantain-Trees" represented the actual opening scene.

It was, of course, the aim of the dramatist to give some novel touch to a prologue, some salt, some pretty fancy or garnish, such as might arrest and hold the attention of an audience. Accordingly all kinds of devices were essayed. It may be remarked that Dryden seldom, if ever, resorted to alien artifice. The introduction of the two Astrologers in the Prologue to *The Wild Gallant*; the entry of a second Prologue before *The Rival Ladies*; the return of the Prologue "to speak the rest" before *Secret Love; or, The Maiden Queen* (and these, it must be remembered, are all his earliest plays); the brief prose induction before honest Mr. Williams came in "half mellow from the *Rose-Tavern*" [29] to speak the prologue to Joseph Harris' *The Mistakes; or, The False Report,* produced at Drury Lane late in 1690, seem legitimate enough in all conscience when we consider such prologues as that triple fare which the Hon. Edward Howard prefixed to *The Womens Conquest,* produced at Lincoln's Inn Fields in the winter of 1670. The first prologue is a dialogue of some length between Edward Angel, Underhill, and Nokes; the second is an address in verse spoken by the ghost of Ben Jonson, an apparition which had been mute whilst the comedians were chattering; the third, the speaker of which is unnamed, is a prologue in verse commencing:—

> *You see what little Arts w'are fain to try*
> *To give a Prologue some variety*; . . .

It must be acknowledged that the Restoration dramatist had precedent for his variety, since the admired Jonson has a Prologue to *The Poetaster* spoken " After the second sounding " by Envy, who " arises in the midst of the stage ", and at the third sounding " As she disappears, enter Prologue hastily in armour ", crying :—

> Stay, monster, ere thou sink—thus on thy head
> Set we our bolder foot.

It will be remembered that the speaker of the Prologue to *Troilus and Cressida* is " A prologue arm'd ", and similarly the prologue to Henry Burnell's *Landgartha,* " A Tragie-Comedy, as it was presented in the new Theater in Dublin with good applause, being an Ancient story," Dublin, 4to, 1641, is delivered by an Amazon wielding a mighty battle-axe. The Induction to *Bartholomew-Fair* is in part a dialogue between the Stage-keeper, the Bookholder, and a Scrivener, who reads out lengthy articles. Those who have had the pleasure of seeing *The Poetaster* and *Bartholomew Fair* [30] acted upon the stage will appreciate how excellent these prologues are. Again the spirited prologue to *Cynthia's Revels* begins with the squabbling of the three Children for the black velvet cloak convention required should be donned by the speaker of the prologue, and the ensuing conversation is very pretty. A prologue in verse follows after the third sounding.

Not infrequently a particular revival was set off with a special Prologue. Thus when Jonson's *Catiline's Conspiracy* was given with great splendour at the Theatre Royal, on Friday, 18th December, 1668, as a *bonne bouche* the tragedy was ushered in with a Prologue " Merrily spoken by Mrs. *Nell* in an *Amazonian* habit ".

Among the more remarkable or famous Prologues of the Restoration theatre delivered in character or which are other than an address in verse to the audience by one single speaker, may be reckoned :—the Prologue " *To the Duke of* Lerma, *spoken by* Mrs. Ellen *and* Mrs. Nepp ". *The Great Favourite; or, The Duke of Lerma* by Sir Robert Howard was produced at the Theatre Royal on Thursday, 20th February, 1668. Pepys was present ; " and Knepp and Nell spoke the prologue most excellently, especially Knepp, who spoke beyond any creature I ever heard." The Prologue to Thomas St. Serfe's *Tarugo's Wiles ; or, The Coffee House,* produced at Lincoln's Inn Fields, Saturday, 5th October, 1667, is a colloquy between a Gentleman, a Player, and a Poet's Servant, and incidentally their talk contains much that is extremely valuable to the Stage historian. The Prologue to Orrery's *Tryphon,* produced at Lincoln's Inn Fields, Tuesday, 8th December, 1668, was spoken by Nokes and Angel.

Pepys who was in a thoroughly bad humour (and perhaps not without reason) thought it "very silly". Duffett's burlesque *The Mock-Tempest; or, The Enchanted Castle,* given at the Theatre Royal in November, 1674, was introduced by a free and frolic dialogue between Joe Haines and Betty Mackarel,[31] a well-known and fair cyprian of the day, who had begun her career as an orange-wench in that very theatre. The lady having made her curtsey and departed, Haines proceeded to a Prologue of more conventional pattern. Dryden's prologue to *Troilus and Cressida; or, Truth Found too late,* Dorset Garden, spring of 1679, was effectively "Spoken by Mr. *Betterton,* Representing The Ghost of *Shakespear*". A very different spectre delivered the Prologue to Mrs. Behn's *The Roundheads; or, The Good Old Cause,* produced at the same theatre in the winter of 1681, since this address was "Spoken by the Ghost of *Hewson* ascending from Hell dress'd as a Cobler". The same lady's pantomime *The Emperor of the Moon,* Dorset Garden, spring of 1687, was equipped with a Prologue given by Tom Jevon, and incidentally the business of "*the speaking Head*" was intercalated. "The Head rises upon a twisted Post, on a Bench from under the Stage. After *Jevern* speaks to its Mouth.

Oh!—Oh!—Oh!
Stentor. *Oh!—Oh!—Oh!*

After this it sings *Sawny,* laughs, crys God bless the King in order."

Stentor answers:—

Speak louder, Jevern, *if you'd have me repeat;*
Plague of this Rogue, he will betray the Cheat.

The Prologue to D'Urfey's *Don Quixote, Part III,* produced in the winter of 1695, presumably at Dorset Garden, is a dialogue between young Hildebrand Horden and Miss Cross.[32] Bevil Higgons, a kinsman of the author, supplied the prologue to Granville's alteration of *The Merchant of Venice,* which as *The Jew of Venice* was given at Lincoln's Inn Fields in the spring—probably May—of 1701. "The Ghosts of *Shakespear* and *Dryden* arise Crown'd with Lawrel."

If it be inquired when the Prologue ceased to be spoken the answer may be found in a letter written by Miss Mitford to Mr. Fields, her American publisher. She tells him: "It is singular that Epilogues were just dismissed at the first representation of one of my plays *Foscari,* and Prologues at another, *Rienzi.*" *Foscari* was first performed at Covent Garden in November, 1826; *Rienzi* at Drury Lane on 9th October, 1828. According to Mr. Planché, however, the first play of any importance presented without a Prologue was his adaptation of William Rowley's old comedy, *A New Wonder, A Woman Never Vext,* produced at Covent Garden on the 9th November, 1824, the performance being embellished, as was Planché's wont, with a grand pageant of the Lord Mayor's Show as it may be supposed to have appeared in the days of Henry VI. During one of the last rehearsals, Fawcett, the stage manager, asked the author if he had written a Prologue? "No." "A five-act play and no Prologue! Why the audience will tear up the benches!" As a matter of fact, the omission passed almost without notice. It must not, however, be supposed that these time-honoured addresses were dropped suddenly at any particular point within a few years. The custom was largely abandoned owing to the fact that the older Prologues being for the most part extremely topical had lost a good deal of their application, one might even say so far as the general public was concerned a good deal of their meaning, and they were not usually delivered at the revivals of plays which might not have been given for some little time. There is an anecdote told of an actor named Wignell, who was it seems a greater favourite in the provinces than in London. When Sheridan revived *Cato* it had been the custom for many years to omit Pope's Prologue. Wignell, who performed Portius, upon the rising of the curtain at once commenced the play with—

> The dawn is overcast, the morning low'rs,
> And heavily in clouds, brings on the day

when he was interrupted with cries for the Prologue. Wignell, renowned for his imperturbability, paused a moment, and then turning his face from Marcus, whom he was addressing, to the audience, said in as lofty a tone and as solemn a heroic measure as if he were yet declaiming lines in his speech—

> Ladies and gentlemen, there has not been
> A Prologue spoken to this play for years

and then, turning to Marcus, he continued—

> The great, Th' important day, big with the fate
> Of Cato and of Rome—

Perhaps it should be mentioned that well-nigh throughout the nineteenth century Prologues have been spoken at performances on special occasions, and it were not untrue to say that the custom although obsolete still lingers. Now and again at the revivals of old comedies the Prologues have been spoken, and having often been excellently delivered they are received with great applause. In fact a revival is very incomplete without this address. It were to be wished that so admirable a practice might become general and that even modern plays should be thus furnished. But then it would be necessary to find someone who was capable of penning such witty lines. When Wycherley's *The Gentleman Dancing-Master* was seen for one performance at the Regent Theatre, London, on 20th December, 1925, it was not helped by the importation of a flat meaningless Prologue and Epilogue, written for the occasion, although these were both delivered by one of our favourite actresses.

Nicolo Sabbatini in his *Practica di fabricar Scene e Machine ne' Teatri* (Ravenna, 1638), speaks of three kinds of curtain which were employed at that time in Italy. There was the curtain which sank beneath the stage and rolled up below; the Roman *aulæum*; there was the curtain which ascended and rolled up above of the fashion in the general modern theatre; there were also the double curtains which were drawn up in loops, parting in the middle, and festooning on either side. This latter kind commends itself least of all to Sabbatini, but none the less these double curtains were those preferred in the public English theatres upon the regular introduction of scenery at the Restoration. They seem to have prevailed until the third decade of the eighteenth century or even longer. It may, of course, be contended that on this point we must not press the evidence of such illustrations as the frontispiece by G. Vander Gucht to *Harlequin Horace* (third edition), 1735; or similar plates which embellish *Beauties of the English Stage,* 1737; and Fielding's *Pasquin,* 1737. But all these show the double curtain, looped, and their evidence is surely not without weight. The same kind of curtain is clearly indicated in the illustration to *Hamlet,* Rowe's Shakespeare, 1709; as also in the plates to *A Wife for a Month; The Mad Lover; The Nice Valour; or, The Passionate Madman* (a particularly good example); *Thierry and Theodoret; The Fair Maid of the Inn; The Knight of Malta*; to instance but half a dozen pieces taken almost at random from the Beaumont and Fletcher of 1711. Attention might also be called to Pierre Le Vergne's frontispieces for Carlile's *The Fortune-Hunters,* 12mo, 1714; and Shadwell's *The Squire of Alsatia,* 12mo, 1715; to the frontispiece of the Twelfth Edition of *The Rehearsal,* 12mo, 1734; to the frontispiece by Basine before Mrs. Centlivre's *The Basset-Table,* Third Edition, 1735; and the junior James Thornhill's drawing to Young's *Busiris,* 12mo, 1735. We have here an accumulation of evidence, and many more such illustrations could easily be instanced. In most cases the artist drew his pictures from the performance on the contemporary stage. *The Squire of Alsatia,* for example, was being played at Drury Lane in 1711 (May and November), 1712, and 1714; *The Rehearsal* was seen nearly every season, Cibber was acting Bayes at Drury Lane in 1733 and 1734. It is perhaps worth remark that a very cursory examination will suffice to show how vastly these earlier drawings, done (as I believe) from the life, differ from the illustrations by J. J. Barralet which are to be found in the Beaumont and Fletcher, ten volumes, 1778. These are spirited and vigorous enough, often indeed extremely pleasing in their design, but they are obviously imaginative work. Yet we may note that not a few (as for example the plates to *The Humorous Lieutenant* and *The Loyal Subject,* vol. iii) display the festooned curtain, although perhaps this may be merely decorative.

Mrs. Centlivre's *The Perjur'd Husband; or, The Adventures of Venice,* Drury Lane, September, 1700, opens thus: "Act I. Scene 1. *The Curtains fly up, and discover a Mask in* Pizalto's *House.*" "Charles Easy" in his letter to *The Spectator,* No. 240 (Steele), Wednesday, 5th December, 1711, describes the beau who at the performance of *Philaster,* "getting into one of the Side-Boxes on the Stage before the Curtain drew, was disposed to shew the whole Audience his Activity by leaping over the Spikes; he passed from thence to one of the ent'ring Doors, where he took Snuff with a tolerable good Grace, display'd his fine Cloaths, made two or three feint Passes at the Curtain with his Cane, then fac'd about and appear'd at the other Door; Here he affected to survey the whole House, bow'd and smil'd at Random, and then shew'd his Teeth (which were some of them indeed very white); After this he retir'd behind the Curtain, and obliged us with several Views of his Person from every Opening."

The usual entrances and exits employed on the Restoration stage were the proscenium doors, that is to say the permanent doors, forming an architectural feature of the building, which were set on either side of the apron stage, between the oval front of the stage which faced the pit and the proscenium arch As the error has been more than once made and is yet repeated, it must be emphasized that there were no such doors, indeed there could not be, on the further side of the proscenium arch, behind the curtain line. Actually the evidence concerning the number of proscenium doors employed in Restoration times is most contradictory and confusing if we attempt to generalize, and the safest plan is to prove the precise number employed in each theatre, so far as the known details admit.

Imprimis, the Vere Street Theatre was from first to last a platform-stage, and therefore had no proscenium doors.[33] The first Theatre Royal in Bridges Street was furnished with no less than six doors, as is proved by a stage direction in Lacy's farce *The Old Troop; or, Monsieur Raggou,* which was produced at this house in 1665, and revived some three years later. (It was first printed, quarto 1672.) In Act II we find the direction: "*Enter twelve* Troopers *at six doors—two at a door.*" It may be remarked that as Lacy was an eminent actor at this very theatre he would most certainly be entirely familiar with the construction and resources of the stage. Again in the Hon. James Howard's *All Mistaken; or, The Mad Couple,* a comedy which was seen at the same theatre by Pepys on Friday, 20th September, 1667, in Act II we have "*Enter six* Ladies, *one after another*". They are seeking to speak with Philidor, but he manages to escape, whereupon the Ladies, each invoking a right royal curse on his head, retire. The stage direction is "*Exeunt at several doors*", that is to say each lady goes off, one immediately after the other at her separate door, and each in succession utters her hearty malediction just as she vanishes. So here we have the complement of six doors in use.

In Edward Howard's *The Man of Newmarket,* produced at the Theatre Royal in March, 1678, the Induction begins with "*Enter* Prologue *at one Door; and just as he addresses to speak; enter* Shatteril *and* Haines *at t'other*". This, on the face of it might seem as if there were two only doors. In Act II, however, Luce peeps out and Passall cries: "Mark these Doors"; a moment later Luce peeps again when Whiffler "*Goes to the Door*" crying "thou pretty Bo-peep thou", but "Luce *appears at another Door*". There are five jockeys, all speaking parts, and in Act III we have "*Enter* Jockeys *at several Doors*", which proves five doors in use. In Act V also we find the stage direction "*Enter* Jockeys *at several Doors*".

From Wren's sectional design for the second Theatre Royal, Bridges Street, it is shown that this house had four proscenium doors, two on each side, and it can be demonstrated that these were all in constant use.

Similarly at Lincoln's Inn Fields and at Dorset Garden at least four proscenium doors were employed.

Thus at the commencement of the second Act of Etherege's *She wou'd if she cou'd,* produced at the Duke's House, Lincoln's Inn Fields, on Thursday, 6th February, 1668, the scene is laid in the Mulberry-Garden, which lay on the site of the present Buckingham Palace and its gardens. It was a very favourite rendezvous, and here come two young ladies, Ariana and Gatty, in masks, to meet their gallants. The scene begins with Courtal and Freeman walking up and down and waiting for the ladies. Then "*Enter* Ariana *and* Gatty *with Vizards, and pass nimbly over the Stage*". The two gentlemen after a word or two follow briskly enough.

They go after the Women.
Enter Women again, and cross the stage.

Aria. Now if these should prove two men of War that are cruising here, to watch for Prizes
Gatty. Would they had courage enough to set upon us; I long to be engag'd.
Aria. Look, look yonder, I protest they chase us.
Gatty. Let us bear away then; if they be truly valiant they'll quickly make more Sail, and board us.

The Women go out, and go about behind the Scenes to the other Door.

Enter Courtal *and* Freeman.

Free. How fleet they are! Whatsoever faults they have, they cannot sure be broken-winded.
Cour. Sure, by that little mincing step they shou'd be Country Fillies that have been breath'd at Course a Park, and Barly-Break: we shall never reach 'em.
Free. I'll follow directly, do thou turn down the Cross-walk and meet 'em.

Enter the Women, and after 'em Courtal *at the lower Door,* and Freeman *at the upper on the contrary side.*

Cour. By your leave, Ladies—

Before further evidence is presented with regard to the doors it should be remarked that over each door was a balcony, or a kind of box, and these balconies were continually used when a character had to appear aloft or above, as at a window; and indeed the terms "window", balcony, and "above" are all convertible.

It is true that the earlier Restoration stage also had at least two permanent windows, one on each side, and these were fairly low down (see the passage from *The Carnival* quoted below)—probably in the space between two of the doors. These were a heritage from the old platform stage, since as at the introduction of scenery in the public play-houses it was initially conceived in Caroline masque style, and there was little foreign influence in the theatre before the building of Dorset Garden. A window is employed in *The Adventures of Five Hours,* Act V, produced at Lincoln's Inn Fields, Thursday, 8th January, 1662–3. The scene is an interior, the house of Don Carlos. "*A Blaze of Light appears at the Window, and a noise without.*"

Porcia. See, *Flora,* at the Window, what's that Light
And noise we hear

[Flora *goes to the Window.*

PLATE XI

MASTER JOE'S UNEXPECTED VISIT TO THE PIT
By George Cruikshank
Dickens, "Memoirs of Joseph Grimaldi," 1838

[*face p.* 128

Flora. O Madam! we are all undone, I see
Henrique, Carlos, and their Servants with Torches
All coming hither; and which is wonderful
Antonio leading them with his Sword drawn.

Camilla. Thou dream'st, distracted Wench; *Antonio* false?
It is impossible.

[Camilla *runs to the Window, and turning back says,*
All she has said, is in appearance true.

In Porter's *The Carnival,* acted at the Theatre Royal, 1663, I, 1, we have: "Enter *Ferdinando, Beatrice,* at a low Window." Ferdinando gives the signal by crying "Hem!" whereupon Beatrice "Opens the door: Enters". Later in the same act Ferdinando "*Knocks softly at the Window*" of another house, whence Elvira comes out on the stage.

The famous scene in *Sr Martin Mar-All,* Lincoln's Inn Fields, August, 1667, where the foolish knight is to serenade his mistress was, I feel assured, played in the proscenium balconies (of which three were required for the business of this episode), not at the windows, although the term window is actually employed. Mrs. Millisent insists that her admirer, who is utterly unskilled in music, shall treat her with a song on the lute, and that he shall meanwhile be placed where she can observe him; "let him stand in the view; I'le not be cheated," she conditions. Warner instructs Sir Martin. "Get up into your Window, and set two Candles by you, take my Land-lord's Lute in your hand, and fumble on't, and make grimaces with your mouth, as if you sung; in the mean time, I'le play in the next Room in the dark, and consequently your Mistress, who will come to her Balcone over against you, will think it to be you; and at the end of every Tune, I'le ring the Bell that hangs between your Chamber and mine, that you may know when to have done." Presently "*Enter* Millisent, Rose, *with a Candle by 'em above*". After a little talk Rose says: "And see, Madam, where your true Knight, Sir *Martin* is plac'd yonder like *Apollo,* with his Lute in his hand, and his Rays about his head." "[*Sir* Martin *appears at the adverse window, a Tune play'd; when it is done,* Warner *rings and Sir* Martin *holds.*" A song is sung; *Blind Love to this hour,* a paraphrase of Voiture's chanson *L'Amour sous la loy*; and "*The Song being done,* Warner *rings agen; but Sir* Martin *continues fumbling, and gazing on his Mistress*". Millisent smokes the trick and cries: "Play louder, Sir *Martin,* that we may have the fruits on't." Warner *peeping*: "Death! this abominable Fool will spoil all . . . [*Rings agen.*" However, the stratagem has failed. Here we have the several balconies referred to in Warner's speech as Balcony; in one stage direction as *above*; in another stage direction as *Window.* Scene 5 of the Second Act of Mrs. Behn's *The Emperor of the Moon,* Dorset Garden, spring of 1687, is a Garden. Scaramouch enters with a ladder to serenade Mopsophil as he deems it "rude to surprize her sleeping, and more gallant to wake her with a Serenade at her Window". He "*Sets the Ladder to her Window, fetches his Lute and goes up the ladder*". After his song, "*Enter* Mopsophil *above.*" They discourse, and Harlequin enters below. "Ha, What do I see?" he cries. "My mistress at the Window, courting my Rival!" Presently "Scar. *going over the Balcony*" he cannot contain his indignation and bawls out; "Scar. *comes down, as* Mopsophil *flings out of the Balcony.*" Window, Balcony, and *above* are employed as indifferent terms for the proscenium-balcony. The balconies must have been considerably larger than the space an actual window could have occupied, and have allowed of the presence of far more characters. In *The City Heiress; or, Sir Timothy Treat-All,* Dorset Garden, 1682, II: "*Enter Lady* Galliard *and* Closet, *above in the Balcony.*" The lady says to her maid: "Prithee let's take a turn in this Balcony, this City-Garden, where we walk to take the fresh Air of the Sea-coal Smoak." Wilding whose attention she wishes to engage is in the street below, and she exclaims:—

> I think he's passing on,
> Without so much as looking towards the Window.

Accordingly she lets fall her fan and requesting him to bring to her into the house, "*Goes out of the Balcony with* Closet."

However the opening tableau of D'Urfey's heroic tragedy *The Siege of Memphis; or, The Ambitious Queen,* Theatre Royal, June, 1676; 4to, 1676; was a built-up scene: "*The Curtain being drawn, an Alarm of Drums and Trumpets are heard, the Scene representing a Turret, besieged by* Moaron, Psamnis, *and Syrians*; Zelmura, Phillopater, Zichmi, *and Egyptians, appearing on the Walls defending, a skirmish of Darts, which done the Scene changes to* Melechadels *Pallace.*"

Just as the proscenium doors were able to be locked, so could balcony doors be fastened in the same way. In a comedy by George Digby, Earl of Bristol, *Elvira; or, The Worst not always True,* which was printed quarto 1667, and probably acted at the Duke's Theatre in 1663–4, it plainly appears that a balcony door could be locked. In Act II we have: "*Scene changes to* Donna Bianca's *antechamber. Enter* Francisca, *and goes to the hanging where* Don Zancho *and* Chichon *are hid*:—

> *Fran.* Ho! trusty servant with his faithful master!
> Come out, the balcony's open, lose no time,

Julio's abed, and fast asleep ere this—
There's nobody in the street, it is so light
One may discover a mile; therefore be quick.

[Don Zancho *and* Chichon *come out from behind the hanging and follow her as leading to the balcony. Exeunt.*
[*And soon after* Don Zancho *and* Chichon *appear as in the balcony, and* Francisca's *head as peeping out of the door into it.*

Scene changes to the prospect of Valencia. *Enter* Fabio *as in the street, and settling himself in a porch.*

Fab. Here is a porch, as if 'twere built on purpose.
[Fabio *looking up, perceives them in the balcony.*
Ha! here's a vision that I little dreamt of.
Stand close, Fabio, and mum!

[Don Zancho *gets over the balcony, and letting himself down at arm's length, leaps gently into the street.* Chichon *offers at the like, but takes a fall as he lights, and (rising) counterfeits lameness.* Francisca *retires, and locks the balcony.*

In Orrery's *Guzman,* produced at Lincoln's Inn Fields, Friday, 16th April, 1669, Act I, Guzman and Francisco enter with Musicians to give a serenade. Francisco directs the fiddlers: "'Tis under that Balcony, you must Play and Sing." Guzman asks: "Are you sure it is *Antonia* and *Pastrana's* Window?" When the song is done "*A Balcony opens, in which* Antonia *appears drest in Pink-Colour, and* Pastrana *in Sky-coloured Gowns*". Presently "Pastrana *and* Antonia *Shut the Balcony, and retire.*"

The scene of the Third Act of Tuke's *The Adventures of Five Hours,* produced at Lincoln's Inn Fields on Thursday, 8th January, 1662–3, is "Don Henrique's House". "Camilla, Porcia, Flora *appear in a Balcone.*" Presently Antonio, Octavio, and Diego enter, and almost immediately after "*Enter on the other side of the Stage* Henrique *and* Carlos."

Hen. Let's go home the shorter way;
The Back-door of my Garden's here at hand . . .
Porc. Would he were come, I fear the Rising Moon
Will give us little time. [*Above in the Balcone.*
[Octavio *knocks upon the Hilt of his Sword.*
I think I hear his usual knock . . .
Hen. Come; we are now hard by the Garden Gate.
Oct. Let's to the door; sure she's there by this time . . .
[*The noise of a Lock*
Car. I think I heard your Garden door open.
Hen. I think so too; Ha! at this time o' th' night?
Why what a devil can this mean? 'Tis so.

Ant. They have open'd the door; 'tis time for me
To follow, surely *Octavio* is gone in.

[Antonio *goes towards the door.*

Porc. What stay you for?

[*Holding the door half open.*

Hen. What's that I hear? sure 'tis *Porcia's* Voice . . .

Porc. You may come in securely, *Octavio.*

[*Setting open the door.*

A *mêlée* ensues. In the Fifth Act of the same play we have: "Don *Carlos's* House. *Enter* Diego, Flora, *and* Pedro *accompanying the Chair, groaping as i' th' dark.*"

Pedr. Dame *Flora*, and Signior *Diego* go in there.
And you, my Friends, set down the Chair, and let
The Lady out; Go, there's money for you.
I'll go fetch a Candle.

Diego *and* Flora *go in, and the Chair being set in the door,* Octavio *goes out into the Room*; Pedro *claps to the Door, and goes away.*

Enter Octavio, Diego, Flora, *at another door.*

Oct. What! Put in all alone here i' the dark!

[*Groaping as i' th' dark.*

And the door shut upon me! *Diego, Flora.*

Die. Here am I Sir, and Mistriss *Flora* too.

Oct. I can't conjecture where we are; I durst not
So much as peep out of the Chair, since *Flora*
Gave me the warning . . .

Flor. You may escape before the Candles come;
The door was wont to open on this side;

[Octavio *goes to the door.*

If not, I have another way in store.

Oct. *Flora*, I cannot make the Lock go back.

[Pedro *unlocks it on the other side, and coming in with a Candle, meets with* Octavio, *and starting back and stumbling, lets the Candle fall, then running out again double-locks the door.*

Die. Nay then, i' faith, w'are fast; I heard him give
The Key a double turn . . .

Flor. W'have yet some room for hope; there's a Back-stairs
Beyond that Inner Chamber, which goes down
Into the Garden, if the door be open,
As certainly it is, the way is easie.

There is a good deal more bustle and stir with locking and unlocking and clapping to doors in the play, and if it be objected that the securing of these various portals and the struggling to open them were merely acted or feigned, a stage sham, that the doors were not really secured, it may be answered that nothing is more difficult or more unsafe to pretend than a piece of business of this kind, if an actor is pulling at a door which the intrigue demands must resist his efforts, he will be bound to exert some force, and most assuredly unless the obstacle is made fast actually and indeed the door will fly open to the spoiling and ridicule of the whole situation. Moreover the Duke's Players at Lincoln's Inn Fields were pretty vigorous in their action as a French visitor, Chappuzeau, remarked: "Estant à Londres il y a six ans, j'y vis deux fort belles Troupes des Comediens, l'une du Roy, et l'autre du Duc D'Yorc, et je fus à deux representations, à la mort de *Montezume,* Roy de Mexique, et à celle de *Mustapha,* qui se defendoit vigoreusement sur le Theatre contu les muets qui le vouloient étrangler." [34]

In D'Urfey's favourite comedy *The Fond Husband; or, The Plotting Sisters,* produced at Dorset Garden in the spring of 1676, Act IV, we have: "*Enter* Rashley *and* Emilia, *Scene a Bed-Chamber.*" But Ranger has previously been concealed by the Governess in a closet adjoining this very room and he steals out softly. Although it is dark he recognizes the lovers by their voices, especially when they begin to jeer himself. Suddenly Bubble, Emilia's husband, who has been warned by his sister Maria of what is performing is heard at the door: "Bawds! Strumpets! Whores! Witches! Break open the Door there, break open the Door—" Emilia seeks to thrust Rashley into the closet, but to her amazement Ranger bars the way whilst Bubble continues shouting: "Quickly, quickly! a Leaver, a Leaver!" Rashley is concealed under the table, and Emilia muttering "This Key may add to my Design. [*Takes out the Key o' th' door*". "Down, down with it, break it open there," clamours Bubble in an extremity of rage. "What think of that, Madam?" Ranger taunts. Emilia, however, "*goes and puts the Key into his Coat-pocket, and then lays hold of him, and cries out*—Help, help there . . . A Rape, a Rape!" By this subterfuge she is eventually able to soothe her husband's suspicions. In this scene we have one proscenium-door serving as the door of the room, and this is locked fast; whilst a second proscenium-door on the opposite side is utilized as the door of the closet.

Another comedy of D'Urfey's, *The Fool's Preferment; or, The Three Dukes of Dunstable,* Dorset Garden, 1688, introduces business with the locking of a proscenium door. In the first scene of the Second Act we are shown the basset-table crowded with gamesters. Justice Grub, Cocklebrain, and Toby enter, and Grub sets about clearing the room. Suddenly Lyonel rushes in and all the card-players are driven out, whereupon Grub orders: "So, so, now lock the Door upon 'm *Toby*. [Toby *locks the Door*."

Otway's Sir Noble Clumsey reeling about drunk as a drum runs against Lady Squeamish and knocks over a table with its china. "Oh help! I am murder'd!" screams the lady. Sir Noble hiccups out: "Look you, Madam, no harm! no harm! you shall see me behave myself notably yet—as for example—suppose now—suppose this the door. [*Goes* to the *Door*.] Very well; thus then I move.—[*Steps forward and leaves his Peruke on one of the Hinges*.] Hah! who was that? Rogues! Dogs! Sons of Whores!"

In Act V of Nevil Payne's *The Morning Ramble; or, The Town-Humours* produced at Dorset Garden in November, 1672, although the scene is laid in the Mulberry Garden we have "[*Exit* Muchland, *and bolts the Door*", and later "[Muchland *locks the door*". In Mrs. Behn's *Sir Patient Fancy*, Dorset Garden, January, 1678, Act III, Scene 7, we have: "*Lady* Fancy's *Bed-chamber . . . Noise at the Door of unlatching it*."

A fastening of the proscenium door occurs in Dryden's *The Indian Emperour*, Theatre Royal, spring of 1665, in the Fifth Act when Montezuma wishes to gain entrance to the tower in which his daughter Cydaria has been left for safety. Almeria who is with him says:—

> My voice she knows and fears, but use your own,
> And to gain entrance feign you are alone.
>
> [Almeria *steps behind*.
>
> *Mont*. *Cydaria!*
> *Alm*. Lowder.
> *Mont*. Daughter!
> *Alm*. Lowder yet.
> *Mont*. Thou canst not sure, thy Father's voice forget.
> [*He knocks at the door, at last* Cydaria *looks over the* Zoty.

The zoty, azotea, is a name of Moorish origin, for the flat roof which is still common and is to-day so called in Spain and Mexico. All editions save the first 4to, 1667, read "balcony". After satisfying herself it is her father who calls "Cydaria *descends and opens the Door,* Almeria *rushes betwixt with* Montezuma.

> *Cyd*. *Almeria* here! then I am lost again.
> [*Both thrust*.
> *Alm*. Yield to my strength, you struggle but in vain.
> Make haste and shut, our Enemies appear.
> [Cortez *and* Spaniards *appear at the other end*.
> *Cyd*. Then do you enter and let me stay here.
> [*As she speaks, Almeria over-powers her, thrusts her in, and shuts*.

Cort. Sure I both heard her voice, and saw her face,
She's like a Vision vanish'd from the place.
Too late I find my absence was too long;
My hopes grow sickly, and my fears grow strong.
[*He knocks a little, then* Montezuma, Cydaria, Almeria *appear above.*

After a brief dialogue Montezuma stabs himself:—

Cyd. Oh my dear Father!
Cort. Haste, break ope the Door.
Alm. When that is forc'd then yet remain two more.
[*The Soldiers break open the first door and go in.*

I have quoted this scene at some length as it so admirably shows the ingenious use of Proscenium Doors and Balconies. In Crowne's *The Destruction of Jerusalem,* I, Act IV, whilst Matthias, the High Priest, and the rest of the Sanhedrin are wrapped in slumber, John the Pharisee is plotting against them. A martial noise is heard: "John, Eleazar, *and their party now break into the room with drawn swords, and chase* Matthias, *&c., off the stage, who retreat fighting as into some other rooms of the palace, and shut the door to hinder* John's *pursuit.*" A few moments later "Matthias, Sagan, Phineas *appear in the balcony*". A dialogue follows, and "Matthias, *&c. go out of the balcony, and* John *&c. break open the door, after which a noise of fighting is heard*". In Shadwell's comedy *The Miser,* Theatre Royal, January, 1672, Act V, old Squeeze who is lodging for the night at Mrs. Cheatly's retires with Lettice. Unfortunately a riot of scowrers beset the house and demand admittance. Timothy Squeeze who is drunk bawls out: "Bounce at the door, break the windowes, hey!" "*They bounce at the doores.*" Squeeze *at window in his cap and undressed.* "Heaven they have almost broke the door, I must venture to escape at this window!" [*He leaps down.*] "Death! I have broke my bones; oh, oh!" "Some body leaped out of a window," cries Ranter. The Constable and Watch hale away old Squeeze, whilst the bullies "*go off, and come in at another door.*" Theodore and Robin enter and with the help of Bellamour drive the rioters off the stage. Here we have four doors in use; the first is that of Mrs. Cheatly's house; the noisy crew withdraw by the second, to return immediately at the third; Theodore Robin, and Bellamour enter at a fourth door.

In Ravenscroft's famous play *The London Cuckolds,* produced at Dorset Garden in the winter of 1681, the intrigue is full of bustle, mistake, and movement, and great use is made of the doors and balconies. The first scene of Act II is laid in a room in Dashwell's house. During the old scrivener's absence his wife Eugenia with her maid Jane in attendance is awaiting a visit from Ramble. However, there first appears in disguise, so that he is unrecognized, Mr. Loveday, "A Young Merchant, one that had formerly been a Lover of *Eugenia*." Bringing with him letters from Dashwell's brother in Hamburg he claims hospitality for a few days, and accordingly a room is got ready, while the lady suggests that since he must be fatigued with his journey he should at once retire to bed, a hint which leaves the coast clear, as she is loath to be interrupted once Ramble has arrived. This gentleman is punctual to the assignation, and then Jane announces: "Madam, Supper is upon the Table." Eugenia bids her, "Draw the Table in here, this room is more private." "Jane *draws the Table in*," and the two lovers sit down to supper. In a few moments there is a repeated knocking at the door, i.e. at a proscenium door. So that her husband shall not discover the gallant, he is hurried into a closet (through an opposite proscenium door), and after him "*Table and all is put into the Closet*". Some little conversation is exchanged when Loveday, who has been on the watch, enters with his letters of credit which he gives to Dashwell. The stranger cleverly contrives to remark that whilst he was at Oxford he studied magic, and recounts the various wonders he can perform. Dashwell shrewdly comments: "I would you cou'd help us to a good Supper to Night, for I am damnable hungry." No sooner said than done, Loveday pretends to conjure, recites a whole string of hard names and then pointing to the proscenium door says: "Let your Servant open that door—and draw in the Table as it is furnished by the Power of my Art." There is no help for it, "Jane *opens the Closset, draws out the Table*." It will be remarked that in this scene two proscenium doors have been employed, the one serving as the door of the room; the other, opposite, serving as the door of an antechamber or powder-closet opening out of the room. In the next scene which is a street before the houses of Wiseacres and Dashwell, Ramble is loitering to be admitted to Eugenia. Attended by a link-boy, for it is night, Aunt and Peggy enter, and soon after Wiseacres appears. The link-boy is given a tester, and dismissed, and "*Exeunt, as into* Wiseacres' *house, he shuts the door*". Ramble wanders a little way down the street (off the stage), and Townly is passing by when Jane peeps out at the door of Dashwell's house. Mistaking him for Ramble she calls softly, and "*Exeunt, as into* Dashwell's *House*". Ramble re-enters, he "*goes and feels out the door and turns back*", muttering to himself: "The Door is shut, and all whist. Will this fusty Alderman ne'er be in bed? Let me see, are there any Lights above in the windows? No; not a glimpse!"

He "*walks about humming a tune, then feels at the door again*". "The door is fast still," he cries, but a moment later "Hark! the door opens, I'll advance". Eugenia having mistaken Townly for Ramble, has granted him the favours designed for her lover and is now hurrying him off ere her husband wake: "*Enter* Townly, Eugenia—*in the street, embracing.* Jane *half out, holding the door.*" At this moment a link appears, and by its light Ramble draws his sword and rushes at Townly. The women scream, "*Run in, and clap the door to.*" We here have two doors in use in a street scene, and they are employed as the doors of two separate houses.

In Act III of the same comedy Ramblc is pursuing an amour with Arabella, Doodle's wife. The gamesome lady and her beau are interrupted by the bracket-fac'd cuckold, but after some complication during a false alarm of fire Ramble gains the street. Engine, Arabella's maid, promises to re-admit him so soon as her master is snoring, and as he loiters we have "Engine *at the window*". She informs him that Doodle has taken the key. "Is there no hole or window to creep at?" he asks. "Just there below is a Cellar-window with a bar out, the shutter on the inside is unpin'd, and will give way, try if you can get in there," she replies. "I have found it here—even with the Ground," he answers. "*Eng.* Try if it be wide enough to get through. *Ram.* I believe it is. *Eng.* I'll come down then and open the Cellar-door. [Engine *goes from the Window.*" Unfortunately in his efforts to pass heels forward through so narrow a space Ramble is stuck fast and his clothes being caught by some hook or staple on the inside he can neither get in nor out and hangs "like a Monkey by the Loins". Meanwhile "Engine *above at the Window*" calls to him that "the Cook-maid has lock'd the Cellar-door and taken out the Key—I can't find it to get down—and if you do get in you can't come up stairs". Misadventures begin to crowd. A link-boy passing by knocks his link on the captive's head. "'Sdeath, how it scalds!" he cries. "Hau! I hear a Casement open above . . . It's so dark I can't see—Oh confound you." "[*A Window opens above, and one throws a Chamber-pot of water upon his head just as he looks up. Eng.* What's the matter, Sir. *Ram.* One Rogue set me on fire with a Link, and another has quench'd me with a stale Chamber-pot, faugh how it stinks. *Eng.* That roguish Prentice at the next house does so almost every night." An even more unsavoury adventure follows with two chimney-sweeps, and finally Ramble is extricated by the watch who first knock up Doodle and tell him: "We have catch'd a Thief creeping in at your Cellar-door." They "*Knock hard at the door* " and " Doodle—*above at the window* " from which Engine has just withdrawn. When Doodle appears on the stage the watchmen who have seized Ramble clamour " See the very Iron bars are bent ", " Here's one we found sticking fast betwixt the Bars in the Cellar grates." There are explanations, and eventually Ramble is allowed to go free but in a fine pickle. It will be noticed that one door is here employed, that of Doodle's house, whilst the balcony above it serves as a window in the house, and a second balcony is utilized as the window of the contiguous house whence the unfortunate gallant is saluted with the stale from the jockum-gage.

The cellar-window, " even with the Ground," which plays so important a part in this scene, must have been a trap in the stage, and in order that the actor who sustained Ramble should slide into it in perfect safety and seemingly stick fast there a special arrangement was required, built up under the stage for him to rest his legs and support his weight during a considerable period. It may be remarked that *The London Cuckolds* was a most popular comedy, frequently performed, and therefore this device would be continually called into requisition, and, we may suppose was managed as adroitly and conveniently as possible.

The situations which require the employment of more than two proscenium doors or balconies not infrequently occur in Restoration plays, but it will suffice that two or three examples should stand for many. Three balconies are employed in Ravenscroft's *The Citizen Turn'd Gentleman,* which was produced at Dorset Garden early in July, 1672, probably on 4th July. It was printed, quarto 1672, and reissued as *Mamamouchi,* quarto 1675. In Act IV we have " Enter Mr. *Jorden,* musick ", obviously in one balcony from the ensuing dialogue. Then " *Cleverwit,* in *Turk's* habit, with *Betty Trickmore* and *Lucia* appear in the Balcony ", number two. A song is sung and " Young *Jorden* and *Marina* in the Balcony against 'em ". Young Jorden remarks, " Now, dearest *Marina,* let us ascend to your Father, he is by this time from his Window convinced of the slight is put on you . . . *They retire,*" and although there has been no exit marked for Mr. Jorden, we find directly, " Enter Mr. *Jorden* and *Trickmore,*" obviously upon the stage itself, to which these characters have descended.

Three doors and two balconies are employed by Crowne in the second act of his comedy *The Countrey Wit,* produced at Dorset Garden in January, 1676. The scene is Pall Mall, where are the houses of several of the characters. Lady Faddle and her maid Bridget appear in the balcony of her house, and presently Bridget enters on the stage. Later, Lord Drybone

PLATE XII

THE ROVER: PART I; ACT V

Collection of the Author

[*face p.* 138

with his mistress Betty Frisque and Cis comes to the window of his house. A song is sung by fiddlers who are giving a serenade, and as soon as it is finished there appears from his house (the third proscenium door) Sir Thomas Rash "*in a buff coat, with a long sword by his side, followed by two or three* Footmen *with long swords*". A few moments later from the door of his house "*Enter* Lord Drybone *in his nightgown with a sword in his hand*". A general muss ensues, they fight helter skelter, and Lord Drybone's servants rush out of the door of his house to assist their master.

The second act of Mrs. Behn's *The Rover; or, the Banish't Cavaliers,* Part I, produced at Dorset Garden in March, 1677, opens with *The Long Street* at Naples. Several characters appear on the stage, many in masquerade, for it is carnival-time. After some dialogue: "*Enter two Bravoes, and hang up a great Picture of* Angelica's, *against the Balcony, and two little ones at each side of the Door.*" Presently "*Enter* Angelica *and* Moretta *in the Balcony, and draw a Silk Curtain*". One proscenium door now does service as the door to the house of Angelica Bianca "a famous Curtezan", and she with her maid is at the window above it. Presently "*Enter at one Door Don* Pedro, *and* Stephano; *Don* Antonio *and* Diego, *at the other Door, with People following him in Masquerade, anticklу attir'd, some with musick*". We have here then the employment of three doors, and one door already doing service as the entrance to Angelica's house, into which later Willmore withdraws.

I would call particular attention to the phrasing of the stage direction "*Enter at one Door Don* Pedro, . . . *Don* Antonio . . . *at the other Door*", since this was a very usual mode of expression, but much liable to be misunderstood. It has indeed been argued from the terms "one door" and "the other door" that there were only two proscenium doors, but this, we have completely demonstrated, is a palpable and gross error. It is true we get such stage directions as the following:—In Orrery's tragedy *Mustapha,* produced at Lincoln's Inn Fields in the spring of 1665, Act V: "*Exeunt* Queen, *and* Haly. *Enter* Zarma *at the other door.*" In Nevil Payne's *The Morning Ramble,* Dorset Garden, November, 1672, Act IV, a stage direction runs: "*Scene the Street. Enter* Merry *at one door, and* Rose *at the other.*" Again, in Otway's comedy *Friendship in Fashion,* produced at Dorset Garden early in April, 1678, the fourth act opens thus: "*Enter* Goodville *at one Door; Mrs.* Goodville *and* Lettice *following her at the other.*" (It may be remarked that the scene is laid in a garden, the time late at night.) Also in Dryden's *All for Love; or, The World well Lost,* produced at the Theatre Royal in the winter of 1677, Act III commences with the following stage direction: "*At one door, Enter* Cleopatra, Charmion, Iras, *and* Alexas, *a Train of* Ægyptians: *at the other,* Antony *and* Romans. *The entrance on both sides is prepar'd by Musick.*" It must be allowed that these and other directions which are conveyed in precisely the same terms are apt to lead—as actually has proved the case—to a certain confusion. Mr. G. C. D. Odell, for example, in his account of the proscenium doors "in the age of Betterton" [35] is far from clear or definite in his ideas but, as has been remarked, the general phraseology of the dramatists is loose, and we get such directions as, in Duffett's farce *The Mock-Tempest* acted at Drury Lane in November, 1674, Act V, Scene 2: "*Enter* Prospero *and* Miranda *at one Door.* Ariel *and* Quakero *at another.*" Again in the last act of Lee's tragedy *Theodosius; or, The Force of Love,* produced at Dorset Garden in the autumn of 1680, we have, Act V, Scene 3: "*The outward Part of the Temple. Enter* Pulcheria *and* Julia *at one Door,* Marcian *and* Lucius *at another.*" In Sedley's dull tragedy *Antony and Cleopatra,* given at Dorset Garden in February, 1677, we have Act IV, "Scene The Second. A Wood. "Enter *Antonius, Canidius, Photinus,* at one door, *Agrippa, Thyreus,* at the other, Fighting." But in Act V, "Scene The First. The Palace," after "*Exeunt* Antonius, Canidius, Lucius", we get "*Enter* Photinus *at another Door*".

We have already noted that the doors were utilized in a garden scene (*Friendship in Fashion*), and here they are employed in a Wood, so that in practice these entrances came to be accepted as purely conventional. However, certain regulations were observed. In a street scene, and such are very frequent in Restoration plays, when a door had been used as the street door of a house it could be employed for no other purpose until the close of the scene. If two or three houses were represented, and the proscenium doors were to stand for the street doors of those houses, they must be used only for an entrance into or an exit from the several houses, all other departures from the stage had to be made by other doors; or "through the scenes", that is to say through the wings. If the scene represented an interior, a room, and one of the doors was to be regarded as the door of that chamber, all the other doors were for the time being suppressed as non-existent, and no exit could be made by means of any one of them. Yet, if required, one other such door might be employed, but only as the entrance to an inner room or closet adjoining, as we have already seen put into requisition by Ravenscroft in *The London Cuckolds.* A similar device commended itself to Mrs. Behn in *The Emperor of the*

Moon, produced at Dorset Garden in 1687. Act I, Scene 3, is "The *Chamber of* Bellemante". The lady is writing poetry. Her lover Charmante enters, but Dr. Baliardo is on his way to the room, and the gallant has to be concealed in a powder-closet. He is quickly thrust through a proscenium door. The previous scene shows a garden, and one of the proscenium doors serves as the garden-gate. We have "A knocking at the Garden-gate". Whereupon Scaramouch "*goes to the Door*".

In 1684 John Banks printed quarto his play *The Island Queens; or, The Death of Mary Queen of Scots, Published only in Defence of the Author and the Play, against some mistaken censures, occasion'd by its being prohibited the Stage.* Genest says "For what reason this prohibition took place it is not easy to conjecture", and certainly the tragedy seems an entirely harmless piece of work. However that may be, it was not produced until it had been altered as *The Albion Queens; or, The Death of Mary Queen of Scotland* when it was first given at Drury Lane on the 6th March, 1704. In this year it was printed, quarto, from the theatre script, and by some happy accident or lucky mischance a number of the prompter's notes and directions were retained in the published copy. In this tragedy the Duke of Norfolk was acted by Wilks; Morton by Mills. On page 2 of the quarto we have: "A LETTER for Mr. *Wilks*". Norfolk actually enters some forty lines later. On page 5 we have in similar fashion: "A LETTER for Mr. *Mills*."[36] Some thirty or forty lines later Morton, Courtiers, Guards, "are discover'd at the throne" in attendance upon Queen Elizabeth. The two letters are, of course, property letters which later in this act are very necessary to the business of the play. Morton hands a letter to Queen Elizabeth exclaiming:—

> behold, a letter
> By *Navus* wrote; and sign'd with her own Hand. (p. 8);

and presently (p. 10) Norfolk also presents a letter from Mary, Queen o' Scots, saying boldly to Elizabeth:—

> Here is a Letter from that Guilty fair one?
> She bid me thus present it on my Knees.

These two letters are all-important to the conduct of the scene.

When Norfolk first comes on the stage we have: "*Enter* Norfolk. V.D.O.P.", and at the commencement of the Second Act: "Act II. Scene I. Norfolk *Solus*. V.D.P.S." He has a speech of nine lines, and "*Enter* Morton. V.D.O.P." At various other entrances of actors throughout the play we find: "V.D.P.S., L.D.O.P., and L.D.P.S." After a double entrance, III, 1, O.P.P.S. is marked. It is plain that P.S. indicates "prompt side"; and O.P. "opposite prompt". V.D.O.P. will therefore be read as Upper Door, Opposite Prompt; L.D.O.P., Lower Door, Opposite Prompt; V.D.P.S., Upper Door Prompt Side; L.D.P.S., Lower Door Prompt Side; and O.P.P.S., Opposite Prompt, and Prompt Side, since for this latter entrance of two characters opposite proscenium doors were employed.

In the Bodleian Library are preserved [37] three original prompt copies of undated and untitled plays, in this order, Theobald's *The Perfidious Brother,* Southerne's *Money The Mistress,* and Elkanah Settle's *The Lady's Triumph.* All were produced at Rich's theatre in Lincoln's Inn Fields; the first on 21st February, 1716; the second on 19th February, 1726; and the third on 22nd March, 1718.

The first of these, *The Perfidious Brother,* commences thus: "New Chamber. Act I. M:D:O:P: Enter Roderick and Serv^{n}: in a Travelling Habit." In the margin we have: "Mr. Smith Mr. Coker." (Smith played Roderick, and Coker the Servant.) A little later marginally is noted: "Mr. Cory," a prompter's warning for that actor, who played Gonsalvo. The next entry is: "M:D:O:P: Enter Gonsalvo." Later we find: "U:D:P:S: Enter Luciana." Next: "Enter Gonsalvo, Sebastian & Beaufort. L:D:O:P:" Towards the end of Act I, "Act ready" is marked in the margin. Act II commences: "M:D:P:S: Mrs. Rogers, Miss Rogers. Enter Luciana & Selinda."

In the prompt book copy of Shirley's *The Sisters,*[38] prepared for performance between 1668 and 1671, the sign ⊙ is used to denote a change of scenery. Thus in Act I at the entry of Giovanni and Stephanio, the second scene commences, shifting from the wood to an interior, and is noted "⊙ Castle". Act II, Scene 1, is "⊙ fabies house & landskape"; Scene 2 "⊙ Presence". The beginning of Act IV again is marked "⊙ wood", and Scene 2 becomes "Angellina's Chamber ⊙". These are only a few of many similar indications for the prompter's use. In the prompt book of *The Perfidious Brother* we also have the conventional sign ⊙, employed throughout and similarly denoting whistle for change of scene,[39] as in Act III when the flats open to an "Inward Apartment. Sebastian discovered at a Table, writing". The prompter had made a marginal note some little while before, "Mr. Keene," to call Theophilus Keene who acted this rôle. It is not necessary to go through the whole play, and it will suffice to point out that the employment of six doors is indicated, namely: (1) U:D:P:S: Upper Door, Prompt Side. (2) U:D:O:P: Upper Door, Opposite Prompt. (3) M:D:P:S: Middle

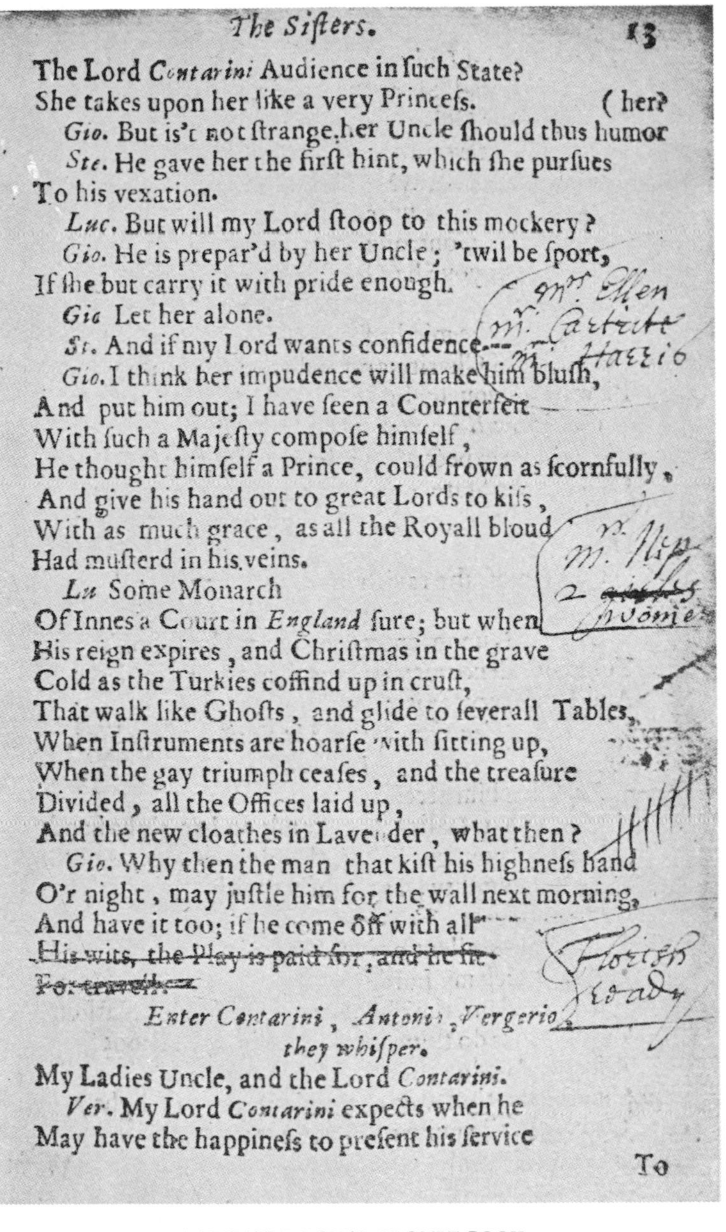

The Sisters. 13

The Lord *Contarini* Audience in ſuch State?
She takes upon her like a very Princeſs. (her?
Gio. But is't not ſtrange, her Uncle ſhould thus humor
Ste. He gave her the firſt hint, which ſhe purſues
To his vexation.
Luc. But will my Lord ſtoop to this mockery?
Gio. He is prepar'd by her Uncle; 'twil be ſport,
If ſhe but carry it with pride enough.
Gio Let her alone.
St. And if my Lord wants confidence---
Gio. I think her impudence will make him bluſh,
And put him out; I have ſeen a Counterfeit
With ſuch a Majeſty compoſe himſelf,
He thought himſelf a Prince, could frown as ſcornfully,
And give his hand out to great Lords to kiſs,
With as much grace, as all the Royall bloud
Had muſterd in his veins.
Lu Some Monarch
Of Innes a Court in *England* ſure; but when
His reign expires, and Chriſtmas in the grave
Cold as the Turkies coffind up in cruſt,
That walk like Ghoſts, and glide to ſeverall Tables,
When Inſtruments are hoarſe with ſitting up,
When the gay triumph ceaſes, and the treaſure
Divided, all the Offices laid up,
And the new cloathes in Lavender, what then?
Gio. Why then the man that kiſt his highneſs hand
O'r night, may juſtle him for the wall next morning,
And have it too; if he come off with all---
~~His wits, the Play is paid for, and he fit~~
~~For travell.~~

Enter Contarini, Antonio, Vergerio,
they whiſper.

My Ladies Uncle, and the Lord *Contarini*.
Ver. My Lord *Contarini* expects when he
May have the happineſs to preſent his ſervice

To

A THEATRE ROYAL PROMPT BOOK
Shirley's "The Sisters,"
Sion College Library

Door, Prompt Side. (4) M : D : O : P : Middle Door, Opposite Prompt. (5) L : D : P : S : Lower Door, Prompt Side. (6) L : D : O : P : Lower Door, Opposite Prompt.

In the two other Lincoln's Inn Fields prompt copies, *Money The Mistress* and *The Lady's Triumph,* we find the same prompter's markings, M : D : P : S :, M : D : O : P :, L : D : P : S :, L : D : O : P :, but the Upper Doors were not utilized. It seems clear that although six doors might be, and sometimes were employed, there was already in evidence a tendency towards simplification in the matter of entrances and exits, and only four doors were generally required. Thus in Banks' tragedy the use of the Middle Doors was avoided, in *Money the Mistress* and *The Lady's Triumph* the use of the Upper Doors was avoided.

Four doors were in use at least as late as 1737 for in Fielding's dramatic satire *The Historical Register, For the Year 1736* produced at the Haymarket about 31st March, 1737, there is a stage direction: "Enter Four Patriots from four different doors, who meet in the centre and shake hands." It has been with much probability suggested that the four proscenium doors were reduced to two when Garrick altered Drury Lane in 1747. In 1763, *Fitzgiggo, A New English Uproar* and *The Second and Last Act of Fitzgiggo* plainly show that at this time Covent Garden had only two proscenium doors.

The history of the proscenium doors, or stage-doors as they were often termed about the middle of the eighteenth century, may be said to extend even to the present day. Occasionally as in Drury Lane, September, 1780, the experiment was tried of taking away the doors, but, one is glad to learn, they were almost immediately restored. Again when Drury Lane was rebuilt in 1793 the doors disappeared, only to be replaced in September, 1797. In 1822 they were finally removed from this house, and a year later Covent Garden followed suit. In 1830 they were, however, still in evidence at the Lyceum, and it warms one's heart to know that in 1853 the doors were restored to the Royal Standard Theatre after a lapse of many years. In 1865 the Surrey still boasted stage-doors, and at Sadler's Wells they persisted until about 1880. Writing of this fine old theatre as he remembered it in the mid-fifties of the nineteenth century Clement Scott says [40]: "The Proscenium was to all intents a little house, and it was fascinating to a child to see on either side of the stage proper a little green door with brass knockers and handles, and over each door a window with lace curtains and a balcony with flower pots on it." This exactly describes the proscenium as so delightfully depicted by George Cruikshank in his illustrations to Dickens' *Life of Grimaldi.*

The gleaming knocker was an indispensable ornament to those most fascinating doors, and we may remember that in Restoration days they seem to have been furnished with a bell-pull, for in *The Feign'd Courtezans* towards the end of the Third Act Sir Signal Buffoon who is lurking in the street at the house door of the fair lorettes says: "Hah—what's this—a String—of a Bell I hope—I'll try to enter; and if I am mistaken, 'tis but crying Con licentia." "[*Rings. Enter* Philippa. *Phil.* Who's there? *Sir Sig.* 'Tis I, 'tis I, let me in quickly . . . *Phil.* I'm glad you're come—give me your hand . . . [Exeunt." The next Act opens in Silvianetta's Apartment, and presently "[Philippa *at the door puts in* Sir Signal".

It is worthy of remark that in the excellent models of stages upon which the plays of Skelt, Pollock, and Webb are to be performed the cardboard proscenium is painted with appropriate stage-doors.

To a fairly recent date the Theatre Royal, King Street, Bristol, retained the proscenium doors. I do not know whether they yet remain. Many years ago, in the nineteenth century, I remember a performance of *Othello* at that historic house. In the last act the Moor entered Desdemona's bedchamber on the prompt side by the proscenium door, and this he locked behind him. It was extraordinarily effective, and although I have seen Shakespeare's great tragedy in vast theatres in many a wealthy capital I have never witnessed a production which was so vigorous, so real, so gripping in its sheer intensity and piteous horror, as that given upon the old stage where the apron yet lingered and the proscenium doors flanked the scene—I for one bitterly regret the passing of the stage-doors, and maybe one day when futurism and cubism and constructivism and freakism have run the whole gamut of nightmare lunacy the theatre will return to sane and simpler methods, perhaps the four proscenium doors and the apron will be adopted. There are indications, slight but significant, that this is not impossible.

Since mention has been made of *The Albion Queens* as printed quarto, 1704, from the prompt copy, it may not be impertinent to mention a few other instances of plays which owing to the occasional insertion of actors' names instead of characters in the stage directions and of marginal notices for actors to be ready and properties at hand were certainly printed from the theatrical scripts.[41]

At the time of publication, 1675, the bookseller Bentley, definitely attributed to Dryden at least one scene of *The Mistaken Husband,* "By a Person of Quality," and hence this remains a piece of particular interest.[42] The opening stage direction of the Fifth Act is: "Scen. I. *A Ship* or *Gunroom. Learcut* and the *Boatswain,* Duke *Watson.*" This is Marmaduke Watson, whose name can first be traced among the list of actors of the Theatre Royal Company in one of the Lord Chamberlain's warrants for liveries of July, 1661. Watson appears in many printed casts, and it may be remarked that in the *Roscius Anglicanus* [43] he is called Mr. *Duke.*

In D'Urfey's alteration of *Cymbeline,* which was printed quarto, 1682, as *The Injured Princess; or, The Fatal Wager,* the stage direction at the commencement of the Second Act is: "*Enter behind* Cymbeline, Queen, *a Purse,* Pisanio, Doctor *and* Guards, *a Viol,* Mrs. Holten, Sue." Mrs. Holten is Mrs. Holden who was, Downes tells us, one of Sir William Davenant's first actresses. Sue is Susanna Percival, who married William Mountford,[44] and *en secondes noces* became Mrs. Verbruggen. The daughter of an actor of the Duke's Theatre she had been on the stage since a young girl of eight or nine years old. There is a curious difficulty connected with *The Injured Princess,* as we have here two actresses of the Duke's company in the cast, although doubtless they played small rôles, probably the waiting-women Sophronia and Aurelia. But on the title-page we have: "As it was Acted at the Theatre-Royal By his Majesties Servants." It appears in the Term Catalogues, November, 1682. It seems extremely unlikely that any member of the Duke's Company would have migrated to Drury Lane either in 1682 or for some time previously since the King's players were notoriously involved in chaotic difficulties. The Companies united in 1682, and commenced acting at Drury Lane on 16th November of that year. I conceive that D'Urfey's play was among the earliest given after the Union, and the author at once dispatched the script to the printers Bentley and Magnes.

D'Urfey, indeed, appears to have been remarkably careless in revising the proofs of his plays, for prompter's notes have in several cases been retained as marginalia in his quartos, of which the pagination is often erratic to a degree. Thus in *A Fool's Preferment,* 4to, 1688, the numeration leaps from p. 56 to p. 65 without any break of continuity in the text, whilst *The Richmond Heiress,* 4to, 1693, passes from p. 36 to p. 41 without any gap or lacuna in the dialogue. Among D'Urfey's printed pieces which indicate the use of the script as copy in *A Fool's Preferment,* Act IV, p. 64, we have: "*Call* Longo, Bewford," as a memorandum some three speeches before the two characters Longovil (indifferently spelled Longevile, Longoville) and Bewford enter. In Act V, p. 75, we find "(*Call* Maria", who enters seven or eight speeches later. On p. 29, III, 3, of *The*

Richmond Heiress; or, A Woman Once in the Right we note: "*Exit Sir.* Quib. *and* Dog.," that is to say Doggett who acted Quickwit and who had just been on the stage; p. 36, IV, 1, "*Exit* Dogget *and* Marm."; p. 41, IV, 1, "*Call* Quickwitt"; p. 48, IV, 4, "*Enter Sir* Quibble, Fulvia, Dogget, *and* Marmalett." In *Bussy D'Ambois; or, The Husband's Revenge,* 4to, 1691; p. 32, IV, 1, are the directions: "*Call* Tamira, Charlot"; p. 38, IV, 3, "*Call* Mount Surry, Monsieur, *and* Guise"; p. 39, "*Call* Charlot *Letter.*" *Squire Oldsapp; or, The Night-Adventurers,* 4to, 1679, p. 38, IV, 2, has "Scene II. *Table, Chairs, and Wine. Enter Sir* Fred. *Col.* Buff, *and* Oldsapp. *Boy*".

During the Second Act of *The Virtuous Wife; or, Good Luck at Last,* Dorset Garden, 1679, Beauford and Brainworm his man are on the stage; Lady Beardly enters, and we find a prompter's marginal note *A Chair set on.* In the following scene Amble says to Beverly: "Sir, my Lady is come back agen I believe suspecting something and is just coming into the chamber —hark you may hear her." At the cue "into the chamber" Downes jotted on the script "Treading", and in the printed quarto we find "[*Treading*". In Act IV of this same comedy we have a stage direction which is purely "in the old *Elizabeth* Way of Plainness". A new scene begins. "*Enter Lady* Beardly *and* Tisick *sitting smoaking.*" Sir Lubberly Widgeon bolts in on 'em and My Lady in the confusion breaks her pipe as she bawls for musk pastilles to sweeten her breath. A similar stage direction occurs in Wycherley's *Love in a Wood; or, St. James's Park,* Theatre Royal, 1671, Act IV: "*Enter Sir* Simon Addleplot, *sitting at a Desk writing as a Clerk, my Lady* Flippant *jogging him.*" In these two instances the use of the word "*Enter*" means nothing more than a discovery; Lady Beardly and her maid are discovered, as in Wycherley's comedy Sir Simon and Lady Flippant are discovered. In Marlowe's *Edward II* (at line 301) the nobles are assembled on the stage and we have: *Enter the King and* Gaueston, but this is really a discovery, and the two friends are seen seated side by side on the throne, since Edward at once speaks:—

> What? are you mou'd that *Gaueston* sits heere?
> It is our pleasure, we will haue it so.
> *Lancaster.* Your grace doth wel to place him by your side,
> For no where else the new earle is so safe.

Dekker and Middleton's *The Honest Whore,* Part I, 1604, has: "*Enter* Bellafront *with lute, pen ink and paper being placed before her.*" She is seated at a table, writing a letter to Hippolito.

Act V of Dekker and Massinger's *The Virgin Martir* licensed by Sir George Bue, 6th October, 1620, commences: "*Enter* Theophilus *in his study. Books about him.*" He is seated, as at line 5 of his first speech we have "*Rises*"; at line 9 "*Sits*"; and at line 36, "*Rise.*" Both these instances are discoveries.

In Crowne's first tragedy, *Juliana; or, The Princess of Poland*, produced at Lincoln's Inn Fields, 1671, and printed 4to, 1671 (licensed for printing 8th September of that year), Act IV, we have a direction "[*Call Osso., Dem., Bat., bound*". A few speeches later: "*Enter* Ossolinsky *and* Guard, *with* Demetrius, *and* Battista *bound.*" It was important that the prompter, John Downes, should remember that the two actors, Young (Demetrius) and Westwood (Battista) must be brought in fast secured by cords, and as the business of the scene is quick action and something complicated he made a special note in the margin of the script. Maidment and Logan in their recension of Crowne (1873), vol. i, p. 77, in spite of the fact that at the point in the scene where the note is printed Ossolinsky, Demetrius, and Battista are not on the stage, very foolishly explain "[*Call Osso., Dem., Bat. bound*" by Cassonofsky "Instructs Osso. to have Demetrius and Battista taken away and bound".

In *Tom Essence; or, The Modish Wife,* 4to, 1677, I, 1, we find: "*Mrs.* Essence *ready above.*" Powell's *The Treacherous Brothers,* 4to, 1690, v, prints "*Enter Mr.* Harris", who played a Bassa.

A striking example of a play hurriedly written, and printed from a copy made, almost it would seem without revision, from the prompt-book is to be found in Ravenscroft's *The Careless Lovers.* This comedy, the author tells us, "was written at the Desire of the young men of the *Stage,* and given them for a *Lenten-Play*; they ask't it not above a Week before *Shrove-Tuesday*: In three dayes time, the three first Acts were Made, Transcrib'd, and given them to write out in Parts—The Two last Acts took me up just so much time: one Week compleated it." In the printed quarto we find such notes and indications as *Ready to shut the Boult* a prompter's warning (p. 15) for Toby to shut the bolt some one-and-twenty lines later when the appropriate stage-direction occurs. On p. 19 we have a marginal note: "*Call* [misprinted *All*] Muchw. Jacinta." Muchworth enters 28 lines later, and Jacinta 5 lines after his appearance. On p. 21 is [*Pass,* a direction to Jacinta and Hillaria to walk up and down whilst Careless observes them. At the end of p. 37 is "[D. Boast. *with a Letter*", a warning to furnish De Boastado with a letter, which soon after his next entrance he pulls from his pocket and reads aloud. Eighteen lines before the entrance of Beatrice on p. 33 we have "[*Call* Beatrice".

There is also a direction " [*Bring* Napkins and stop their Mouths] " which refers to a piece of business not specified in the text. The Fourth Act has " [*Hall continues* ", the scene being unchanged. There are notes of properties: p. 39, " *A Bottle of Sack and Glass ready for* Beatrice," who enters on p. 41 when Muchworth says: " Come *Beatrice,* Fill my Lord a Glass of Sack." On p. 48 we have: " *Tables, Chairs, Candles, Bottles. Enter* Mrs. Breeder, Clappam, *Drawer in Tavern.*" On p. 50 a warning occurs " [*Musick ready below* ", and on p. 51, [*Musick playes,* Hilaria cries: " Come in you sons of Melody," and the fiddlers appeared on the stage. On p. 58 we have " [*Call* Lovel, Careless ", and eleven lines later " [*Call* Hilaria ", warnings for the subsequent entrances of these characters. On p. 64 " [*Beat. on the Beir ready* " is a warning for the mock funeral procession which enters on p. 66. On p. 67: " *Hall-Table and Candles,* 4 *Chaires. Enter* Lovel, Jacinta, *the Scene changes, and a Room in* Muchworth's *House.*" There are other disconnected and irregular points in the printing of this interesting play, but further investigation is the peculiar province of Ravenscroft's future editor.

Once the curtains had been drawn at the commencement of the First Act they remained up until the Epilogue was spoken, and (with very rare exceptions) all scenic changes were made in full sight of the audience. Even tables and chairs necessary for the business of a play were thus brought on or carried off as required, quiet simply and without any attempt to cloak or disguise. So in Mrs. Behn's *The City Heiress; or, Sir Timothy Treat-All,* produced at Dorset Garden in the spring of 1682, III, a stage direction plainly says [*Enter Bottles and Glasses.* A table must have been carried on at the same time, for a little later " [*The Men go all to the drinking Table* ". Reference has just been made to the chair which was brought on the stage at the entrance of Lady Beardly, *The Virtuous Wife,* Act II, and although the stage-directions are certainly a little obscure I am inclined to believe that in *The Fond Husband,* Dorset Garden, spring of 1676, Act V, Sneak's chair which betrayed the nature of his malady to Cordelia although Sir Roger manfully endeavoured to explain it away as " a Mathematical Engine they use at *Cambridge* ", was exhibited to the audience, that is to say carried on to the stage, or else surely the scene must have lost much of its point. In the quarto, 1675, of Otway's *Alcibiades,* produced at Dorset Garden, September, 1675, Act V, we have: " *Enter a Chair of State, with a Table by it, and upon that the Crown and Scepter. Enter* King *and* Lords."

The last scene of Act IV of Mrs. Behn's *Sir Patient Fancy,* Dorset Garden, January, 1678, is the Lady Fancy's Bedchamber, and it is an episode particularly full of some complicated business, during the course of which use is made of the bed, table, chairs, the dressing-table which is covered with all the dressing-things, so we see that the stage was amply furnished. At the conclusion Sir Patient goes off with his wife, "[*Exeunt, leading her,*" and Maundy, her woman, following them. The flats then drew over to represent the next scene, Act V, 1, a room in Sir Patient Fancy's house. "*A Table, and six Chairs.*" These must have been brought on and set whilst the music was playing in full sight of the audience. *The Mall; or, The Modish Lovers,* a comedy which may be assigned to John Dover, printed quarto 1674, and produced (probably in January or February of that year) at Lincoln's Inn Fields by the King's Company, has such stage-directions as: III, 2, "*A Bed-chamber, a Table out, and a Chair.*" The flats draw, "*A Bed-chamber discover'd, with* Peg *and* Mr. Easy *in't.*" The table and chair here served for two scenes without change. IV, 2, "Scene Second. *Chairs set out,*" that is they were brought on to the stage. In *The Mistaken Husband,* Theatre Royal, 1675, similar directions are found: Act I. "*Enter* Hazzard, Underwit, *and* Drawer. *Table out.*" "Act III. Scen. 1. *A Chamber with a Bed in it. Enter* Hazzard *and* Underwit *with a Pillow under his Cloak. On a Cupboard Plate and Jewels.*" It should be remarked that in the preceding scene Hazzard has left the stage "[*Between the Scenes*". Very occasionally in a modern music-hall properties chairs, tables, are brought in and carried off by spruce footmen in bag and knot or by liveried attendants, and I can remember the same contrivance in pantomime.

NOTES TO CHAPTER IV

[1] "The Origin of the English Picture-Stage," *The Elizabethan Playhouse,* Second Series, 1913, p. 146.

[2] First edition, 1740, pp. 240–1.

[3] Thus Mr. Granville-Barker, in his *On Dramatic Method,* "being the Clark lectures for 1930," 1931, chapter iv, "Wycherley and Dryden," girds and sneers for three and forty pages at the Restoration dramatists, and their modern editor in the most supercilious and offensive vein. He is particularly huffed at their technique—"blunderingly exhibited too!" To clinch his argument and top his tirade he proclaims: "There is a stage direction in Wycherley's *Love in a Wood* ('prentice work truly, but it has earned from its latest editor glowing praise), *They all go off in a huddle, hastily.* The play's stagecraft is summed up in that—" (p. 117). This stage-direction occurs in Act V, Scene 1, *St.* James'*s Park* at night. The intrigue of the comedy is complicated but clear, and if Mr. Granville-Barker had read *Love in a Wood* with any perspicacity he must have appreciated that this stage-direction at which he jeers is, as it stands (not wrested from the script), perfectly explicit and intelligible. There are plays of Mr. Granville-Barker's own writing —'prentice work truly—which appear to me at any rate far more blunderingly exhibited than anything I have ever met in a Restoration dramatist. Stagecraft forsooth! The whole sum of the matter lies in this, that Mr. Granville-Barker is utterly and

lamentably ignorant of the technique of the Restoration theatre, and it seems a very deplorable thing that a Clark lecturer should so jauntily deliver himself of such a burthen of undiluted nonsense as cumbers these three and forty pages *On Dramatic Method.*

[4] *Tethys Festival; Or, The Queenes Wake* . . . Deuised by Samvel Daniel, 4to, 1610. *The Lords Maske* was presented on the marriage night of the County Palatine with Princess Elizabeth, being the first day of the carnival week, 1613. *The Description, . . . Of The Lords Maske,* 4to, 1613, sig C.

[5] Edition, 12mo, 1751, p. 163.

[6] *Guzman* was originally played at Lincoln's Inn Fields on Friday, 16th April, 1669.

[7] *Studies of the Greek Poets,* Second Series, 1876, *Aeschylus,* p. 201.

[8] Mr. G. C. D. Odell, *Shakespeare from Betterton to Irving,* 1921, vol. i, p. 10, misinterprets the allusions in this Prologue, which he takes " to refer to the stage set with scenes ". The Theatre " shining all with Gold " is, of course, a flick at the ornate and gilded proscenium of Dorset Garden.

[9] Second edition, 1702, p. 5.

[10] The Epilogue was spoken by Mr. Ion Swinley who played Rhodophil. At a later production of *Marriage A-la-Mode* at the Lyric Theatre, Hammersmith, on Thursday, 9th October, 1930, the Epilogue was given to Melantha! I have no doubt that the brilliant actress who sustained this rôle delivered the Epilogue with the utmost vivacity and charm, but what are we to think of a producer who assigns the verses which should have been spoken by Rhodophil to Melantha! Dryden, however, had (I understand) been pretty generally tinkered at, mammocked, and " improved " for this revival.

[11] Malone, *Prose Works of John Dryden,* 1800, vol. i, part i, pp. 455–6. The " two instances " to which Malone alludes are the Epilogue " Written by a Person of Honour " to *Secret Love*; and the Epilogue " By a Friend of the Author's " to *The Spanish Fryar.* The witty Prologue " *Sent to the Author by an unknown hand* [Sir Harry Sheeres], *and propos'd to be spoken by Mrs.* Montford *drest like an Officer* ", was not allowed owing to its reflection upon the political situation of the moment. See *Dryden The Dramatic Works,* edited by Montague Summers, 1932, vi, pp. 133–4, and Explanatory Notes, pp. 534–7.

[12] See Warburton's note, published in 1751, upon Pope's lines on Southerne's birthday.

[13] Bodley, Ashm. G. 15 (147), 1689, folio.

[14] Forsythe, p. 47. G. C. D. Odell, *Shakespeare from Betterton to Irving,* 1921, vol i, pp. 68–9, was misled by this Prologue.

[15] " The Music of Shadwell's ' The Tempest ' ". *The Musical Quarterly,* vol. vii, No. 4, October, 1921, pp. 365–378.

[16] *New History of the English Stage,* 1882, vol. i, p. 431.

[17] O'Keeffe's *Recollections,* ii, 422.

[18] The Works of Ben. Jonson . . . with Notes . . . By Peter Whalley. 7 vols., 1761; vol. i, p. 141.

[19] *Ionsonus Virbius; Or, The Memorie of Ben: Johnson,* 4to, 1638, p. 39 (misprinted p. 31).

[20] Part ii, Act v, scene 1; the siege of Babylon.

[21] Act ii, Scene 1.

[22] *New History of the English Stage,* i, p. 137.

[23] Webster's *Appius and Virginia.* " Acted at the Dukes Theater under the name of The Roman Virgin or Unjust Judge." 4to, 1620. The Bodleian copy, 4to, 1679, is the Webster *Appius and Virginia,* 4to, 1659, with a new title-page. Langbaine and Downes say the alteration was due to Betterton. There are further contemporary allusions which bear out this ascription.

[24] 4to, 1672; and 4to, 1710.

[25] Underhill played Amble; Jevon, Sir Frolick Whimsey; Betty Currer, Jenny Wheadle; Leigh, Sir Lubberly Widgeon; Nokes, Lady Beardly, " An amorous impertinent old Woman, one that has buried three Husbands, yet still very desirous to be courted."

[26] See the present writer's " A Restoration Prompt-Book ", *Times Literary Supplement,* Thursday, 24th June, 1920, p. 400; reprinted in *Essays in Petto,* 1928.

[27] In *The Prompter,* No. I, Tuesday, 12th November, 1734, Aaron Hill describes among a prompter's *Instrumenta Regni* " a little Bell, which hangs on his Arm:

By the tinkling of this Bell, if a Lady in Tragedy be in the Spleen for the Absence of her Lover, or a Hero in the Dumps for the Loss of a Battle, he can conjure up soft Musick to sooth their Distress ; nay, if a Wedding happens in a Comedy, he can summon up the Fidlers to dispel *Care* by a Country Dance ".

[28] Sloane 4455, f. 26[b].

[29] The Rose, or Will's Coffee House, Covent Garden. Joseph Williams, according to Cibber, had great merit, yet his industry "was not equal to his Capacity for he loved his Bottle better than his Business ".

[30] *The Poetaster,* produced by Mr. William Poel, was played at the Apothecaries Hall, Wednesday, 26th April, 1916. *Bartholomew-Fair* was revived for two performances by the Phoenix, 26th and 27th June, 1921.

[31] The gentleman who is responsible for the 1926 reprint of the *Works* of Rochester (and Others), writing a note on the line

May *Betty Mackrell* cease to be a Whore ;

has: " Mackrell seems to be a nickname ; the word is better known in French, ' maquereau, maquerelle ' ; the meaning in this case seems to be ' Betty, the procuress, or the bawd '—possibly the well-known Betty Morris." It were certainly desirable that anyone who undertook to edit the *Works* of Rochester should have at least some slight knowledge of the persons not infrequently mentioned in the satires and lampoons of the day, or should at any rate avoid the more flagrant and obviously incorrect forms of guessing.

Mackarel or Mackrell (the name is indifferently spelled) is not a nickname, and there are continual references to the lady. See, for example, Philip's *Don Quixote,* 1687, p. 184 and p. 412 ; *The Whole Works of Walter Moyle, Esq.,* 1727, p. 242. Also Duffett's farce, *The Empress of Morocco,* 4to, 1674, the Epilogue where Heccatie says :—

Where's *Mack'rel* back and Jilting *Sue*?

See further my *Shakespeare Adaptations,* pp. 107–8 and pp. 261–2.

[32] " Miss," it may be noted, as signifying a very young girl.

[33] It should be remarked that the text, 4to, 1669, of Dryden's first play *The Wild Gallant,* originally produced at Vere Street in February, 1663, is that of the revised and altered play as given at the Theatre Royal, Bridges Street. Some indications of a platform-stage performance, however, yet remain. In Act IV, Scene 1, we have, for example, an allusion in the dialogue to the arras with which Vere Street, in common with all platform-stages, was hung. See *Dryden The Dramatic Works,* 1931, edited Montague Summers, vol. i, p. 111, where Nonsuch says : " These Walls can get no Children ; nor these Hangings ; though there be Men wrought in u'm," and note p. 433.

Richard Flecknoe in his *A Short Discourse of the English Stage,* attached to his *Love's Kingdom,* 8vo, 1664, emphasizes the differences between the platform and the picture stages. " Now for the difference between our Theaters and those of former times, they were but plain and simple, with no other Scenes, nor Decorations of the Stage, but onely old Tapestry, and the Stage strew'd with Rushes (with their Habits accordingly) whereas ours now for cost and ornament are arriv'd at the heighte of magnificence."

[34] *Le Théâtre François,* Paris, 1674 ; p. 55. *La Mort de Montezume* is Dryden's *The Indian Emperour.*

[35] *Shakespeare from Betterton to Irving,* vol. i, pp. 103–6.

[36] Amongst other bad blunders the writer of an article " Doors and Curtains in Restoration Theatres ", *Modern Language Review,* April, 1920, vol. xv, No. 2, pp. 137–142, absurdly says : " The ' letter ' seems to have been a contemporary theatrical phrase for a ' call ' ! "

[37] MS. Rawl. Poet. 136. *The Perfidious Brother* was published 4to, 1715 ; *Money the Mistress,* 8vo, 1726 ; *The Lady's Triumph,* 12mo, 1718.

[38] " A Restoration Prompt Book," see above, n. 25.

[39] In *The Prompter,* No. I, Tuesday, 12th November, 1734, Aaron Hill describing a prompter at the play-house writes : " Another Tool of his Authority is a Whistle, which hangs about his Neck. This is an Instrument of great Use and Significance : . . . Dr. *Faustus*'s celebrated Wand has not a more arbitrary and extensive Power, than this musical Machine : At the least Blast of it, I have seen Houses move, as it were, upon Wings, Cities turned into Forests, and dreary Desarts converted into superb Palaces : I have seen an audience removed, in a Moment, from *Britain*

to *Japan,* and the frozen Mountains of *Zembla* resembling the sunny Vales of *Arabia Fœlix* . . . and all by the powerful magic Influence of this Wonder working Whistle."

[40] *English Illustrated Magazine,* Christmas, 1898. "The King of Clownland."

[41] There are very many similar prompt warnings in the printed copies of Pre-Restoration plays. Examples from a couple of plays in the Beaumont and Fletcher, folio, 1647, may serve for many similar instances. In *The Mad Lover,* Actus Secundus, we have: *Enter Stremon and his Boy Ed. Hor.,* i.e. Edward Horton, who also played a female rôle in Carlell's *The Deserving Favourite.* In *The Mad Lover* again, *Actus Quartus, Scœna Prima* commences: *Enter a Servant and R. Bax, and Stremon at the doore.* R. Bax. is Richard Baxter. In Act V of the same play we have a marginal note *The Hearse ready* forty-two lines before *Enter Funerall.*

In *The Chances,* Actus Tertius, Scæna Prima, is a marginal note *Bowls of wine ready,* 135 lines before *Ent. Rowl. with wine,* which entrance is actually in Scene 2. *Rowl.* is Rowland Dowle, a member of the King's Men from 1628 to 1636, an actor who played very small parts. In the same play, *Actus Quartus,* Scæne 2, a marginal note has: *Bawd ready above.* Fifty-four lines later in Scæne 3, *Enter Bawd* (*above*).

[42] It has been reprinted and for the first time annotated, in *Dryden The Dramatic Works,* edited by Montague Summers, 1932, vol. iv, p. 1.

[43] Edited by Montague Summers, p. 2; and note pp. 77–8.

[44] William Mountford of St. Martin-in-the-Fields, bachelor, 22, and Mrs. Susanna Peircivall, of St. Giles-in-the-Fields, spinster, 19, consent of parents—at St. Giles-in-the-Fields, 2 July, 1686. Licence issued by the Bishop of London's office. *London Marriage Licences,* 1521–1869, excerpts by Colonel Joseph Lemuel Chester, edited by Joseph Foster; 1887, col. 950.

Chapter V

THE EPILOGUE

As Country Vicars, when the Sermon's done,
Run huddling to the Benediction;
Well knowing, though the better sort may stay,
The Vulgar Rout will run unblest away:
So we, when once our Play is done, make haste
With a short Epilogue to close your taste.
In thus withdrawing we seem mannerly,
But once the Curtain's down we peep, and see
A Jury of the Wits who still stay late,
And in their Club decree the poor Plays fate;
Their Verdict back is to the Boxes brought,
Thence all the Town pronounces it their thought.

Epilogue to *Sr Martin Mar-all*, 4to, 1668.

The evidence that the curtain once drawn up after the Prologue did not fall until the last word of the Epilogue had been spoken is so overwhelming that this circumstance may of a certainty be pronounced to have been the prevailing practice. Those few exceptions which speak of the curtain falling between the Acts, or at any other time during a play, are excessively rare, and when a little later we come to examine them in detail it will be found that far from indicating a normal variant they are so wholly exceptional and their particularity is so stressed that they do indeed by their very singularity prove the general rule. The end of an act was shown by a clear stage; one of the characters came down to the front and spoke a rhyming tag, generally a couple of lines, but sometimes four verses, and sometimes even more. All the characters then went off the stage, a conclusion which may seem stiff and unnatural, but which, as is abundantly clear to those who have been concerned with the revivals of Restoration plays in the original mode or who have witnessed such productions, is actually vastly remote from anything inelegant or ineffective. When every play can furnish us with examples it were entirely superfluous to quote more than two or three instances of the conclusions of Acts, and these may all be selected from one dramatist. At the end of Act IV of Dryden's *An Evening's Love; or, The Mock-Astrologer* produced at the Theatre Royal, in June, 1668, Maskall speaks the tag—

With all my heart; and when our loves are veering,
We'll make no Words, but fall to privateering.

Exeunt, *the men leading the women.*

In Dryden's and Lee's tragedy *The Duke of Guise,* given at Drury Lane, November, 1683, Act IV concludes with a short dialogue between the King and Marmoutiere, Grillon also being on the stage. The scene is written in blank verse, which four lines before the end in the very middle of the King's last speech of eight lines changes to rhyme:—

Not *Greece,* nor hostile *Juno* cou'd destroy
The Hero that abandon'd burning *Troy,*
He scap'd the dangers of the dreadful Night,
When loaded with his Gods he took his Flight.

[*Exeunt, King leading her.*

The second scene in Act III in Dryden's *Don Sebastian, King of Portugal,* Drury Lane, December, 1689, is one of the lighter episodes, written in prose. Towards the end Morayma and Antonio are left on the stage together, and the gentleman kissing the lady's hand, says:—

Thus Conquer'd Infidels, that Wars may cease,
Are forc'd to give their hands, and sign the Peace.
Mor. Thus Christians are out-witted by the Foe;
You had her in your pow'r, and let her go.
If you release my hand, the fault's not mine;
You shou'd have made me seal as well as sign.
She runs off, he follows her to the door; then comes back again, and goes out at the other.

There are but few plays of which the Acts omit to conclude with the traditional tag, but we may remark that a couplet was not particularly favoured by Shadwell, and this ending until the conclusion does not occur throughout *The Humorists,* Lincoln's Inn Fields, early in 1671. In *The Libertine,* given at Dorset Garden in June, 1675, Acts I and II have no couplet to round them off, but Acts III and IV are duly provided. So also is Act I of *The Virtuoso,* Dorset Garden, May, 1676, but Acts II, III, and IV of this comedy lack the final verse. Until the conclusion, again, there are no tags at the ends of the Acts of a *True Widow,* Dorset Garden, December, 1678. But it may be noticed that the printed copy, quarto, 1679, has "*The End of the First* (*Second—Third—Fourth*) *Act*". In *The Sullen Lovers; or, The Impertinents,* Lincoln's Inn Fields, May, 1668, Acts I and III conclude with the usual couplet, but Acts II and IV have a special arrangement. Act II finishes thus: "*Emilia* and *Stanford*

MARRIAGE A-LA-MODE: THE COURT SCENE

Designed by Hugh Owen, Birmingham Repertory Theatre, April 1928

[*face p.* 154

run out at several doors, the Impertinents divided follow 'em." In Act IV Sir Positive has been discoursing at some length of his many interests and activities. At last Stanford and Emilia are able to bear it no longer. "*They run.*" But he detains them, and the scene ends with "Ex. omnes, *and he goes out talking as fast as he can*". Probably Shadwell was endeavouring to introduce this more natural way of rounding off an Act in imitation of his great idol, Jonson. It is true that Dryden's comedy *The Kind Keeper; or, Mr. Limberham,* quarto, 1680, has no traditional couplets at the conclusion of the first four acts, but this can very probably be accounted for since we know that the printed copy of the play is mutilated and incomplete. Yet there are other examples which might be cited. Nevil Payne's comedy *The Morning Ramble,* Dorset Garden, November, 1672, has no tags until the end of the Fifth Act. After Act I the quarto, 1673, notes *The end of the first Act,* but the conclusion of other Acts is not thus marked. Incidentally it may be noted that at the conclusion of the Fourth Act of Shadwell's opera *Psyche* the two jealous sisters are left on the stage. Cupid descends, and threatens vengeance in a speech which ends with the couplet:—

> Arise ye Furies, snatch 'em down to Hell.
> No place becomes such envious Hags so well.
>
> [Aglaura *and* Cidippe *sink.*

A little before Furies had arisen and then descended with Psyche, and the same business was obviously repeated here.

As it might possibly appear a little clumsy, especially in a tragedy, for any number of characters to have remained upon the stage until the conclusion of an act, so that it was necessary for several persons to go off through the doors, a practised dramatist would endeavour to contrive that in some natural way his persons should as it grew towards the close of an act go off gradually, one by one, and that the stage was eventually left with a single actor to conclude the scene and retire. In Otway's *Don Carlos, Prince of Spain,* Dorset Garden, 1676, towards the end of the third act the King goes off, proffering as it were some kind of excuse for his withdrawal with the lines:—

> Whilst I retiring hence, my self make fit
> To wait for Joyes, which are too fierce to meet.

The Queen, the Duchess of Eboli, and Don Carlos are left on the stage. After the dialogue the Prince "Leads her to the Door". Two or three lines are exchanged and she goes out supported by Eboli. Don Carlos is left to declaim:—

Thus long I wander'd in Loves crooked way,
By hope's deluding meteor, led astray;
For e're I've half the dang'rous desart crost,
The Glimm'ring light's gone out, and I am lost.

[*Exit* D. Carlos.

The End of the Third Act

The conclusion of the fourth act of *The History and Fall of Caius Marius,* Dorset Garden, autumn, 1679, is a trifle clumsy. It will be remembered that in this tragedy Otway has incorporated not a little of *Romeo and Juliet,* and this scene corresponds to the drinking of the potion. The Priest of Hymen (Friar Laurence) has supplied Lavinia (Juliet) with the opiate, and she is left alone. Juliet's fine speech is shortened and mangled. Lavinia concludes:—

What? *Sylla*? Get thee gone, thou meager Lover;
My Sense abhors thee. Don't disturb my draught;
'Tis to my Lord (*Drinks.*) Oh! *Marius! Marius! Marius!*

[*Exit.*

The End of the Fourth Act

The same poet far more adroitly managed the conclusion of the Fourth Act of his first play *Alcibiades,* Dorset Garden, 1675. The King and Queen of Sparta are on the stage attended by their full court. Alcibiades and Timandra have just been arrested on a false charge of conspiring against the throne. They are removed in custody. "*Exeunt several ways, Guarded, looking back at each other.*" [1] Whereupon the King speaks seven lines and goes off, leaving the Queen to declaim a short speech of eight lines and then take her departure, the stage thus being clear of characters, and the end of the act denoted.

There is an important passage in the Prologue to Thomas St. Serfe's comedy *Tarugo's Wiles; or, The Coffee House,* produced at Lincoln's Inn Fields on Saturday, 5th October, 1667, which shows that the audience counted upon the rhymed couplet to denote the conclusion of an act. The Prologue consists of a dialogue between a Gentleman, a Player, and a Poet's Servant. After some preliminary discussion about the play to be produced, the conversation proceeds:—

Gent. But tell me friend, without any more circumlocutions, what way is the Play drest?

P. Serv. What do you mean by that?

Gent. That's whether it be set off with Blank verse, Rhyme, or Prose.

P. Serv. My Master is no Arithmetician, and so defies all numerical composition.

Gent. This is the first Poet that ever I heard of, cou'd not make Verse ; But how shall the Expectations of the Audience and the Musick be prepar'd at the ending of Acts?

P. Serv. I am appointed with an Engine to do that.

Gent. Which way?

P. Serv. This way.

(*The Poet's man takes out a Rattle and whirles it about his Head.*

Play. 'Slife, I think this Prose Poet's fancy will take ; for if I be not mistaken, a Rattle will be better understood by a great many here then the best kind of Rhyme.

(*Aside. The Gentleman takes the Rattle and whirles it about.*

Gent. I see no reason but this same Engine ought to alarum the Minstrills to tune their Fiddles, and advertise the Audience to refresh their hams as well as a couplet of Rhyme.

Play. But Sir it may scare the Ladies from eating their fruit.

It is quite obvious from this pleasant piece of mild satire that the curtain did not fall between the acts ; the conventional couplet delivered by one of the characters, the clear stage and the music (an Act tune), were indications regarded as amply sufficient for their purpose. Perhaps it is not too much to surmise from St. Serfe's dialogue that in theatrical circles the question had been mooted whether some other way might be found to make it clear to the audience that an Act was over. A quarter of a century later we have evidence which is even more conclusive that the end of an act was marked by a clear stage. In the fifth dialogue of *The Impartial Critic* by John Dennis, 1693, Beaumont and Freeman are discussing the question of the classical Chorus in tragedy, and Beaumont is quoting the opinions of his friend Wild :—

Beaum. A Tragedy, said he, is the imitation of an Action, which must be one and entire ; and therefore there must be a Chorus : For without it the Acts can never be joyn'd, there will be a solution of continuity, and Tragedy can never be one entire Body.

Freem. . . . Then Mr. *Wild* and you fancy, that the Action breaks off every time that the Musick plays between the Acts?

Beaum. That is Mr. *Wild*'s Opinion.

Freem. But then I could tell you, that the Action is suppos'd to be continued behind the Scenes.

Beaum. How can an Audience be sure of that? Or when the Stage is left empty upon the end of the First Act, what grounds has a Company to believe the Actors will return ? What grounds, I say, can they have but Custom? . . . Whereas a Chorus naturally keeps the

Company together, till the return of the principal Actors . . .

Beaum. You say the Song of the Chorus is very absurd and unnatural; but are not the Fiddles between the Acts a great deal more absurd and unnatural? . . . Is it probable that *Oedipus*, or any other Prince, should four times in the height and fury of his Passion, leave the Scene of Action, purely to give leave to a Company of Musitians to divert the Spectators four times, least they should be too much shaken by the progress of the terrible Action?

There must now be examined certain stage directions in printed plays which specifically require that the curtain should be let fall during the progress of a play, and these exceptions must be assigned a reason, which in truth will not be found far to seek. In the first place, we may take the plays of that very important and prominent writer Roger Boyle, Earl of Orrery, whose dramas and comedies are particularly valuable for their ample and detailed stage directions. The Fourth Act of *King Henry The Fifth,* produced at Lincoln's Inn Fields in August, 1664, and which was noticed as a new play by Pepys on Saturday, the 13th of that month, opens as follows: "*The Curtain being drawn up, the Duke of* Burgundy, *the* Constable, *Earl of* Charaloys, *and the Bishop of* Arras *are seen sitting at one side of a Table, attended by the French Officers of State; on the other side, are seated the Duke of* Exeter, *Duke of* Bedford, the Archbishop *of* Canterbury, *and the Earl of* Warwick, *attended by the* English."

Towards the end of the Fifth Act, "*The Curtain falls. Two Heraulds appear opposite to each other in the Balconies near the Stage.*" It should be noticed that these are the two proscenium balconies nearest the curtain-line. The Heralds summon all the Powers and Potentates of England and France, whereupon "*The Curtain is drawn up. The Curtain being lifted up, there appear the* King, Princess Katherine, Queen *Mother,* Princess Anne, Chareloys, *and all the* English, *and the* French *Nobility and Officers of State; and others according to their places*".

At the end of the First Act of the same author's *The Black Prince,* produced at the Theatre Royal on Saturday, 19th October, 1667, we have the stage direction "*The Curtain fals*". The Second Act opens with the following elaborate spectacle.

"*The Curtain being drawn up, King* Edward *the Third,* King *John of* France, *and the Prince of* Wales *appear, seated on one side of the* Theater; *waited on by the Count of* Guesclin, *the Lord* Latymer, *the Lord* Delaware, *and other Lords, with the King's Guards. On*

THE SQUIRE OF ALSATIA: ACT V
Collection of the Author

[*face p.* 158

the other side of the Theater, *are seated* Plantagenet, Alizia, Cleorin, Sevina, *and other Ladies. The Scene opens; two Scenes of Clouds appear, the one within the other; in the hollow of each Cloud are women and men richly apparell'd, who sing in Dialogue and Chorus, as the Clouds descend to the Stage; then the Women and Men enter upon the* Theater, *and dance; afterwards return into the Clouds which insensibly rise, all of them singing until the Clouds are ascended to their full height; then onely the Scene of the Kings magnificent Palace does appear, all the Company arise.*"

In *Queen Catharine; or, The Ruines of Love* by Mrs. Pix, produced at Lincoln's Inn Fields in September, 1698; 4to, 1698; Act V, the scene is in Ludlow Castle, a full stage set. Isabella is dead upon the boards; Warwick orders:—

Carry this fair Maid to the Queens apartment.

After less than a dozen lines, the speakers, Clarence and Warwick, *exeunt*: "*The Curtain falls; Enter Lord* Dacres *and* Esperanza." After a dialogue of one and twenty lines: "*Curtain rising, discovers Queen* Catharine *sitting on a Couch, with Herbs and Flowers by her, attended.*" Dacres and Esperanza have obviously entered through a proscenium door on the apron; a striking picture of the sorrowful Queen is discovered when the curtain rises a moment or two later. Dacres addresses Queen Catharine and converses with her; at the end of the scene *Exeunt omnes,* after which other characters appear and in some seventeen lines conclude the play.

In each of these cases it will be remarked that the curtain was let fall and afterwards drawn up to reveal an elaborate and magnificent tableau requiring the presence of a large number of characters, a piece of special staging which could not have been effected in any other way. If a discovery of two or three persons was required this, being a far simpler matter, could be managed by the drawing of the scene, that is to say the opening of a pair of flats. Such an arrangement as that in Powell's *The Cornish Comedy,* produced at Dorset Garden in June, 1696, is quite exceptional. In this play the Curtain fell at the end of Act III. Act IV commences: "*Curtain drawn, discovers* Swash *and* Sharper *at Cribbidge.*" We have then the reason for the exceptional falling of the curtain during the progress of a play; there was to be presented some tableau or masque which demanded this uncommon and unusual expedient. On the contemporary French stage the use of the curtain between the acts was considered a poor expedient. This is clearly brought out in a note of Claude Perrault in his translation *Les Dix Livres d'Architecture de Vitruve,* folio 1673. In Book V, Chapter 7 (pp. 168–9), Perrault, commenting upon the various kinds of scene-shifting described by Vitruvius as employed in the ancient theatre, remarks: " Il est neanmoins difficile de croire que ces changemens fussent aussi prompts que ceux de nos Theatres, qui se font presque en un moment & sans qu'on s'en apperçoive: car nous lisons que lors que les Anciens vouloient changer les ornements de leur Scene, ils tiroirent un rideau qui estoit apellé *Siparium,* derriere lequel ils faisoient à loisir ce qui estoit necessaire au changement." I believe that throughout the whole period from 1660 to 1700, scarcely more than a dozen and a half examples all told of this dropping of the curtain may be found, and almost in every case the reason for such an expedient is as we have explained. Thus in the third act of Sir Robert Howard's *The Surprisal,* produced at Vere Street, Wednesday, 23rd April, 1662, a masque of Cupid, Hymen, Charon, and the Parcae is introduced, and "*As soon as the Masque begins the Curtain draws*". At the conclusion of the entertainment, after a short dialogue: " *The Curtain draws. Manet* Miranzo."

At the commencement of the second act of Mrs Behn's *The Forc'd Marriage; or, The Jealous Bridegroom,* given at Lincoln's Inn Fields, December, 1670, was displayed a tableau which certainly seems suggested by the Elizabethan dumb-show. "Act II. THE REPRESENTATION OF THE WEDDING. *The Curtain must be let down, and soft Musick must play: The Curtain being drawn up, discovers a scene of a Temple: The* King *sitting on a Throne, bowing down to join the hands of* Alcippus *and* Erminia, *who kneel on the steps of the Throne; the Officers of the Court and Clergy standing in order by, with* Orgulius. *This within the Scene.*

" *Without on the Stage,* Philander *with his Sword half-drawn, held by* Galatea, *who looks ever on* Alcippus: Erminia *still fixing her eyes on* Philander; Pisaro *passionately gazing on* Galatea: Aminta *on* Fallatio, *and he on her:* Alcander, Isillia, Cleontius, *in other several postures, with the rest, all remaining without motion, whilst the Musick softly plays; this continues a while till the Curtain falls; and then the Musick plays aloud till the Act begins.*"

Particular attention should be drawn to the wording of this direction for the phrase of itself shows that it is unusual, " *The Curtain* must *be let down and soft Musick* must *play.*" A similar tableau or discovery occurs in the same lady's play *The Young King; or, the Mistake,* produced at Dorset Garden in the spring of 1679. " Act III, Scene 1. *The Curtain is let down——— being drawn up, discovers* Orsames *seated on a Throne asleep, drest in Royal Robes, the Crown and Scepter lying by on a Table.* Geron *near the Throne. On either side of the Stage, Courtiers ready drest, and multitude of Lights. Above is discovered the* Queen, Olympia, *and Women,*

Pimante, Artabazes, Ismenes; *Soft Musick plays; whilst he wakes by degrees, and gazes round about him, and on himself with Wonder.*"

In Settle's *Cambyses, King of Persia,* Lincoln's Inn Fields, January, 1670–1, at the conclusion of Act III Mandane is left upon the stage. She is gazing at a Table upon which lies the body of Osiris beheaded, whilst an Executioner stands by with the supposed head in a vessel of Blood. She utters the lines—

> that I could but melt in Tears away;
> That when our rising Sun proclaims the day,
> With Morning dew I by his Rays might be
> Exhal'd, and snatcht up to his Heav'n, and Thee.
> [*Exit.*
>
> *Finis Actus Tertii. The Curtain falls.*

We then have: "ACTUS QUARTUS. Scena prima. *The Scene drawn,* Cambyses *is discover'd seated in a Chair Sleeping.*" A vision with a dance of Spirits is shown: "*In the midst of the Dance arises a Woman with a Dagger in her hand; at which the Scene shuts.*" It is plain that an especial use of the curtain was demanded here by the exigencies of the situation. The execution tableau had to be removed and the representation of spirits who appear to Cambyses prepared.

In Mrs. Manley's *Almyna; Or, the Arabian Vow,* a play most elaborately produced at the Haymarket, 16th December, 1706, Act II, Scene 1, is a Garden, which remains unchanged throughout the act. The locale of Act III is not specified, but from Zoradias' concluding speech it would seem to remain the same, the sofa to which she is led being the "*Repose of Flowers*". After Act III the curtain evidently fell, and the apron now represented "An Antichamber, to the Royal Bed-Chamber". Morat is in waiting. He must have entered by a proscenium-door. To him enter Alhador. They exchange a brief dialogue, and "*The Curtain rises, and shows the Emperor a Sleep, upon a Sofa, according to the Custom of the East*"; large wax Flambeaux are burning; "*the Eunuchs waiting in Ranks like Statues*"; evidently from its impressiveness a full stage set. At the end of the act the flats close to represent "*The Prince's Appartment in the* Seraglio". Zoradia enters and demands audience from an Officer who comes on to her. The Scene draws to a set in the second grooves "*and shews* Abdalla *Lying on the Ground dejected; he rises*". Zoradia joins him, and after some dialogue they go off; the flats then open to show the full stage. During this final scene the Sultan "*ascends to the Window*", that is he goes up to the proscenium balcony.

There occurs in *The Rehearsal,* produced at the Theatre Royal,

7th December, 1671, a passage which is very valuable in its bearing upon the point under consideration and which completely bears out the explanation advanced. At the end of the Fourth Act Bayes says "Let down the Curtain", a reminder which would have been entirely superfluous had it been the custom to lower the curtain at the conclusion of an act. The characters go off and the stage is clear. Act V commences. Bayes and the two Gentlemen come on to the apron by way of a proscenium door and the poet expounds: "Now, Gentlemen, I will be bold to say, I'l shew you the greatest Scene that ever *England* saw: I mean not for words, for those I do not value; but for state, shew, and magnificence. In fine I'll justifie it to be as grand to the eye every whit, I gad, as that great Scene in *Harry* the Eight, and grander too, I gad; for instead of two Bishops, I bring in here four Cardinals." [*The Curtain is drawn up, the two usurping Kings appear in State, with the four Cardinals, Prince,* Pretty-man, *Prince* Volscius, Amarillis, Cloris, Panthenope, &c. *before them, Heralds and Serjeants at Arms with Maces.*] Buckingham is here directly burlesquing Orrery's singular use of the curtain which to the wits appeared a sorry enough expedient.

In the Prologue to *She Wou'd and She Wou'd Not; or, The Kind Impostor,* produced at Drury Lane, 26th November, 1702, Colley Cibber with reference to his observance of the unities in this comedy says:—

> *Our humble Author thinks a* Play *should be,*
> *Tho' ty'd to Rules, like a good* Sermon *free*
> *From Pride, and stoop to each Capacity . . .*
> *His* Action's *in the Time of Acting done*
> *No more than from the Curtain, up and down.*
> *While the first* Musick *plays, he moves his Scene*
> *A little space, but never shifts again.*

This is strictly the case. Act I takes place at an Inn in Madrid. Act II is Don Manuel's House; before Acts III, IV, and V is prefixed the direction "*The* Scene *continues*". The action of these four Acts is exactly the time of the representation on the stage, and the unity is preserved with a strictness that would have delighted the great Mr. Curdle. So Don Manuel, who is to give his daughter in marriage first declares we'll "e'en clap up the Wedding to-morrow morning", but a little later informs Rosara "you shall marry Don *Philip* this Evening". Obviously "the Curtain, up and down" means the time from the rising of the curtain after the Prologue until the fall of the curtain after the Epilogue. So it is plain that at least as late as 1702 the act-intervals were not otherwise distinguished than they had been in the palmy days of old Rowley himself.

However interesting, and perhaps not altogether impertinent, it were to inquire into the use of the curtain during the eighteenth century, it must suffice but briefly to review a lengthy period. Act III of Mrs. Centlivre's *The Bassett-Table,* Drury Lane, November, 1705, commences: "*The* SCENE *draws, and discovers* Valeria *with Books upon a Table, a Microscope, putting a Fish upon it, several Animals lying by.*" At the conclusion of Act I of *Mar-Plot; or, The Second Part of the Busie-Body,* Drury Lane, December, 1710, Marplot is left alone upon the stage. He "*Goes into the Chimney, and the Scene Shuts*", which is to say two flats representing Donna Perriera's Apartment, the first scene of Act II, drew over and met in the centre. The Fifth Act of *The Cruel Gift,* Drury Lane, December, 1716, opens with "SCENE *draws, and discovers* Leonora *sitting on a Couch, her Women weeping round her*". It is obvious from these directions that as yet the curtain had not begun to fall between the acts. In May, 1717, was produced at Drury Lane, Mrs. Manley's *Lucius, the First Christian King of Britain,* and this tragedy exhibits in Act V, 1, a tableau in much the same manner as similar representations were arranged by Mrs. Behn: "*The Curtain drawn up discovers an Altar to* Jupiter; *Flamens attending*; Lucius *and the* Queen *under the* British *Guard.*" A decade later at the end of Philip Frowde's *The Fall of Saguntum,* Lincoln's Inn Fields, January, 1727, we have "*Curtain falls*", a direction which would hardly have been particularized were act-intervals also thus generally distinguished. The rhyming tag still rounded off and proclaimed the end of an Act. So in Gay, Pope, and Arbuthnot's *Three Hours after Marriage,* Drury Lane, January, 1717, Mrs. Phoebe Clinket, who has an itch for scribbling plays, bewails the loss of "the tag of the Acts of a new Comedy".[2]

The employment of the curtain by Fielding in his farces and burlesques is so irregular that we cannot, I think, glean much from their evidence, save some assurance that no systematic service had as yet either suggested itself to the dramatists or been introduced in the theatre. Indeed the stage directions of *Pasquin,* produced at the Haymarket in March, 1736, are rigidly conservative. Fustian is at the rehearsal of his tragedy, and cries: "Come, Prompter, will the tragedy never begin?" "Yes, Sir," replies that official, "they are all ready; come draw up the curtain." A mock act of the new piece is performed, and the author directs: "Come, begin the second act." "*The Scene draws, and discovers* Queen Common-Sense *asleep.*" The curtain does not fall until after the Epilogue. Again in *The Historical Register for the Year* 1736, Haymarket, spring of 1737, Medley remarks, "My first scene, Mr. *Sourwit,* lies in the island of

Corsica . . . Enter Prompter. *Prompter*: Sir, they are ready. *Medley*: Then draw the scene and discover them. *Scene draws and discovers five* Politicians *sitting at a table*." In the next act of the play Medley directs: "Come draw the scene and discover the ladies in council . . . *The scene draws and discovers four* Ladies." A little later the Prompter warns those who are on the stage watching the rehearsal: "Gentlemen, you must make room, for the Curtain must be let down, to prepare the Auction-Room." Presently he announces: "Sir, every thing is ready." Medley: "Then draw up the Curtain . . . THE AUCTION. SCENE.—*An Auction-Room, a Pulpit and Forms, plac'd, and several People walking about, some seated near the Pulpit*." As in the days of Hart and Betterton the curtain was let down if a tableau had to be arranged with many characters. *A Criticism of* The Foundling *in a Letter to the Author* (1748), has an interesting reference: "the Act ended as I have seen many others do, with all the Performers leaving the Stage, and the Music striking up." Some twelve years later in the twenty-first letter of Goldsmith's *Citizen of the World* (1760), Lien Chi Altangi describes a visit to a London theatre.[3] "As the curtain was not drawn before my arrival, I had an opportunity of observing the behaviour of the spectators. . . . The expected time for the play to begin at length arrived, the curtain was drawn, and the actors came on . . . " The heroine of the piece was a queen, who is represented as overwhelmed with sorrow for her son whom she had lost as a child fifteen years before. "Her lamentations grew loud. Comfort is offered, but she detests the very sound . . . After thus grieving through three scenes, the curtain dropped for the first act." The Chinese visitor criticizes the play. "I had scarce finished this observation, when the curtain rose, and the king came on in a violent passion. . . . After he had thus fretted, and the queen had fretted through the second act, the curtain was let down once more." There are various comments on the third act, and in the fourth act the queen finds her son. But the king resolves that he must die. "The queen exclaims at his barbarity; is frantic with rage, and at length overcome with sorrow, falls into a fit; upon which the curtain drops, and the act is concluded." The fifth act is described as all bustle and stir. From this account it is obvious that the curtain now fell in the act intervals as a regular thing. Yet it were a mistake to attempt a generalization for any given year or period concerning this use of the curtain to divide the acts. (We may remark, however, that as early as 1760 a dramatist was able to let his curtain fall upon a picture, the swooning queen.) The several houses varied in their practice, but perhaps it is not too hazardous to say that the modern employ of the curtain was admitted and began to prevail about the middle of the eighteenth century. It may be observed that at the revivals by the Phoenix Society of plays by Dryden, Wycherley, Congreve, Otway, and others, the end of an Act was marked by a clear stage, and the old method was found to be not merely quite intelligible to an audience of to-day, but never in the slightest degree awkward, frequently extremely effective and elegant.

Before we consider in detail the speaking of the Epilogue and the final fall of the curtain attention must be drawn to the traditional dance, which if not invariably, at least most frequently proclaimed the finish of a comedy. A dance was by no means unknown to round off the Fifth Act in Pre-Restoration plays. One may recall the Bergomask in *A Midsummer Night's Dream*; the terminal dance of *As You Like It*; Benedick's " Strike vp, pipers ", and the dance which concludes *Much Ado About Nothing*. The last speech of Momford in *Sir Giles Goosecap, Knight,* 4to, 1606, runs :—

> Now will we consecrate our ready supper
> To honour'd Hymen as his nuptial rite;
> In form whereof first dance, fair lords and ladies,
> And after sing; So we will sing and dance,
> And to the skies our virtuous joys advance.
>
> *The Measure.*

"Again again : set, set !" cries Lord Rainbow half a dozen lines before the end of *The Ball,* that comedy which gave Herbert such trouble in November, 1632, and then follows a dance. In the days of Charles I the dance at the conclusion of a play was vastly in favour, and so popular a writer as Brome did not fail often to satisfy the public taste. The dance which is given at the ending of *The Antipodes* (acted in 1638; 4to, 1640) is introduced by means of a small masque or " by-play "; that which concludes *A Mad Couple Well Match'd* (8vo, 1653) is more naturally led up to by a speech of Lord Lovely, " Come Madam, I finde here's Musick, let's leade the Brides a Dance to stirre their appetites to Dinner." At the conclusion of *The New Academy; or, The New Exchange* (8vo, 1658) when old Matchil cries—

> But heark, before you break up school; lets have
> One frisk, one fling now, one cariering dance.
> And then pack up,

all shout "Agreed, Agreed, Agreed ", and call for *Les tous ensembles,* whilst Nehemiah Nestlecock begins to boast—

I and my mother,
My Aunt and all can daunce in't, as well as the best,
With everyone in their own footing. Now observe.
[*Daunce.*

After the Restoration, Dryden in *The Wild Gallant* (acted Vere Street, 1663; revived, Theatre Royal, 1667) has an allusion to the popularity and purport of the dance. "Come Nuncle," says Isabella, "'tis in vain to hold out now 'tis past remedy: 'Tis like the last Act of a Play, when People must marry; and if Fathers will not consent then, they should throw oranges at 'em from the Galleries; why should you stand off to help us from a Dance?" A few moments later Loveby urges Bibber, "Chear up thy Wife, *Will.* Where are the Fiddles? A Dance should do it." "Strike up Fiddles," commands Mrs. Bibber and the regulation dance follows. Buckingham showed considerable ingenuity when he wished to conclude *The Rehearsal,* Theatre Royal, December, 1671. Bayes has walked off in hot anger, the players are left alone on the stage. "Let's see *Haynes* and *Shirley* practise the last dance; for that may serve us another time," says one. "I'll call 'em in. I think they are but in the Tiring-room," a second replies. *The Dance done.* "Come, come; let's go away to dinner," and all exeunt. It may be remarked that by "the last dance" is meant the dance which was to have concluded Mr. Bayes' play. Buckingham also here had in mind the conclusion of Thomas Thomson's *The English Rogue,* 4to, 1668:—

Plot-thrift. Come, let's have a dance or two and so to dinner.
All. Agreed! Agreed!
[*Dance.*]
Arantius. Well, now let's in to dinner.

It would be possible to give a very long list of comedies that conclude with a dance, in some cases introduced very appositely and with a certain felicity; in other instances dragged in and awkwardly obtrusive. That comedies whose intrigue takes place in carnival-time, such as Dryden's *An Evening's Love,* where the scene is Madrid, the last evening of the Carnival, and Mrs. Behn's *The Rover* (I) with locale at Naples during the carnival, should conclude with a dance is wholly in character and in keeping. Again a tale of light amours at Montpelier, lightly told by Southerne in *Sir Anthony Love,* and concluding with more than one venture in matrimony, may aptly be rounded off by Valentine's "Come, come, we must have a dance to all these weddings". Not dissimilar is the situation at the end of *Bury*

Fair. " Call in the Fiddlers " : cries Oldwit, " I am Transported ! I am all Air ! Sirrah, go you and set the Bells a going in both Churches : Call in all my Neighbours, I'll have him hang'd that's Sober to Night : let every Room in my House Roar, that it may keep the whole Town awake. Here are the Fiddles : fall to Dancing presently ; lose no time." The dance here is natural and proper.

A dance, however, seems to me a little impertinent at the conclusion of Sedley's *The Mulberry-Garden,* where it is merely consequent upon Sir John Everyoung's : " Now you are all pair'd, let's have a dance." Nor is it better contrived in *Bellamira ; or, The Mistress,* for Keepwell says : " These Roguish Fidlers smell a Wedding already ; since— They are come. Let's dance— " *They Dance.* In Betterton's *The Amorous Widow ; or, The Wanton Wife* the terminal dance is a palpable intrusion. A servant enters and tells Lady Laycock : " Madam, the Parson's come." Merryman chips in with " That's well—bid my Servants strike up, we'll go merrily to this business ". "*A Dance.*" At the conclusion of Nevil Payne's *The Morning Ramble ; or, The Town-Humours,* Merry gives the cue for the dance as an accepted convention : "All this I see is a meer contrivance for a Dance, lets without any more ado have it then. (*Dance.*)" Nor is the dance at the end of the Fifth Act more adroitly managed in Carlile's *The Fortune Hunters ; or, Two Fools well Met.* Young Wealthy somewhat abruptly remarks : " But come, I have provided an entertainment." The dance follows, and two songs conclude the play. It is plain that Congreve had no liking for the traditional dance, and it is most summarily imported with a word or two of dialogue into *The Old Batchelour, Love for Love,* and *The Way of the World,* in which last play the movement breaks off upon Lady Wishfort's " As I am a Person I can hold out no longer ". From *The Double-Dealer* it is wholly omitted, nor does the piece suffer by the loss. Although Wycherley bowed to custom in his first comedy *Love in a Wood, The Plain-Dealer* has no such feature wholly alien to the scene, and at the conclusion of *The Country-Wife* we have "*A Dance of Cuckolds* ", presumably an antic. Shadwell at the conclusion of *The Sullen Lovers* provided some novelty. Carolina says : " in stead of a grand Dance according to the laudable Custom of Weddings, I have found out a little Comical Gentleman to entertain you with." " *Enter a Boy in the habit of* Pugenello, *and traverses the Stage, takes his Chair, and sits down, then Dances a Jigg.*" Pepys notes under Saturday, 2nd May, 1668, his visit to the first performance of *The Sullen Lovers* : " But a little boy, for a farce, do dance Polichinelli, the best that ever anything was done in the world, by all men's report: most pleased with that, beyond anything in the world, and much beyond all the play."

Among comedies which omit the dance at the end of the Fifth Act are Shadwell's *The Virtuoso, A True Widow, The Woman-Captain, The Lancashire Witches, The Amorous Bigotte,* and *The Scowrers;* Otway's three comedies, *Friendship in Fashion, The Souldiers Fortune,* and *The Atheist*; Ravenscroft's *The London Cuckolds* and *Dame Dobson*; Crowne's *The Countrey Wit, City Politiques, Sir Courtly Nice,* and *The English Frier*; Dryden's *The Kind Keeper*; Mountfort's *Greenwich-Park*; Mrs. Behn's *The Town-Fopp, Sir Patient Fancy, The Feign'd Curtizans, The City-Heiress, The False Count,* and *The Luckey Chance*; D'Urfey's *A Fond Husband, Squire Oldsapp, The Royalist,* and *Love for Money*; Southerne's *The Wives Excuse*; Vanbrugh's *The Relapse, The Provok'd Wife, The Confederacy,* and *The Mistake.* These thirty odd titles which have been quoted do not, of course, in any way pretend to be a complete list; they are merely a few examples of well-known and popular plays in which the traditional concluding dance was not a feature. It is difficult in many cases to say why the dance should have been omitted; why, for instance, Shadwell's *The Humorists* and *The Volunteers* should both be rounded off with the dance, somewhat arbitrarily introduced, and why *A True Widow* and *The Amorous Bigotte* should not thus be provided; why Southerne's *The Wives Excuse* has not the terminal dance which duly appears at the conclusion of *The Maid's Last Prayer,* his following comedy. Sometimes truly we can appreciate that the introduction of the dance would have been altogether too incongruous and inappropriate, as in *The Plain-Dealer*: sometimes it is plain that a dramatist misliked the artificiality of the custom, and this, there is reason to think, was Congreve's attitude.

In the eighteenth century Cibber for a while, Mrs. Centlivre, and others stoutly maintain the old tradition. In *The Beau's Duel,* Lincoln's Inn Fields, 1702, her first, and in *The Artifice,* Drury Lane, October, 1722, her last comedy the dance holds its place at the end of Act V. In the first named play a servant enters with "Sir, here's the Musick without come to congratulate your Marriage". "Bid 'em come in," says Careless, "we'll have a Dance." "[*Here's a Dance.*" A couple or so of speeches and Mrs. Plotwell speaks the tag, a triplet. At the conclusion of *The Artifice* the dance is dragged in, *ui et armis,* for à propos of nothing Ned Freeman exclaims: "Let's have a Country Dance." There is no stage-direction but a brief speech from Sir John and a tag of seven lines spoken after the dance and the play. Cibber's *Love Makes a Man; or, The Fops*

Fortune, Drury Lane, December, 1700; *The Double Gallant; or, The Sick Lady's Cure,* Haymarket, November, 1707; and *The Rival Fools,* Drury Lane, January, 1709; are all concluded with the traditional dance, although the action in none of these can be said naturally to lead up to this. Thus in *The Double Gallant,* Old Wilfull cries: "Odzooks, here's a great deal of good Company, ho! and 'tis a Shame the Fiddles should be idle all this while." "Oh! by no means! Come strike up, Gentlemen," rejoins Careless. "*They Dance.*" At the end of *The Rival Fools,* Young Outwit says: "And, lastly, Sir, this memorable hundred Pounds worth of Musick, which to crown my Triumph, Sir, are very generously return'd to play just one Dance at my Cousin *Cunningham's* Wedding." Sir Oliver takes the cue: "And now strike up Musick." Charles Johnson in his *The Country Lasses; or, The Custom of the Manor,* Drury Lane, February, 1714–15, emphasized the terminal dance more particularly and at the end of the Fifth Act makes Sir John English almost eloquent: "Come, come, all is made up; let us have one Trip for it now, I beseech you: What, a Wedding without a Fiddle, Man, is like a Troop without a Trumpet. Codso, we will Foot it till a good Capermonger shall be able to copy the Figure of the Dance from our Impressions on the Pavement." A Dance follows. Benjamin Griffin in his comedy *Whig and Tory,* Lincoln's Inn Fields, January, 1720, is more frankly conventional and gives Charles Heartfree the following: "And now, as Custom requires, on these Occasions, let's begin our Mirth with a Dance." "[*After the Dance, a Servant enters with Wine.*" A dance is introduced at the conclusion of Hoadly's *The Suspicious Husband,* Covent Garden, February, 1747, but the tradition was soon to be on the wane. As a variant in some instances a masquerade or presented masque had been employed. Thus in Act V of Cibber's *Love's Last Shift; or, The Fool in Fashion,* Drury Lane, January, 1696, there is a masque with Love seated on a Throne; Fame, Reason, Honour, Marriage. *She wou'd, and She wou'd not,* Drury Lane, November, 1702, is concluded with an Entertainment. Into the action of *The Provok'd Husband,* Drury Lane, January, 1728, scenes of an elaborate masquerade are introduced towards the end of the play.

At the conclusion of Fielding's *The Miser,* Drury Lane, February, 1733, it is announced: "There are some people in masquerading habits without." They enter and dance. But shortly after the middle of the eighteenth century the time-honoured dance of the Fifth Act rapidly began to disappear from the stage. In 1776–7 was published a collection of plays entitled

The New English Theatre, and of these many are "Marked with the Variations in the Manager's Book at the Theatre-Royal in Covent-Garden". In each case the terminal Dance and all dialogue leading up or relating to it have been drastically cut. Thus in Volume I we notice that several speeches and the Dance are between inverted commas, that is to be omitted, in Mrs. Centlivre's *The Busy-Body.* In Volume VII the Dance has disappeared from *Love Makes a Man* and Steele's *The Funeral*; in Volume IX Old Wilfull's speech and the rejoinder of Careless with the direction for the Dance are not merely marked for omission but more, not even printed at the end of *The Double Gallant.* From *The Provok'd Husband* the masquerade has been deleted with the dance of Masks in various Characters.

These alterations and excisions are certainly significant. It is worth remarking that Anthony Aston in his "A Brief Supplement to *Colley Cibber,* Esq.; His Lives Of the late Famous Actors and Actresses" says of Betterton: "He was incapable of dancing, even in a Country-Dance; as was Mrs. *BARRY*: But their good Qualities were more than equal to their Deficiencies.—While Mrs. *BRACEGIRDLE* sung very agreeably in the LOVES of *Mars* and *Venus,* and danced in a Country-Dance as well as Mr. *WILKS,* though not with so much Art and Foppery, but like a well-bred Gentlewoman." And again writing of Mrs. Barry he insists: "She could neither sing, nor dance, no, not in a Country-Dance." Thomas Jevon, however, had actually been a dancing-master before he came on the stage, and Charlotte Butler was allowed "to sing and dance to great Perfection". In Tom Brown's *The Ladies Lamentation for their* Adonis; *Or, an* Elegy *on the death of Mr.* Mountford *the Player* there are allusions to his excellent dancing:—

> His face, and his voice, and his dancing are rare,
> And wherever they meet they prevail with the fair.

Even more famous names are John Lacy, originally a dancing-master and pupil of the celebrated John Ogilby; Joe Haines, whom Pepys terms "the incomparable dancer of the King's house"; Nell Gwyn; and Moll Davies, whom Flecknoe in a poem "*on her Excellent dancing*"[4] thus compliments:—

> Dear Mis: delight of all the nobler sort;
> Pride of the Stage and darling of the Court,
> Who wou'd not think to see thee dance so light,
> Thou wert all air? or else all soul and spirit?

The traditional dance at the end of the Fifth Act was by no means the only, perhaps not the most important occasion in the theatre when actors were required to foot it merrily. There survived from Pre-Restoration days that curious entertainment or interlude known as the jig. Although the term boasts at least three distinct meanings it may for our purpose be defined as a brisk song and dance, often elaborated and expressing some dramatic action. These jigs, not unseldom partaking of the nature of a masque, sometimes merely a dance in character, were retained in high favour on the Restoration stage. Davenant in his Prologue for the revival of *The Wits* in 1661, writes—

> So country Jigs and Farces, mixt among
> Heroic scenes, make plays continue long.

On Thursday, 7th March, 1666–7, Pepys saw Caryl's *The English Princess; or, The Death of Richard the III* at Lincoln's Inn Fields, "a most sad, melancholy play, and pretty good; but nothing eminent in it, as some tragedys are; only little Mis. Davis did dance a jig after the end of the play,[5] and then telling the next day's play; so that it come in by force only to please the company to see her dance in boy's clothes." Mrs. Evelyn writing on 10th February, 1668–9, to Mr. Tyrrell in Ireland tells him of various attractions at the theatres, and amongst others "Horace, with a farce and dances between every act, composed by Lacy and played by him and Nell, which takes". On Tuesday, 19th January, of this year Pepys had seen the play: "to the King's house to see 'Horace'; this the third day of its acting—a silly tragedy; but Lacy hath made a farce of several dances—between each act, one: but his words are but silly, and invention not extraordinary, as to the dances; only some Dutchmen come out of the mouth and tail of a Hamburgh sow." On Thursday, 4th February, Evelyn notes: "I saw the tragedy of *Horace* (written by the *virtuous* Mrs. Philips) acted before their Majesties. Betwixt each act a masque and antique dance." These jigs were assuredly popular, and the Hon. Edward Howard in the preface to *The Women's Conquest*, 4to, 1671, girds at the "Scenes, Machines, Habits, Jiggs, and Dances" which had found their way even into tragedies. In his first Prologue he makes Angel say scommatically: "We are to act a farce to-day that has sixteen Mimics in it . . . with two and thirty Dances and Jiggs à la mode." Nevertheless in his First Act he himself has a Masque of Diana, Echo, Thetis, Cupid, and a Dance of Nereids.

The extraordinary Epilogue—a burlesque of *Macbeth*—which was presented after Duffett's farce *The Empress of Morocco*, produced at the Theatre Royal in the winter of 1673, may be said to have been a species of dramatic jig. "EPILOGUE Being a new Fancy, after the old and most surprising way of MACBETH Perform'd with new and costly MACHINES, Which were invented and managed by the most ingenious Operator Mr. *Henry Wright,* P.G.Q." The actual Epilogue follows. Even the Epilogue to *The Clandestine Marriage,* produced at Drury Lane, 20th February, 1766, a miniature play, spoken and sung by nearly a dozen characters, is a dramatic jig, although by this time the word was long since obsolete in that sense.

It may be remarked that in William Mountford's *The Successful Straingers,* produced at Drury Lane in the winter of 1689; 4to, 1690; we find: "*The End of the Third Act. Mrs.* Butler's *Dance.*" Charlotte Butler had no rôle in the piece. A few references to the early play-bills and advertisements will amply show how the jig had assumed a position of very considerable importance, although it was usually announced as an Entertainment of Dancing and Singing. A Drury Lane bill for 18th May, 1703, of *The Relapse,* sets out at length such attractions as "Singing in Italian and English by Mrs. Campion. Also several Entertainments of Dancing by the Famous Monsieur Du Ruel, particularly an Extraordinary Comical Country Man's Dance never perform'd before. And Signior Gasperini will perform several Sonata's on the Violin, one between Mr. Paisible and him, and another between him, and a Scholar of his, being the last time of his performance". In 1704 an ample announcement proclaims: "At the New Theatre in *Little-Lincoln's-Inn-Fields,* this present Thursday, being the 25th of *January,* will be reviv'd a Comedy call'd Like Master Like Man. With several Entertainments of Singing and Dancing in and between the Acts, viz. That celebrated Dialogue by Mr. *Boman* and Mr. *Pack,* representing a Drunken Officer and a Town Miss, originally perform'd in the Opera of the Mad Lover. As also a Country Dialogue by Mrs. *Willis* and Mr. *Short.* A new Trumpet Song by Mr. *Davis,* compos'd by Mr. *Eccles.* Likewise the last new Entry by Mr. *Prince* and Mrs. *Clark*; and several other Comick Dances by him and others. Also a right *Irish* trot by a child of 5 years of Age. By her Majesty's Sworn Servants."

The curtain then finally fell after the Epilogue had been spoken, a practice which is amply and certainly established by very many references and which prevailed as long as these terminal addresses continued to be delivered.

Any variation from this use is always very distinctly marked as exceptional. Thus the Epilogue to Banks' *Cyrus The Great; or, The Tragedy of Love,* produced at Lincoln's Inn Fields early in December, 1695, is headed: "Epilogue, Spoken by a Boy and Girl, by way of Dialogue." *Curtain falls.*

Girl. *Hold, is the Play done?*
Boy. *Ay, pretty Rogue.*
Girl. *What, a new Play without an Epilogue! . . .*
Why, what d'you make of Mr. Betterton?
Boy. *The Curtain's dropt, and he's glad he's gone.*

In Motteux' comedy *Love's A Jest,* produced at Lincoln's Inn Fields in 1696, at the end of the Play Underhill advances with Bowen:—

Mr. *Underhil.* Now for the Epilogue.
Mr. *Bowen.* There's none I think!
Mr. *Underhil.* Let down the Curtain then, and let's go drink.

To take an example from the eighteenth century the Epilogue to Mottley's tragedy *Antiochus,* produced at Lincoln's Inn Fields on the 13th April, 1721, commences thus: Epilogue. The Curtain falling, Mrs. *Seymour* comes forward with Mr. *Quin* and Mr. *Egleton.*

Mrs. *Seymour.* *What now! Pray hold, there's something more to say,*
There ought to be an Epilogue to th' Play.
Are you to speak it, Sir, or Mr. Quin?
The Company expects you should begin:
They look as if they long'd to be dismiss'd;
At least I do, I'm sure, to be undress'd.

The Epilogue to Fielding's comedy *The Miser,* Drury Lane, 17th February, 1733, an address which was written by Colley Cibber and spoken by Kitty Clive, ends with the following triplet:—

Madam, these things than you I'm more expert in,
Nor do I see no Epilogue much hurt in,
Zounds! When the play is ended—Drop the Curtain.

The business at the end of the fifth act varied, sometimes all the characters withdrew and the speaker of the Epilogue then entered, or if it was a person who had taken part in the play and was on in the last scene returned, and delivered the address to the audience. In Drake's *The Sham-Lawyer; or, The Lucky Extravagant,* produced at Drury Lane, 31st May, 1697; 4to, 1697; Spade the sexton, acted by Joe Haines, speaks the epilogue. He is on the stage at the end of the play and we have "Exeunt Omnes". Then follows "Epilogue. Spoken by *Spade*". This commences:—

On Business I'm return'd so quick this way,
Sent by the Author to interr his Play . . .

Sometimes, and perhaps this was the more usual way, the Epilogue was spoken before the dramatis personae departed; indeed, as will be seen, it was not infrequently a dialogue between two or more of the actors. In any case it must be emphasized that, save with the rarest exceptions, it was delivered before the curtain fell.

At the conclusion of the fifth act of Orrery's *The Black Prince,* produced at the Theatre Royal, Saturday, 19th October, 1667, we have a stage direction " *The Curtaine Falls* ". At the end of the Fifth Act of *Mustapha* (Bodley MS. Rawl. Poet. 27, f. 54) after the final *Exeunt* we have " The Curtaine Falls ". This direction does not occur in the folios. Again at the close of the same author's *Tryphon,* Lincoln's Inn Fields, December, 1668, we have " *The Curtain Falls* ". (The same direction appears at the end of *Herod the Great,* folio 1694, but since this play was not acted the point is merely valuable as showing that the stage direction was written in by the author and is not due to the practical experience of the producer or actors.) Again in the operatic version of *The Prophetess; or, The History of Dioclesian,* put on by Betterton at Dorset Garden, June, 1690, after Dioclesian has spoken the tag, " *The Curtain Falls.*" There will not I think be traced many other examples of this stage direction in this place, and it was obviously a most exceptional piece of business. The reason why it was so employed is that Orrery's dramas are largely spectacular, and on account of their magnificent mounting, scenic displays, pomp and crowds, they demanded special production and a particular use of the curtain. They are altogether singular. The same remarks apply to the operatic *The Prophetess,* which was notably " set out with Coastly Scenes, Machines and Cloaths ".

The final episode of Shadwell's *The Libertine,* produced at Dorset Garden in June, 1675, exhibits the interior of a church, where is seen the statue of Don Pedro and the ghosts of Don John's victims. Don John, his two profligate companions, with the trembling Jacomo in attendance, enter. After vain exhortations to repentance there is a song of Devils with a chorus of fearful doom. Jacomo creeps away, and presently the three impious wretches are swallowed up quick. The Statue speaks:—

> Thus perish all
> Those men, who by their words and actions dare,
> Against the will and pow'r of Heav'n declare.
>
> [*Scene shuts.*

The Epilogue was delivered by Jacomo (Underhill). This particular arrangement of the flats closing was due to the elaborate details of the final scene and the crowded stage.

THE AMOROUS WIDOW: ACT V
Collection of the Author

[*face p.* 174

For a like reason D'Urfey wrote "Curtain falls" at the conclusion of the Third Part of his *Don Quixote,* Theatre Royal, winter of 1695. The last scene was the Don's bed-chamber. He is in bed with his friends and servants about him. They suggest a diversion for his melancholy. "*Here follows the last Entertainment of Singing and Dancing, which Ended,* Don Quixote *sleeps.*"

It is true that at the conclusion of Nevil Payne's *The Fatal Jealousie,* Dorset Garden, August, 1672, when the Captain of the Watch speaks the last lines :—

For Lust may be excus'd since flesh is frail,
But Murder on the Soul does guilt Entail,

The Curtain Falls.

Admittedly this tragedy does not come within the category represented by Orrery's heroic plays and the dramatic opera, nor is there any spectacular finale, wherefore we can but look upon this fall of the curtain as an exception, sufficiently curious and unusual.

The final direction at the close of the fifth act *Exeunt Omnes* which occurs in so many plays must, I apprehend, more often be taken quite literally; all the characters did withdraw. Occasionally, indeed, there is some particular allusion or further reference which shows that such was indubitably the case. Thus, at the conclusion of Dryden's *The Kind Keeper; or, Mr. Limberham,* Dorset Garden, March, 1678, Woodall says: "Now, let's to Dinner: Mrs. *Saintly,* lead the way, as becomes you in your own house."

[*The rest going off.*

Pleasance. Your Hand, sweet Moiety.
Woodall. And Heart too, my comfortable Importance.
Mistress and Wife, by turns, I have possess'd:
He who enjoys 'em both in one, is bless'd.

At the end of D'Urfey's *Love for Money; or, The Boarding School,* produced at Drury Lane in the winter of 1689, we have the regular "*Exeunt Omnes*", but as the characters were going off Mrs. Butler, the script in her hand, entered from a proscenium door and called back Mountford. This piece of business began the Epilogue :—

Butler. *D'ye hear me, Mr.* Mountford, *pray come back.*
D'ye know what I've done here?
Mount. *Yes, play'd a Crack.*

Mrs. Butler has played Betty Jiltall, who flounces angrily from the stage in her final exit some little while before the end of the piece, but Mountford (Jack Amorous) was on until the last.

In the rare *Poems On Affairs of State,* 1698,[6] without assignation to any particular play is printed "An Epilogue *By Mrs.* Butler, *spoken immediately after the others running Out*".

Reference should be made to the famous Epilogue which was spoken by Dogget to the First Part of D'Urfey's *Don Quixote,* produced at Dorset Garden in 1694. Doggett played Sancho Panca, and the Epilogue was spoken "By Sancho, riding upon his Ass". Don Quixote and Sancho had been carried off the stage before the end of the fifth act, which after the tag is duly furnished with the conventional *Exeunt Omnes.* So it is plain that Sancho must have returned riding upon Dapple. Incidentally it may be remarked that a number of other comedians copied this piece of business, the delivery of an Epilogue from the back of an ass. Joe Haines in the habit of a Horse-officer, mounted on a donkey upon whose head he had placed a wig, thus spoke the Epilogue to Scott's *The Unhappy Kindness,*[7] a tragedy produced at Drury Lane in 1697. In the quarto, 1697, the title is: "The EPILOGUE written, and spoke by Mr. *Haynes,* in the Habit of a *Horse Officer,* mounted on an Ass." There are illustrations of this Epilogue, but the details of the engravings differ very considerably, and I do not think that they can be considered of any value as a representation of the interior of the Theatre Royal. It is surprising that this piece of tomfoolery, the introduction of a donkey upon the stage, should have commended itself to any actor, but we find that both Pinkethman and Liston (at Covent Garden, 9th June, 1818) delivered Epilogues in this manner.

It may be observed that the direction *Exeunt Omnes* does not invariably occur at the end of plays. It is for example omitted from Dryden's *The Duke of Guise,* 4to, 1683; from Lee's *Mithridates,* 4to, 1678; *Caesar Borgia,* 4to, 1680; *Lucius Junius Brutus,* 4to, 1681; The *Princess of Cleve,* 4to, 1689; from Ravenscroft's *Dame Dobson,* 4to, 1684; from Sir Robert Howard's *The Great Favourite; or, The Duke of Lerma,* 4to, 1668; from Shadwell's *The Miser,* 4to, 1672; *The History of Timon of Athens,* 4to, 1678; *A True Widow,* 4to, 1679; *The Lancashire Witches,* 4to, 1682; *Bury-Fair,* 4to, 1689; *The Amorous Bigotte,* 4to, 1690; and *The Volunteers,* 4to, 1693; rrom *The Mall; or, The Modish Lovers,* 4to, 1674; from *The Counterfeit Bridegroom,* 4to, 1677; from Duffett's *The Fond Lady,* 4to, 1684; from Mrs. Behn's *The Roundheads,* 4to, 1682; from Burnaby's *The Lady's Visiting Day,* 4to, 1701; and from many others. *The*

Mistaken Husband, 4to, 1675, has a curious misprint: "*Exit omnia.*"

There are very frequent examples of the Epilogue having been spoken before the characters left the stage, whilst they remained in a conventional group. This appears to me to have been by far the most effective method, but a few examples may stand for many. The Epilogue to Ravenscroft's popular *The London Cuckolds,* produced at Dorset Garden in the winter of 1681, is spoken by no less than seven actors, Smith (Ramble), Mrs. Currer (Eugenia), Leigh (Dashwell), Mrs. Barry (Arabella), Nokes (Doodle), Underhill (Wiseacre), and Mrs. Petty (Peggy). Yet *The London Cuckolds* has "*Exeunt omnes*", in this instance an error, as also is the same direction at the end of the Fifth Act of D'Urfey's *Squire Oldsapp; or, The Night-Adventures,* 4to, 1679, since the Epilogue is spoken by Mrs. Currer (Madam Tricklove) and the line

May you all live, till y'are as dull as he

was given "*Pointing to* Oldsapp".

The Epilogue to Shadwell's *The Lancashire Witches,* Dorset Garden, autumn of 1681, was spoken by Mrs. Barry and Anthony Leigh, who acted Tegue. The Epilogue to Mountford's *The Successful Straingers,* Drury Lane, winter of 1689, was "Spoke by Mr. *Nokes,* Mr. *Lee* and Mr. *Mountfort*".

Mr. *Nokes* pulling Mr. *Mountfort.*
Nay, Prithee come forward and ben't so asham'd,
Mr. *Lee.* *Time enough to be sad, when thou'rt sure thy Play's damn'd;*
Nokes. *A Player and bashful, 'tis as senseless I'm sure,*
As that Vizards should swear they come here not to whore,
Lee. *Or that Sharpers won't pay, yet deny they are poor.*

Fourteen lines later Nokes says: *Well, make your Leg.* [Mount. bows to Audi. and Exit.]

In March, 1682, was produced at Dorset Garden Mrs. Behn's *Like Father, like Son; or, The Mistaken Brothers,*[8] an adaptation of Randolph's *The Jealous Lovers.* The Epilogue was spoken by Jevon with the whole company grouped about him, and to several of the actors the lines make direct allusion:—

There's *Joe* and *Jack* a pair of Whining Fools
And *Leigh* and I, Dull, Lavish, Creeping Tools. { Pointing at Mr. *Williams,* Mr. *Wiltshire.*

Bowman's for Mischief all, and carry's on
With Fawn and Sneer, as Gilting Whigg has done,
But like theirs too, his Projects are o'er thrown.
Sweet Mistris *Corall* here has lost her Lover,
Pshaw *English* or *Irish* ground shall find another.

Poor Madam *Butler* too, are you defeated, To Mrs. *Butler.*
You never were before so basely Cheated.
Here Mistris *Petty,* Hah! she's grown a very Woman,
Thou'st got me Child, better me than no man.
Here's Blundering *Richards* is my Huffing Esquire,
Damn me, the best in *England's* for't, d'e hear.
Is that your Cue come nearer, Faith thy Face
Has Features not unlike *Joe Hains's* Grace.
Impudence assist thee, and boldly try
To speak for us, and for the Comedy.

Mr. Richards *Speaks.*

I'le do't Gallants, I'le Justify this Play;
Od Zoons 'tis Good, and if you lik'd you may.

Mistris *Corall* is Berry Currer. Mrs. Petty [9] had joined Dorset Garden in 1676, when she was very young and played the rôles of girls in their earliest teens. Of Richards, Chetwood writes: "Mr. *Ashbury* informed me, that Mr. *Richards* was a very good Actor, both in Tragedy and Comedy, but not over-happy in his personal Appearance."

An earlier play of Mrs. Behn's, *The Amorous Prince; or, The Curious Husband,* produced at Lincoln's Inn Fields in the spring of 1671, 4to, 1671, presents a peculiarity. At the conclusion there is no *Exeunt* but the direction "*Curtain Falls*". The Epilogue is "*Spoken by* Cloris", obviously with all the characters who were on the stage at the end of the Fifth Act remaining in their places, whilst "Guilliam *advances*" to round off the valedictory address with six comic lines and a *double entendre.*

The poets often endeavoured to give an extra spice and savour to their prologues and epilogues by entrusting the delivery of these addresses to a young girl. It appears to have been considered something especially piquant that wanton rhymes should be pronounced by lips which if not innocent were at any rate tender and bland, and a smutty jest was winged with far livelier point if given with seeming simplicity and ingenuous artlessness. The Prologue to Dryden and Howard's *The Indian Queen* was spoken by an Indian Boy and Girl, as we have before remarked, but the dialogue is unexceptionable. Little Mrs. Ariell was famous for imping a poet's sauciest rhymes with the jauntiest élan. Thus she spoke the Epilogue to Mrs. Behn's *Abdelazer; or, The Moor's Revenge,* produced at Dorset Garden during the late autumn of 1676. It commences:—

With late success being blest, I'm come agen;
You see what Kindness can do, Gentlemen,
Which when once shown, our Sex cannot refrain.

Yet spite of such a Censure, I'll proceed,
And for our Poetess will intercede:
Before a Poet's wheedling Words prevail'd,
Whose melting speech my Tender Heart assail'd,
And I the flatt'ring Scribler's Cause maintain'd;
So by my means the Fop Applauses gain'd.

And concludes:—

Your Kindness, Gallants, I shall soon repay,
If you'll but favour my Design to Day:
Your last Applauses, like refreshing Showers,
Made me spring up and bud like early Flow'rs;
Since then I'm grown at least an Inch in height,
And shall e'er long be full-blown for Delight.

The "late success" to which allusion is here made is that of Mrs. Ariell's delivery of the Epilogue to Otway's *Don Carlos, Prince of Spain,* produced at Dorset Garden a few months before *Abdelazer.* When *Don Carlos* was printed, quarto 1676, the Epilogue is given as "Spoken by a Girle".

The Epilogue to Settle's *The Heir of Morocco With the Death of Gayland,* produced at Drury Lane, 11th March, 1682, was "spoken by Mrs. *Coysh's* Girl, as a *Cupid*".

Shadwell commences his *A Lenten* Prologue *refus'd by the Players,* a furious political lampoon which was published 11th April, 1683, with a very frank admission:—

Our Prologue-Wit grows flat, the Nap's worn off;
And howso'ere we turn and trim the Stuff,
The Gloss is gone, that look'd at first so gaudy;
'Tis now no Jest to hear young Girls talk Baudy.

The Epilogue (quoted pp. 172–3) to Banks' *Cyrus the Great; or, The Tragedy of Love* produced at Lincoln's Inn Fields, about the second week of December in 1695, was "spoken by a Boy and Girl, by way of DIALOGUE".

The witty and amusing Prologue to D'Urfey's *The Comical History of Don Quixote,* Part III, Drury Lane, November, 1695, is a duologue between young Hildebrand Horden and Miss Letitia Cross. The Epilogue to Powell's *Bonduca; or, The British Heroine,* Drury Lane, 1695, was "Spoken by Miss *Denny Chock,* But Six Years Old". The following year Denny Chock delivered the Epilogue, written by Joe Haines, to the same author's *The Cornish Comedy,* produced at Dorset Garden. When the play was printed, 4to, 1696, the valedictory address had "Spoken by Miss *Chalke,* Seven Years Old". Two years later she was entrusted with the Epilogue to William Philips' tragedy *The Revengeful Queen.*

Miss Howard did the same service at Lincoln's Inn Fields in 1695 for Dilke's comedy *The Lover's Luck,* archly delivering an epilogue which commences:—

> *What makes our Poet fasten still on me,*
> *To speak the* Exit *of his Poetry?*
> *He tells me, 'tis because he'd finish well,*
> *And Charm your Censures with a Virgin Spell.*

Miss Bradshaw spoke the Epilogues to Mrs. Manley's *The Royal Mischief* at Lincoln's Inn Fields in 1696, and to *The Deceiver Deceiv'd* by Mrs. Pix in the following year. A great favourite, Miss Maria Allison, delivered the Epilogue to Dennis' *A Plot, and No Plot* at Drury Lane in May, 1697. It may be remarked that when Cibber's *Richard III* was produced at Drury Lane late in 1699, probably in December, Miss Allison played the Prince of Wales and Miss Denny Chock the little Duke of York. The taste for these Epilogues did not soon die out, for on the 3rd July, 1703, at Drury Lane when *The Pilgrim* was acted for the benefit of Mrs. Lucas, a new Epilogue was spoken "by the little Girl who played Queen Bess" in Banks' *Anna Bullen.* This was probably Miss Younger, who according to a letter written by Mrs. Saunders the actress to Curll and published in his *History of the Stage,* was born 2nd September, 1699, and made her first appearance on the boards when about seven years old as the little Princess Elizabeth.[10]

Dramatists indeed varied their Epilogues as much as possible to make them novel and attractive. Thus, on Thursday, 26th March, 1668, Pepys went to the first performance of Davenant's *The Man's The Master* at Lincoln's Inn Fields. His comment is: "The play is a translation out of French,[11] and the plot Spanish, but not anything extraordinary at all in it . . . the prologue but poor, and the epilogue little in it but the extraordinariness of it, it being sung by Harris and another in the form of a Ballet." Downes, however, remarks: "This Comedy in general was very well Perform'd, especially, the *Master,* by Mr. *Harris*; the *Man,* by Mr. *Underhill*; Mr. *Harris* and Mr. *Sandford,* Singing the Epilogue like two Street Ballad-Singers." One of the most curious Epilogues was that spoken to Sir Robert Howard's *The Vestal Virgin*; *or, The Roman Ladies,* Theatre Royal, 1664. "Just as the last Words were spoke Mr. *Lacy* enter'd and spoke the *Epilogue,*" which commences:—

> *By your leave, Gentlemen—*
> *After a sad and dismal Tragedy,*
> *I do suppose that few expected me.*

Sir Robert Howard altered the play, and it was " *Acted the Comical Way* ". We then have " *Epilogue* spoken by Mr. *Lacy,* who is suppos'd to enter as intending to speak the Epilogue for the Tragedy ".

> *By your leave, Gentle . . . How! what do I see!*
> *How! all alive! Then there's no use for me.*
> *'Troth, I rejoice you are reviv'd agen;*
> *And so farewel good living Gentlemen.*
> I. *Nay,* Mr. Lacy. La. *What wou'd you have with me?*
> *I can't speak Epilogues* ex tempore.

There is a passage in Davies' *Dramatic Miscellanies* [12] which has often extremely puzzled writers upon Congreve, but which is quite clear when we remember that at the end of a play it was frequently the custom for the actors to remain grouped upon the stage whilst the speaker of the Epilogue advanced or entered, as the case might be. Davies writes: " The Stage, perhaps, never produced four such handsome women, at once, as Mrs. Barry, Mrs. Bracegirdle, Mrs. Mountford, and Mrs. Bowman: when they appeared together in the last scene of the Old Batchelor, the audience was struck with so fine a groupe of beauty, and broke out into loud applauses." Sir Edmund Gosse, referring to this anecdote says [13]: " No doubt the fact is correct, except in one particular: Mrs. Barry had nothing to do on the stage in the last scene. She acted Letitia Fondlewife; but if we replace Mrs. Barry by Mrs. Leigh, the quartet is again complete." No such change is necessary. Mrs. Bracegirdle (Araminta), Mrs. Mountford (Belinda), Mrs. Bowman (Sylvia) were on the stage when Betterton (Heartwell) spoke the last lines, and Mrs. Barry, entering to deliver the Epilogue, completed the quartet of beautiful actresses, although Letitia Fondlewife is not seen after Act IV of the comedy.

Appropriately to deliver a Prologue or Epilogue would require a certain particular quality and verve. Such famous figures as Hart, Mohun, Lacy, Betterton, Smith, Mrs. Marshall, Nell Gwyn, Mrs. Mary Knepp, Mrs. Barry, Lady Slingsby, Anne Quin, were continually entrusted with the delivery of these important addresses to the audience. But there were also other actors and actresses who were great favourites, and who were at least equally applauded for the skill and felicity with which they imped some cynic fleer or dry bawdy bob.

The facetious Joe Haines afforded the theatre endless delight when he came forward to speak a poet's lewder rhymes, or haply some pasquil of his own, for he was extremely adept in this kind of composition. A point is made of this in the Prologue (spoken by Haines) to *A Plot, and No Plot*, the first comedy by John Dennis produced at Drury Lane, 8th May, 1697: This commences :—

> *Do you hear? You Prompter! You may spare your pains,*
> *The Devil shall hearken to you, before* Jo Hains.
> *Whine out your Prologue in your canting tone,*
> *But tell your Poet I shall speak my own.*

Nor was he vastly troubled by notions of respect and decorum, and his arrest on 18th June, 1677, for reciting "a Scurrilous & obscoene Epilogue" was not the only occasion when he gave such offence. This wicked wag, who under James II had loudly professed himself a Catholic, when, after the Revolution, he played Bayes in *The Rehearsal,* came upon the stage "*in a white Sheet with a burning Taper in his Hand*" and uttered a scandalous and profane lampoon, verses such as could only have been penned and pronounced by men who had abandoned the slightest affectation of religion, honour, principle, and common decency. Mrs. Boutell was greatly in request at the Theatre Royal; and Sarah Cook was celebrated for her pointed delivery of saucy and political epilogues. It was to this lady that Dryden entrusted the clever and pointed Epilogue to *The Duke of Guise,* and she also spoke the same author's excellent Epilogue to Lee's *Constantine the Great,* as well as the Prologues upon the first and second days of *Valentinian.* William Mountford and his wife; Charlotte Butler; Thomas Jevon; and above all the fascinating Mrs. Bracegirdle "for Prologues fam'd"; by their talent or their charm saved many a piece whose fate was trembling in the balance.

It would appear that a few decades later the favourite Epilogues were even repeated when the house made this demand. At least *The Spectator,* No. 341, asserts that such was the case with the Epilogue to *The Distrest Mother.* "The Audience would not permit Mrs. *Oldfield* to go off the Stage the first Night till she had repeated it twice: the second Night the Noise of *Ancoras* was as loud as before, and she was again obliged to speak it twice; the third Night it was still called for a second time: and in short, contrary to all other Epilogues, which are drop'd after the third Representation of the Play, this has already been repeated nine times."

Since the curtain did not fall until after the Epilogue had been delivered, and, at the conclusion of a tragedy, it was seldom that two or more of the characters were not left dead upon the stage, it must be inquired how these bodies were removed from the sight of the audience. Incidentally, it should be remarked that the stabbing or poisoning or whatever violent method was employed had taken place down stage upon the apron.

The question then arose how decorously to dispose of the corpses who could not rise up and walk off *coram populo*. The solution was easy; the old system of bearers for the dead was continued, and nobody seemed to regard it as in any way awkward or absurd, indeed it was this circumstance which gave point to the most famous of all Epilogues, that to Dryden's *Tyrannick Love; or, The Royal Martyr,* a tragedy produced at the Theatre Royal, Bridges Street, about the end of June, 1669. In the last act Valeria, the Emperor's daughter, has stabbed herself and expires in true heroic fashion with the lines:—

> "*Porphyrius,* do not swim before my sight;
> Stand still, and let me, let me, aim aright.
> Stand still but while thy poor *Valeria* dies,
> And sighs her Soul into her Lover's Eyes."

At the end, after *Exeunt Omnes* we have the Epilogue, "Spoken by Mrs. *Ellen,* when she was to be carried off dead by the Bearers." Suddenly jumping up she gave one of the men a box on the ear with the words:—

> "*Hold, are you mad? You damn'd confounded Dog,*
> *I am to rise, and speak the Epilogue.*"

Running down to the front of the stage, she directly addressed the theatre:—

> "*I come, kind Gentlemen, strange News to tell ye,*
> *I am the Ghost of poor departed* Nelly."

And after some exceedingly clever verses she wound up with her mock epitaph:—

> "Here *Nelly* lies, who, tho' she liv'd a Slattern,
> Yet dy'd a Princess acting in St. *Cath'rin.*"

retired to where the cercueil was awaiting her, reclined gracefully thereon, and was borne away amid thunders of applause.

In *The Spectator,*[14] 1st April, 1712, reference is made to the persons "Whose Business it is to carry off the Slain in our *English* Tragedies". Although perhaps this was not always possible owing to the business of the scene, a clever dramatist would sometimes adroitly arrange that the dead bodies should be conveyed from the stage before the conclusion. Thus in Nevil Payne's *The Siege of Constantinople,* Dorset Garden, November, 1674, Act V, Irene and Udoxia have been poisoned. Presently *Mutes carry in the Ladies.* In the last act of Congreve's *The Mourning Bride,* the King in a small inner dungeon has not only been slain but in order that the murder may be concealed Alonzo an officer, crying: Who can wound the Dead?

> from the Body
> Sever'd the Head, and in a Corner of
> The Room dispos'd it, muffled in the *Mute's*
> Attire; leaving alone to View, the bloody
> And undistinguishable Trunk.

Zara enters followed by two mutes, who discover the mutilated carcass and expose it to their mistress. *They go to the Scene which opens and shews the Body.* No doubt, as Restoration methods were extremely realistic, a very unpleasant and gory spectacle was here presented. A little later, when Alphonso rescues Almeria, he commands—

> "Let 'em remove the Body from her Sight,"

which served as a cue for the bearers to fulfil their office.

In 1719 was published "The Tragedy of Julius Caesar: With the Death of Brutus and Cassius; Written Originally by Shakespear, And since alter'd by Sir William Davenant and John Dryden late Poets Laureat. As it is now Acted by His Majesty's Company of Comedians at the Theatre Royal". The changes of diction which occur during the first four acts are for the most part simply stupid and impoverishing, but with Act Five the alterations become more serious and even worse. It is safe to say that neither Dryden nor Davenant had anything whatsoever to do with this version which bears every mark of having been tinkered at during the earlier years of the eighteenth century, and to me the thing smells suspiciously of Colley Cibber. However that may be, in Act V when Cassius has slain himself and Brutus uttered his vale over the body:—

> *Enter* Caesars *Ghost.*
> *Ghost.* Cassius, my three and thirty wounds are now reveng'd.

Brutus questions the spectre, who cries:—

> The Ides of March Remember—I must go,
> To meet thee on the burning Lake below.
> [*Sinks.*
> *Brutus.* . . . Come, let's to the field—Flavius, set our
> Battles on—and Romans, yet e're night,
> We shall try fortune in a second fight.
> *Take off* Cassius.
> [*Alarm here. Exeunt.*

Evidently the dead body of Cassius was conveniently borne off by the soldiers.

An episode in the Fifth Act of Southerne's tragedy *The Fate of Capua,* Lincoln's Inn Fields, February, 1699–1700; 4to, 1700; might seem to offer some difficulty. In the second scene of Act V, Virginius' House, Favonia, who has poisoned herself, lies dead, whilst Virginius and Junius, both mortally wounded in a duel, expire but a little after. The last line of Virginius is:—

I've lost my Wife, and Friend, and now my self.

(*Dyes.*

SCENE Pacuvius *House.*

Pacuvius, Vibius Virius, Marius Blosius, *with Seven or Eight Senators rising from a Feast.*

The question then is how were the bodies of Favonia, Virginius, and Junius disposed of, in plain English got off the stage, since if flats closed over in the usual way it would not be possible to make a discovery of characters "*rising from a Feast*". It may be that the flats closed over to reopen almost immediately, simultaneously with the second pair of flats behind which was set the feast, but just giving time for Favonia, Virginius, and Junius to leave the stage. Possibly, if this were a little clumsy, we may take the stage direction to mean *as* rising from a Feast, and the actual banquet was not shown. The scene of Pacuvius's House merely drew over and concealed the bodies.

At the opening of *The Double-Dealer,* Theatre Royal, October, 1693, we have: "*Enter* Careless, *Crossing the Stage, with his Hat, Gloves, and Sword in his Hands; as just risen from Table.*" It may be observed that the commencement of Act II of Shadwell's *The Woman-Captain,* Dorset Garden, 1679, "*Enter Sir* Humphry [*and company*]. *Servants waiting at Dinner,*" is a discovery, two flats being drawn apart to reveal the guests seated at table.

We further remark that in the tragedy *Henry the Second, King of England,* produced at Drury Lane, November, 1692 (attributed to John Bancroft, but published 4to, 1693, with an Epistle Dedicatory by Mountford) Mrs. Bracegirdle acted Fair Rosamund, who poisoned by Queen Eleanor dies in the arms of the King. At the end of this drama all the characters withdrew, and after the bodies had been borne off Mrs. Bracegirdle returned to speak the Epilogue.

It appears that this business of the bearers did not commend itself to at least one important dramatist, the Earl of Orrery, and he contrived other devices for his tragedies, although indeed it is an open question whether his directions were ever put into actual practice in the theatre. In *Mustapha,* Act V, the scene is the Sultan's pavilion, where enters Solyman. Shortly before, his son Mustapha, accused of treason, has been strangled by the bow-string in the inner apartment of the tent. Zanger, his other son, now presents himself at the command of Solyman, who informs him what has happened :—

> Behold then the revenge which I did take
> On him who kept me many Months awake.

The scene opens and shows Mustapha sitting dead on a Couch: at which sight Zanger starts back :—

Zanger. My brother dead? . . .

A few lines later " Zanger goes towards Mustapha ". The printed copies of *Mustapha* curiously enough omit the stage-direction " The scene opens . . ." although they retain " Zanger *goes towards* Mustapha ". Zanger stabs himself and falls at Mustapha's feet. At the exit of the Sultan the scene shuts upon the two dead bodies. I have quoted above from the Bodley MS. (M.S. Rawl. poet. 27, ff. 45, 46).[15]

In Orrery's *Tryphon* the last scene of Act V is the royal chamber in the palace. " Tryphon *goes to an elevated place like a Throne, seats himself in it, then draws a Ponyard,*" stabbing himself to the heart as Nicanor, Demetrius, Aretus, Seleucus, and the Guards break into the room. Soon afterwards the faithful Arcas, who is led in, runs to Tryphon, seizes the bloody dagger, and kills himself, falling at his master's feet. A moment later Cleopatra, Stratonice, Hermione, and Irene enter, having received the news of the tyrant's end. The printed text follows :—

> *Cleopatra.* The news of Tryphon's Death hath brought us here,
> We heard that he by his own Hand did Dye.
> *Seleucus.* See where he now Pale as his Guilt does lye.
> (*They all goe towards the dead Body.*
> *Cleopatra.* This sight at once my Joy and Grief does raise.
> *Stratonice.* 'Tis an ignoble Triumph thus to gaze,
> Sir, let his Body be from hence convey'd;
> He by his Death for all his Crimes has paid.

It might reasonably be adduced that Orrery intended the bearers to enter here and carry off the two dead bodies, and probably this is what actually happened in the theatre. True, there is no direction to that effect, but these particular stage-directions are not always noted. Be that as it may, Orrery suggested a deviation from the general use. In the Bodley MS. of *Tryphon* (Malone MSS. 11) we read :—

> hee by his death for all his crimes has paid.
> {A Curtaine is drawne afore the dead bodyes.}

In the second Bodley MS. (MS. Rawl. poet. 39) of this play, we read:—

he by his death for all his Crimes has paid.

A Curtaine is drawne before Tryphon & Arcas.

It may be remarked that it is obvious Orrery did not here require the stage curtain to fall since *Tryphon,* folio 1669, has at the end of Act V, before the Epilogue,[16] the unusual direction "*The Curtain falls*".

NOTES TO CHAPTER V

[1] For a parody of this and similar conventional exits see the burlesque of the separation of a hero and his mistress in heroic drama by Colley Cibber, at the end of the Third Act of *The Comical Lovers,* as quoted on p. 94. Celadon (Cibber) and Florimel (Mrs. Oldfield), who are standing centre stage, gradually backed with appropriate gesture and looks towards the proscenium doors on either side, through which they darted swift as lightning when the last words were spoken and the music played.

[2] Act I, 8vo, 1717, p. 25.

[3] *The Citizen of the World,* 2 vols, London, 1762; vol. i, Letter XXI, "The Chinese goes to see a play," pp. 76–82.

[4] *Epigrams Of All Sorts.* I. Book. Written by Richard Flecknoe. London, Printed for the Author. 1669, pp. 5–6. In the *Epigrams of All Sorts . . . By Richard Flecknoe,* 1670, p. 43, there are some variations in the text. Here the poem commences:—

Dear Mis,
Who woud not think to see thee dance so light,
Thou wer't all *air,* or else all *soul* and *spirit?*
Or who'd not say, to see thee onely tred,
Thy *feet* were *Feathers,* others *feet* but *lead?*

[5] It may be noted that in the printed quarto, 1667, there is no indication of this jig.

[6] Epilogue, p. 189. That this proceeding—a clear stage for the epilogue—was unusual is shown by the first couplet:—

How contrary soe're to Form—I crave
Humbly to pay my Thanks, and take my leave . . .

[7] See *The Second Volume of the Works of Mr. Tho. Brown,* 1719. Also Tom Brown's *Works,* 1730, vol. iv, p. 313.

[8] Not printed.

[9] Aubrey in his *Brief Lives,* ed. Andrew Clark, 1898, vol. ii, p. 143, tells us that Mrs. Petty was the daughter of Sir William Petty, of whom it is said: "He has a naturall daughter that much resembles him, no legitimate child so much, that acts at the Duke's play-house, who hath had a child by . . . about 1679. She is (1680) about 21."

[10] Since it is quite possible that the date given by Mrs. Saunders is not exact to a year or more. Curll in his theatrical Biographies was often careless and worse.

[11] Of *The Man's the Master* "the Design, and part of the Language is borrow'd from *Scarron's Jodelet, ou Le Maistre Valet*; and (as I remember) part from *L'Heritier ridicule,* a Comedy of the same Authors", as Langbaine does not fail to point out, *English Dramatick Poets,* Oxford, 1691, p. 109.

[12] 1784; vol. iii, p. 391.

[13] *Life of William Congreve,* first edition, 1888, p. 37; second edition, 1924, p. 26.

[14] No. 341; Budgell.

[15] The B.M. MS. (Add MS. 29280) has the same direction.

[16] *Tryphon,* folio 1669, p. 57.

CHAPTER VI

REALISM ON THE STAGE; THE SCENERY

" Il y a donc à Londres trois Troupes d'excellens Comediens ; la Troupe Royale qui jouë tous les iours pour le public, & d'ordinaire tous les Ieudys aprés soupé à Vvitthal: la Troupe de Monsieur Frere vnique du Roy dans la place de Lincolne, qui reüssit admirablement dans la machine, & qui va maintenant du pair auec les Italiens: & vne troisième en Drury-lane, qui a grand abord . . . Il faut ájoûter, Que ces trois Maisons de Londres sont pouruûes de gens bien faits, & sur tout de belles femmes ; Que leurs Theatres sont superbes en decorations & en changemens: Que la Musique y est excellente & les Ballets magnifiques ; Qu'elles n'ont pas moins de douze violons chacune pour les Preludes & pour les Entr-actes ; Que ce seroit vn crime d'employer autre chose que de la cire pour éclairir le Theatre, & de charger les Lustres d'vne matiere qui peut blesser l'odorat ; & enfin, quoy qu'on iouë tous les iours, que ces Maisons ne desemplissent iamais & que cent carrosses en barricadent les áuenues."—SAMUEL CHAPPUZEAU, *L'Europe Vivante,* Genève, 1667, pp. 214–15.

> Now empty shows must want of sense supply,
> Angels shall dance, and *Macbeths* VVitches fly:
> You shall have storms, thunder & lightning too
> And Conjurers raise spirits to your view:
> The upper Gall'rie shall have their desire,
> Who love a Fool, a Devil and a Friar:
> Damn'd Plays shall be adorn'd with mighty Scenes,
> And Fustian shall be spoke in huge Machines:
> And we wil purling streams and fire-works show,
> And you may live to see it rain and snow,
> So Poets save their wit they care not how.

Epilogue to *The Ordinary*. *A Collection of Poems,* 1673, p. 167.

Mention has been made of the realism of the Restoration Theatre, and even Equestrian Spectacle here had its remotest ancestry, as we learn from Pepys, who on Saturday, 11th July, 1668, went to the Theatre Royal " to see an old play of Shirly's called ' Hide Parke ' ; the first day acted ; where horses are brought upon the Stage ". This tradition of realism, especially as regards the exhibition of most gruesome effects, was a legacy from the Elizabethans, whom the later theatre may have equalled but could not possibly have surpassed. In 1668 Chappuzeau, being in England, paid a visit to Lincoln's Inn Fields where he saw a performance of Orrery's *Mustapha.* The title-rôle was played by Henry Harris. In the fifth Act, "*Enter six Mutes, one of them advances before the rest and kneels down, delivers* Mustapha *a black Box with a Parchment, the* Sultan'*s Great Seal hanging at it in a black Ribband. Then he holds up a Bow-string, and makes signs that he should kneel and submit to the* Sultan'*s sentence.*" The Prince, however, wishes to justify himself, and refuses to obey until he has had the opportunity of doing this. The executioners deny: "*The Mutes draw their Scemitars and assault him; he draws too and kills two of them.*" Chappuzeau was extremely struck by the realism of the scene, and he especially notes the energy of Mustapha, "Qui se defendoit vigoureusement sur le Theatre contre les muets qui le vouloient étrangler." [1]

Voltaire, who, it may be remembered, himself sought to remedy the classical coldness of French tragedy by such inventions as the red robes of the senators in *Brutus* and the firing of a cannon in *Adélaïde,* writing to George, Lord Lyttelton emphasizes the brutality of English dramas: "Y^r^ nasion two hundred years since is us'd to a wild scene, to a croud of tumultuous events, . . . to murtherss, to a lively representation of bloody deeds, to a kind of horrour which seems often barbarous and childish, all faults which never sullyed the greak, the roman, or the french Stage; and give me leave to say that the taste of y^r^ politest countrymen in point of tragedy differs not much in point of tragedy from the taste of a mob at Bear-garden." [2]

Before we more particularly consider the realistic presentation of tragedy in the Restoration theatre it will not be impertinent to observe that even the racier scenes of comedy were given with a breadth and a vigour which would, I apprehend, be infinitely surprising to a modern audience. When that capital play *The Luckey Chance; or, An Alderman's Bargain* was censured on account of its easy freedom, Mrs. Behn defended herself stoutly in the preface which she wrote for the printed text, 4to, 1687, and it is plain that the mettle and gusto of the action had much to do with the cavilling and dispraise. After some reference to the witty and conceited sparks who have cried out upon her, she continues: "When it happens that I challenge any one, to point me out the least Expression of what some have made their Discourse, they cry, *That Mr.* Leigh *opens his Night Gown, when he comes into the Bride-chamber*; if he do, which is a Jest of his own making, and which I never saw, I hope he has his Cloaths on underneath? And if so, where is the Indecency? I have seen in that admirable Play of *Oedipus,* the Gown open'd wide, and the Man shown in his Drawers and Waist coat, and never thought it an Offence before. Another crys, *Why we know not what they mean, when the Man takes a Woman off the Stage, and another is thereby cuckolded*; is that any more than you see in the most Celebrated of your Plays? as the *City Politicks,* the *Lady Mayoress,* and the *Old Lawyer's Wife* who goes with a Man she never saw before, and comes out again the joyfull'st Woman alive, for having made her Husband a Cuckold with such Dexterity, and yet I see nothing unnatural nor obscene: 'tis proper for the Characters. So in that lucky Play of the *London Cuckolds,* not to recite Particulars. And in that good Comedy of *Sir Courtly Nice,* the *Taylor to the young Lady*—in the fam'd Sir *Fopling Dorimant* and *Bellinda,* see the very Words—in *Valentinian,* see the Scene between the *Court Bawds.* And *Valentinian* all loose and ruffld a Moment after the Rape, and all this you see without Scandal, and a thousand others, The *Moor of Venice* in many places. The *Maids Tragedy*—see the scene of undressing the Bride, and between the *King* and *Amintor,* and after between the *King* and *Evadne*— All these I Name as some of the best Plays I know; If I should repeat the Words exprest in these Scenes I mention, I might justly be charg'd with course ill Manners, and very little Modesty, and yet they so naturally fall into the places they are designed for, and are so proper to the Business, that there is not the least Fault to be found with them."

Owing to the inebriety of Powell, a notorious tippler, at the *première* of Vanbrugh's *The Relapse; or, Virtue in Danger,* produced on 21st November, 1696, at Drury Lane, scandal was but narrowly escaped. In the Preface to the printed play[3] Vanbrugh writes: "I own the first night this thing was acted, some indecencies had like to have happen'd, but 'twas not my Fault. The fine Gentleman of the Play, drinking his Mistress's Health in *Nants* Brandy, from six in the morning, to the time he wadled on upon the Stage in the Evening, had toasted himself up, to such a Pitch of Vigor, I confess I once gave *Amanda* for gone and am since (with all due Respect to Mrs. *Rogers*) very sorry she scap't; for I am confident a certain Lady (let no one take it to herself that is handsome) who highly blames the Play, for the barrenness of the conclusion, wou'd then have allowed it, a very natural Close."

When Mrs. Behn's *The Rover; or, The Banish'd Cavaliers,* Part I, was revived at Covent Garden on 19th February, 1757, Shuter who acted Blunt exactly followed the old realistic traditions and in Act III as the business requires during the scene in Lucetta's bed-chamber he undressed to his very shirt and drawers. Moreover in the following episode which "*discovers* Blunt *creeping out of a Common Shore, his Face, &c., all dirty*", he resorted to the original methods and covered himself with chawed gingerbread, an unsavoury and sufficiently curious artifice.

The machines and many devices for producing illusion of sounds which were well known in the Elizabethan theatre passed as a popular heritage to the Restoration Stage. They were indeed a legacy from the miracle plays themselves. Stage pyrotechnics in Jacobean times were already developed to a fine point, and in spectacular dramas such as Heywood's quinary Red Bull series [4] *The Golden Age, The Silver Age, The Brazen Age,* and the two parts of *The Iron Age* startling effects were demanded, such as "Thunder, lightnings, Iupiter descends in his maiesty, his Thunderbolt burning"; "Fire-workes all over the house"; "a shower of raine"; "Medea with strange fiery-workes, hangs above in the Aire in the strange habite of a Coniuresse." In *The Second Maiden's Tragedy*; "On a sodayne in a kinde of Noyse like a Wynde, the dores clattering, the Toombstone flies open, and a great light appeares in the midst of the Toombe." Ben Jonson in a Prologue to *Every Man In His Humour,* first printed in the folio of 1616, and probably written for a Jacobean revival, jeers at the theatrical tricks, and takes pride that in his play—

> Nor nimble squibbe is seen, to make afear'd
> The gentlewomen; nor roul'd bullet heard
> To say, it thunders; nor tempestuous drumme
> Rumbles, to tell you when the storme doth come;
> But deedes, and language, such as men doe vse . . .

In many Restoration plays we meet various indications of atmospheric effects, and it is certain that owing to their study of Italian, and even more particularly of French, theatrical mechanism, Killigrew, Davenant, and Betterton would have improved upon and elaborated the old Elizabethan way. In such a tragedy as Nevil Payne's *The Siege of Constantinople,* Dorset Garden, November, 1674, Act III, we have the direction "*Noise of a Storm*". When in Crowne's *Thyestes,* Drury Lane, spring of 1681, at the Atrean banquet Thyestes quaffs the vast bowl of wine which is the blood of his own son, "*a Clap of Thunder, the Table oversets and falls in pieces; all the Lights go out.*" Towards the conclusion of the Second Act of Nahum Tate's *The History of King Lear,* Dorset Garden, September, 1680, there is the stage direction *Lightning and Thunder,* and eight lines after, *Thunder again.* The Duke of Cornwall concludes the Act with a line slightly varied from Shakespeare: "'Tis a wild Night, come out o' th' Storm." The opening of Act III in Tate is: "Scene

A Desert Heath. Enter Lear *and* Kent *in the Storm*." At the end of the scene we have "Loud *Storm*". There is a change to Gloster's Palace, and after this Scene III commences: "*Storm still. The Field Scene. Enter* Lear *and* Kent." It may be noted that later in the play we have the Field Scene in fair weather. In Davenant's alteration of *Macbeth* the three witches during Act I are heralded by *Thunder and Lightning*, whilst when Hecate appears there is *Thunder*. These effects were parodied in the extraordinary Epilogue, a burlesque of the supernatural scenes in *Macbeth*, which followed Duffett's farce, *The Empress of Morocco* produced at Drury Lane in the winter of 1673. The Scene opens: "Thunder and lightning is discover'd, not behind Painted Tiffany to blind and amuse the Senses, but openly, by the most excellent way of Mustard-bowl and Salt-Peter." The old story about John Dennis will be readily remembered. He had invented a far better way than the traditional mustard-bowl of producing the illusion of stage thunder, and the new method was accordingly employed for the first time at the production at Drury Lane of his dull tragedy *Appius and Virginia*, on 5th February, 1709. The piece expired on the fourth day. A little later when Dennis was in the pit at a performance of *Macbeth* he was astounded to hear the rolling of his thunder. Starting to his feet in a fury he cried: "Look you, these damned rascals will not act my plays and yet they steal my thunder!"[5] A note upon the *Dunciad*, ii, 225–6, has: "The old way of making Thunder and Mustard was the same, but since, it is more advantageously performed by troughs of wood with stops in them. Whether Mr. Dennis was the inventor of that improvement, I know not; but it is certain, that being once at a Tragedy of a new author, he fell into a great passion at hearing some, and cried, "S'death! that is *my* Thunder."[6]

In Tate's *Brutus of Alba; or, The Enchanted Lovers*, Dorset Garden, early summer of 1678, the sorceress Ragusa raises foul weather, "The storm's on wing, comes poud'ring from the Nore," and during the royal chase "a dark Storm gathers. *Lightning and Thunder*". Ragusa appears in the Storm, and shrieks: "I, this is Musick! . . . Ha! art thou there my Melancholy Sister?" *An Owl cries*. This too-whit, too-whoo was thus plainly heard above the din and fury of the tramontane. John Bate in his *The Mysteries of Nature and Art* (2nd edition, London, 1635) speaks of instruments and pipes whereby the song of birds and the hoot of the owl could be exactly imitated. In Shadwell's *The Lancashire Witches*, the beldames at their infernal rites "*cry like Screetch Owls, hollow like Owls*". During the

THE INTHRONIZATION OF QUEEN MARY OF MODENA

[*face p.* 192

Incantation Scena in *Der Freischütz*, produced at the Lyceum on Thursday, 22nd July, 1824, according to the libretto 1825, an owl sitting on a withered tree opens and shuts its eyes and flaps its wings during the chorus of Invisible Spirits. When Zamiel is seen the bird vanishes.

The storm at sea with which opens the Third Act of Shadwell's favourite *The Libertine*, as produced at Dorset Garden in June, 1675, was without a doubt most realistically presented. The Captain of the Ship exclaims: "Such dreadful claps of Thunder I never yet remember'd . . . The Heav'ns are all on fire." A few moments later "*A Thunder-clap strikes* Don John *and* Jacomo *down*". At the conclusion when the doom of the three profligate wretches is about to fall upon them, "*It Thunders,* Don Lopez *and* Don Antonio *are swallow'd up*." A few moments later after the defiance of Don John "*It Thunders and Lightens, Devils descend and sink with* Don John, *who is cover'd with a Cloud of fire as he sinks*". To top the first Sabbat Scene in Shadwell's *The Lancashire Witches,* Dorset Garden, autumn of 1681, the hags raise a magic tempest. *The Storm begins,* and during their Song of Three Parts we have the stage direction "*It Thunders and Lightens*" thrice repeated.[7]

Whether there was any attempt to simulate rain is doubtful. Perhaps the "fierce hail of pease" which Pope mentions in *The Dunciad*[8] was employed. Settle in *The Empress of Morocco,* Dorset Garden, 3rd July, 1673, IV, 2, has: "*The Scene open'd is presented a Prospect of a Clouded Sky, with a Rain bow. After a shower of Hail enter from within the Scenes* Muly Hamet *and* Abdelcador." The shower fell within the curtain line, and attention is drawn to it by Muly Hamet:—

> Such Storms as these the Climate never knew:
> A show'r of Hail's an Object strange and new.

In the accounts of an old miracle play *The Day of Judgement* an item runs: "Payd for starche to meke the storm . . . vi*d*." One suspects that something similar was used in Settle's drama for the hailstones.

In Act V of *The Lancashire Witches,* when the witches are abroad, we have "*Thunder softly here*", and a minute later: "*Thunder and Lighten*." "Here's a great Storm arising," says Tom Shacklehead. Indeed Shadwell is very lavish with his fulminations and his gales but then, as Downes points out, *The Lancashire Witches* was "A kind of Opera", and an opera in Restoration days must always be a crowded vehicle for every sort of elaborate stage effect. Thus, when Circe in Charles Davenant's opera of the same name (Dorset Garden, May, 1677) summons her spirits it thunders terribly and, in the Fifth Act, we have an almost continual battle of the elements. Such directions as the following appear in quick succession: "*Storm within, Thunder, &c.; Thunder again; Storm here; Storm and Lightning; Loud Storm; It Thunders; Darts of Lightning, Thunder; Thunder and Lightning here; Horrid musick. It Thunders; The Stage is wholly darken'd, and the City of a sudden is a Fire; It Thunders.*" But perhaps the most popular of all dramatic operas, that is to say *The Tempest; or, The Enchanted Island* was also the most rackety and reboant. Shadwell's version commences with a Scene, "*which represents a thick Cloudy Sky, a very Rocky Coast, and a Tempestuous Sea in perpetual Agitation . . . And when the Ship is sinking, the whole House is darken'd, and a shower of Fire falls upon 'em. This is accompanied with Lightning, and several Claps of Thunder, to the end of the Storm.*" The frontispiece to *The Tempest* in Rowe's Shakespeare, 1709, so exactly represents the scene as described in detail by Shadwell that there can be little doubt it was drawn from the actual stage setting of the time rather than from Shakespeare's unadulterated text. That the confusion and the bellow of this opening greatly impressed the audience, is obvious from an allusion in an anonymous poem *The Country Club*, 4to, 1679:—

> Such noise, such stink there was you'd swear
> The *Tempest* surely had been acted there.
> The cryes of Star-board, Lar-board, cheerly boys,
> Is but as demy rattles to this noise.

Many more examples and details might be added to show that illusions of sound were common and popular in the Restoration play-houses, but probably sufficient evidence has been advanced, and we may now turn to one or two other particulars of staging which serve to illustrate actual conditions in the theatre of the day.

An interesting, if minor, detail is suggested by a stage direction in Tuke's *The Adventures of Five Hours*, Lincoln's Inn Fields, 8th January, 1663. We are walking in a garden, and "*The Rising Moon appears in the scene*". There is no doubt that the effect of moonlight was actually simulated, for Octavio says:—

> 'Twill not be long,
> Now that the Rising Moon lends us some light.

A moonlight effect upon the stage is certainly one of the loveliest and by no means the most difficult.

Although perhaps there are not many definite directions to be traced it seems certain that moonlight was simulated by means of transparencies on the Restoration Stage. In Mrs. Behn's posthumous *The Widdow Ranter; or, The History of Bacon in Virginia,* Drury Lane, November, 1689, Act V opens with: "*The* Sevana *in sight of the Camp; the Moon rises.*" In Orrery's *The Tragedy of King Saul,* 4to, 1703, but written at least twenty-five years before, in Act IV, we have: "Several great Clouds appear, the Moon partly seen." If it be argued that this play was never performed we may at least say that it was written for actual production and the stage-directions are eminently practical. Another interesting scene in Act IV is Saul's camp, "Thro' a dark Scene several lights are discovered at a distance." Act III of Mountford's comedy *Greenwich-Park,* Drury Lane, 1691, commences: "Scene I. *The Park. The Moon: Enter* Dorinda *and* Aunt." "Has not the Clock struck Eleven yet?" asks Dorinda. A few moments later young Reveller appears, and not only are his first words "'Tis a fine Moon-shine Night", but he thus freely apostrophizes the chaste Cynthia: "Shine out thou Pale-fac'd Bawd to Midnight Wooers; blush, if thou canst, to make thy Flame more chearful, for I will do a Deed, if she will let me, shall make thy Cheeks glow, little *Luna,* and wish instead of lighting the World, thou wer't in her Condition of Peopling it."

The mock inventory of "the Moveables of *Ch—r R—ch,* Esq.", published in *The Tatler,* Number 42, 16th July, 1709, has an item: "A new Moon something decay'd."

In the operatic *The Fairy-Queen,* Dorset Garden, April, 1692, Act IV, we have a truly magnifical dawn: "*A Sonata plays while the Sun rises, it appears red through the Mist, as it ascends it dissipates the Vapours, and is seen in its full Lustre; then the Scene is perfectly discovered.*" Act II of the same opera begins: "SCENE *a Wood, by Moon-light.*" Settle in his opera *The World in the Moon,* Dorset Garden, 1697, calls for the most ornate and elaborate mechanism. During the First Act: "*a Circular part of the back Clouds rolls softly away, and gradually discovers a Silver Moon, near Fourteen Feet Diameter: After which, the Silver Moon wanes off by degrees, and discovers the World within, consisting of Four grand Circles of Clouds, illustrated with* Cupids, etc." *Arsinoe, Queen of Cyprus,* the opera adapted by Motteux from Stanzani's *Arsinoe,* and produced at Drury Lane, 16th January, 1705, opens with "Arsinoe *Sleeping in a Garden. The Time Night, the Moon Shining*".

When at the conclusion of Mrs. Behn's *The Emperor of the Moon* Cinthio appeared in a chariot, made like a silver crescent, I have no doubt that some device was employed such as graced Jonson's masque of *Oberon the Fairy Prince* (1611) where the moon rose above the horizon and by its argent ray revealed the satyr. Even if one were to seek to press Gravelot's illustration to Dryden's *The Assignation* into the argument as an actual drawing from the stage, since the latest revival of this comedy during the eighteenth century seems to have been that of 1744, it would of course be observed that his picture is sixty years later than the original production, but I am not altogether certain whether this mutual recognition of Aurelian and Laura does not represent the scene pretty much as it was played by Hart and Mrs. Boutell. True Aurelian's costume is that of 1730; but I suspect the background, a garden at night with terraces and shadowed trees seen through an arch, whilst a new moon rides high in the heavens, to be little different from the painted flats the actors used in 1672.

In the same way when both Shakespeare's Lorenzo and Granville's Lorenzo whispered each to his several Jessica:—

> "The Moon shines bright. In such a Night as this . . ."

the lovers in the Belmont garden were bathed in silver radiance. When "The most lamentable comedy, and most cruel death of Pyramus and Thisby" was acted by Quince's company the question how to bring moonlight into a chamber greatly exercised the producer, until he settled that "one must come in with a bush of thorns and a lanthorn, and say he comes to disfigure, or to present the person of Moonshine"; in which rôle Starveling, the tailor, shone with a good grace. That Shakespeare was laughing at some clumsy presentation of moonlight in the theatre does not admit of doubt. Again, it is hardly possible that in Dekker's old play *If it be not Good, the Devil is in it,* when the Sub-Prior begins his speech "Blest Star of light . . ." there was not some reflection of rays and beams, although actually we have no stage direction and there is no mention of the moon in the text. A similar effect must have been produced in Act IV, Scene 3, of *The Second Maidens Tragedy* (1611), when the Tyrant pacing the Cathedral aisle murmurs:—

> "O, the moon rises! What reflection
> Is thrown upon this sanctified building,
> E'en in a twinkling! How the monuments glister
> As if death's palaces were all massy silver,
> And scorn'd the name of marble."

Several elaborate effects of lighting were introduced into this play, and it hardly seems likely that one which was so important, so emphasized, and so easily wrought should have been here omitted.

Upon the Elizabethan stage vision scenes were very frequently introduced by the dramatists who ever had their fingers upon the popular pulse, and the dream, actually presented, proved an equal favourite in the Restoration Theatre. The vision scenes in *Cymbeline* and *Henry VIII* will at once occur to the mind, whilst reference might also be made to Massinger's *The Roman Actor*; Brome's *The Queen's Exchange; The Atheist's Tragedy,* and very many other plays.

In the later theatre, to name but a few dramas which introduce similar visions, we have Dryden and Sir Robert Howard's *The Indian-Queen,* Theatre Royal, January, 1664; Crowne's *The History of Charles the Eighth,* Dorset Garden, November, 1671; the same author's *The Destruction of Jerusalem,* Part I, Drury Lane, January, 1677, where the ghost of Herod appears to the sleeping Sanhedrin; and *Thyestes,* Drury Lane, spring of 1681, which opens amid claps of thunder to show the tortured ghost of Tantalus and the fury Megæra perturbing with their horrid presence the evil dreams of slumbering Atreus; Lee's *The Tragedy of Nero,* Theatre Royal, May, 1674, Act IV, Scene 4, "Nero *sleeping in a Couch,* Caligula's *Ghost appears*"; *The Rival Queens,* Theatre Royal, March, 1677, when the spirits of her father and mother appear to Statira who "*is discover'd sleeping in the Bower of Semiramis*"; *Constantine the Great,* Theatre Royal, winter of 1683, which commences thus: "Constantine *sleeping in a Pavilion,* Silvester *standing at distance, two Angels descend with Banners in their Hands.* This Motto, *In hoc signo vince,* writ in Gold"; *The Massacre of Paris,* Theatre Royal, October, 1689, Act V, where the Genius appears to King Charles IX; Otway's *Alcibiades,* Dorset Garden, September, 1675, the scene of an Elyzium; and above all the famous episode in Dryden's *Tyrannick Love,* which was produced at Drury Lane, about the end of June, 1669. In Act IV we have the vision of Saint Catherine. By the magic of Nigrinus the Saint is shown asleep in her bed, and "*A* Scene *of a Paradise is discovered*". Placidius cries:—

> "Some pleasing Objects do her Mind employ;
> For on her Face I read a wandering Joy."

Nakar, Damilcar, and other spirits throng around only to be dispersed by the descent of the Guardian Angel of Saint Catherine, Amariel, who appears in glory and in radiant flame. It is remarkable that this scene of Paradise was the cause of a Chancery Suit. Isaac Fuller the painter brought an action against Hart and Mohun to recover payment for his work,[9] and in fine he was awarded £335 10*s*., which in consideration of the proportional value of money at that time seems an enormous sum, particularly as this scene in Dryden's drama was only used during the vision. However that may be, it took mightily with the Town for the Duke of Buckingham did not neglect prominently to parody this episode of the spirits in *The Rehearsal*.

At the commencement of Act III of Orrery's tragedy *Herod the Great*, folio 1694, probably unacted, Herod is shown us asleep, and during his dream the ghosts of Hircanus and Aristobulus appear attended by various other spectres who "*dance Antick Dances*". In the same author's unpublished and unacted *The Tragedy of Zoroastres*,[10] Act II opens as follows: "The scene drawn Oroandes is discouer'd laying asleep uppon a Couch." A vision appears of the Temple of Cupid, who descends "with 2 darts in his hand, one of Jealousey, ye other of despair, hee goes round Oroandes at last sticks 'em both in him". A song is given for Cupid "How sweet is revenge to our Godship above", and in his dream Oroandes sees Polynice, smiling and beautiful.

Episodes which gave unusual opportunity for much bustle and business upon the stage and for striking spectacular effects were scenes of conflagrations, when a house, a street, or even a whole town was set ablaze. In this twentieth century the stage has borrowed from science, and the most realistic illusions of fire can be given without the introduction of the element itself, and without risk, but in former days it must have been a dangerous business, and in some cases, it is difficult to see how it was managed at all. We have some fairly late but valuable evidence, for in the Tonson Beaumont and Fletcher of 1711 is an illustration of the famous scene in Act II of *The Island Princess*, which represents the capital of Ternata in flames. It will be found in volume vi at p. 3005. Obviously the flats are painted with a city bursting into flames and a frenzied crowd of the inhabitants in various attitudes of horror and dismay. On the stage itself the characters rush wildly to and fro and by their piercing cries and woeful gestures, create an illusion of stampeding terror before the background of the panorama. It may be remembered that on 7th January, 1669, Pepys who saw this play was particularly struck by "a good scene of a town on fire". The presentation of the naval engagement in *The Double Marriage* was arranged in precisely the same manner. (See Beaumont and Fletcher, 1711, vol. v, p. 2427.)[11] On the flats two galleons are depicted in a confusion of flame and smoke; whilst upon the stage itself the Master, Boatswain, Gunner, and sailors are shouting their commands and hallooing courage as the wide-mouthed cannons sing and trumpets blare. Elkanah Settle's *The Siege of Troy*, a Bartholomew Fair droll (1707), has a town on fire with "*near forty Windows or Port holes*" spreading the blaze "*from House to House*" and "*all performed by Illuminativations and transparent Paintings seen scatter'd thro' the Scenes*".[12]

Amongst other plays in which conflagrations find a place we have Sir Robert Howard's *The Vestal Virgin; or, The Roman Ladies,* Theatre Royal, 1664, "Act III. Scene 1. *The* Scene *appears a Burning house.*"

Enter Artabaces.

Artab. What Noise is this!—How!— [*Noise.*
A House in Flames!

Also Settle's *Love and Revenge,* Dorset Garden, 1674, "Act the Third. *After* [*Fire*] *cryed, Enter* Clotair, Nigrello, Lords *and* Guards:—

Nigr. Look how it flames, I fear some Treachery:
Beat at her Chamber door, cry it aloud,
And let your voyce be Thunder to this Lightning.
Guards. Fire, Fire.

The Queen enters above, and calls: "What art thou?

Clot. Look!
The fire will give you light; 'tis I, your Son.
Fly from that Chamber or you're lost: The Court
Is all on Fire.
Queen. . . . Curse on this blazing light.

It is evident that the flames were contrived to blaze and glare amain. We have already remarked the spectacular scenes of fire in Charles Davenant's *Circe* and in other operas. In Shadwell's *The Libertine,* Dorset Garden, June, 1675, Don John amongst other atrocities commits arson and fires a convent, and in a moment the place is full of people and as light as day. Crowne concluded his Second Part of *The Destruction of Jerusalem,* Theatre Royal, January, 1677, with the burning of the Temple immediately before the sentimental parting of Titus and Berenice; Banks in *The Destruction of Troy,* Dorset Garden, 1678, has: "Scene *opens, and discovers* Troy *Burning,*" a final tableau which was probably not very unlike the town aflame in *The Island Princess* at the other house. There is a very sensational scene of fire in Settle's *The Female Prelate,* Theatre Royal, 1679. Two heretics set fire to the prison in order to obtain their escape.

1. *Heretic.* this night,
This dead dark hour, the Prison's to be fired . . .
2. *Her.* Most excellent!
1. *Her.* And by this happy Plot
'Tis possible some of us may escape . . .
Bernardo, look, yon dauning streaks of light
Tell us the happy Train has taken fire . . .

It may be remembered that in *Justine* (chapitre iii) la Dubois gains her freedom with Justine by the same device. "Entre sept et huit heures, poursuivit-elle, le feu prendra à la conciergerie: c'est l'ouvrage de mes soins . . . Le feu prit; l'incendie fut horrible; il y eut soixante personnes de brûlées. Mais Justine, la Dubois, et ses complices se sauvèrent." The following episode in *The Female Prelate,* points to some very realistic illusion—*The Third Scene is the Duke of* Saxony'*s Bed-chamber within the Prison. Enter* Saxony *in his Night-gown as newly risen from Bed.*

Sax. Good Heav'n! what misty damp disturbs my sleep?
Sulphur and Pitch? What poysonous smoaky stench
Offends my aking Eyes?
Within. Fire! fire! fire!
Sax. Horrour and Death! the place is all on fire! . . .
Within. Fire! fire! fire!
Sax. By Heav'ns, we are almost circled in with flames!

Whether here they really misted the stage with fume it would be hazardous dogmatically to decide, but in my opinion such actually was the case. The effect is easy, and it is hardly possible that it would have been omitted. It was employed on the Elizabethan Stage, and in the Gray's Inn Masque of 3rd January, 1594–5 there was "troubled smoke and dark vapour". In *The Maid's Tragedy,* an extremely popular play under the Restoration, at the wedding masque "Night rises in mists", and in *The Triumph of Honour* (*Four Plays in One, circa* 1619–1625) there is a direction "Solemn music, a mist ariseth, the rocks remove". In the dumb show which introduces the Fourth Act of *The Prophetess,* licensed May, 1622, Delphia raises "a foggy mist". When *The Prophetess* was turned into an opera, Dorset Garden, June, 1690, Delphia in her relation to Drusilla refers to this mist but it is not visualized. A few spirals of smoke would have added no mean touch to the tumult and disorder in Settle's melodramatic episode. Steele in *The Spectator,* No. 14, Friday, 16th March, 1711, writes humorously of the effects in *Rinaldo and Armida,* produced at the Haymarket, 24th February, 1711: "We had also but a very short Allowance of Thunder and Lightning; tho' I cannot in this Place omit doing justice to the Boy who had the Direction of the two painted Dragons and made them spit Fire and Smoke: He flash'd out his Rosin in such just Proportions and in such due Time, that I could not forbear conceiving Hopes of his being one Day a most excellent Player. I saw indeed but Two things wanting to render his whole Action compleat, I mean the keeping his Head a little lower, and hiding his Candle."

In comedy, as we might suppose, scenes of fire are infrequent, but such an effect is introduced in Mrs. Behn's posthumous *The Younger Brother; or, The Amorous Jilt,* ushered on to the stage by Gildon in December, 1696. Scene III of Act III shows "*A Garden by Night*". An alarm of Fire is given: "*Enter Lady* Blunder *in her Night-Gown.*" She shrieks: "Fire! Fire! Fire!" Servants run in and out carrying trunks from the house; Manage cries "Oh Heavens! My Lady *Mirtilla's* Chamber's all on Flame". At this point there must have been a blaze of light at the balcony, for "*Prince* Frederick *and* Mirtilla *appear at the Window, the Flame behind 'em*". A ladder is hastily brought and the lady rescued, the Prince descending immediately after her.

It has already been emphasized that the Elizabethans literally revelled in scenes of death and torture; they demanded the crudest realism; real blood must be used, the blood of sheep or calves, and it must flow in a thick slab stream. Their nerves were strong as whip-cord, and they thoroughly enjoyed an accumulation of horrors which have revolted and sickened later generations. In this respect there was little to choose between a Restoration and an Elizabethan audience. The playhouse, as we have seen, on occasion became the arena of fierce brawls and the deadly duello; it was not for folk to shrink from mimic murder on the boards when mortal frays were waging in the pit.

Before the so-called Reformation there was annually presented at Canterbury on the day of the Saint's Martyrdom, 29th December, "the pagent of St. Thomas," and various items connected therewith are to be found among the records of the Corporation's expenses from 1504–5 until "far on in the reign of Queen Elizabeth". In the earlier years we may note the following: "For two bagges of leder: For payntyng of the awbe and the hedde; For the hyre of a sworde: For wasshynge of an albe and an amys." In later years are recorded: "Pro le yettyng sanguynem: Pro le payntyng capitis Sci Thomae: For a new leder bag for the blode: For Wasshyng of the albe and other clothys abowte the Auter, and settyng on agayn the apparell." [13] Until 1529 the pageant stood in the barn of S. Sepulchre's convent; thereafter in a convenient place in the archiepiscopal palace. In 1536–7 the piece was suppressed for a decade and a half, but happily revived under Queen Mary I. Whether dialogue was spoken or whether it was a dumb-show, this pageant evidently represented in realistic action the Martyrdom of S. Thomas. The "leder bag" would have been a bladder filled with blood which when the Saint was struck across the head by the knight's sword was suddenly pricked or burst by some adroit prestidigitation, so that the contents gushed out red over the amice and alb of the Martyr, also apparently sprinkling the linen altar-cloths. Accordingly we find that these together with the alb must needs be laundered, and for this washing the rich broidered apparel was untacked from the *caputium* (head opening) of the alb and afterwards sewn on again in its place.

Similar devices for a flow of blood were employed on the Elizabethan stage, and the contrivance persisted. The more manageable sponge took the place of a bag or bladder, a trick yet in use when required, and of most ghastly effect, although to-day red paint or some water deftly cochinealed is preferred to actual blood. The horror of a scene in *Sweeny Todd* still lives fresh in my memory, when the demon-barber drew his razor with terrific force across the white throat of Mrs. Loveit, and as he leaped back the lady's fair skin seemed to be streaming with blood that welled from a deep crimson gash. Very pertinent are two stage directions to be found in a couple of Killigrew's plays, *The Princess; Or, Love at First Sight,* folio, 1663; and *Thomaso; Or, The Wanderer* (Part I), folio, 1663; both included in the *Comedies and Tragedies,* folio, with general title-page, 1664. In *The Princess,* IV, 10, is a marginal note: "Bragadine *shoots,* Virgil *puts his hand to his eye, with a bloody spunge and the blood runs down.*" The ninth scene of the Fifth Act of *Thomaso* (Part I) is a darkened bedchamber, and a grand scuffle is in progress. "Edwardo *strikes him, and they cuff in the Bed;* Edwardo *throws him down, there they cuff and struggle upon the floore, and are both bloody, occasion'd by little spunges ty'd of purpose to their middle fingers in the palmes of their hands.*" [14] In Dryden's dramatic opera *King Arthur; or, The British Worthy,* Dorset Garden, spring of 1691, the stage direction for the combat between Arthur and Oswald is: "*They Fight with Spunges in their Hands dipt in Blood; after some equal Passes and Closeing, they appear both Wounded.*" A little earlier in the enchanted wood when about to fell the magic oak, Arthur *strikes at the Tree, and cuts it; Blood spouts out of it, a Groan follows, then a shreik:—*

> Good Heav'ns, what Monstrous Prodigies are these!
> Blood follows from my blow; the Wounded Rind
> Spouts on my Sword, and Sanguine dies the Plain.
>
> [*He strikes again: A Voice of* Emmeline *from behind. Em. from behind.*]
>
> Forbear, if thou hast Pity, ah forbear!
> These Groans proceed not from a Senceless Plant,
> No Spouts of Blood run welling from a Tree . . .
>
> [Emmeline *breaks out of the tree, shewing her Arm Bloody.*

There are realistic scenes of the gallows. In *A Warning for Faire Women,* 1599, "*Enter maister Browne to execution with the Sherriffe and Officers.*" There is some dialogue; he mounts the ladder to the triple tree, and "*leapes off*":—

Enter a Messenger.

Messen. It is the Councels pleasure master Shiriff
The bodie be conuaide to Shooters hill,
And there hung up in Chaines.
Shiriff. It shal be done.

We have the gossip of Tom Peart and Will Crow, "*two Carpenters under Newgate*", who are setting up a gibbet "a swinger". Robert Yarington in his *Two Lamentable Tragedies* (4to, 1601) spares us no pitiable and distressing detail. "*Enter* Merry *and* Rachel *to execution with Officers with Halberdes, the Hangman with a lather, &c.*" Merry goes up the ladder, and after his dying speech, "*Turne of the Lather*; Rachel *shrinketh.*"

Officer. Nay shrinke not woman, haue a cheerefull heart.

She also climbs, utters a pathetic lamentation, and "*Dyeth*".

In the anonymous *Edward the Fourth,* Part II (1599; 4to, 1600) which is by practically all authorities assigned to Heywood, towards the conclusion, "Jocky *is led over the stage to be whipt. Then* Ayre *is brought forth to execution by the Sheriff and Officers,* Jane Shore *weeping, and* Shore *standing by.*" Ayre is executed and his body, which must have remained suspended for some minutes, bestowed on his friends. Shore reveals himself to Jane, and says:—

Lend me thy hand to bury this our friend,
And then we both will hasten to our end.

[*They put the body of* Ayre *into a Coffin, and then he sits down on one side of it and she on the other.*

It is exceedingly difficult to divine how these hangings were managed without awkwardness on the stage. Actually a dummy figure was employed. Thus in Sir David Lindsay's *Ane Satyre of the Thrie Estaitis,* performed on the Play-field at the Greenside on the lower slopes of Calton Hill, Edinburgh, on Sunday, 12th August, 1554, before Marie de Lorraine, Queen-Regent,[15] Thift, Dissait, and Falset, are brought out to be hanged. "*Heir sal the Sergeants lous the presoners out of the stocks and leid them to the gallows.*" A little later: "*Heir sal Thift be drawin up, or his figour.*" Dissait meets the same end: "*Heir sal Dissait be drawin up or ellis his figure.*" Falset has a long speech, which is interrupted by: "*Heir sall thay festin the coard to his neck with ane dum countenance.*" Presently: "*Heir sal he be heisit up, and not his figure, and an Craw or ane Ke salbe castin up, as it wa his saull.*" These very early stage directions are of no little interest.

In Lillo's *The London Merchant; or, The History of George Barnwell* (produced at Drury Lane, 22nd June, 1731), V, 11, we have: "*The Place of Execution. The gallows and ladders at the farther end of the Stage. A crowd of Spectators. Blunt and Lucy.*" Barnwell, Millwood, Officers, and Executioners enter. There is a short but intensely vivid scene, and they go off the stage. Trueman enters to Blunt and Lucy. Some six or seven brief speeches end the play. Sir Adolphus Ward conjectured that "Apparently the remaining lines are given as Barnwell and Millword are led to the gallows". [16]

In the later prompt-books (as indeed in the first edition, 8vo, 1731, and also in the fourth octavo, 1732), Scene 11, *The Place of Execution* is excised. The text given in *The New English Theatre,* vol. vi, "Marked with the Variations in the Manager's Book At The Theatre-Royal in Drury Lane," 1782, distinguishes the whole scene with inverted commas as a sign it was omitted in representation. By 1825 in Dolby's edition it is not even printed. The text is "from the Acting Copy, with Remarks, to Which are Added A Description of the Costumes, Cast of the Characters (Covent-Garden, 1825; Cooper, Barnwell; Mrs. Faucit, Millwood); Sides of Entrance and Exit, Relative Positions of the Performers on the Stage, and the Whole of the Stage Business". The last scene is the Prison. Thorowgood has his interview with Barnwell and leaves. Trueman and Maria are next admitted. A few moments elapse; Bell tolls; the Keeper enters and announces: "The officers attend you, sir. Millwood is already summoned." Barnwell has a final speech, he embraces Maria, and with some highly moral remarks utters the tag, nine lines of verse to the effect that if the story impresses the audience

> Then must you own you ought not to complain;
> Since you nor weep, nor shall I die, in vain.

The play ends. This scene is V, 10, of the original.

It is worth remark that when on 2nd June, 1927, at the Lyric Theatre, Hammersmith, was produced the Dickensian *When Crummles Played,*[17] in the course of which Lillo's tragedy was given in broadest burlesque the later scenes were so poignant and painful that the farcical interpretation completely broke down, and the audience was harrowed by the final moments of a very real and piteous tragedy, which is no small tribute to Lillo's power.

Episodes of torture applied upon the stage in sight of the

audience are not uncommon in Elizabethan dramatists. Thus in Chapman's *Bussy D'Ambois,* V, 1, the unhappy Tamyra is racked at her frantic husband's command; in *The Double Marriage* at the tyrant Ferrand's bidding Juliana, the matchless wife of Virolet, is stretched upon the rack by Ronvere and the executioners;

I will be
Ten Days a killing thee,

yells the infuriated lord of Naples. *A Larum for London; or, The Siedge of Antwerpe* (1602), is a veritable repository of horrors, and amongst other Transpontine episodes a wretched factor is put to the strappado by Sancho Davila, who bids "so hoise the peasant up". "[*Hoise him up, and let him down again,*" "a very Tragicall and dolefull spectacle," says Coryat who at Venice had witnessed such a public torture in the Piazza San Marco. In *The Virgin Martir,* a play which was at the Restoration revived with great applause, S. Dorothy is haled by the hair, tortured, and beheaded on the stage; Theophilus is racked; Calista and Christeta stabbed. Gifford runs quite off the track when he supposes that "there is too much horror in this tragedy" and that its popularity must wholly be attributed to the scenes—exquisite as they are—of the bright Angel who vanquishes the demon, and the "most glorious vision" of S. Dorothy emparadised.

Scenes of torture, the rack, and the wheel, pincers and fire, were as frequent in the Restoration play-house as in Elizabethan theatres. Nor need we be over nice for such episodes have won vast popularity in our own day. What was more thronged than the Grand Guignol at the Little Theatre, Adelphi, with its appeal to mere physical horror? There is a scene of tensest agony in *La Tosca* which reaches its climax when the doors are flung open and the victim, his mashed head swathed in a blood-boltered napkin, falls swooning into the room. Crowded houses thrilled again and again during *The Sign of the Cross,* a piece of neither artistry nor merit, when the house rang with the shrieks of the Christian boy who was conveniently tortured in the wings.

"I must own," says Steele, *The Tatler,* No. 134, "there is something very horrid in the publick Executions of an *English* Tragedy. Stabbing and Poisoning, which are performed behind the Scenes in other Nations, must be done openly among us to gratify the Audience.

"When poor *Sandford* was upon the Stage, I have seen him groaning upon a Wheel, Stuck with Daggers, impaled alive, calling his Executioners with a dying Voice, Cruel Dogs, and

Villains! And all this to please his judicious Spectators, who were wonderfully delighted with seeing a Man in Torment so well acted."

Malignii in Porter's *The Villain,* Lincoln's Inn Fields, October, 1662, was one of Sandford's most famous rôles, and at the conclusion he is hurried away to execution. Screams are heard from within "O, O! ye cruel Dogs!" and presently "Malignii *discover'd pierct with a stake*". There is a prolonged scene, V, 2, in Dryden's *The Indian Emperour,* Theatre Royal, 1665, when Montezuma and the Indian priest are tortured in order to compel them to discover the Aztec treasures. Pizarro gives order:—

> Fasten the Engines; stretch 'um at their length,
> And pull the streightned Cords with all your Strength.
>
> [*They fasten them to the rack, and then pull them.*

A little later he shouts to the executioners:—

> Increase their Pains, the Cords are yet too slack.

The Indian priest expires, and Montezuma is taken down "*Endeavouring to walk, and not being able*". The scene of the wheel in *Tyrannick Love,* Act V, is from the history of S. Catherine. The Angel "Amariel *descends swiftly with a flaming Sword, and strikes at the Wheel, which breaks in pieces, then he ascends again*".[18] The tortures, again, which are exhibited in *Amboyna,* Lincoln's Inn Fields, 1673, by Killigrew's company, are carefully collected from the authentic accounts.[19] In Act V, "*The* Scene *opens, and discovers the* English *tortur'd, and the* Dutch *tormenting them.*"

> *D'Alva,* whom you
> Condemn for cruelty, did ne're the like;

exclaims Towerson; and "*Enter* Beamont *led, with Matches ty'd to his Hands*".

Settle in *The Empress of Morocco,* Dorset Garden, 3rd July, 1673, obliged the audience with the punishment of his villain Crimalhaz; "*Here the Scene opens, and* Crimalhaz *appears cast down on the Gaunches, being hung on a Wall set with spikes of Iron,*"[20] a sufficiently ghastly spectacle if we may judge by Dolle's copper-plate which illustrates this tableau in the quarto of 1673. The same author could not resist regaling his Whig patrons with some twopenny-coloured melodrame in Act III of *The Female Prelate,* Theatre Royal, 1679. *The Scene the Prison, which opening, discovers variety of Hereticks in several Tortures.*

From the description given by the Constable in Crowne's *The Ambitious Statesman,* Theatre Royal, spring of 1679, no circumstance of grisly horror was omitted when "*The Scene*

PLATE XVIII

THE EMPRESS OF MOROCCO: ACT V, 4to, 1673

[*face p.* 206

drawn, the Duke is shew'd wrack't, Louize *dead by him* ". A similar exhibition in Southerne's *The Fatal Marriage; or, The Innocent Adultery,* Drury Lane, February, 1694, was heralded by piercing screams from the mangled wretch.

Frederick. What cries are those?
Villeroy. Open that door:
SCENE *opened, shews* Pedro *on a rack.*
Here's one can tell you all.
Pedro. All, all: take me but from the rack, I'll confess all.
I can hold out no longer.

Nahum Tate in the last act of his *The Ingratitude of a Common-Wealth,* Drury Lane, winter of 1681, when Coriolanus inquires for his son, produces the Young Martius " Mangled, Gash't Rack't, Distorted ". The boy expires on the stage.

The display of Masaniello's mangled corpse drawn by horses at the conclusion of D'Urfey's *The Famous History of the Rise and Fall of Massaniello,* Part II, Drury Lane, 1699, is historical. " The Scene opens and discovers the trunk of *Massaniello,* headless and handless, dragged by horses, his head and hands fastened to a pole, with an inscription, and behind these the bodies of *Blowzabella,* and *Pedro,* hanging upon gibbets." The dummy bodies here exhibited in horrid mutilation were very exactly modelled and naturally coloured to correspond in detail with the players who acted Masaniello, Blowzabella, and Pedro. So also when in Part I of this same tragedy the severed heads of Don Peppo di Caraffa and the brigand Perone are produced, these counterfeits were made to the particular likeness of the actors. The features were distorted and smeared with seeming blood. This device was not uncommon in Elizabethan theatres. In *Measure for Measure* the Provost enters bearing the head of Ragozine. More remarkable and important is the conclusion of *Macbeth*: Re-enter Macduff with Macbeth's head:—

Macduff. Hail, king! for so thou art. Behold, where stands
The usurper's cursed head.

Not so Davenant. Macbeth fell cut down by Macduff in the sight of the audience crying as he expired:—

Farewell, vain world, and what's most vain in it, ambition!

On 7th January, 1744, at Drury Lane, Garrick revived *Macbeth* " as written by Shakespeare ", and yet, Genest truly remarks, he " added a contemptible dying Speech to his part ". The criticism of Francis Gentleman, *The Dramatic Censor,* 1770, is so buffle-headed that it compels quotation. " Why the author chose to execute so great a culprit behind the scenes, thereby depriving the audience of a most satisfactory circumstance, is not easy to imagine ; death certainly is made, in this instance, too modest ; and the bringing on a head defeats every trace of the author's new-born false delicacy—the present mode of representation is much better . . . As *Macbeth,* in representation, dies before the audience, it appeared necessary, according to dramatic custom, to give him some conclusive lines, which Mr. *Garrick,* as we have been told, has happily supplied, as nothing could be more suitable, or striking, than to make him mention, with dying breath, his guilt, delusion, the witches, and those horrid visions of future punishment, which must ever appall and torture the last moments of such accumulated crimes." Succurrite ! io ciues !

At length on 27th September, 1847, Phelps restored *Macbeth,* and upon the following day *The Times,* amongst other improvements and blemishes removed noted " last, but not least, Macbeth is killed *off* the stage in the orthodox manner, and his head is brought on the pole ". Unhappily Charles Kean in his ornate production at the Princess's Theatre, 14th February, 1853, restored the combat and the killing of Macbeth on the stage.

In *King Henry VI,* Part II, IV, 4, Queen Margaret is seen mourning over Suffolk's head :—

> Here may his head lie on my throbbing breast,
> But where's the body that I should embrace ?

And in Crowne's *King Henry the Sixth,* Dorset Garden, 1681, a gentleman brings in the bloody head to the Queen.

As might be supposed dummy heads were much utilized for decapitation scenes, and in *The Imperial Tragedy,* folio 1669, which is ascribed by Langbaine to Sir William Killigrew, when Pelagius is to lay his head on the block, " He puts up a false head, which is cut off." Such a piece of business would require some neat sleight in performance. A yet more realistic detail is introduced in *The Rebellion of Naples,* 12mo, 1649, where the mob yell for Masaniello's head. In despair he submits. " He thrusts out his head, and they cut off a false head made of a bladder filled with blood. Exeunt with his body." In the Fifth Act of *The Insatiate Countess,* generally attributed to Marston and Barksted, a Whitefriars play of *circa* 1610 (4to, 1613, " Written by Iohn Marston "), we are at Pavia, " a scaffold laid out," and presently " Enter Isabella, with her hair hanging down, a chaplet of flowers on her head, a nosegay in her hand ; Executioner before her, and with her a Cardinal." Her hair is tied up ; her eyes blinded with a napkin; and "The executioner strikes off her head".

None the less these decapitations were ticklish devices and the smallest hitch would reduce the pathos and agony to a jesting sham. Whilst they could be and were often essayed with good effect we find that on occasion when the scaffold has been set up and all is ready for the end some unexpected turn will bring pardon and release to the condemned. Towards the conclusion of *The Faire Maide of Bristow*, acted before James I and his Queen at Hampton Court during the winter of 1603–4; quarto, 1605; "Enter the King, Richmond, Liester, Sir Eustice, Sir Godfrey, to the execution." And a little after: "Enter the officers with the prisoners":—

King. Dispose yong *Vallenger* the first to death,
That done, send hence the other to their sentence domd.

But at the last moment the execution is stayed by the entrance of Anabell "disguised like a man" at one door, and at another Challener. The lady is recognized and the king commands:—

we are content her husband haue his life,
But she shall lay her head upon the block,
And she shall haue no executioner,
But *Vallenger* him selfe, shall strike it off.

In pudding-time the Gordian knot is undone by Sentloe, who supposed murdered, is present disguised in a friar's habit which he puts off and reveals himself.

Thus in Tourneur's *The Atheist's Tragedy* (4to, 1611), Charlemont is on the scaffold, his head laid upon the block, and D'Amville is about to deal the blow, but "*As he raises up the Axe, strikes at his own Brains—Staggers off the Scaffold*". In *The Knight of Malta,* II, 5, we have "*The Scaffold set out, and the Stairs*", and "*Enter* Oriana, Ladies, Executioner, Abdella, *and* Guard". However Oriana's champion vindicates her innocence by right of arms. In Shakespeare and Fletcher's *The Two Noble Kinsmen* after the lists "*Enter* Palamon *and his Knights pinion'd; Jailor, Executioner, and Guard*". They bid farewell, and Palamon "*Lies on the Block*" when "*A great Noise within, crying, Run, save, hold*". A messenger enters in hot haste hard followed by Perithous, who relates that Arcite has been thrown from his steed and lies a-dying. In Dryden's *Tyrannick Love,* Act V: "*Here the* SCENE *opens and discovers* Berenice *on a Scaffold, the Guards by her, and amongst them* Porphyrius *and* Albinus, *like Moors, as all the Guards are.* Placidius *enters, and whispers the Emperor.*" Porphyrius and Albinus attempt to stab Maximin, but are seized, and the furious monarch orders them all to be taken away "to suffer in another Place". "*Exeunt* Berenice, Porphyrius, *and* Albinus *carried off by Guards*."

Before the artifice of the dummy head with a neat fetch to sprinkle blood came into practice the earlier method of presenting a decollation was for the character to bid a last farewell, sometimes even to be blindfolded, and then to leave the stage as if stepping on to the scaffold. A few moments later the executioner would enter with the head. This is the arrangement in *The Life and Death of Thomas, Lord Cromwell* (1602), where after a pathetic leave-taking Cromwell proceeds to the block, and four lines later: "Enter one with Cromwel's head." *The Famous History of Sir Thomas Wyat,* by Webster and Dekker (1602; printed 1607) concludes with the death of Lady Jane Grey, which curiously enough is made to precede that of Lord Guildford Dudley. The Headsman enters and with the usual formula craves forgiveness; Lady Jane's women assist her to doff her surmantle; she utters the couplet:—

> Now blind mine eyes never to see the sky:
> Blindfold thus lead me to the block to die.

There is no stage direction, but obviously she must have been conducted off here, as six lines after:—

> *Enter* Headsman, *with* Jane's *head.*

Bishop of Winchester. Here comes the headsman with the head of Jane.
Guildford. Who spake of Jane? who nam'd my lovely Jane?
Winchester. Behold her head.

Chapman concludes *The Tragedie of Charles Duke of Byron,* a Blackfriars play of 1608, with Byron on the scaffold, his eyes blindfolded, his head laid on the block. He cries to the executioner:—

> Strike, strike, O strike; fly, fly, commanding soul,
> And on thy wings for this thy body's breath
> Bear the eternal victory of death.

There is no exeunt, but the play ends abruptly without any sign or direction. If there has not been some excision or tampering with the text (and owing to a complaint of the French ambassador, Antoine Lefèvre de la Boderie, a good deal of the drama was wholly suppressed) one can only imagine that the action took place on the inner stage and that the curtains closed over a tableau.

In the Restoration theatre any attempt to show actual decapitation was entirely forgone, and I apprehend that this was the case owing to the enormous difficulty of manipulating a dummy head with dignity or any semblance of reality. In Settle's *Cambyses, King of Persia,* produced at Lincoln's Inn Fields January, 1670–1, towards the conclusion of Act III, Cambyses orders: "Draw back that Curtain," and "*The Scene appears, and on a Table appears the Body of* Osiris, *beheaded; & an Executioner with the suppos'd head in a vessel of Blood*". Probably for this effect the trick described by Reginald Scot in *The Discoverie of Witchcraft,* Book XIII, chapter 34,[21] was practised. This author explains how "*To cut off ones head, and to laie it in a platter, &c: which the jugglers call the decollation of John Baptist*". "This was doone by one Kingsfield of London, at a Bartholomewtide, An. 1582, in the sight of diverse that came to view this spectacle." An illustration of the trick table is furnished and very full directions. It may be remarked that Act III of *Cambyses* ends very shortly after this spectacle is exhibited, and Scot in his "Necessarie observations to astonish the beholders" particularly bids "Not to suffer the companie to staie too long in the place".

But in the historical tragedies of John Banks the characters simply walk off the stage to the scaffold. In Act V of *The Unhappy Favourite; or, The Earl of Essex,* Theatre Royal, autumn of 1681, Essex (Clarke) bids farewell to his swooning Countess (Sarah Cooke) and leaving her senseless in the arms of her women, "*Exit* Essex *to Execution,* Burleigh, Raleigh, *Lieutenant and Guards.*" So in *Vertue Betray'd; or, Anna Bullen,* Dorset Garden, 5th April, 1682, "*Enter* Queen *going to Execution all in white*; Diana, *Women in Mourning; Guards.*" Rochford, who is on the stage, after a short dialogue is led away to execution; and when the young Princess Elizabeth has been introduced and received her mother's embrace, "*Exit Queen to Execution, with* Northumberland *and Guards.*" Nine lines later, "*Enter a Gentleman with a Handkerchief stain'd with the Queen's blood.*" In *The Albion Queens; or, The Death of Mary Queen of Scotland,* Drury Lane, 6th March, 1704, Queen Mary (Mrs. Oldfield) says:—

> Come near, and you two take me by the Hands;
> For to the last with Decency I will,
> Though little Port, the Majesty retain
> Of what I am, the rightful Queen of *Scotland,*
> Queen Dowager of *France,* and *England's* Heir; . . .
> —Weep not
> But take me by the Hands, . . .
> So lead me to the Place where I may gain
> Immortal Pleasures, and immortal reign.
>
> [*Exit led by two Gentlemen.*

Otway in *Venice Preserv'd; or, A Plot Discover'd,* produced at Dorset Garden, 9th February, 1682, presents the death of Pierre. "*Scene opening discovers a Scaffold and a Wheel prepar'd for the executing of* Pierre ; *there enter Officers,* Pierre *and Guards, a Friar, executioner, and a great Rabble.*" There is some converse between Pierre and the Friar, when Jaffier appears. The friends talk, and are interrupted by the Officer with " The day grows late, Sir ". Pierre and Jaffier ascend the scaffold, and the executioners bind the doomed man when Jaffier suddenly stabs him to the heart and next turns the dagger on himself. " Heav'n grant I dye so well," cries the Officer. "*Scene shuts upon them.*"

Precisely the same arrangement was employed by Rowe in *The Tragedy of Lady Jane Grey,* Drury Lane, 20th April, 1715. Lord Guildford Dudley (Booth) and Lady Jane Grey (Mrs. Oldfield) take their last farewell. " Guildford *is led off by the Guards.*" Bishop Gardiner (Cibber) endeavours to persuade the lady who rejects his counsel. "*The Scene draws, and discovers a Scaffold hung with Black, Executioner and Guards.*" The final preparations made "*Lady* Jane *goes up to the Scaffold: The Scene closes* ", and Pembroke (Elrington) enters to Gardiner. After a speech or two, *Exeunt Omnes* ; Mrs. Porter speaks the Epilogue, and the curtain falls.

✓ The drawing together of two flats meeting in the centre was then the conventional method of ending a scene, and not infrequently hereby characters were concealed from view when they could not easily be got off the stage, so that " Scene closes " came to be almost equivalent in its effect to the modern dropping of the curtain.

To talk of a " box-set " in connection with the Theatre Royal or Dorset Garden is not merely to display egregious ignorance but to set rolling a mischievous blunder to boot. In an article that appeared in *The Stage,* 13th August, 1925, Dr. W. J. Lawrence was at some pains to point out that the provision of proscenium doors obviated the necessity for doors in the scene and delayed the arrival of the box set. He first traced a practicable door in a flat in 1767, at Drury Lane, in *Cymon* (produced 2nd January), Garrick's " dramatic romance ". The full box set, with enclosed sides, instead of wings, came much later.[22]

Both Davenant and Killigrew were intimately acquainted with the principles and functions of the scenery which had been employed in Caroline masques, and although scenes when first introduced on the public English stage, that is to say at Lincoln's Inn Fields and the first Theatre Royal, Bridges Street, were illustrative and dioramic rather than realistic and exact, a background rather than a set, there is no reason at all to think that they were crude and rough-hewn. In fact there is good ground for supposing the contrary. On Thursday, 15th August, 1661, Pepys notes: " to the Opera, which begins again to-day with ' The Witts ', never acted yet with scenes; and the King and Duke and Duchess were there . . . and indeed it is a most excellent play and admirable scenes." Saturday, 24th August, following he has: " to the Opera, and there saw ' Hamlet, Prince of Denmark ', done with Scenes very well, but above all, Betterton did the prince's part beyond imagination."

At first, of course, the stock of scenes at each house would necessarily be small, and no doubt a few flats did yeomen service. Dramatists, unless they were prime favourites, would be chary of introducing some unusual episode or effect. Thus Flecknoe in the preface to his *The Damoiselles a la Mode,* 4to, 1667, emphasizes that the play could be easily produced, " the scaenes and cloaths being the least considerable in it; any *Italian* scaenes with four doors serving for the one, and for the other any French cloaths à la mode." In the earlier plays we have an occasional reference to new pieces of scenery. Thus in Porter's *The Villain,* produced at Lincoln's Inn Fields, Saturday, 18th October, 1662, Act IV, Scene 1, was " The new Scene of the HALL ". In this connection the Prologue to Tuke's *The Adventures of Five Hours,* produced at Lincoln's Inn Fields on Thursday, 8th January, 1662–3, may be quoted. " THE FIRST SCENE IS THE CITY OF SEVIL. *The Prologue Enters with a Play-Bill in his hand, and Reads,* This Day being the 15th of *December,* shall be Acted a New Play, never Plai'd before, call'd *The Adventures of Five Hours.*

A New Play.

Th'are i' the right, for I dare boldly say,
The *English* Stage ne'er had so New a Play;
The Dress, the Authour, and the Scenes are New.
This ye have seen before ye'l say; 'tis true.

It would be difficult, perhaps impossible to name the play or plays in which the scene of " The City of Sevil " had been used before. The probable date for the opening of the first Duke's Theatre, Lincoln's Inn Fields, is Friday, 28th June, 1661, but we have not anything like a complete list of the plays which were given between that date and the 8th January, 1663. Moreover, it is quite possible that the view of Seville may have been very well employed in Davenant's *The Spanish Lovers* (otherwise *The Distresses*) the locale of which is Cordova, a drama there is reason to suppose was revived nearly about this time. Again, it is likely enough that Seville had been presented as almost any other Spanish or Italian city. However, we fairly presume that the new scenes in Tuke's play included the following: Don *Henrique's* House, Act I, Act III (bis), Act V; *A Garden* (with moonlight effect), Act III; Don *Octavio's* House, Act IV. *Don* Antonio's *Apartment in Don* Henrique's *House,* Act IV; Don *Carlos's* House (bis), Act V. It can, I think, be taken as certain that the scenes would be utilized in other productions; for example the interiors and the garden would admirably serve in Davenant's *The Man is the Master,* produced at Lincoln's Inn Fields, on Thursday, 26th March, 1668. This also is a Spanish play, the plot comes from Spain *via* Scarron, and the scene is laid in Madrid. I have no doubt that the same garden scene was used in *Romeo and Juliet, Twelfth Night, The Rivals, The Villain, The Dutchesse of Malfey, Love in a Tub, The Sparagus Garden, Love Tricks, The Witty Fair One, The Grateful Servant, A Woman is a Weathercock*; and a number of other revivals and new plays requiring such a scene, which it were superfluous and tedious to list. Most, if not all, of these plays also demand interior scenes, rooms and bedchambers, and assuredly an almost infinite number of changes might be rung upon some four or five pairs of flats which could be used indifferently for tragedy or comedy, in England, Italy, Spain, France, Illyria, or where you will.

Occasionally in this connection very illuminating notes have found their way into the printed copy of a play, a circumstance to be made abundantly clear by an inspection of Orrery's *Guzman,* folio 1693, which was produced at Lincoln's Inn Fields, on Friday, 16th April, 1669. It will be profitable to review this in some detail. Act I, "*The First Scene is a Piazza, with Walks of Trees, and Houses round about it.*" This occupies the whole of the Act. Act II opens with "*The Scene with the Chimny in it*". This scene was probably again called into requisition in the production of Mrs. Behn's *The Feign'd Curtezans; or, A Night's Intrigue,* Dorset Garden, March, 1679, since in Act IV of this comedy, when Sir Signal, having found his way at night into the house of Silvianetta, supposed a cyprian, begs Philippa to hide him, she cries: "Here, step behind this Hanging—there's a Chimney which may shelter ye till the Storm be over—If you be not smother'd before." And she "*Puts him behind the Arras*". In a few moments we see him "*Peeping out of the Chimney, his Face blackt*", and a little later "*Peeping out with a Face more smutted*". Eventually, his countenance is that of an Ethiop.

In Ravenscroft's *Dame Dobson; or, The Cunning Woman,* Act IV, the cunning Dame gives the Colonel some proof of her skill which involves a clever stage trick. "*Dame* Dobson *walks about with precipitation, looks upward and downward, mutters to her self. After that Thunder and Lightning is seen to flash down the Chimny.*"

In a few moments "*The other parts of the Body fall down the Chimny*". "A Humane Body torn Limb from Limb," cries the astounded Colonel. But "*She waves her wand in the Air, the Thunder and Lightning redoubles, during which the Parts of the Body approach and joyn together. The Body rises and walks to the middle of the Stage*". Immediately after which "*The Body vanishes*". A device something similar had been employed in Mrs. Behn's *The Rover* (Part II, Dorset Garden, February, 1680), Act III, when Harlequin "*ushers in* Hunt *as a Giant*". Since the new colossus is too tall to pass through the door "Hunt *being all Doublet, leaps off from another Man who is all Breeches, and goes out; Breeches follows stalking.*" So at the conclusion of Mountford's farce *The Life and Death of Doctor Faustus,* "SCENE *discovers* Faustus'*s Limbs*":—

Scholar. O help us, Heav'n
See here are *Faustus*'s Limbs,
All torn asunder by the Hand of Hell . . .

SCENE *changes to Hell.* Faustus *Limbs come together. A Dance, and Song.*"

I suspect that we should not be far out if we were to say that the same chimney scene was used in Mrs. Centlivre's *Mar-Plot; or, The Second Part of The Busie-Body,* produced at Drury Lane, 30th December, 1710, for at the close of the first Act, Marplot, who is in Colonel Ravelin's Lodgings, makes his way out by means of the chimney. "So, now for the Art of Chimney-sweeping," he chuckles to himself, "*Goes into the Chimney, and the Scene shuts.*"

In the next Act, Scene, Donna Perriera's *Apartment,* "Marplot *flaps down the Chimney*" to the amaze of the whole company.

As early indeed as Killigrew's *The Pilgrim,* possibly unacted and certainly not given later than by the English players at Paris in 1646, when Fidelia, Act III, 8,[23] throws away the letter: "*The Scene must present a Chimney, in which she throws the Letter and goes out.* (Victoria *snatches up the Letter.*) [Exit *Fidelia.*"

It may be remarked that, at the commencement of Act II of *Guzman* we have prompter's notes, "*Two ready*" and "*Knocking prepar'd*". The next scene is: "A Table and Two Swords. *Enter* Oviedo *to* Pirracco *in his Chamber.* [*A flat Scene of a Chamber.*" There is a short dialogue, and another marginal note intrudes, "*Leon. Pastra. Anton.*" This reminds the prompter to call the three actresses, since the next scene is, "Enter Leonora, Pastrana, and Antonia. [*The Q. of* Hungary's *Chamber.*" Accordingly we perceive that this interior had already been employed in *The Tragedy of Mustapha* produced at the same theatre in April, 1665, a drama in which the Queen of Hungary plays an important rôle. The Chamber is Act I, Scene 2. During the dialogue of this scene in *Guzman* we have a note "*Maria, Lucia, Sala. Ferd*". Although Maria and Lucia did not enter until the following act it was necessary that they should have ample notice since they had to make their appearance "*drest like good Spirits, . . . in glittring Habits*" for the mock incantation. The prompter further notes "*A little Bell ready. Flashes of Fire ready. Boy ready*". It may be remarked here that throughout the play we have calls for actors some little time before they make their appearance, and also notes of properties and effects such as: "*A Purse* (Act III). A Periwig for *Francisco.* A Paper like a Bond" (Act V), as also "*Trampling ready*" (Act III), "*Rapping ready*" (Act IV).

The scene after the interior, the Queen of Hungary's Chamber, is "*The new Black Scene*". Apparently this was "painted about with Mathematical Instruments and Grotesque Figures", but if needed I imagine that these could easily have been obliterated, and therefore it seems likely that this scene was used later in the Fifth Act of William Whitaker's *The Conspiracy; or, the Change of Government,* produced at Dorset Garden early in 1680, where a "*Room hung all with Black*" is required. It may be observed that the stage direction for the Fifth Act of Rowe's *The Fair Penitent,* produced at Lincoln's Inn Fields in March, 1703, runs: "Scene *is a Room hung with Black; on one side,* Lothario's *Body on a Bier; on the other, a Table with a Skull and other Bones, a Book, and a Lamp on it.*"

Act III of *Guzman* is "Alcanzar's *Astrological Cabinet*", and at the conclusion of a variety of somewhat elaborate business the flats draw over and we have "*A Flat Scene of a Chamber*". This changes to "*The Scene the* Piazzo. [The new flat Scene". After which we have "*The Scene a Field with Trees.* [The Forest."

Act IV opens with "*The New Flat Scene*". There is a brief dialogue of eight speeches between Maria and Lucia, and we return to the "*Q. of* Hungary's *Chamber*". Then "*The Scene is* Francisco's *House.* [The Chamber with the Chimney in't". There follow "*The New Flat Scene*" and "*The Scene a Grove of Trees.* [The Forest". Next we have: "*The Scene a Garden.* [The Garden in *Tryphon* as a Back Scene." Lord Orrery's *Tryphon* was produced at Lincoln's Inn Fields on Tuesday, 8th December, 1668. The opening Scene "is the Garden of *Tryphon's* Palace in *Antioch*". The penultimate scene of the fourth Act of *Guzman* is "*the Piazzo.* [The New Flat Scene", and the last scene is "*the Astrological Cabinet.* [The new black Scene". Act V commences with "*The New Flat Scene*" which changes to the "*Queen of* Hungary's *Chamber*". From every point of view the script of *Guzman* deserves careful study, and it seems a pity that when this comedy was reprinted in the collected edition of Orrery's *Works,* two volumes, 1739, the prompter's marginal notes were omitted, and the stage directions were altered, so that from a literary point of view it may be more elegant and easy to read, but distinctly it is far less interesting.

Downes notes that when *Mustapha* was produced the play was "new cloath'd with New Scenes", and naturally the house could not afford merely to lay these scenes by, but was obliged to employ them in other plays as opportunity offered. Thus in the anonymous *Tom Essence; or, The Modish Wife* produced at Dorset Garden about June, 1676, Act IV, Scene 2, a chamber in old Monylove's House is indicated as "*Malfey's Chamber*". This points to a particular revival with special scenery, early in 1676, of Webster's tragedy, and indeed *The Dutchesse of Malfey* took its place in the repertory of Dorset Garden for it was published late in 1677 (with date 1678) quarto, "as it is now Acted at the Duke's Theatre" (*Term Catalogues,* Michaelmas, 26th November, 1677). In D'Urfey's comedy *Squire Oldsapp; or, The Night-Adventurers,* produced at Dorset Garden during the spring of 1678, and printed 4to with date 1679, Act V, Scene 2, we have: "Carlo's *Bed-Chamber.*" That is to say the scene was utilized which had been presented as the last scene in Otway's *Don Carlos,* first given at the same house in June, 1676, and frequently acted.

New and important productions would put the Company to considerable expense, and in these matters each theatre endeavoured to outdo the rival playhouse. In the third week of December, 1663, *Henry VIII* was given at Lincoln's Inn Fields, with the utmost splendour. Downes emphasizes the magnificence of the show, "it being all new Cloath'd and new Scenes; it continu'd Acting 15 Days together with general Applause." But the Theatre Royal capotted with a paramount attraction. On Wednesday, 27th January, 1664, Pepys accompanied his wife to Covent Garden, "in the way observing the streete full of coaches at the new play, 'The Indian Queene'; which for show, they say, exceeds 'Henry the Eighth'." The Howard and Dryden tragedy was set forth with every resource of splendour and brilliant ornament. On Thursday, 4th February, 1664, Evelyn, the nicest of critics, has: "I saw *The Indian Queen* acted, a tragedy well written, so beautiful with rich scenes as the like had never been seen here, or haply (except rarely) elsewhere on a mercenary theatre."[24]

That the Theatre Royal expended large sums on their scenes is very certain, and among the more important productions prior to Thursday, 25th January, 1672, on which day occurred the calamitous fire " which half burned down the house, and all their scenes and wardrobe . . . 20,000*l* damage ", were such ornate spectacular pieces as *Catiline,*[25] *Tyrannick Love,* and *The Conquest of Granada.*

It seems hardly possible that the expenses of the production of *Tyrannick Love* were proportionate throughout to the huge sum (£335 10*s*.) paid for the one *Scene of a Paradise,* which after all was only shown to the audience for a short time—the vision of S. Catharine is quite brief, although a very important episode—and, one supposes, there cannot have been a very great number of tragedies in which this painting could be introduced, popular as this kind of spectacle proved.[26]

Of other scene-painters of this period, besides Isaac Fuller, whose art was represented by this famous *Paradise,* we know John Webb, the pupil of Inigo Jones, and the designer of the first scenery for *The Siege of Rhodes.* Robert Aggas (or Angus) and Samuel Towers worked for the second Theatre Royal, and on occasion appear to have been treated in much the same way as Fuller. The admired Stephenson painted scenery for Dorset Garden, and he particularly distinguished himself by the decorations of *Psyche* produced at that house on 27th February, 1674–5. In the Preface to the printed copy of this opera, 4to, 1675, Shadwell says, " *The Scenes were Painted by the Ingenious Artist, Mr.* Stephenson." Robert Robinson undertook the scenery for Settle's opera *The Virgin Prophetess ; or, The Fate of Troy,* a most elaborate spectacle which had a belated production at Drury Lane in May, 1701. Robert Streeter, whom we have already met, was " his Majesty's Sergeant Painter ", and in 1671 and 1672 was painting scenes for the Court Theatre in Whitehall. Streeter, who is several times mentioned with high praise by Evelyn, died in 1680.

From Streeter's brush came the splendid and ornate scenes of Dryden's most famous heroic tragedy *The Conquest of Granada by the Spaniards,* the first part of which drama was produced at the Theatre Royal in December, 1670, whilst the second part followed in January, 1671. From all accounts the decoration, although perhaps not strictly correct, appears to have been sumptuously oriental, and we are shown the Alhambra, the Albayzin, and the Vivarambla, which latter " *appears fill'd with Spectators* ". Under 9th February, 1671, Evelyn notes : " I saw the great ball danced by the Queen and distinguished ladies at Whitehall Theatre. Next day, was acted there the famous play, called *The Siege of Granada,* two days acted successively; there were indeed very glorious scenes and perspectives, the work of Mr. Streeter, who well understands it."

Revivals also were rendered attractive by splendid scenes, and as early as 1663 Fletcher's *The Faithful Shepherdess* was given with a decor that drew large houses, for Pepys on Saturday, 13th June, of that year notes: "to the Royall Theatre . . . Here we saw 'The Faithfull Shepheardesse', a most simple thing and yet much thronged after, and often shown, but it is only for the Scene's sake, which is very fine indeed and worth seeing."

Modern comedies would not, of course, need an elaboration of scenery, but it is interesting to inquire whether typical London resorts, the rendezvous of court and society, places probably well known to every member of the audience were faithfully rendered by the artists, or did imagination sway. When Sedley's *The Mulberry-Garden* was produced on 18th May, 1668, was the scene of the Mulberry Garden (I, 3; IV, 1) a lively representation of the original? Most certainly, Yes. The presentment of any well-known centre, part of the town or other view was very exact. Unless this were the case much of the dialogue between Victoria and Olivia as they walk in the Mulberry Garden would miss its point, and not only is there mention, but in the business of the play use is made, of various arbours. Moreover Wildish "meets *Modish* in a Walk". Wycherley's lively comedy, *Love in a Wood,* produced autumn of 1671, concludes in "*the Dining-room, in Mulberry-Garden-house*".

We know that the rival house, Lincoln's Inn Fields, had a scene of Mulberry Garden, for it was utilized in the Duke of Newcastle's *The Humorous Lovers* (II, 1) seen by Pepys, Thursday, 11th April, 1667, and also by Etherege, *She Wou'd if She Cou'd* (II, 1), produced on 6th February, 1668.

It should be remarked that *Love in a Wood* requires "*St.* James's *Park at night*" (II, 1).

Dryden's directions to his opera *Albion and Albanius,* produced at Dorset Garden on Saturday, 6th June, 1685, sufficiently show what exactitude was employed in painting the Scenes. Describing the "Decorations of the Stage in the First Act" the poet writes: "*The Scene, is a Street of Palaces, which lead to the Front of the* Royal-Exchange; *the great Arch is open, and the view is continued through the open part of the* Exchange, *to the Arch on the other side, and thence to as much of the Street beyond, as could, properly be taken.*"

In Act II after the "Poetical Hell" with Pluto, Democracy, and the rest, "*The Scene changes to a Prospect taken from the middle of the* Thames; *one side of it begins at* York-Stairs, *thence to* White-Hall, *and the* Mill-bank, &c. *The other from the* Saw-Mill, *thence to the* Bishop's Palace, *and on as far as can be seen in a clear Day.*"

Act III opens with "*a View of* Dover, *taken from the Sea: a row of Cliffs fill up each Side of the Stage, and the Sea the middle of it, which runs into the* Peer: *beyond the* Peer, *is the Town of* Dover: *on each side of the Town is seen a very high Hill; on one of which is the Castle of* Dover; *on the other, the great Stone which they call the* Devils drop.[27] *Behind the Town several Hills are seen at a great Distance which finish the view.*"

The opera concludes with a charming panorama. "*The Scene changes to a walk of very high Trees: At the end of the Walk is a view of that part of* Windsor, *which faces* Eaton: *In the midst of it is a row of small Trees, which lead to the Castle-hill: In the first Scene, part of the Town and part of the Hill: In the next, the Terrace Walk, the King's Lodgings, and the upper part of St.* George'*s Chappel, then the Keep; And, lastly, that part of the Castle, beyond the Keep.*"

Scene-painting for the public theatre had greatly advanced in the quarter of a century or rather more since John Webb drew the designs for the landscapes which illustrated Davenant's *The Siege of Rhodes,* although it may not be impertinent to remind ourselves that even these were by no means inaccurate so far as the general disposition of the town with its harbour, and the island are depicted. Indeed these designs are certainly based on topographical authority, probably upon the engravings in G. F. Carnotti's *Rodi Città,* Venice, 1571, and Daniel Meisner's *Thesaurus Philo-Politicus* (tertia pars), 4to, 1625.

One might, however, incline to think that the exquisite scenery of Dryden's opera more closely resembled the prospective of Ferrara which Raphael painted for the performance of Ariosto's *I Suppositi* when it was played at Rome on 6th March, 1519, the Sunday of the Carnival, in the apartments of the Apostolic Palace of Cardinal Innocenzo Cibo. Ser Tomà Lippomano [28] says that the scene represented "Ferrara precise come la è", and the Pope, Leo X, who was present expressed himself as particularly delighted with the view.

Even with regard to interiors, I have very little doubt that when Killigrew's *The Parson's Wedding* was given on 5th or 6th October, 1664, and Act III, Scene 5, has "*Enter* Careless, Wild, *and a* Drawer, *at the Devil*", a room (possibly the actual Half-Moon) in this famous Tavern was closely copied on the stage. In the same way when they presented Shadwell's *The Miser,* "the last Play that was Acted at the King's Theatre in *Covent-Garden,* before the fatal fire there" and Rant, Hazard, Lettice, and Joyce appeared at Chatolins, the audience certainly were able to recognize the French house in Covent Garden.

During their temporary occupation of Lincoln's Inn Fields, which commenced 26th February, 1672, Killigrew's company must indeed have been hard put to it by the difficulty of procuring adequate scenes. It is hazardous to speculate what provision they were able to make and how. Dryden in the Prologue to *Arviragus and Philicia* which was revived there shows himself sorry and sore:—

> With sickly Actors and an old House too,
> We're match'd with glorious Theatres and new,
> And with our Ale-house scenes and Cloaths bare worn
> Can neither raise old Plays nor new adorn.

Again in his Prologue, *for the Women When they Acted at the Old* Theatre *in* Lincoln's Inn Fields he wittily says:—

> The worse the Lodging is, the more the Love.
> For much good Pastime, many a dear sweet hug
> Is stol'n in Garrets, on the humble Rugg.

Moreover in the Prologue, spoken at the opening of the second Theatre Royal, Bridges Street, 26th March, 1674, Dryden cannot spare his reflections upon the splendour of the rival Dorset Garden, at which he girds thus:—

> 'Twere Folly now a stately Pile to raise,
> To build a Play-house, while you throw down Plays;
> Whilst Scenes, Machines, and empty *Opera's* reign,
> And for the Pencil you the Pen disdain; . . .
> I would not prophesie our Houses Fate;
> But while vain Shows and Scenes you over-rate,
> 'Tis to be feared—
> That, as a Fire the former House o'erthrew,
> Machines and Tempests will destroy the new.

The allusion in the last line is to the splendid series of dramatic operas which were so great a feature of the Dorset Garden attractions, and especially to the outstanding success of *The Tempest*. Incidentally this clever sarcasm supports the belief that the operatic version of *The Tempest* is due to Shadwell, since it is unlikely that Dryden would have a flick at the popularity of one of his own plays.

In the *Shakespeare Society Papers* [29] Mr. Collier printed a deed of 23rd March, 1673–4, which shows that the actors of the Theatre Royal formed a combination to raise money to build na adequate scene-house for their new theatre, the second Drury Lane. This annex was to serve " for the makeing and providing of Scenes, Machines, Cloathes, Apparell, and other things to be used in or relating to the acting of Comedies, Tragedies, and other Interludes at the said Theatre, or in any other place where the Company . . . shall act ".

As we have already seen, large sums of money were expended upon the productions at the Theatre Royal, and we may be sure that during the eight years from 1674 to 1682 the actors would have endeavoured to maintain the same standard of magnificence. It is known that for some three or four years at least prior to the Union of the two Companies in 1682, things were in a bad state at the Theatre Royal, but nevertheless, considerable efforts must have been made to present with a certain degree of sumptuousness the heroic tragedies for which this house was famed. Thus John Crowne's *The Destruction of Jerusalem* in two parts, produced in January, 1677, according to a letter entitled " Some Memoirs of the Earl of Rochester " and supposed to have been written by St. Evremond to the Duchess of Mazarin, " met with as wild and unaccountable Success as Mr. DRYDEN's *Conquest of Granada*."[30] Crowne's drama requires the most ornate display. It opens with a view of the brazen gates of Herod's Temple, which presently are flung wide as a solemn procession of priests and Levites issues from the sanctuary. Later we have the outward courts of the Temple ; the altar is discovered, and the Holy Place. The veil of blue, and purple, and crimson, and fine linen is mysteriously rent asunder showing the Sanctum Sanctorum whilst an Angel descends in flames and glory. The second part of the drama concludes with the burning of the Temple and the final capture of Jerusalem by the Romans. It is obvious that all this must have taxed theatrical resources to the utmost, and we have proof that a great deal of money was expended since in a petition addressed by Charles Killigrew, Hart, Burt, Goodman, and Mohun to the Lord Chamberlain, the Earl of Arlington, which may be dated 1678, complaint is made that Dryden has collaborated with Lee in a play called *Oedipus* for Dorset Garden. They further state that "Mr. Crowne, being under the like agreement with the Dukes House, writt a play called *The Destruction of Jerusalem,* and being forced by their refusall of it to bring it to us, the said Company compelled us after the studying of it, and a vast expence in scenes and cloathes, to buy off their clayme, by paying all the pension he had received from them ; amounting to One hundred and twelve pounds paid by the Kings Company, besides neere Forty pounds he the said Mr. Crowne paid out of his owne pocket ".[31]

It is possible that when on 8th August, 1677, the two scene painters Aggas and Towers petitioned the Lord Chamberlain for Forty Pounds due to them from the Kings Company "for worke done in ye Theatre Royall" they were seeking to recover payment on account of the canvases they had painted for *The Destruction of Jerusalem.*

Since we have spoken of the scenery at the Theatre Royal at some length it is hardly necessary to consider the scenery of the rival company at Lincoln's Inn Fields and Dorset Garden in like detail. We need only remark that as a matter of course the company headed by Betterton would have endeavoured to surpass the novelties and splendours of their rivals, and there is every reason to suppose that, since financially they were far more sound, and domestically they were under the guidance of a far more equable management, they certainly succeeded in outshining the rival playhouse, which indeed was rapidly on the wane. Naturally enough there were certain stock scenes which must have reappeared time after time at the Duke's indifferently in comedy and tragedy alike, as occasion demanded. Such were streets, interiors, gardens, palaces, prisons, groves, and woods, *cum multis aliis.* To name all the plays which exhibited these and similar conventional scenes would be to write a pretty extensive and quite superfluous list. It will, I think, suffice if we select some two of these scenes and name about half a dozen or eight plays apiece in which they appear. We may take, for example, a prison, a garden, and a grove, and show how these three locali were repeatedly presented in various productions. I have selected plays prior to the Union in 1682, since of course after this date the scenery of the two companies was naturally joined in one common stock.[1]

Prison scenes are shown in Davenant's *The Law against Lovers,* seen by Pepys, Tuesday, 18th February, 1662; Shadwell's *The Royal Shepherdesse,* Lincoln's Inn Fields, 25th February, 1669 (V. Enter Neander, Geron, *and* Phronesia *in Prison*); Settle's *Cambyses, King of Persia,* Lincoln's Inn Fields, January, 1670–1; the same author's *Love and Revenge,* Dorset Garden, November, 1674 (III. Scene the Second. *The Scene a Dungeon*; and Act the Fifth. Scene the First. The Scene a Prison. *Clarmount* and *Fredigond* appear bound); Mrs. Behn's *Abdelazer; or, The Moor's Revenge,* Dorset Garden, autumn of 1676 (V, 3. *A Prison*); Pordage's *The Siege of Babylon* (II, 2), Dorset Garden, 1677; Mrs. Behn's *The Young King; or, The Mistake,* Dorset Garden, spring of 1679 (II, 1, *A Castle or Prison on the Sea*; II, 2, *Another room in the Prison*; V, 3, *A Prison*); Betterton's *The Revenge; or, A Match in Newgate,* Dorset Garden, 1680 (Act V: "*Great-gate.* SCENE changes to the Front of *New-gate* at the Grate two or three Prisoners, one a beging, a Box hangs out." The next scene is "*the inside of the Prison*"); Tate's *King Lear,* Dorset Garden, 1680 (V. Scene, *A Prison.* Lear *asleep, with his Head on* Cordelia's *Lap*). In the final episode of Crowne's *The Misery of Civil-War,* produced at Dorset Garden early in 1680 the scene is that room in the Tower where Richard of Gloster murders King Henry VI; and Tate in his *History of King Richard the Second (The Sicilian Usurper),* acted three times at Dorset Garden late in 1680, in the last scene shows Richard in Pontefract Castle and his assassination by Exton and servants. It seems very probable that in these two scenes a prison setting was employed.

A Garden is required in the following plays: Thomas Porter's *The Villain,* October, 1662 (IV, *Enter* Malignii, *as in the Garden*); Shadwell's *The Humorists,* early in 1671 (IV, Enter *Lady* Loveyouth *in the Garden*); Crowne's *Juliana; or, The Princess of Poland,* 1671 (Act the First. *The Scene a* Grove *and* Gardens. Paulina *sleeping under a tree*; and II, Scene, the Gardens). The preceding three plays were given at Lincoln's Inn Fields; the following pieces were produced at Dorset Garden. Crowne's *The History of Charles the Eighth of France,* November, 1671 (IV, *the Scene is drawn and a fair garden* is presented); Nevil Payne's *The Fatal Jealousie,* August, 1672 (IV, *Enter* Antonio *and* Jasper *in the Garden*); *The Dutch Lover,* February, 1673 (III, 4, *The Garden*); Shadwell's *The Virtuoso,* May, 1676 (I, *Enter* Miranda *and* Clarinda *in the Garden*; and several times during the play); Mrs. Behn's *Sir Patient Fancy,* 1677–8 (Act II, Scene 1, *A Garden to Sir* Patient Fancy's *House*); Otway's *Friendship in Fashion,* April, 1678 (the Fourth Act, Scene, *Night-garden*); D'Urfey's *Squire Oldsapp,* spring of 1678 (III, 2 and 4, *The Garden*); Ravenscroft's *The London Cuckolds,* winter of 1681 (V, *Enter* Doodle, Arabella, *and* Engine, *in the Garden.* A little later: Dashwell *and* Jane *upon a Mount, looking over a Wall that parts the two Gardens*); Mrs. Behn's *The False Count,* autumn (before the end of October), 1682 (IV, 2, *A Garden,* which locale continues until the end of the play).

A Grove appears in Mrs. Behn's *The Amorous Prince,* Lincoln's Inn Fields, spring of 1671 (I, 2, *A Grove,* at night; V, 2, *A Grove,* by day); and in Crowne's *Juliana,* at the same house, 1671 (which as cited above has Act the First. *The Scene a* Grove *and* Gardens). Again after 9th November, 1671, when Dorset Garden was opened, in Mrs. Behn's *The Dutch Lover,* February, 1673, Act I, Scene 3, is *A Grove,* Act III, Scene 2, is *A flat Grove,* and when this draws off Scene 3 is *A Grove.* In Shadwell's *The Libertine,* June, 1675, IV, after the dialogue of Clara and Flavia, "The SCENE is a delightful Grove." This was probably used

MRS. BRACEGIRDLE
Collection of Kenneth W. Sanderson, Esq.

W. Vincent

[*face p.* 224

in Otway's *Alcibiades,* autumn of the same year, II, 1, "*A Grove adjoyning to the* Spartan *Camp,*" which I make no doubt was also the opening scene of Mrs. Behn's *The Young King,* spring of 1679, Act I, Scene 1, *A Grove near the Camp,* which lies between the Dacians and the Scythians. Otway's *Don Carlos,* June, 1676, Act II, has SCENE An ORANGE GROVE. In Act III The GROVE continues. D'Urfey's *Squire Oldsapp; or, The Night Adventurers,* spring of 1678, Act I, Scene 2, is *Wood or Grove,* and the Second Act begins with *Grove continues.* In Dryden's and Lee's *Oedipus,* January, 1679, III, 1, is *A dark Grove.*

With the Duke's Company scenes of popular centres of contemporary life were as greatly favoured as at the Theatre Royal, and their presentation was meticulously exact and detailed. A very few examples, which might be almost indefinitely multiplied, will serve. The scene of Dryden's *Sr Martin Mar-All,* Lincoln's Inn Fields, 15th August, 1667, is Covent Garden. The same general stage direction is given in D'Urfey's *Madam Fickle,* Dorset Garden, autumn of 1676, and curiously enough in a play of the same author's to which attention may be drawn although acted after the Union and at the Theatre Royal, *A Commonwealth of Women,* produced about June, 1685, where as in *Madam Fickle* following the Dramatis Personae we have a direction, "SCENE, *Covent-Garden,*" although after the First Act we are transported to a ship at sea, and then for the remainder of the play to some far tropic isles where Amazonians rule.

Covent Garden is the locale of Act V, 1, of Mrs. Behn's *The Town-Fopp,* Dorset Garden, winter of 1676. Otway places the first scene of Act III of *The Souldiers Fortune,* Dorset Garden, 1680, in Covent Garden, and in Act IV of the same comedy the scene *changes to* Covent-Garden *Piazza.* Covent Garden also appears as the last scene of Act III and in Act IV of Leanerd's *The Rambling Justice; or, The Jealous Husbands,* which was given at the Theatre Royal early in 1678.

"The Pall Mall—In the year 1675" is the general scene of Crowne's *The Countrey Wit,* Dorset Garden, January, 1676. Scene 3 of the Fourth Act of Etherege's *The Man of Mode,* Dorset Garden, March, 1676, is "*The* Mail", and Otway commences two of his comedies, *Friendship in Fashion,* Dorset Garden, April, 1678, and *The Souldiers Fortune* in the same place.

Nevil Payne in *The Morning Ramble,* Dorset Garden, November, 1672, has scenes in Hyde Park and the Mulberry Garden. The first scene of the Fifth Act of D'Urfey's *Squire Oldsapp,* Dorset Garden, spring of 1678, is Clarendon House. St. James appears in Act II of a Theatre Royal play, Leanerd's *The Rambling Justice,* 1678.

A very favourite spot both on and off the stage was the New Exchange, an arcade on the south side of the Strand with two long galleries of shops, in double tier one above the other. Act III of Etherege's *She wou'd if she cou'd,* Lincoln's Inn Fields, February, 1668, opens in this resort: " *Mrs.* Trinckit *sitting in a Shop, people passing by as in the* Exchange." Otway has also shown the New Exchange in the Second Act of *The Atheist,* Dorset Garden, 1683. Beaugard and Courtine are strolling there and the latter remarks: " Methinks this Place looks as it were made for Loving: The Lights on each hand of the Walk look stately; and then the Rusling of Silks Petticoats, the Din and the Chatter of the pretty little party-colour'd Parrots . . ." Beaugard is there to keep an assignation and as he lingers near Mrs. Furnish's shop she hails him with " Gloves or Ribbands, Sir? Very good Gloves or Ribbands, Choice of fine Essences. Captain *Beaugard,* shall I sell you nothing to-day?" So in Carlile's *The Fortune-Hunters,* Drury Lane, 1689, Act II, Scene 2, is " *The* Exchange. *Discovers Mrs.* Spruce *in her Shop.*" Presently Sophia and Maria enter, whereupon Mrs. Spruce cries: " Ribbonds or Gloves, Madam; Gloves or Ribbonds."

Coffee-houses scenes in St. Serfe's *Tarugo's Wiles,* Lincoln's Inn Fields, October, 1667, and D'Urfey's *The Royalist,* Dorset Garden, January, 1682, are very life-like and vigorous and were most realistically presented. *The Way of the World,* Lincoln's Inn Fields, March, 1700, opens in a Chocolate-House.

During the last decade of the seventeenth century Southerne and Congreve show us the modish world sauntering in S. James' Park and trysting at Rosamund's Pond. Southerne too in *The Maid's Last Prayer; or, Any Rather than Fail,* Drury Lane, January, 1693, lays one of his scenes at the fashionably notorious Indian house kept by Mrs. Siam,[32] where also Cibber places the first scene of Act V of *Womans Wit; or, The Lady in Fashion,* produced at Drury Lane in December, 1696.

Although heroic tragedies in particular and serious drama in general were presented with sumptuous scenery and effects the most elaborate and the most prized decorations were reserved for Operas. It should be noted that this word, which actually is not far removed from slang being an abbreviation of the term *opera musicale,* was only beginning to become generally known and accepted in England. At first the precise signification seems to have been a little undetermined. Downes, on account of the machines, flyings for the witches, singing and dancing, introduced into Shakespeare's tragedy, regarded *Macbeth* as " being in the nature of an Opera"; and he also speaks of Shadwell's *The Lancashire Witches,* as " a kind of Opera". As late as 1685,

Dryden in his printed *Albion and Albanius* (folio, 1685) discusses the nature of an opera at great length, and defines an opera as "a poetical Tale, or Fiction, represented by Vocal and Instrumental Musick, adorn'd with Scenes, Machines, and Dancing". He also speaks of that part of an opera "which (for want of a proper *English* Word) I must call *The Songish Part*"; and adds that in his opinion whoever undertakes the writing of an opera "is obliged to immitate the Design of the *Italians*, who have not only invented, but brought to perfection, this sort of Dramatique Musical Entertainment".

The way to these musical representations set out with scenery had been admirably paved by *The Siege of Rhodes*, and as we have already shown in some detail it was not long before painted perspectives of no little skill and art began to adorn the English theatre. Yet in his *Discourse of the English Stage*, addressed to the Duke of Newcastle, and printed with the pastoral tragicomedy *Love's Kingdom*, 8vo, 1664, a preface which may have been written a year or two earlier, Richard Flecknoe says: "Now for the difference betwixt our Theaters and those of former times, they were but plain and simple, with no other Scenes, nor Decorations of the Stage, but onely old Tapestry, and the Stage strew'd with Rushes (with their Habits accordingly) whereas ours now for cost and ornament are arriv'd at the heighth of Magnificence; but that which makes our Stage the better, makes our Playes the worse perhaps, they striving now to make them more for sight, then hearing." A little later he adds: "For Scenes and Machines they are no new invention, our Masks and some of our Playes in former times (though not so ordinary) having had as good or rather better then any we have now."

The masque, which at Whitehall had been so much admired and so often presented in former reigns, did not achieve any great popularity under Charles II. The reasons for this are not far to seek. In the first place the King and his Queen were in no wise disposed to take part in these gorgeous shows, as had been the delight of Anne of Denmark, and had not been disdained by Charles I and Henrietta Maria. Again for his entertainment the King far more frequently visited the public theatres than had been the custom of former monarchs. The magnificence of the masque was incorporated in the opera, and thence long afterwards it passed as a heritage to the pantomime. John Crowne's *Calisto; or, The Chaste Nimph*, "designed for the pleasures and divertisements of their Majesties and Royal Highnesses," a masque set to music by Nicholas Staggins which was produced at Court in February, 1675, was an exceptional entertainment, and it does not appear to have been followed by any other court pieces of the same nature.[33] Colley Cibber in his *Apology* says in reference to masques: "After the Restoration of *Charles* II, some faint attempts were made to revive these Theatrical Spectacles at Court, but I have met with no Account of above one Masque acted there, by the Nobility; which was that of *Calisto,* written by *Crown.*" [34]

The very detailed and elaborate stage directions which are given in the printed texts of these "dramatic operas" clearly indicate what elaborate spectacular effects were presented, and indeed when Dorset Garden was built it was especially designed to allow of such exceptional representations. In 1661 the French players had given at the old Cockpit, in Drury Lane, Chapoton's *Le Mariage d'Orphée et d'Eurydice,* which required Great Machines and extraordinary effects. No doubt the hint did not fall on stony ground and whilst the splendid new theatre was being built Betterton paid a visit to Paris in order that he might personally investigate and learn from the conditions of the French Theatre. James Wright in his *Historia Histrionica,* 1699, speaks of scenes having been "introduced upon the publick Stage by Sir *William Davenant* at the *Duke's Old Theater* in *Lincolns-Inn-Fields,* but afterwards very much improved, with the Addition of curious Machines, by Mr. *Betterton* at the New *Theater* in *Dorset-Garden,* to the great Expence and continual Charge of the players".

The Tempest; or, The Enchanted Island, an alteration from Shakespeare by Dryden and Davenant, had been produced at Lincoln's Inn Fields on Thursday, 7th November, 1667, and had proved a great success. With whom this suggestion originated one cannot precisely say although it is strongly to be suspected that Betterton himself launched the idea, but, however that may be, some half a dozen years after, *The Tempest* was "made into an Opera by Mr. *Shadwell*", and thus produced at Dorset Garden *circa* 30th April, 1674. "The chief differences between the comedy *The Tempest* and the opera *The Tempest* may be summed up very briefly as—"new songs, dances, and spectacular effects, in particular the gorgeous masque of Neptune, fair Amphitrite, Oceanus, Tethys, the Tritons, and Nereides." "The first alteration of *The Tempest* seems immediately to have been absorbed in the opera, which was extraordinarily popular, indeed few pieces upon the Restoration stage proved so great and so continued an attraction." Both the Prologue and the Epilogue insist upon the extravagant outlay and cost of the production. The Prologue commences:—

> Wee, as the ffathers of the Stage have said,
> To treat you here a vast expense have made;

What they have gott from you in chests is laid,
Or is for purchas'd Lands, or houses paid,
You, in this house, all our estates may find,
Wch for your pleasures wholly are design'd.

The Epilogue is even more emphatic:—

When you of Witt, and sence, were weary growne,
Romantick, riming, fustian Playes were showne,
We then to flying Witches did advance,
And for your pleasures traffic'd into ffrance.
From thence new Arts to please you, we have sought
We have machines to some perfection brought,
And above 30 Warbling voyces gott.
Many a God & Goddesse you will heare
And we have Singing, Dancing, Devills here
Such Devills, and such gods, are very Deare.

On the 22nd August, 1673, James Vernon, writing a letter from Court to Sir Joseph Williamson at Cologne mentions that "the Dukes House are preparing an Opera and great machines. They will have dansers out of France, and St. André comes over with them".[35] On the 27th February, 1675, "The long expected Opera of *Psyche,* came forth in all her Ornaments; new Scenes, new Machines, new Cloathes, new *French* Dances; This Opera was splendidly set out, especially in Scenes; the charge of which amounted to above 800*l.* It had a Continuance of Performance about 8 Days together. It prov'd very Beneficial to the Company; yet the *Tempest* got them more Money." When we remember that Isaac Fuller was adjudged £335 10*s.* for one scene, a Paradise, it must be confessed that even above £800 seems very reasonable for the elaborate scenery of such an Opera as Shadwell's ornate *Psyche.* The first scene "is a very deep Walk in the midst of a mighty Wood, through which, is seen a Prospect of a very pleasant Country". The Second Act opens upon a most elaborate spectacle: "*The Scene is the Temple of* Apollo Delphicus, *with Columns of the* Dorick *Order, inrich'd with Gold, in the middle a stately Cupolo, on the top of it the Figure of the* Sun; *some distance before it an Altar lin'd with Brass; under it a large Image of* Apollo, *before which stands the Tripod.*" This scene changes "to a Rocky Desart full of dreadful Caves, Cliffs, and Precipices, with a high Rock looking down into the Sea". One of the chief scenic effects was reserved for Act III, the Palace of Cupid "*Compos'd of wreath'd Columns of the* Corinthian *Order; the Wreathing is adorn'd with Roses, and the Columns have several little* Cupids *flying about 'em, and a single* Cupid *standing upon every Capital. At a good distance are seen Three Arches, which* *divide the first Court from the other part of the Building: The middle Arch is noble and high, beautified with* Cupids *and* Festoons, *and supported with Columns of the foresaid Order. Through these Arches is seen another Court, that leads to the Main Building, which is at a mighty distance. All the* Cupids, *Capitals and Inrichments of the whole Palace are of Gold, Here the* Cyclops *are at work at a Forge, forging great Vases of Silver. The Musick strikes up, they dance, hammering the Vases upon Anvils*". It was this scene with the chorus of bedizened Cyclops at their aureate furnaces that Rochester gibed in his Epilogue to Sir Francis Fane's *Love in the Dark; or, The Man of Bus'ness,* produced at Drury Lane in May, 1675, some three months later than Shadwell's opera:—

> As Charms are Nonsense, Nonsense seems a Charm,
> Which hearers of all Judgement does disarm;
> For Songs, and Scenes, a double Audience bring,
> And Doggrel takes, which *Smiths* in Sattin sing.
> Now to Machines, and a dull Mash you run,
> We find that Wit's the Monster you would shun,
> And by my troth 'tis most discreetly done . . .
> For since with Vice and Folly Wit is fed,
> Through Mercy 'tis, most of you are not dead.
> Players turn Puppets now at your desire,
> In their Mouth's Nonsense, in their Tail's a Wire,
> They fly through Clouds of Clouts, and Showres of Fire.

A little later, in Act IV, when at the instigation of her two sisters Psyche is imprudent enough to ask her lover his name, and he declares himself to be the God of Love, the punishment of her untoward curiosity swiftly follows his disappearance. "*The Garden and Palace vanish, and* Psyche *is left alone in a vast Desert, upon the brink of a River in Marish, full of Willows, Flags, Bullrushes, and Water-flowers; beyond which, is seen a great open Desert.*" Agalura and Cidippe who have arrived at the place mock her despair and when with bitter taunts they have left her, "She offers to throw her self into the River. The God of the River arises upon a seat of Bullrushes and Reeds, leaning upon an Urn. The *Naiades* round him sing." In his analysis of *Psyche* Professor Dent well observes: "One of the most effective moments is the appearance of the river-god. Molière shows us the river-god reclining on his urn throughout the scene, and his remonstrance to Psyche is spoken. Shadwell causes him to rise from the river just at the moment when she is about to throw herself in, and heightens the effect enormously by making him sing, with the nymphs to echo his words. The music gives a much greater impressiveness to his entry, and adds a touch of mystery and solemnity to his prediction of her immortality." [36]

In due course the angry Venus dispatches Psyche to Hades in order to procure from Proserpine the mysterious box of beauty. Furies rise, and then descend with Psyche. Act V opens with the mythological concept of the fabled underworld. "The *Scene* represents Hell, consisting of many burning Ruines of Buildings on each side: In the foremost Pieces are the Figures of *Prometheus* and *Sisyphus, Ixion* and *Tantalus*. Beyond those are a great number of Furies and Devils, tormenting the damned. In the middle arises the Throne of *Pluto,* consisting of Pillars of Fire; with him *Proserpina*; at their feet sit *Minos, Æacus,* and *Rhadamanthus*. With the Throne of *Pluto* arise a great number of Devils and Furies, coming up at every rising about the House. Through the Pillars of *Pluto's* Throne, at a great distance is seen the Gate of Hell, through which a Lake of Fire is seen; and at a huge distance, on the farther side of that Lake, are vast Crowds of the Dead, waiting for *Charon's* Boat." After a return "*to the Marish which was in the former Act*", we have a grand finale. "The SCENE *changes to a* Heav'n. In the highest part is the Palace of *Jupiter*; the Columns and all the Ornaments of it of Gold. The lower part is all fill'd with *Angels* and *Cupids,* with a round open *Temple* in the midst of it. This *Temple* is just before the *Sun,* whose Beams break fiercely through it in divers places: Below the Heav'ns, several Semi-circular Clouds, of the breadth of the whole House, descend. In these Clouds sit the Musicians, richly Habited. On the front-Cloud sits *Apollo* alone. While the Musicians are descending they play a *Symphony* till Apollo begins, and sings." (The width of the Dorset Garden stage was about thirty feet, so these semi-circular clouds were of no mean dimensions.) A most elaborate concerted piece with a chorus and various symphonies of pipes, hautboys, and recorders follows. "Then *Jupiter* descends in a Machine, with *Cupid* on one side, and *Psyche* on the other. Then a Dance of six *Elizian* Princes, gloriously habited." After a song by Mars and a lively catch by Bacchus with appropriate music and refrains, there is a general chorus whilst the dancers mingle with the singers. "Six Attendants to the *Elizian* Princes bring in Portico's of Arbours, adorn'd with Festoons and Garlands, through which the Princes and they dance; the Attendants still placing them in several Figures." Jupiter speaks six lines of rhyming platitudes and the opera ends.

I have quoted the stage directions to *Psyche* very fully to show what great demands were put upon the theatre in February, 1675, for it must be remembered that Shadwell was not writing his directions from the pictures he saw in his imagination nor was he merely detailing what he would have liked to present upon the stage, but he was working in conjunction with the musicians Matthew Locke and Giovanni Baptista Draghi; with the ballet-master St. Andrée; and with the scene-painter, Stephenson; whilst the whole production was at every point most carefully supervised by the eminently practical Betterton himself. So we may certainly take it that in the libretto of Shadwell's opera we have a pretty accurate description of the spectacle the audience beheld. There is no need for me to insist upon the magnificence of these ornate and elaborate panoramas with their effects of vanishing and sudden changes; that they must have called into play every resource of the theatre, and that, I would venture to add, they must have been exceedingly beautiful, is obvious even to one who reads the bare printed account set forth without much attempt at grace or elegance of style.

No doubt many of the machines and much scenery would be utilized, as required, in later operas, for Downes tells us that all was new for this particular production and the scenes alone cost above £800, a very large sum for those days. But Betterton, it must be remembered, had recently returned from Paris where he had closely studied French stage decoration; and he was, certes, filled with a spirit of emulation and native competition.

It is by no means necessary so amply to quote from other operas and spectacular pieces. Stage directions, unless we can clearly visualize the picture, are apt to be a little arid in their accumulation. Brief references to some of the more notable productions will no doubt suffice. Charles Davenant's *Circe* was given at Dorset Garden in March, 1676–7, with music by Banister, and " being well Perform'd,[37] it answer'd the Expectation of the Company ". When I read the libretto I am strongly reminded of Italian opera; the whole tragedy is to my thinking most baroquely impregnated with that pseudo-classical atmosphere born of temples, sacrifices, choruses of Furies, dances of combatants, dragons whirling aloft enchanted chariots, Iris (with song) appearing on a rainbow, and all those many fascinations that are so conspicuous a feature of these grand teatri for which scenery was designed by Buontalenti, Alfonso Parigi, Vigarani, and the great Giovanni Maria Bibiena, the first of that famous family with whom artistry seemed a veritable heritage. Although the stage directions of *Circe* are not quite so elaborately set out as those of *Psyche* such a scene as that which opened the Fourth Act of Charles Davenant's opera would have proved very effective.

"Circe's *Inchanted Palace, with a beautiful Garden: In the middle is seen the Hill* Parnassus, *on which* Orpheus *is discovered a playing on his Lute, while* Orestes *is sleeping on a Bed of Flowers, with* Circe's *Women singing about him.*" Various concerted pieces follow and there is something like a miniature masque, which concludes by the entry of Bacchanals. "*They fling their Darts at* Orpheus, *who falls dead; they Dance, then the Mountain disappears.*" Later King Thoas makes his way to the garden and Circe wishes to conceal Orestes in an arbour. He refuses to withdraw, whereupon the lady summons supernatural aid; "*Spirits appear, who force* Orestes *into the Arbor,*" which obviously by some mechanical means closed over him since during her interview with the King Circe cries:—

> Oh sacred Bow'r! unfold thy leafie Arms,
> And be no more protected by my Charms.

"*The Bower opens,* Orestes *comes out, who is seiz'd by the Guards.*" There is some elaborate business in the Fifth Act. "*The Cave of the God of Sleep arises, with him* Phobetor *and* Morpheus." There are various entries of pleasant Dreams and with a change of scene of frightful Dreams, all of which must have called for no little skill in stagecraft.

When he has occasion to record the production of an opera Downes never omits to mention the great expense involved, and should the performance not prove successful it was little less of a disaster. Certainly the failure of Dryden's *Albion and Albanius* meant a very considerable loss to all concerned. Unhappily at the sixth, and last, performance the news reached London that the Duke of Monmouth had landed in the West, and the whole nation was thrown into such a stir as proved fatal to the piece.

If Dryden had been unlucky with *Albion and Albanius,* and this miscarriage was owing to circumstances beyond the poet's control, he scored a very great and thoroughly deserved success with *King Arthur; or, The British Worthy,* which was produced at Dorset Garden in January, 1692. The music is by Purcell, and is justly celebrated and admired, the Frost Scene being one of that master's most famous achievements.

A year or two previously Betterton also had retrieved anything that he might have lost either of reputation or money by the ill-fortune of 1685. In 1689–1690 he engaged Purcell to compose the music for a new opera which he himself adapted from *The Prophetess,* a play belonging to the 1647 folio Beaumont and Fletcher.[38] Betterton's version *The Prophetess; or, The History of Dioclesian,* printed 4to, 1690, chiefly differs from the original in the somewhat drastic curtailment of the dialogue to admit of a number of songs and dances, musical interludes and similar *divertimenti* embellished with a good deal of intricate business. Thus in Act III the opening scene is "*A Room, Chairs in it, the Hangings and Figures* Grotesk". Later Delphia, the prophetess, charms the figures in the arras, which are spirits who do her bidding. She waves her wand, and "*The Figures come out of the Hangings and Dance: And Figures exactly the same appear in their places: When they have danc'd a while, they go to sit on the Chairs, they slip from 'em, and after joyn in the Dance with 'em*". This seems an episode which was very popular. In Mrs. Behn's Italian pantomime *The Emperor of the Moon,* produced at Dorset Garden in the spring of 1687, a number of characters who are dressed in carnival habits in order to avoid Doctor Baliardo take their places in the hangings of the room, and standing there without motion appear as the figures in the tapestry. *The Spectator,* No. 22 (Steele), Monday, 26th March, 1711, has a humorous reference to this. William Screne writes: "I have acted several Parts of Houshold-stuff with great Applause for many Years; I am one of the Men in the Hangings in the *Emperor of the Moon;* I have twice performed the third Chair in an *English* Opera." Ralph Simple also sends a letter to Mr. Spectator: "I have several times acted one of the finest Flower-pots in the same Opera wherein Mr. *Screne* is a Chair; therefore upon his Promotion, request that I may succeed him in the Hangings, with my Hand in the Orange-Trees."

The Prophetess concludes with a masque, and although the stage direction is somewhat lengthy it will not, I think, be impertinent to quote at length, as there are few better examples of the elaborate stage mechanism which could be and was employed in the English theatre at the end of the seventeenth century.

"While a Symphony is Playing, a Machine descends, so large, it fills all the Space, from the Frontispiece of the Stage to the farther end of the House; and fixes it self by two Ladders of Clouds to the Floor. In it are Four several Stages, representing the Pallaces of two Gods, and two Goddesses: The first is the Pallace of *Flora*; the Columns of red and white Marble, breaking through the Clouds; the Columns Fluted and Wreath'd about with all sorts of Flow'rage; the Pedestals and Flutings inrich'd with Gold. The Second is, The Pallace of the Goddess *Pomona,* the Columns of blue Marble, wound about with all kind of Fruitage, and inrich'd with Gold as the other. The Third is, The Pallace of *Bacchus,* the Columns of green Marble, Wreath'd and Inrich'd with Gold, with Clusters of Grapes hanging round 'em. The last is the Pallace of the Sun; it is supported on either Side by Rows of *Terms,* the lower part white Marble, the upper part Gold. The whole Object is terminated with a glowing Cloud, on which is a Chair of State, all of Gold, the Sun breaking through the Cloud, and making a Glory about it: As this descends, there rises from under the Stage a pleasant Prospect of a Noble Garden, consisting of Fountains, and Orange Trees set in large Vases: the middle Walk leads to a Pallace at a great distance. At the same time Enters *Silvanus, Bacchus, Flora, Pomona, Gods* of the Rivers, *Fawns, Nymphs, Hero's, Heroines, Shepherds, Shepherdesses,* the *Graces,* and *Pleasures* with the rest of their followers. The Dancers place themselves on every Stage in the Machine: the Singers rang themselves about the Stage."

Several interesting operas and operatic versions of older plays are passed over here, but a brief word must be given to *The Fairy-Queen,* an alteration, sometimes attributed to Elkanah Settle, of *A Midsummer Night's Dream.* Here we have a very riot of magic and glamour. It was, says Downes, even superior in ornaments to *The Prophetess* and *King Arthur.* The same artists were responsible for the music and the ballet, Henry Purcell and Josias Priest. The clothes, singers and dancers, scenes, machines and decorations were all "most profusely set off; and excellently perform'd". Accordingly "the Court and Town were wonderfully satisfy'd with it; but the Expences in setting it out being so great, the Company got very little by it". Certain it is that *The Fairy-Queen* is second to none for mechanical marvels, which if one may judge must have been of the most entrancing and exquisite beauty. Fairyland itself is exhibited to the audience. Probably not the least lovely effect was the Garden of Fountains.[39] "*A Sonata plays while the Sun rises, it appears red through the Mist, as it ascends it dissipates the Vapours, and is seen in its full Lustre; then the Scene is perfectly discovered, the Fountains enrich'd with gilding, and adorn'd with Statues: The view is terminated by a Walk of Cypress Trees which lead to a delightful Bower. Before the Trees stand rows of Marble Columns, which support many Walks which rise by Stairs to the top of the House; the Stairs are adorn'd with Figures on Pedestals, and Rails; and Balasters on each side of 'em. Near the top, vast Quantities of Water break out of the Hills, and fall in mighty Cascade's to the bottom of the Scene, to feed the Fountains which are on each side. In the middle of the Stage is a very large Fountain, where the Water rises about twelve Foot. Then the 4 Seasons enter, with their several Attendants.*"

In Act V "Juno *appears in a Machine drawn by Peacocks*", and presently "the Peacocks *spread their Tails, and fill the middle of the Theater*", which is taken from *Albion and Albanius,* Act I:

"Juno *appears in a Machine drawn by Peacocks . . . it opens and discovers the Tail of the Peacock, which is so Large, that it almost fills the opening of the Stage between Scene and Scene While the Scene is darken'd, a single Entry is danced; Then a Symphony is play'd; after that the Scene is suddainly Illuminated, and discovers a transparent Prospect of a* Chinese *Garden, the Architecture, the Trees, the Plants, the Fruit, the Birds the Beasts quite different from what we have in this part of the World. It is terminated by an Arch, through which is seen other Arches with close Arbors, and a row of Trees to the end of the view. Over it is a hanging Garden, which rises by several ascents to the top of the House; it is bounded on either side with pleasant Bowers, various Trees,*[40] *and numbers of strange Birds flying in the Air, on the Top of a Platform is a Fountain throwing up Water, which falls into a large Basin.*" A man and a woman from Cathay, robed in curious oriental silks, sing and dance together in this appropriate setting.

The monkey ballet is famous; "*Six Monkeys come from between the Trees, and Dance.*" Equally antic is the business during and at the conclusion of Hymen's song: "*Six Pedestals of* China-*work rise from under the Stage; they support Six large Vases of Porcelain, in which are six* China-*Orange-trees. . . . The Pedestals move toward the Front of the Stage, and the Grand Dance begins of Twenty-four Persons.*"

George Powell's opera *Brutus of Alba; or, Augusta's Triumph,* produced at Dorset Garden in 1696, seems to have utilized some of the scenery both of *Albion and Albanius* and of *The Fairy Queen,* but it is only right to add that several new effects were introduced and the production is from all points of view one of no small interest. D'Urfey's *Cinthia and Endimion; or, The Loves of the Deities* had originally been designed to be acted at Court before Queen Mary II, but upon the death of that lady it was produced at the Theatre Royal in 1697. It may be remarked that it is something exceptional for an opera to be given at Drury Lane rather than at Dorset Garden, since the latter house was in every way the better adapted for elaborate spectacle. The reason, no doubt, lies in the fact that, although quite sufficiently ornate, *Cinthia and Endimion* does not scale the heights of magnificence which were essayed in some of the operas we have been considering. The form of the Prologue is unusual. "The Scene is a pleasant Country, in which appears, by an artificial Sun just setting Mount *Latmus,* with pleasant Valleys round it; some full of Corn, others with Fruit; a Gloominess on the suddain o're-spreads the Stage, till after a while *Saturnia,* representing Night, ascends from the Stage, and Sings." After the song the Pleiades enter, and "joyn in a Figure like the Seven

Stars ; as they appear, the Scene becomes more light ". Merope, who is the seventh and least visible star of the constellation, has a charming song, and after a ballad by Zephyrus the first Act commences. "*The* SCENE *appears more lightned ; Variety of Birds are heard Singing ; and several Flutes, as suppos'd, play'd on by the Inhabitants, Shepherds then.*" At the finale the stage is filled with Nymphs, Stars, and Rivers ; there is a grand dance of Gods and Goddesses, " Endimion *is chang'd into a Star, and with a Chorus the* Opera *concludes.*"

As we have noticed, Betterton visited Paris for the sake of studying the decoration of the French theatre, and the famous comedian Joseph Haines in company with Thomas Wright, the chief machinist of the Duke's Theatre and in these matters Betterton's most trusted auxiliary, took a journey to the French capital for the same purpose. It is somewhat curious to find that in the Dedicatory Letter to Christopher Rich that appears before the printed copy of Settle's Dramatic Opera *The World in the Moon,* 4to, 1697, the poet not merely suggests but emphasizes the native origin of this kind of spectacle. He says " That never was such a Pile of Painting rais'd upon so Generous a Foundation ". More, he adds, " I have remov'd a long Heap of Rubbish, and thrown away all our old *French* Lumber, our Clouds of Clouts, and set the Theatrical Paintings at a much fairer Light." In the Epilogue he is no less insistent :—

> *tis all home-spun Cloth ;*
> *All from an* English *Web, and* English *Growth.*
> *But if we'd let it make a costly Dance*
> *To* Paris, *and bring home some Scenes from* France,
> *I'm sure 'twou'd take : For you, Gadzooks, are civil,*
> *And wish them well, that wish you at the Devil.*

Perhaps this last line betrays the true reason for Settle's attitude. It must be remembered that at this time England and France were on very ill terms. The allusion to "*an* English *Web*", being a play upon the name John Webb, the assistant of Inigo Jones, and the artist who designed not only the famous scenery for *The Siege of Rhodes,* but for many other of Davenant's pieces, is distinctly interesting, and Settle vaunts himself truly patriotic in most native vein. Not that *The World in the Moon* was without its elaborate spectacular effects. For example in the first act " The Flat-Scene draws, and discovers Three grand Arches of Clouds extending to the Roof of the House, terminated with a Prospect of Cloud-work, all fill'd with the Figures of Fames and *Cupids* ; a Circular part of the black Clouds rolls softly away, and gradually discovers a Silver Moon, near Fourteen Foot Diameter :

After which, the Silver Moon wanes off by degrees, and discovers the World within, consisting of Four grand Circles of Clouds, illustrated with *Cupids*, &c. Twelve golden Chariots are seen riding in the Clouds, fill'd with Twelve Children, representing the Twelve Celestial Signs. The Third Arch intirely rolling away, leaves the full Prospect terminating with a large Lanschape of Woods, Waters, Towns, *&c.*" In Act IV the Scene is "a Wood, near Thirty Foot high, the Paintings meeting in Circle; all the Side-Pieces and Back-Scene cut through, to see a farther Prospect of a Wood, continued to the Extent of the House". In the last great scene is exhibited "*A Prospect of Terras Walks on Eight several Stages, mounted one above another*" and "*Above Fifty Figures are seen upon the several Terras's*".

It must not be supposed that all this expense and elaboration passed without criticism from the purer classicists. It will be sufficient to quote the following passage from the famous Rymer's *A Short View of Tragedy*[41]: "*Horace* was very angry with these empty *Shows* and Vanity, which the Gentlemen of his time ran like mad after.

Insanos oculos, et gaudia vana.

What would he have said to the *French Opera,* of late so much in vogue? There it is for you to bewitch your *eyes* and to charm your *ears*. There is a Cup of Enchantment, there is Musick and Machine; *Circe* and *Calipso* in conspiracy against Nature and good Sense. 'Tis a Debauch the most insinuating, and the most pernicious; none would think an *Opera* and Civil Reason, should be the growth of one and the same Climate." It may be remarked that the correct Dacier condemned Opera as "the Grotesque of Poetry", whilst actually it was not until 1705 that the Italian Opera was introduced into England in its entirety, although for many years the way had been most amply and admirably prepared.

It cannot have escaped notice that in all these multifold variations and changes of operatic scenery, rivalling in their coruscations the transformation scenes of Victorian pantomime, large set pieces are often directed to rise or to sink. For example in Act III of *Albion and Albanius,* "*The Cave of* Proteus *rises out of the Sea, it consists of several Arches of Rockwork adorn'd with mother of Pearl, Coral, and abundance of Shells of various kinds. Thro' the Arches is seen the Sea, and Parts of* Dover *Peer; In the middle of the Cave is* Proteus *asleep on a Rock adorn'd with Shells, &c. like the Cave.* Albion *and* Acacia *seize on him; and while a Symphony is playing, he sinks as they are bringing him forward, and changes himself into a Lyon, a Crocodile, a Dragon, and then to his own Shape again ; He comes toward the front of the Stage, and Sings.*" later " *A Machine rises out of the Sea : It opens and discovers and* Albanius *sitting in a great Scallop-shell, richly adorn'd : is attended by the Loves and Graces,* Albanius *by* Hero's ; *T is drawn by Dolphins : It moves forward, while a Simphony of uts-Doux, &c. is playing, till it Lands 'em on the Stage, and then it closes and sinks* ".

In *King Arthur,* produced at the same house in January, 1692, during the terminal masque, " *The Scene opens, and discovers a calm Sea, to the end of the House. An* Island *arises, to a soft Tune* ; Brittania *seated in the Island, with Fishermen at her Feet, &c.*" In the same opera as King Arthur is making his way through the enchanted wood and about to cross the bridge, " *two Syrens arise from the Water* " and sing that song " *Two Daughters of this Aged Stream are we* ", where exquisitely beautiful words have been set to exquisitely beautiful music. A little later when the King destroys the magic oak he " *Strikes twice or thrice, and the Tree falls, or sinks* ".

These stage directions involve the employment of an elaborate and intricate system of trap doors, some of which must have been of very considerable size ; and such indeed actually did cut up the stage of Dorset Garden. The boards of Drury Lane were equally honeycombed, and in the ludicrous account which is given in *The Tatler,* No. 99, 26th November, 1709, of the retirement of Rich from Drury Lane it is humorously related how Divito (Rich) rallied all his subjects of the theatre : " Door-Keepers came out clad like Cardinals, and Scene-Drawers like Heathen Gods. *Divito* himself was wrapped up in one of his black clouds, and left to the Enemy nothing but an empty Stage, full of Trap-Doors, known only to himself and his Adherents."
✓In the Restoration theatre very great use was made of the traps, and a point that must be most carefully borne in mind is that the large traps through which set pieces of scenery of some size, often with characters grouped upon them, rose or sank, were on the further side of the proscenium, that is to say within the curtain line ; whilst the apron stage had smaller traps through which one character, or perhaps two characters together, might sink or appear from below. Restoration tragedy is very lavish in its employment of the supernatural, and it would, I think, hardly be any exaggeration to say that unless there be some specific stage direction to the contrary, all apparitions, all ghosts and demons, one might almost say all supernatural visitants, rose on to the stage through a trap-door. This is merely a continuance of the Elizabethan practice, of which there are innumerable examples.

Incidentally it may be remarked that in Dryden's tragedy *Tyrannick Love* the Angel Amariel descends. In Act IV he "*descends to soft Musick, with a flaming Sword*". When he has driven away the spirits he ascends. Again in Act V when the torture of the wheel is about to be inflicted, "Amariel *descends swiftly with a flaming Sword, and strikes at the Wheel, which breaks in pieces, then he ascends again.*" When Pepys was at the revival of *The Virgin Martir,* at the Theatre Royal on Thursday, 27th February, 1668, what pleased him beyond anything in the whole world "was the wind-musique when the Angel comes down, which is so sweet that it ravished me".

In Nahum Tate's *Brutus of Alba; or, The Enchanted Lovers,* Dorset Garden, 1678, Ragusa and her four attendant witches vanish down the traps. Thus in Act V when the Queen cries: "Pernicious Hagg! a Guard here, seize the Witch." "*Guard Entring,* Ragusa *vanishes,*" obviously down a trap. It is a little uncertain how in Act III "Ragusa *appears in the storm*", probably she rose through a trap, but witches for the most part were distinguished by flying in machines, an aerial transvection eminently appropriate to the infernal sisterhood. Downes tells us that when *Macbeth* was produced as "alter'd by Sir *William Davenant*" one of the principal features was "Machines, as flyings for the Witches". He even considered Shadwell's *The Lancashire Witches,* Dorset Garden, autumn (probably September) of 1681, "a kind of Opera," since it had "several Machines of Flyings for the Witches, and other Diverting Contrivances in't". When the play was revived at the Haymarket, 1st July, 1707, by the Summer Company, it was announced as "with all the risings, sinkings, and flyings of the Witches, as they were originally performed". In Act I of *The Lancashire Witches* "*Mother* Demdike *rises out of the ground*", and a little later during the storm, when Clod enters with his candle and lanthorn, "One of the Witches flies away with the Candle and Lanthorn, Mother Demdike sets him upon the Top of a Tree, and they all fly away Laughing." At the end of Act II the visit of the hags to Sir Edward's cellar, all the witches "*sink and vanish*". In Act III after the admission of Madge into their horrid society, "*They all vanish,*" probably by flying off in the air as Tom Shacklehead fires his gun at them. Upon the next occasion when the whole crew is heard above Shacklehead who is crossing a field shoots, "M. Spencer *shrieks and falls down.*" Clod ensorcells her by repeating the magic couplet and throwing a bridle over her; then "*He flies away upon her*". In the gallery of the manor Teague O'Divelly is talking in the dark to Mother Dickenson, whom he has mistaken for another, and when Susan enters with a light, "*The Witch sinks.*" When candles are brought "*two Spirits fly away with 'em*".

This elaborate business of flyings was very often not accomplished without certain risks to the actors. *The Spectator,* No. 141, Saturday, 11th August, 1711 (Steele) has a supposed letter from a member of the audience at the revival of Shadwell's play. He says: "*Ben. Johnson* was almost lamed; young *Bullock* narrowly saved his Neck." In the preamble it is reported: "I am informed, that while I was out of Town the Actors have flown in the Air, and play'd such Pranks, and run such Hazards, that none but the Servants at the Fire-Office, Tilers and Masons, could have been able to perform the like." That there is a serious undercurrent in the jest is plain from what we are told by Chetwood, who after relating an accident which happened during the Pantomime Entertainment of *Dr. Faustus* at Lincoln's Inn Fields when a Machine broke killing two of the occupants and maiming a third, so that in future only dummy figures were allowed to be thus conveyed, continues: "Another Accident of the same Kind happened in *Smock-Alley,* which gave me much Concern as having a Hand in the Contrivance. The late Mr. *Morgan* being to fly on the Back of a Witch, in the *Lancashire Witches,* thro' the Ignorance of the Workers in the Machinery, the Fly broke, and they both fell together, but thro' Providence they neither of them were much hurt; and such Care was taken afterwards, that no Accident of that Kind *could* happen."

The operatic *The Tempest* has many flyings of the "aiery Spirits" Ariel and Milcha, and at the conclusion the "*Scene changes to the Rising Sun, and a number of Aerial Spirits in the Air,* Ariel *flying from the Sun, advances towards the Pit*". After the song, *Where the Bee sucks, there suck I,* "Ariel *speaks, hovering in the Air.*" There is an amusing reference to the flyings in D'Urfey's *The Marriage Hater Match'd,* produced at the Theatre Royal early in January, 1692, where in answer to Lord Brainless' "thou toldst me her Breeding was such, that she had been so familiar with Kings and Queens", Darewell replies: "Ay my Lord in the Play-house, I told ye she was a High Flyer, too, that is, I have seen her upon a Machine in the *Tempest.*" In the *Daily Courant,* 13th February, 1707–8, a performance of *The Tempest* is announced with "all the original Flyings and Musick". Great use was also made of the trap-doors. In Act II, Scene 3, "*The Stage opens in several places,*" and presently a number of Devils arise singing a chorus. As Alonzo, Antonio, and Gonzalo are going out "*a Devil rises just before them*". One of the great features of the opera was, according to Downes, the disappearance of the table just as Trinculo and his company were about to seat themselves to the banquet, IV, 2: "*A Table rises, and four Spirits with Wine and Meat enter, placing it, as they dance, on the Table: The Dance ended, the Bottles vanish, and the Table sinks agen.*"

The trap-door is one of the oldest, as it can be one of the most effective pieces of theatrical mechanism, and it is interesting to note that in Jean Michel's *Le Mistere de la Resurrection de Nostre Seigneur,* which was given in 1491, the Risen Saviour suddenly appeared through the stage without any indication of the place whence He emerged.[42] Turf had been carefully arranged all round the edges of the trap as well as upon the trap itself.

Early examples of the use of traps may be found in *Gorboduc,* given at Whitehall early in 1562, where in the fourth dumb-show the Furies issue forth from the underworld. In Gascoigne's and Kinwelmershe's tragedy *Jocasta,*[43] 1566, we have what is possibly the first example of the use of that large oblong trap which is still employed on the stage, and still known by its old name " grave-trap ". " The *grave-trap* is the one in centre of the stage, or nearly so, and is so called on account of its use in the grave-scene in ' Hamlet '." [44] In the second dumb-show of *Jocasta* mourners appear bearing two biers, " and after they had caried the coffins about the stage, there opened and appeared a grave, wherein they buried the coffins, and put fire to them . . . After the funerals were ended and the fire consumed, the grave was closed up again, the mourners withdrew them off the stage." In the third dumb show " there opened and appeared in the stage a great gulfe ". There is then shown the story of Mettus Curtius who came in like " a knighte with his sword drawen, armed at all poyntes ", and walking twice or thrice about it (the Lacus Curtius), " sodeinly lepte into the gulfe, the which did close up immediately."

Attention has been drawn to the scene in Dryden's *King Arthur* where the tree that is felled sinks through the earth, that is to say through a trap, and there are some episodes in Elizabethan plays in which, generally as the result of the conjuror's art, trees rise or descend through the earth. In Greene and Lodge's *A Looking Glasse for London and England* (*circa* 1590; 4to, 1594), " The Magi with their rods beate the ground, and from vnder the same riseth a braue Arbour." Again in Greene's *The Honorable Historie of frier Bacon, and frier Bongay,* 4to, 1594 (*circa* 1589), Scene 8, " *Heere Bungay coniures and the tree appeares with the dragon shooting fire.*" In *A Warning for Fair Women,* 4to, 1599, in a dumb-show when lovers offer to embrace " suddenly riseth vp a great tree betweene them ".

The grave-trap was also used in river scenes, when as so often a character leaped into the stream and was drowned, or was thrown into the water. The trap was masked from view by an imitation bank of sedge and rushes or a mossy slope with flowers, properties possessed by every theatre. In Henslowe's inventory of the properties of the Admiral's Men, 10th March, 1598, we find "ij moss banckes and j snake". (This no doubt was used in *Locrine* [45].) In this connection we may remark a scene in *The Divils Charter,*[46] a robustious and singularly unhistorical melodrama by Barnaby Barnes which was acted in 1607, and printed quarto that year. The episode in question presents the murder of the Duke of Gandia, a crime which, as is well known, romantic writers attribute to Caesar Borgia, but which more sober historians consider to be the result of a vendetta of Orsini. In Barnes' tragedy, Act III, Scene 5, it is black night and Frescobaldi is already concealed upon the stage. "*Enter a Page with a torche, Duke of* Candie *and* Caesar Borgia *disguised.*" The torch is put out and the boy dismissed, whereupon Gandia remarks that it is very dark. Caesar picks a sudden quarrel with his brother and then "*trips up* Candies *heels*", at the same time giving the concealed bravo the watchword "Col nuvolo la pioggia". Thereupon they both stab their victim, and Caesar says:—

> Helpe *Frescobaldi* let vs heaue him ouer,
> That he may fall into the riuer *Tiber,*
> Come to the bridge with him.

The body is thrown into the water and Caesar, in order to get rid of a witness, as the bravo is stooping over the brink "*casteth* Frescobaldi *after*".

I think that we may definitely say that a realistic splash was heard, for certainly such was the case when the same episode was presented upon the Restoration stage, and the parallel scene in Lee's tragedy *Caesar Borgia; The Son of Pope Alexander the Sixth,* produced at Dorset Garden in the late summer or early autumn of 1679, is so interesting that it may be quoted in full.[47]

Enter one Executioner with a dark Lanthorn, follow'd by another at a distance; they part often, look up and down, and hem to the rest.

1 *Exec.* The Coast is clear, and all the Guards are gone.
2 *Exec.* Hark, hark; what noise was that?
1 *Exec.* The Clock struck three.
2 *Exec.* See, the Moon shines; haste, and call our Fellows.
Hem to 'em; that's the Sign.
1 *Exec.* They come, they come.

Enter four Executioners more; two carry the Body of the

Duke of Gandia *in a Chair; the others follow, and scout behind.*

1 *Exec.* So—set him down, and let 'em bear their part;
For I am weary—
4 *Exec.* And so am I: I sweat; but 'tis with fear.
1 *Exec.* Make no more words on't; take him from the Chair.
2 *Exec.* A ghastly sight. The Weight about his Neck
Has bent him almost double: I'll not touch him—
3 *Exec.* Cowardly Villain—Come, my Princely Master,
The Fishes want their Break-fast.
4 *Exec.* Joyn all together,
And hurl him o're this Wall into the *Tyber*.
2 *Exec.* Fly, fly—I hear a noise: The Guards, the Guards.
3 *Exec.* He lies, he lies; the Coynage of his fears;
Once more, I say, joyn all your hands together.
Remember the Reward, two thousand Crowns
A Man: but for that Milk-sop, I suspect him;
Therefore let's watch our time, decoy him on;
And when this business is a little o're,
Strangle him in some Corner, lest he prate
Of what is done. Now, now's the time, away—

They joyn all together; take him by the Legs and Arms, and hurl him over the Wall into the Tyber: *A noise is heard, as of a Body falling into the Water—They look about once more, then start, take up the Chair, and run out—Scene shuts.*

The grave-trap was employed in Nevil Payne's *The Fatal Jealousie,* Dorset Garden, 1672,[48] Act III, the scene at the witch's house, when Jasper, fearful of a surprise, asks:—

What's that? No stratagem to help it?
Have you no hole near us, Aunt?
Witch. Yes, here is one, but should we go into 't
The other taken once, will soon betray us.

A little after Jasper "*Runs her through often, then throws her into the hole she shew'd him*".

A little previously reference has been made to the scene in *A Looking Glasse for London and England,* where Rasni, King of Nineveh, commands the Magi to exercise their sorceries for his pleasure.

Magi, for loue of Rasni by your Art,
By Magicke frame an Arbour out of hand;
For faire Remilia to disport her in.
Meane-while, I will bethinke me on further pomp.

Whereupon, as indeed has already been noted, "The Magi with their rods beate the ground, and from vnder the same riseth a braue Arbour." The striking of the earth with their wands was of course an effective gesture of the incantation, but it also served another purpose, it gave the cue to the men working the trap to send up the arbour from below. In fact this method of striking upon the ground, or more usually of stamping upon the ground with the foot, very often occurs to give the cue for the men to be ready with the trap. Thus at the commencement of Jonson's *Cynthia's Revels,*[49] I, 2, when Mercury wishes to summon Echo he says:—

> Make haste, sad *Nymph,* thrice shall my winged rod
> Strike th' obsequious earth, to giue thee way.
> Arise, . . .

and thereupon Echo ascends. In Middleton's *A Mad World, My Masters,*[50] the succubus on being commanded to depart, "Stamps—and *Exit,*" which of course implies that she vanishes down a trap. Again in *The Witch of Edmonton,* produced at the Cockpit in 1621, but not printed until 1658, when Mother Sawyer summons the spirit, "*She stamps. Enter the Dog; he fawns and leaps upon her.*" It is plain that he appears from below through a trap, and a moment later he vanishes in the same way.

In Rawlins' curious tragedy *The Rebellion,* 4to, 1640, Act IV, when Aurelia saves Antonio, who is seated in a chair contrived suddenly to sink through an oubliette, "*She takes a Dogge and tyes it to the Chaire, shee stampes: The Chaire and Dogge descends, a Pistoll shot within: a noise of a Mill.*"

Precisely the same method of giving this particular cue was employed in the Restoration theatre. Thus in Ravenscroft's comedy *Dame Dobson; or, The Cunning Woman,* produced at Dorset Garden in the early autumn of 1683, Act V, Dame Dobson showing a cast of her craft, "*Whistles. Thunders and Lightnings, stamps with her foot and sinks down.*" Similarly in Mrs. Manley's *The Lost Lover,* a comedy produced at Drury Lane in January, 1695–6, in Act III the sharking fortune-teller, Knowlittle, raises a spirit for his clients. Timothy his man is ready, waiting the summons. Knowlittle "*uses postures of Conjuration, Stamps with his Foot: then* Tim *arises, dress'd like a Fury, with a Wand in his Hand,*" exclaiming: "From Hell's deep Center, hither am I come." Again in Dryden's *Amphitryon; or, The Two Socias,* produced at Drury Lane early in October, 1690, Act IV, when Mercury gives Phaedra a cast of his office, "*He stamps upon the ground: some Dancers come from underground: and others from the sides of the Stage: A Song, and a fantastick Dance.*" After the entertainment he says to the lady "Thou art wishing, now, for the same Power I have exercis'd; that thou mightest stamp like me; and have more Singers come up for another Song". Phaedra exclaims: "Gad, I think the Devil's in you. Then I do stamp in some body's name, but I know not whose; (*stamps.*) Come up, Gentle-folks, from below; and sing me a Pastoral Dialogue, where the Woman may have the better of the Man; as we always have in Love matters. [*New Singers come up and sing a Song.*"

When we find that Prologues and Epilogues are spoken by characters who rise from below we have direct evidence of the employment of the traps in the apron stage. A few examples of this will serve for the very many that might be quoted. The Prologue to Dryden's *Troilus and Cressida; or, Truth Found too Late,* Dorset Gardens, spring of 1679, was "Spoken by Mr. *Betterton,* Representing the Ghost of *Shakespear*".

> *See, my lov'd* Britons, *see your* Shakespeare *rise,*
> *An awfull ghost confess'd to human eyes!*

The Prologue of Mrs. Behn's *The Roundheads; or, The Good Old Cause,* Dorset Garden, January, 1682, was "Spoken by the Ghost of *Hewson* ascending from Hell dress'd as a Cobler". To speak the Prologue to Lord Lansdowne's *The Jew of Venice,* Lincoln's Inn Fields, spring of 1701, "The Ghosts of Shakespeare and Dryden Arise, Crown'd with Lawrel." The Prologue to *Iphigenia* a tragedy by Dennis produced at Lincoln's Inn Fields in November, 1699, was "*Spoke by Mr. Verbruggen.* The Genius of *England* rises to a Warlike Symphony". When he has delivered the Prologue, "He sinks to the same Symphony that he rose."

The Epilogue, to Tate's *Brutus of Alba,* Dorset Garden, 1678, is delivered "by *Ragusa* rising from under the stage". In order to speak the Epilogue to D'Urfey's opera *Cinthia and Endimion,* Theatre Royal, 1697, "*Mr.* Dogget, *dress'd like* Collin, *rises from under the Stage as frighted.*" The Epilogue to George Powell's *The Imposture Defeated; or, A Trick to Cheat the Devil,* produced at Drury Lane in the autumn of 1697, was "Spoken by Mr. *Mills* ascending from under the Stage". Mills played the familiar Artax, and in Act I of the comedy, Artax "*a Spirit rises in the Habit of a Scholar*".

With regard to the actual mechanism and working of the trap doors, especially of that trap which in and after the eighteenth century was known as the ghost-trap, it is certain that there was a very extensive cellarage of some considerable depth under the Restoration theatres.

Incidentally it may be remarked that another kind of trap, the vampire-trap did not come into existence until the nineteenth century. Actually it was invented for the production of Planché's

The Vampire; or, The Bride of the Isles,[51] which was produced at the English Opera House, 9th August, 1820. " A Vampire trap consists of two or more flaps, usually india rubber, through which the sprite can disappear almost instantly, where he falls into a blanket fixed to the under surface of the stage. As with the star trap, this trap is secured against accidents by placing another piece or *slide,* fitting close beneath when not required, and removed when the prompters bell gives the signal to make ready."

It must be borne in mind that a character could ascend or descend gradually by means of a trap. Thus in Peele's extraordinary *The Famous Chronicle of king Edward the first* when Queen Elinor has wished that the earth may gape and swallow her if she has been the Autor of the Mayoress's tragedy, instantly she exclaims: " On *Ione,* helpe *Ione* thy mother sinckes. *Ione.* Oh mother my helpe is nothing, oh she is suncke, and here the earth is new closde vp againe, ah Charinge greene for euer change thy hew . . . because that beauteous *Elinor* sincke on thee." Presently " *Enter the Potter and the Potters wife called the Potters hive dwelling there, and Iohn her man* ". We are now at Potters Hive. Queen Elinor rises gradually out of the earth to the great alarm of goody who bawls out in a sad fright: " Staie *Iohn,* what's that riseth out of the ground, Iesus blesse vs, *Iohn;* look how it riseth higher and higher." " Be my troth mistres tis a woman," answers John, " good Lord do women grow, I neuer saw none grow before." There are no stage directions, but it is quite plain that Queen Elinor, who addresses the Potter's wife with " Welcome good woman, what place is this ", rose gradually from the trap and by degrees.[52] In the Fifth Act of *The Virgin Martir,* 4to, 1620, when Theophilus holds up the Cross of flowers, Harpax the demon " *Sinkes a little* " yelling " Keepe from me ". " Art poasting to thy center? down hel-hound, down," cries Theophilus as the fiend disappears.

At Dorset Garden, and no doubt at the Theatre Royal, the same mechanical contrivance for a gradation of descent or ascending was employed. In Charles Davenant's opera, *Circe,* Dorset Garden, March, 1677, Act V, the mad Orestes is charmed to sleep, and as he slumbers both pleasant and frightful Dreams appear, also Clytemnestra's Ghost ascends. At length " Orestes *wakes, the* Scene *vanishes, the Dreams and Ghost sink down by degrees* ". In the Fifth Act of Dryden and Lee's *Oedipus,* Dorset Garden early in 1679, " *The Ghost of* Laius *ascends by degrees, pointing at* Jocasta."

At the conclusion of Shadwell's *The Libertine,* Dorset Garden, June, 1675, " *It Thunders and Lightens, Devils descend and sink with* Don John, *who is cover'd with a Cloud of fire as he sinks.*"

Flashes of fire also generally heralded the arrival and accompanied the departure of demons and hobgoblins. On the Elizabethan stage in *The Divil's Charter,* IV, 1, there is a scene of conjuring with many suffumigations. "*Fiery exhalations lightning thunder ascend a King, with a red face crowned imperiall riding upon a Lyon, or dragon.*" Various exorcisms follow: "*The diuell descendeth with thunder and lightning and after more exhalations ascends another all in armor.*" When Theophilus in the Fifth Act of *The Virgin Martir* is eating of the fair fruit from Paradise sent to him by S. Dorothy the fiend would prevent him, and "*Enter* Harpax *in a feareful shape, fire flashing out of the study*". At the end of the play Harpax is dinged to perdition by Angelo who cries: "Haste to thy place appointed cursed fiend, . . ." and "*the diuell sinkes with lightning*".

On the Restoration stage, in Dryden and Lee's *The Duke of Guise,* Theatre Royal, November, 1682, Act IV, the warlock Malicorn is alone at night. "*A flash of lightning. Enter the Spirit* Melanax." "*Enter*" is here equivalent to ascends, and at the conclusion of the scene the familiar descends by the same trap. When the wizard's fatal contract is out, the fiend appears to fetch his prey. Melanax jeers the wretch's horrid despair, and as the last grain of sand runs through the hour-glass, "*A flash of Lightning, they sink together.*" Again, in Act II of Dryden's *King Arthur,* Dorset Garden, June, 1691, the fiend Grimbald has endeavoured to mislead the Britons who are following hard upon their conquered foe. He would guide them into some quagmire or dangerous morass when Philidel, the good spirit, by her warnings of sweet song sets them in the right path. Grimbald howls out in rage—

> Curse on her Voice, I must my Prey forego;
> Thou, *Philidel,* shalt answer this below.
> [Grimbald *sinks with a Flash.*

In Nevil Payne's *The Fatal Jealousie,* Dorset Garden, 1672, III, when the supposed Witch exercises her charlatanry to deceive Antonio, and summons her Spirits, little boys in devil disguises, we have: "*Enter first Spirit, second Spirit Ascends. After some flashes of fire they sing.*" Presently "Third Spirit Ascends", and the Song with Chorus concluded, "*They Descend.*"

Sebastiano Serlio for "the beames of the lightning" recommends hanging down over the scene a piece of wire "whereon you must put a squib (*un rocchettocò*) couered ouer with pure gold or shining lattin which you will", and then if fire is suddenly set to the squib "it will worke the effect which is desired"—*sarà buono effetto.*[53]

Nicolo Sabbatini in his *Practica di Fabricar Scene e Machine ne' Teatri* (Ravenna, 1638) [54] advises the blowing of Greek pitch and rosin through a torch or candle by means of long tubes. This is probably how the effect was generally procured on the Elizabethan stage, since this method seems to have prevailed until the eighteenth century. This device was by no means new, having formerly been utilized in the miracle plays, for the Glories of the Resurrection were thus simulated. An old account book of Reading in the year 1507 records a payment on account of "rosyn to the resurrecyon play".[55] Comedy in the Induction to *A Warning for Faire Women,* 4to, 1599,[56] has a fleer at various businesses of Tragedy:—

> And then a Chorus too comes howling in,
> And tels us of the worrying of a cat,
> Then of a filthie whining ghost,
> Lapt in some fowle sheete, or a leather pelch,
> Comes skreaming like a pigge halfe stickt,
> And cries *Vindicta,* revenge, revenge:
> With that a little Rosen flasheth forth,
> Like smoke out of a Tabacco pipe, or a boyes squib.

In the Epilogue to Lovelace's comedy *The Scholars,* an address preserved among his poems [57] although the actual play is unprinted, the gallery is said ever to be overjoyed at—

> The rosin-lightning flash, and Monster spire
> Squibs, and words hotter then his fire.

No doubt in the course of years any awkwardness or crudity was improved upon, and the mechanism manipulated with considerable adroitness. Unless it had been truly effective it is difficult to think that this business should be so often introduced by dramatists skilled in stage illusion and pyrotechnical device.

NOTES TO CHAPTER VI

[1] Chappuzeau, *Le théâtre François,* 1674, p. 44. There is a reprint of Chappuzeau, Bruxelles, 1861.

[2] *Memoirs and Correspondence of George, Lord Lyttelton,* 2 vols, ed. by Robert Phillimore, 1845, vol. i, pp. 323–5. This letter is dated from Paris, 17th May, 1750. This letter is not included in the *Lettres de M. de Voltaire a ses Amis de Parnasse,* Geneve, 1766, nor in the *Oeuvres Completes,* 1785, where it should appear in the *Lettres,* 1744–1752, tom. liv.

[3] 4to, 1697.

[4] *The Golden Age,* 4to, 1611; *The Silver Age,* 4to, 1613; *The Brazen Age,* 4to, 1613; *The Iron Age,* 2 parts, 4to, 1632. These plays were probably produced 1610–12.

[5] "Mr. Dennis happened once to go to the play, when a tragedy was acted, in which the machinery of thunder was introduced, a new artificial method of producing which he had formerly communicated to the managers. Incensed by this circumstance, he cried out in a transport of resentment, 'That is my thunder, by G–d; the villains will play my thunder, but not my plays.' This gave an alarm to the pit, which he soon explained." *The Lives of the Poets* . . . by Mr. Cibber, and other Hands, London, 1753, vol. iv, p. 234.

Sebastiano Serlio gives the following directions for theatrical thunder: "you must make thunder in this manner: commonly all Scenes are made at the end of a great Hall, where as usually there is a Chamber aboue it, wherein you must roule a great Bullet of a Cannon or of some other great Ordinance, and then counterfeit Thunder." *The second Booke of Architecture, made by Sebastian Serly* . . . London, folio, 1611, The third Chapter, Fol. 26. *Tutte l'Opere d'Architettura* . . . di Sebastiano Serlio, In Vinegia, MDC, p. 52: "De'Lumi artificiali delle Scene."

[6] *The Dunciad,* published by Mr. Warburton, 1749, p. 91. The two lines, 225–6, run:—

'Tis yours to shake the soul
With thunder rumbling from the mustard bowl.

[7] See my edition of Shadwell's *Works,* 1927, vol. iv, p. 177.

[8] Book III, 262: "Mid snow of paper, and fierce hail of pease." The note tells us that John Rich of Covent Garden "was the first that excelled this way".

[9] See Hotson, *The Commonwealth and Restoration Stage,* 1928, pp. 250–3.

[10] First noticed and described in my article "Orrery's 'The Tragedy of Zoroastres'", *Modern Language Review,* vol. xii, No. 1, January, 1917, pp. 24–32.

[11] Although this is, of course, forty years after the date on which Pepys writes the traditional décor had been in a large measure preserved.

[12] *The New History of the Trojan Wars,* 12mo, 1751, p. 163.

[13] E. K. Chambers, *Mediaeval Stage,* 1903, vol. ii, pp. 344–5.

[14] *The Princess,* iv, 10, p. 48; *Thomaso,* Part I, Act V, 9, p. 377.

[15] *The Works of Sir David Lindsay of the Mount,* 1490–1555. Edited by Douglas Hamer, The Scottish Text Society, vol. ii, 1931, pp. 357–375. It will be remarked I quote from the version of 1554. In 1552 there are variants. The text of 1554 was published at Edinburgh by Robert Charteris in 1602.

[16] *The London Merchant,* ed. A. W. Ward, 1906, p. 111.

[17] The last performance, the 115th, was on 10th September. *When Crummles Played,* "Being the Full Original Text of Lillo's Tragedy of The London Merchant, or George Barnwell, acted by Mr. Vincent Crummles's Company at the Lyric Theatre, Hammersmith, under the Direction of Mr. Nigel Playfair, With an Introduction by F. J. Harvey Daston," was published, June, 1927.

[18] This is historically accurate. See *Dryden The Dramatic Works,* 1931, edited by Montague Summers, ii, pp. 530–1, with the quotations from Symeon Metaphrastes.

[19] Ibid., iv, 1932, pp. 572–7.

[20] There is a similar scene of this horrid Moorish punishment, the ganches, in Powell's tragedy *The Treacherous Brothers,* Drury Lane, February, 1689–1690; 4to, 1690, towards the conclusion of the Fifth Act, when "*The Scene drawn discovers* Men[aphon] *Executed, being flung from a* Battlement *upon Spikes*".

[21] Reprinted, with an Introduction by Montague Summers, folio, 1930, p. 198: "*To cut off ones head, and to laie it in a platter, &c.*"

[22] In his very indifferent and indeed disserviceable book *The Shakesperian Stage,* 1909, Mr. Victor E. Albright talks of the use of *drops* in Restoration days, and writes that scenery was on occasion set plumb in the proscenium opening, as a background to acting on the apron. These are very bad blunders, and in fact Mr. Albright's whole chapter iv, "Some Principles of Restoration Staging," is literally honeycombed with errors, which seem to have been a fruitful source of misconception and mistakes. For hence, I suppose, Mr. de Sola Pinto in his edition of Sedley, 2 vols, 1928, when annotating *The Mulberry-Garden,* Act II, at the stage direction "[*They enter the Widows house*", derived his idea that "The previous scene was probably a 'carpenter's scene', or perhaps only a painted back cloth set immediately within the proscenium!" (i, p. 302). The Restoration stage knew nothing of painted back cloths, and I am very certain that Mr. Pinto does not know what is implied by a "carpenter's scene", which is indeed a nineteenth century

term denoting a front scene inserted as padding into a play, in order to give the carpenters time to build up behind a more or less elaborate set scene.

Again in Sedley's *Antony and Cleopatra,* Dorset Garden, February, 1677, Act IV, Scene 3, is A Wood. After a short speech of Antony and some business of fighting we have " [Exeunt. *Enter* Photinus *as within the Town* ". Mr. Pinto notes (vol. i, p. 311): " Probably a back cloth representing Alexandria was dropped in front of the ' wood ' ! " A stage direction in Act V in the same play is : " *Enter* Antonius, Cleopatra, Charmion, *and* Iras *in the Monument.*" Mr. Pinto comments : " There must have been a change of scene here. Perhaps a back cloth or curtains were removed and the interior of the ' monument ' revealed," i, p. 312.

The fact is that the editing of Restoration plays demands a particular study of the theatrical conditions of the day, and without some knowledge of the kind ineptitudes such as the above are hardly to be avoided.

In a Prologue which Mr. Pinto prints, vol. i, p. 47, the line occurs :—

Ballon and Tumblers please, tho' Poets fail.

This he proceeds to annotate : " The Ballon or Balloon was the seventeenth-century football, which appears from this passage to have been used by clowns on the stage," i, p. 289. This is, of course, just nonsense. Luttrell, on 8th April, 1699 (*Brief Relation,* ed. 1857, iv, pp. 502–3), notes : " Monsieur Ballon, the famous French dancing master . . . having leave to come hither for 5 weeks is allowed by the playhouse 400 guineas for that time, besides which the lord Cholmley has sent him a present of 100 more." There are many allusions to Monsieur Ballon, as for example in *A Comparison between the Two Stages,* 1702, p. 49 : " 'Twas otherwise lately with *Balon* ; the Town ran mad to see him, and the prizes were rais'd to an extravagant degree to bear the extravagant rate they allow'd him."

[23] Killigrew's *Comedies And Tragedies,* folio (general title-page), 1664, p. 190.

[24] In the printed text, folio, 1665, there are few indications of a change of scene. The same scenery was utilized in Dryden's sequel, *The Indian Emperour.*

[25] There was a particularly splendid revival of Jonson's tragedy at the Theatre Royal on Friday, 18th December, 1668, with Hart in the title-rôle. See Pepys, 11th December, 1667 ; 11th January, 1667–8 ; and 19th December, 1668.

[26] The *Scene of a Paradise* would certainly have been employed in performances—subsequent to June, 1669—of *The Virgin Martir,* a tragedy which kept its place in the repertory chiefly perhaps owing to the fine acting of Rebecca Marshall as S. Dorothy. Lacy in his farcical comedy *The Dumb Lady,* Theatre Royal, autumn of 1669, introduced a conjurer who exhibits *Elysium.* (No doubt Fuller's painting was utilized.) At Dorset Garden in Otway's *Alcibiades,* during Timandra's vision, Act V, the Scene " changes to *Elyzium* ".

[27] Such a detail shows Dryden's exactitude in respect of these scenic details. In the Preface to *Albion and Albanius,* however, he speaks of having had the " descriptions of the Scenes, and other decorations of the Stage " from Betterton, to whom may be due this precision. The Devil's drop is really the remains of a Roman Town which topped the Western Heights of Dover. See *Dryden, The Dramatic Works,* edited by Montague Summers, 1932, v, p. 540.

[28] Sanudo, xxvii, col. 73.

[29] Vol. iv, pp. 147 sqq.

[30] *The Works of the Earls of Rochester, Roscomon, and Dorset,* London, 2 vols, 12mo, 1731 ; vol. i, p. xxvi.

[31] Malone, *Prose Works of John Dryden,* 1800, vol. i, part i, pp. 73–5, n. 4.

[32] To Mrs. Siam, whose India House for the sale of tea, bric-à-brac, shawls, oriental cabinets, screens and the like, was in St. James' Street, there are many allusions. Scandal gave these India Houses—or as they were originally called—China Houses an extremely indifferent reputation. In his comedy Southerne even introduces as characters Mrs. Siam, played by Mrs. Elinor Leigh, and Captain Drydrubb, " married to Siam," a rôle acted by Cave Underhill.

[33] Miss E. Boswell, *The Restoration Court Stage,* 1932, devotes particular attention to the Whitehall production of *Calisto.* There is some difficulty about the exact dates of the performances of Crown's masque.

[34] Chapter xvi, first edition, 1740, p. 316.

[35] For *Psyche* see my edition of Shadwell, 1927, vol. ii, pp. 271–340, with the notes, pp. 398–403. Also vol. i, Introduction, pp. cix–cxxii.

[36] *Foundations of English Opera,* 1928, chapter vi, p. 116.

[37] The cast was magnificent. Orestes, Betterton; Pylades, Joseph Williams; Ithacus, Smith; Thoas, King of Scythia, Henry Harris; Iphigenia, Mrs. Betterton; Osmida, Mrs. Twyford; and Circe, Lady Slingsby.

[38] Licensed 14th May, 1622, *The Prophetess* is now very generally ascribed to Fletcher and Massinger.

[39] 4to, 1692, Act iv, p. 40.

[40] 4to, 1692, misprints: "*variours Trees.*"

[41] 8vo, 1693, p. 9.

[42] "On pouvait aussi passer sous la scène, qui s'ouvrait à certains endroits au moyens de trappes dissimulées . . . Dans la *Résurrection* de Jean Michel, on voyait Jésus 'soudainement et subtilement saillir de dessous terre par une petite trappe de bois recouverte de terre, laquelle se recloait (refermait) sans qu'on s'aperçoive'. C'est sans doute par le même procédé que dans le même mystère les pélerins d'Emmaüs voient Jésus 's'évanouir subitement de leurs yeux par un engin'." *Les Mystères,* by Louis Petit de Julleville, 1880, i, pp. 398–9.

[43] I have used the reprint, 1906, of *Supposes* and *Jocasta* edited by G. J. W. Cunliffe, pp. 184 and 268.

[44] *Stage Gossip,* 1886, p. 69.

[45] *The Tragedy of Locrine,* 4to, 1595. Act III, Scene 1: *Dumb Show. The Works of Mr. William Shakespear,* vol. ix, 1728, p. 390.

[46] I have used the facsimile reproduction, 1913, of the 4to, 1607 (Dyce Library). *Old English Drama: Students' Facsimile Edition.*

[47] 4to, 1680, pp. 60–1. A dummy body was, of course, carried in the chair.

[48] 4to, 1672, p. 44. There is a misprint, *shun'd* for *shew'd,* which I correct.

[49] Acted in 1600. First edition, 4to, 1601.

[50] 4to, 1608; sig. F2 verso.

[51] For an account of this play see my *The Vampire: His Kith and Kin,* 1928, pp. 306–8.

[52] "The Famous Chronicle of king Edward the first . . . with . . . the sinking of Queene *Elinor,* who sunck *at Charingcrosse, and rose againe at Potters*-hith, now named Queenehith," 4to, 1593. There are no stage-directions in the original edition, and these were (I suspect) introduced by Dyce. The business, of course, is sufficiently clear from the dialogue, but it is incorrect to write that "the earth", according to the direction, "opens and swallows her."

[53] *Tutte l'Opere d'Architettura,* In Vinegia, MDC, p. 52, *De'Lumi artificiali delle Scene.* I quote from the English translation, folio, 1611, "The Second Booke of Architecture made by Sebastian Serly," The Third Chapter, Fol. 26.

[54] Book II, chapters xxii and xxiii. The title-page of this edition has: "Restampa di nouo coll'Aggiunta del Secondo Libro."

[55] E. K. Chambers, *The Mediaeval Stage,* 1903, vol. ii, p. 393.

[56] I have used the facsimile reproduction, 1912, from the Dyce Library. *Old English Drama, Students Facsimile Edition.*

[57] *Lucasta,* 1649. *The Scholars* was written in 1634, during Lovelace's first year of residence at Oxford, and acted at the Salisbury Court play-house, London.

CHAPTER VII

COSTUME

Now, for the difference betwixt our Theaters and those of former times, they were but plain and simple, with no other Scenes, nor Decorations of the Stage, but onely old Tapestry, and the Stage strew'd with Rushes, (with their Habits accordingly) whereas ours now for cost and ornament are arriv'd to the heighth of Magnificence.
—RICHARD FLECKNOE: *A short Discourse of the English Stage,* 1664.

HIGH o'er the Stage there lies a rambling Frame
Which Men a Garret vile, but Play'rs the Tire-room name;
Here all their Stores (a merry Medley) sleep,
Without Distinction huddled in a Heap.
HUNG on the self same Peg, in Union rest
Young TARQUIN's Trowsers, and LUCRETIA's Vest,
Whilst without pulling Quoives ROXANA lays
Close by STATIRA's Petticoat her Stays;
Hard by a Quart of bottled Light'ning lies,
A Bowl of double Use, and monstrous Size;
Now rolls it high, and rumbles in its Speed,
Now drouns the weaker Crack of Mustard-seed;
So the true Thunder all array'd in Smoak,
Launch'd from the Skies now rives the knotted Oak,
And sometimes nought the Drunkerd's Pray'rs avail,
Ah sometimes condescends to sower Ale.
Near these sets up a Dragon-drawn Calash,
There a Ghost's Doublet delicately slash'd
Bleeds from the mangled Breast, and gapes a frightful Gash,
In Crimson wrought the sanguine Floods abound,
And seem to gutter from the streaming Wound.
Here IRIS bends her various painted Arch,
There artificial Clouds in sullen Order march,
Here stands a Croun upon a Rack, and there
A WITCH's Broomstick by great HECTOR's Spear;
Here stands a Throne, and there the CYNICK's Tub,
Here BULLOCK's Cudgel, there ALCIDE's Club.
Beads, Plumes, and Spangles, in Confusion rise,
Whilst Rocks of Cornish Diamonds reach the Skies.
Crests, Corslets, all the Pomp of Battle join,
In one Effulgence, one promiscuous Shine.

The Stage: A Poem. By Mr. WEBSTER, of Christ Church, Oxon. 1713, pp. 22–4.

The wealth of evidence we have been investigating amply shows that the scenery, effects, and other properties of the theatre in the reign of Charles II were costly, elaborate, and beautiful, and it must not be thought that there was any neglect of another essential feature, the dresses.

Although the costumes of Restoration actors in most cases may not have been, indeed certainly were not, exact, at any rate the principal characters donned finery of considerable richness and show, and it should be remarked that upon the stage an ornate sumptuousness of apparel is often far more effective than the nicest details of an historical pedantry. A costume correct in every antiquarian particular will prove less striking than an appropriate dress which is by no means so precisely authentic. In some ways this is largely due to the fact that minutiae escape the majority of the audience who are seated at a distance, and what is conveyed to their senses and impresses itself upon their imagination is the general appearance of a figure dressed for the boards. It is, in fine, a kind of symbolism. Of course there must be no glaring incongruity, no inharmonious tone. Hazardous as the suggestion may be I do not hesitate to posit that a jejune exactitude of attire theatrically will sometimes prove less satisfactory than habiliments to the fashioning of which a discreet imagination has been suffered to lend ornament and even it may be shape. There is at Knole a full length portrait by Kneller of Anthony Leigh in the character of Father Dominic, the title-rôle of Dryden's *The Spanish Fryar,* produced at Dorset Garden in March, 1680. The picture shows Leigh wearing an ample black habit falling in many folds and confined at the waist by a leathern girdle from which hangs a mighty string of beads. A voluminous black Brandenburgh is secured at the neck. The whole swart costume is most effective, but it is also entirely incorrect. Father Dominic is supposed to be of the Order of Friar Preachers and should wear a white tunic, scapular, and capuce with the *cappa nigra,* and white stockings. Even the string of beads which Leigh has is not a rosary. His habit is not merely not Dominican, but it is not the habit of any religious, monk, friar, canon, or clerk regular. It is purely fanciful, yet as a stage dress none the worse for that. Father Ignatius of Llanthony was wont to appear a very striking figure of a friar. Yet his habit was far from exact. For to the Benedictine tunic and scapular he had superadded the Franciscan cord and sandals, a curious commixture. Notwithstanding he looked the typical " monk ". Incidentally upon the stage even to-day the most ludicrous mistakes are continually being made with regard to ecclesiastical costume. None the less they pass unnoticed. Perhaps Leigh's dressing of Dominic is to be preferred to any scrupulously correct design.

✓It may be borne in mind that many plays of the Restoration period are essentially romantic, and the scene may be laid in some imaginary Court of France (*The Forc'd Marriage*); in Dacia and Scythia where we met with Shepherds, Amintas, Shepherdesses, Urania, Dancing Swains, and a Druid (*The Young King*); in Arcadia (*The Royal Shepherdesse* and many other pastorals); or in a Scythia with fair Amazons (*The Women's Conquest*); or at "*Luds*-Town, alias *London*" with Silvio, Don Michael, Eugenia, Aurelia (*The Injured Princess*); or in Britain about A.D. 430, with Filamor, Sylvanus, Brianella, and Violinda (*The Stepmother*). In any of these plays, however rococo the costumes they would serve without reference to period or clime. At the revival by the Phoenix for two performances in February, 1920, of Dryden's *Marriage A-la Mode* a most delightful effect was obtained since the romantic characters, Polydamas, Leonidas, Argaleon, Palmyra, Amalthea, and the rest, wore the very exquisite baroque dresses which had been originally designed by Albert Rutherston for the production of *A Winter's Tale* at the Savoy Theatre, London, in 1912, whilst Rhodolphil, Palamede, Doralice, and Melantha were attired in the height of fashion of the year 1672. The thing was exactly right.

In Elizabethan days the sour Puritan critics of the theatre were already complaining of the fine clothes worn by actors. John Northbrooke in his *Treatise wherein . . . Vaine playes or Enterludes . . . are reprooued*[1] exclaims of players: "What prodigious apparel . . . is among them, it is a wonder to see," and recommends that if a schoolmaster very rare and seldom should permit his lads to perform Latin scenes "for learning, and utterance sake" the boys "be not pranked and decked up in gorgious and sumptuous apparell in their play". Stephen Gosson in *The Schoole of Abuse* (1579),[2] declares: "Ouerlashing in apparell is so common a fault, that the verye hyerlings of some of our plaiers, which stand at reuersion of vi.s. by the weeke, iet vnder gentlemens noses in sutes of silke."

We know that in the Shakespearean playhouse, although many characters wore contemporary costume, there were also in use a very large number of conventional dresses, and to these there are constant references in Henslowe's *Diary*. It is clear that particular habits were assigned to Turks and Orientals generally; to Greek and Roman personages; to certain traditional figures, either of legend or of history; to ecclesiastics, Christian bishop or pagan priest; to deities; to professions and trades of particular distinction; and also it must not be forgotten that animal disguises and masks were donned. The turban was a great feature of the sooty barbarian, a "turkish bonnet", as Kyd terms it in *Soliman and Perseda.* In *The Merchant of Venice,*[3] Actus Secundus, we have: "*Enter Marochus a Tawnie Moore all in white, and three or four followers accordingly,* and he swears "By this Symitare". Aaron also in *Titus Andronicus* exclaims:

> He dies upon my scimitar's sharp point
> That touches this my first-born son and heir.

For Greek or Roman clothes, gowns and flowing cloaks of toga-like draperies were adopted. "I have lost my gown," complains the Fourth Lord when Timon of Athens has driven out the company from the smoke and lukewarm water feast. Antony exhibits to the citizens Caesar's mantle all cut and stabbed. Coriolanus puts on "a gown of humility", and it may be noted that a little earlier he enters crowned with an oaken garland. Inigo Jones' designs[4] give us a good idea of the very baroque but pleasing semi-classical dress which was worn in the Caroline masques and (perhaps with slight modifications) upon the public stage, a costume which curiously enough many seventeenth artists and engravers, both English and foreign, considered highly suitable for Scriptural scenes.

Among inventories of costumes by Henslowe we find "j green gown for Maryan . . . vj grene cottes for Roben Hoode . . . Roben Hoodes sewte . . . Merlin gowne and cape",[5] whence it is clear that popular figures, Robin Hood, Maid Marian, Merlin, were traditionally attired. In the frontispiece to *The Wits, or Sport upon Sport,* 1663, Sir John Falstaff and the Hostess are attired in much the same fashion as they appear in the frontispiece to II *Henry IV,* in Rowe's Shakespeare, 1709.

Henslowe has several references to "freyers gownes",[6] and no doubt Bacon, Bungay, Friar Hugh Ap David, Peele's Friar "with a chine of beef and a pot of wine", Barnardino, Jacomo, Friar Lawrence, Friar Comolet, Friar Bonaventura, Friar Bernard, Friar John, Crab and Cole, and the numerous fraternity were suitably if not accurately attired. In Greene's *Alphonsus, King of Aragon,* 4to, 1599, we have: "*Rise Calchas up in a white Cirples and a Cardinals Myter.*" In Samuel Rowley's *When You See Me, You know me* we have Enter "*Bonner in his Bishops Robes*". Towards the end of that lurid melodrame *The Divils Charter,* "Alexander *draweth the Curtaine of his studie where hee discouereth the diuill sitting in his pontificals.*" "j poopes miter" occurs in an inventory.[7] For deities Henslowe notes "j sewtte for Nepton", "Junoes cotte", "Mercures wings", which point to appropriate habits. He also notes: "pd. . . . the 7 of marche 1602 vnto the tayller wch made the blacke satten sewt for the woman kyld wth kyndnes the some of . . . xs." "A whitte satten dublette for phayeton" cost forty shillings. A tafety "Rochet for the beshoppe in earlle goodwine" twenty-four shillings.[8]

Judges and senators wore distinctive gowns. "j senetores gowne, j hoode, and 5 senetores capes,"[9] Henslowe enters. In *The Little French Lawyer* La-Writ appears in his long barrister's gown carrying a large buckram bag stuffed with documents. Bartolus the old lawyer in *The Spanish Curate* wears a long cloak and hat and legal bands to which reference is made.[10] In *The Elder Brother,* Charles the scholar contrasts his scurvy old University gown with his brother's "gold and gawdie" clothes, III, 5. Volpone in the First Act of Jonson's play when feigning sickness lies on a couch wrapped up in a loose gown, furs, and night-caps on his head.[11] In the Fifth Act Mosca appears in the habit of a Clarissimo, a Venetian nobleman, that is to say a robe of silken damask, rose, crimson, or blue, with a sash and the distinctive stolone of cloth of gold, whilst Volpone is disguised as a commendadore, an officer of justice, whose uniform was a black stuff gown and a red cap with two gilt buttons in front.

The tradition of costumes passed on from the Elizabethan to the Restoration theatre, and the various habits designed by Inigo Jones and others for the Court masques must have to some extent have influenced the dresses utilized upon the public stage. It is not, of course, to be supposed that, save in exceptional circumstances, the actors would have been able to furnish themselves with such gorgeous panoply as was admired in Court revels, yet no doubt occasionally the masquing suits when no longer required became the property of the playhouses.[12] It is recorded that when his play *Aglaura* was given at the Blackfriars during the Christmas of 1637 Suckling, who was notorious for his extravagance, bore all the expenses of the production which was on a very splendid scale, and not only "had some scaenes to it, which in those days were only used at masques" but "he bought all the cloathes himselfe, which were very rich".[13] They were, in fact, composed of the costliest materials, Genoa velvets and figured silks, the very lace embroidered upon them being of pure gold and silver, no copper nor tinsel. In a letter from the Reverend Mr. Garrard to Lord Strafford, 7th February, 1637–8, it is said: "Two of the King's Servants, Privy-Chamber Men both, have writ each of them a Play, *Sir John Sutlin* and *Will. Barclay,* which have been acted in Court, and at the *Black Friars,* with much Applause. *Sutlin*'s Play cost three or four hundred Pounds setting out; eight or ten Suits of new Cloaths he gave the Players; an unheard of Prodigality." [14]

Although the chief characters might strut their hour in tissue and brocade, and vaunt " the gaudy Plume, the purple Train ", it would appear that often the smaller parts were dressed in shoddy and bombazeen. At least such is the conclusion from Pepys' comments, although truly in *Psyche* the operatic smiths at their forge wore satin habiliments.[15] Perhaps the Dorset Garden wardrobe was superior to that of the Theatre Royal, for Pepys visiting the latter on Monday, 19th March, 1666, when it was closed to the public, notes: " after dinner we walked to the King's play-house, all in dirt, they being altering of the stage to make it wider. But God knows when they will begin to act again; but my business here was to see the inside of the stage and all the tiring-rooms and machines; and, indeed, it was a sight worth seeing. But to see their clothes, and the various sorts, and what a mixture of things there was; here a wooden leg, there a ruff, here a hobby-horse, there a crown, would make a man split himself to see with laughing; and particularly Lacy's wardrobe, and Shotrell's. But then again, to think how fine they show on the Stage, by candle-light, and how poor things they are to look now too near hand, is not pleasant at all. The machines are fine, and the paintings very pretty." On Saturday, 5th October, 1667, Pepys makes his way to the King's house, " and there, going in, met with Knepp, and she took us up into the tireing-rooms: and to the women's shift, where Nell was dressing herself, and was all unready and is very pretty, prettier than I thought. And so walked all up and down the house above, and then below into the scene-room . . . But, Lord! to see how they were both painted would make a man mad, and did make me loath them; and what base company of men comes amongst them, and how lewdly they talk! and how poor the men are in clothes, and yet what a shew they make on the stage in candle-light, is very observable." Yet this cannot always have been the case for on Wednesday, 11th December, 1667, Pepys heard that *Catiline* was " to be suddenly acted at the King's house ", and " The King gives them £500 for robes, there being, as they say, to be sixteen scarlett robes ". A few weeks later on Saturday, 11th January, 1668, Mrs. Knepp told Pepys that *Catiline* " for want of the clothes which the King promised them, will not be acted for a good while ". At length Jonson's tragedy was revived on Friday, 18th December, 1668. Pepys was present on the following day and judged the production " most fine of clothes; and a fine scene of the Senate, and of a fight ". It must not escape remark that £500 would represent an exceedingly large sum appraised at modern values.

Downes tells us that Charles II was not less generous in his encouragement of the Duke's Theatre. Amongst the earliest successes of Lincoln's Inn Fields was "Love and Honour, wrote by Sir *William Davenant*: This Play was Richly Cloath'd; The King giving Mr. *Betterton* his Coronation Suit, in which, he Acted the Part of Prince *Alvaro*; The Duke of *York* giving Mr. *Harris* his, who did Prince *Prospero*; And my Lord of *Oxford,* gave Mr. *Joseph Price* his, who did *Lionel* the Duke of *Parma's* son". In August, 1664, was produced at the same theatre "King *Henry* the *5th*, Wrote by the Earl of *Orrery*. Mr. *Harris, Acted* the King: Mr. *Betterton, Owen Tudor*: Mr. *Smith,* Duke of *Burgundy*". "This Play was Splendidly Cloath'd: The King, in the Duke of *York's* Coronation Suit: *Owen Tudor,* in King *Charles's*: Duke of *Burgundy,* in the Lord of *Oxford*'s, and the rest all New." It may reasonably be objected that the Coronation robes of 1660 are not very accurate for the earlier decades of the fifteenth century, but after all these magnificent garments are traditional and of no particular period. Moreover Orrery's heroic drama is unhistorical to a degree.

It would appear that upon the famous revival of Henry VIII in the third week of December, 1663, some attempt at accuracy was made. "This Play, by Order of Sir *William Davenant,* was all new Cloath'd in proper Habits: The King's was all new, all the Lords, the Cardinals, the Bishops, the Doctors, Proctors, Lawyers, Tip-staves, new Scenes: . . . Every part by the great Care of Sir *William,* being exactly perform'd; it being all new Cloath'd and new Scenes; it continu'd Acting 13 Days together with general Applause."[16] The title-rôle was sustained by Betterton, and there is good reason to think Henry VIII wore a costume something resembling Holbein's portrait. At any rate the particular dress of bluff King Hal was well known. He appears upon the title-page of Samuel Rowley's *When You See Me, You know me,* 4to, 1613; and it is notable that in the frontispiece to *Henry VIII* in Rowe's Shakespeare, 1709, the King is pretty correctly garbed; Wolsey wears a habit which theatrically may well suffice for a Cardinal; but the three Lords have the modish periwigs, coats, breeches, and square-toed shoes of any minister of Queen Anne. In the later edition of Tonson's Shakespeare, 1728, the engraving is modified in a few minor details, whilst the King and the Cardinal remain practically identical figures, and in the rare copperplate which illustrates the fourth edition[17] of Banks' *Vertue Betray'd; or, Anna Bullen,* King Henry is in the same tradition yet not so correctly attired; and Wolsey has a similar but not numerical flowing red cassock and cape; for in Act V the young Princess Elizabeth cries "what's that huge, tall, bloody Man?" and later:—

Child. You'll never hear me . . .
As long as he, that Devil there, stands by
Your Elbow.
King. Ha! what Devil?
Child. That red Thing there.
King. Oh Child, he is no Devil, he's a Cardinal.
Child. Why does he wear that huge, long Coat then,
Unless it be to hide his cloven Feet?

The Duke of Northumberland in this scene wears a costume which if it recall any particular period might be deemed not wholly unlike a dress of the reign of Charles I. Lady Diana Talbot's costume is entirely nondescript. There seems to be a ruff or Medici collar to the bodice, but otherwise it is plain and undistinguished.

There is a picture by Greenhill of Henry Harris as Cardinal Wolsey from which a fine mezzotint has been engraved. The costume, in itself most striking, is an anomaly. The actor is vested in a rochet with a lace-edged rabat, a chimere, the full lawn sleeves favoured by Protestant bishops, and a satin-lined almuce or it may be cappa. A beretta is placed on the full flowing locks; it should be noted that no perruque is worn. It is doubtful whether the portrait of Michael Mohun is in character or no. It may be a mere reminiscence of his soldiering days. It certainly represents him in younger manhood, possibly shortly after his return to the stage. As Cethegus in *Catiline* was one of his most famous rôles it is not unlikely that he may have been painted as he appeared in that part.

The figures which can be seen on the stage in the frontispiece to *Ariane* and in the engravings that illustrate *The Empress of Morocco* seem two minute for detail, and are hardly of any value as evidence for costume. But the mezzotint by J. Smith entitled *The Indian Queen,* representing Mrs. Bracegirdle as the "*Indian Queen,* call'd *Semernia*" in Mrs. Behn's posthumous *The Widdow Ranter; or, The History of Bacon in Virginia,* produced at Drury Lane in the winter of 1689, is of considerable interest. (It may be remarked that this plate has, I believe without exception, always been described as the character of Zempoalla, in Sir Robert Howard and Dryden's *The Indian Queen,* as erroneous an ascription as is the oft-repeated blunder, initiated perhaps by Bernbaum,[18] echoed by Odell and others, that Nell Gwyn created Zempoalla. The original representative of this part was Anne Marshall.)

PLATE XXI

VERTUE BETRAY'D; OR, ANNA BULLEN

Collection of the Author

[*face p.* 260

In addition to her silken robes, "very glittering and rich," Mrs. Bracegirdle is wearing as a fontange, a forest of feathers, no doubt from the suit which Mrs. Behn brought from Surinam as she tells us in her novel *Oroonoko; or, The Royal Slave.* "We trade for Feathers, which they order into all Shapes, make themselves little short Habits of 'em, and glorious Wreaths for their Heads, Necks, Arms and Legs, whose Tinctures are unconceivable. I had a Set of these presented to me and I gave 'em to the *King's Theatre*; it was the Dress of the *Indian Queen,* infinitely admir'd by Persons of Quality; and was inimitable." [19] Semernia's dress has a flowing tabby train which is held by a little black page. Apparently it was towards the end of the seventeenth century that a tragedy queen was duly attended by a page to support her gorgeous trailing robes. A little later when ladies' costumes, if not more elaborate certainly became more formal and stiff with the increasing hoops and farthingales, the page was an invariable concomitant of the royal heroine, and the wits not infrequently amused themselves by observing that whilst a princess raved in madness and despair the only concern of her lackey was to see that she did not disorder the long folds and falls of her ermined train, and even when she died he carefully arranged the satins and brocades lest they should be soiled as she sank lifeless on the stage. It is said that Mrs. Oldfield preferred comedy to more serious rôles, and Chetwood tells us of this great actress: "I remember, in her full Round of Glory in Comedy, she used to slight Tragedy. She would often say, *I hate to have a Page dragging my Tail about. Why do they not give* Porter *these Parts? She can put on a better Tragedy Face than I can.*" [20]

When personating Oriental characters the actors wore some sort of turban. This makes a considerable point in Dryden's *Don Sebastian, King of Portugal,* produced at Drury Lane in November, 1689. The renegade, Dorax, now Alcalde or Governor of Alcazar, but formerly Don Alonzo de Sylvera, is attired in Moorish costume and is unrecognized by Don Sebastian until towards the end of Act IV when *Re-enter* Dorax, *having taken off his Turbant and put on a Perruque, Hat and Cravat.*

> *Dorax.* Now do you know me?
> *Sebastian.* Thou should'st be *Alonzo.*

In Act I of the same tragedy we have: "*Enter* Sebastian *conducted in mean habit, with* Alvarez, Antonio, *and* Almeyda; *her face veil'd with a* Barnus." The more usual modern form of "Barnus" (Arab. *burnus*) is "burnous", the hooded cloak worn by Arab and Moorish ladies. Thus in Act III, Scene 2, "*Enter* Johayma *wrapt up in a Moorish Mantle,*" and a little later Antonio by " *throwing off her* Barnus " discovers who she is. After a while " *Enter the* Mufti *in his Night-gown* ". Antonio has been dressed as a slave, and in order to catch him the Mufti by a subtle fetch dons " the habit of a Slave ". " *Enter the* Mufti *alone, in a Slave's habit like that of* Antonio," but " *Enter* Antonio *in an* Affrican *rich habit* ".[21]

In Mrs. Behn's *The False Count ; or, A New Way to Play an Old Game,* Dorset Garden, early autumn of 1682, Guzman and a numerous company are disguised as Turks. As old Francisco, who imagines he has fallen into the hands of Mahometan, flies into a rage, " Guzman *throws his Turbant at him.*" In Ravenscroft's *The Citizen Turn'd Gentleman,* produced at Dorset Garden, 4th July, 1672, Cleverwit masquerading as the Grand Seignioı (Act IV) enters " *in Turkish habit, his train carried up by three Blacks, Turkish attendants, and three Turks with Vest, Turbant, Cemiter, and Shoes* ". Immediately after the ceremony of making Old Jorden, a Mamamouchi there is a wonderful amount of undressing and dressing, whilst the presiding Mufti has his head coiffed with " *a Turbant stuck full of Lights* ". With this particular head-gear perukes could hardly have been donned, and they were not worn in some other characters, prelates and the like. As we have noted, Henry Harris in Cardinal Wolsey has no peruke ; and Antony Leigh as the Spanish Friar has a tonsured wig. But generally Addison's " monstrous Bush of Hair, which covers their Head, and falls down in a large Fleece below the Middle of their Backs " was the mode for Greek or Roman, Briton or Scythian, mediaeval gallant and Pall Mall fop alike. The scene of John Wilson's *Andronicus Comnenius,* a tragedy printed 4to, 1664, but not acted, is Byzantium and the date 1182–5, the return and reign of Andronicus. In Act I, Scene 3, Manuel, the son of Andronicus, enters disguised. During a struggle his dress is disordered, and he bids Philo—

> Take up that, and help me
> To put it on again. So—so ! 'Tis well !
> [Philo *takes up his grey Perriwig, and helps him on with it again.*

When it was necessary for a woman to appear dressed in male attire a peruke was adopted. Salome (Mrs. Mary Lee) in Pordage's *Herod and Mariamne* produced at the Duke's Theatre in October, 1673, is disguised as a man. She engages in a duel with Tyridates (Smith), and " *her Perriwig falls off in making a pass at* Tyridates ". In Settle's tragedy *Love and Revenge,* Dorset Garden, 9th November, 1674, Mrs. Mary Lee played Nigrello, " a Moor and Favourite to the Queen, *Clotair,* being *Chlotilda* in disguise." The Epilogue was " Spoken by *Nigrello* in a Mans Habit, but in a white Wig, and her Face discover'd ". In Dryden's *Marriage A-la-Mode,* given by Killigrew's company at their temporary house, Lincoln's Inn Fields, about Easter, 1672, Act IV, Scene 3, when Doralice is in boy's clothes and wishes to make herself known to Palamede, " *She plucks off her Perruke, and puts it on again when he knows her.*" So in *Secret Love; or, The Maiden Queen,* Theatre Royal, March, 1667, Act V, Florimel, created by Nell Gwyn, enters " *in Man's Habit* ". " Save you *Monsieur Florimell,*" she cries, " Faith methinks you are a very *janty* Fellow, *poudré* & *ajusté,* as well as the best of 'em. I can manage the little Comb,—set my Hat, shake my Garniture, toss about my empty Noddle." A little after Celadon " *Plucks off her Hat and Perrucke, and discovers* Florimel ". In these two latter instances the characters are, of course, disguised in contemporary attire. In Killigrew's *The Pilgrim,*[22] III, 5, Cosmo adopts for his disguise, " this Periwigg and a Pilgrims Weed." In *The Plain-Dealer,* Drury Lane, winter of 1676, Fidelia is dressed as a man, but Vernish discovering her to be a woman " *Pulls off her Peruke* ". At the conclusion Manly exclaims: " More strange things ! [*Observing* Fidelia's *hair unty'd behind, and without a Peruke, which she lost in the scuffle.*" Addison in describing French opera at Paris tells us: " I have seen a Couple of Rivers appear in red Stockings; and *Alpheus,* instead of having his Head covered with Sedge and Bull-Rushes, making Love in a fair full-buttomed Perriwig, and a Plume of Feathers." [23]

Even in comedy the peruke played its part. Thus in Etherege's *The Man of Mode,* Dorset Garden, March, 1676, Sir Fopling's suit is commended at length and in every detail even to his orangerie gloves, and the whole is crowned by his Chedreux periwig. In Dryden's *The Kind Keeper; or, Mr. Limberham,* Dorset Garden, March, 1678, Woodall who throughout the first act has been wearing a riding suit and black periwig in order to appear as a stranger to Limberham shifts his clothes and dons a flaxen Chedreux. Miss Prue in *Love for Love,* Lincoln's Inn Fields, April, 1695, fell into raptures over the fragrance of Beau Tattle's peruke and gloves. In *The Way of the World,* Lincoln's Inn Fields, March, 1700, Witwoud was " so Becravated and so Beperriwig'd " that Sir Wilfull did not recognize him. Cibber in his *Apology* [24] tells how Henry Brett first ventured behind the scenes, and although he may have been allured by the Theatrical Nymphs " the most visible Cause of his first coming, was a more sincere Passion he had conceiv'd for a fair full-bottom'd Perriwig which I then wore in my first Play of the *Fool in Fashion* in the

Year 1695" (i.e. January, 1696). Davies writing in 1784 says: "The heads of the English actors were, for a long time, covered with large full-bottomed perriwigs, a fashion introduced in the reign of Charles II, which was not entirely disused in public till about the year 1720. Addison, Congreve, and Steele, met at Button's coffee-house, in large, flowing, flaxen, wigs; Booth, Wilks, and Cibber, when full-dressed, wore the same. Till within these twenty-five years, our Tamerlanes and Catos had as much hair on their heads as our judges on the bench . . . I have been told that he [Booth] and Wilks bestowed forty guineas each on the exorbitant thatching of their heads."[25]

There long persisted a tradition that "actors who were cast into the parts of conspirators, traitors, and murderers" should "disguise themselves in large black wigs; and distort their features, in order to appear terrible; in short to discover that which their art should teach them to conceal". Thus in Killigrew's unacted *Cicilia & Clorinda* (folio, 1663, in *Comedies and Tragedies,* folio, 1664) the villain of the drama "Orante *is cloathed in black, with black Feathers, black Perriwig, his person is crooked and ugly, with a Dagger by his side*"; but "*His habit must be good*".[26] Davies notes[27]: "I have seen Hippisley act the first Murderer in Macbeth: his face was made pale with chalk, distinguished with large whiskers, and a long black wig. This custom, of dressing so preposterously the hateful implements of the tragic scene, is now [1784] almost worn out." In the mock Inventory of Drury Lane, *Tatler,* No. 42, 16th July, 1709, is listed: "The Complexion of a Murderer in a Band-box; consisting of a large Piece of burnt Cork, and a Coal-black Peruke." The mot of Charles II is well known as recorded by Cibber. "In King *Charles*'s time, this low Skill was carry'd to such an Extravagance, that the King himself, who was black-brow'd, and of a swarthy Complexion, pass'd a pleasant Remark upon his observing the grim Looks of the Mutherers in *Mackbeth*; when, turning to his People, in the Box about him, *Pray, what is the Meaning,* said he, *that we never see a Rogue in a Play, but, Godsfish! they always clap him on a black Perriwig? when, it is well known, one of the greatest Rogues in* England *always wears a fair one?* Now, whether or no Dr. *Oates,* at that time wore his own Hair, I cannot be positive: Or, if his Majesty pointed at some greater Man, then out of Power, I leave those to guess at him, who, may yet, remember the changing Complexion of his Ministers. This Story I had from *Betterton,* who was a Man of Veracity."[28] The King alluded to the Earl of Shaftesbury, who always wore a flaxen wig, such indeed being extremely modish in that day.

The "Plume of Feathers" to which Addison refers was a

coiffure greatly favoured by actors in heroic tragedy. Davies commenting upon Hamlet's "forest of feathers" says: "The *forest of feathers* alludes to large plumes of feathers which the old actors wore upon their heads in characters of heroism and dignity. This practice was adopted at the Restoration, and continued in force until Mr. Garrick's æra of management. His superior taste got rid of the incumbrance." [29] That admired poetess, Mrs. Katherine Philips, writing from Dublin on 23rd December, 1662, says: "We have Plays here in the newest Mode, and not ill acted; only the other Day, when Othello was play'd, the DOGE of VENICE and all his Senators came upon the Stage with Feathers in their Hats, which was like to have chang'd the Tragedy into a Comedy." The lady adds, "Judge then by what happen'd once to your self, when we saw the Maid's Tragedy together." [30] Both Melantius and Amintor when Mohun and Hart played these rôles were duly furnished with a forest of feathers. No doubt in exotic plays, and it is surprising how many Restoration tragedies have an Oriental flavour, plumes were exceptionally in evidence, and they would not only be flaunted by Moors and Indians, but by classical heroes, by Timon of Athens and Alexander the Great, by Trojan and Persian, by ancient Egyptians of Memphis, by Tartars, and Chinese. It may be remembered that one of the attractions of Voltaire's *L'Orphelin de la Chine* (1755) was "the costuming of Lekain as a Tartar, with a great bow in his hand and hideous feathers waving on an impossible helmet". In the humorous inventory of the "Moveables of *Ch—r R—ch,* Esq.", of Drury Lane, which was given in *The Tatler,* No. 42, 16th July, 1709, one may note: "A Plume of Feathers, never used but by *Œdipus* and the Earl of *Essex.*"

One of the last recorded revivals of Dryden and Lee's tragedy *Oedipus* was at Covent Garden, 10th January, 1755, when Thomas Sheridan played the title-rôle. There was published a portrait of this famous actor in the part (*I. Roberts, del., Reading sc.*). He wears buskins with a pseudo-classical short-sleeved tunic and mantle both ornately guarded with ermine. A small crown surmounted with nodding French plumes is upon his hair, which hangs loose and somewhat dishevelled. A sword is girded at his side. On 17th December, 1790, John Bell of the British Library, Strand, published an engraving (*De Wilde pinx^{t}. Thornthwaite sculp.*) "Mr. Kemble as Oedipus". [31] The scene represented is the conclusion of Act II, "Oedipus *Enters, walking asleep in his shirt, with a Dagger in his right hand, and a Taper in his left.*" He is uttering the cry:—

> I challenge Fate to find another wretch
> Like *Oedipus.*

Kemble is depicted as wearing a short white tunic; his head, arms, and legs are bare. The sandals are loose. In one hand he holds a naked sword, in the other a Pompeian lamp. The gesture is magnificent, and the expression grand and truly awful.

It may be noted that in *Oedipus* Dryden drew particular attention to the dress of Tiresias and the brotherhood of priests. In Act III Haemon says :—

> For see the Prophet comes with Vervin crown'd,
> The Priests with Yeugh, a venerable band; . . .

"*Enter* Tiresias, *led by* Manto: *The Priests follow; all cloathed in long black Habits.*" [32]

In Settle's *The Empress of Morocco,* Dorset Garden, 3rd July, 1673, Act III opens with *Scene the Palace.* Muly Hamet speaks three lines and Exit. Then: "Scene a Bed-Chamber. *The Scene opens, and discovers* Crimalhaz *and Queen Mother sleeping on a Couch, a Table standing by, with* Crimalhaz's *Plume of Feathers, and his Drawn Sword upon it.*" The Fourth Act of Mrs. Behn's *Abdelazer; or, The Moor's Revenge,* Dorset Garden, autumn of 1676, commences in Abdelazer's Tent. "*Enter* Abdelazer, Osmin *bearing his Helmet of Feathers,* Zarrack *with his Sword and Truncheon.*" The Second Scene of Act I of the same lady's rococo *The Young King; or, The Mistake*, Dorset Garden, spring of 1679, is "*A Grove of Trees. Within the Scene lies* Thersander *sleeping, his Cap and Feather at a distance from him.* Presently "Semiris *looks about, finds the Cap and Feathers*" :—

> *Semiris.* See, Madam, what I've found.
> *Cleomena.* 'Tis a fine Plume, and well adorn'd,
> And must belong to no uncommon Man.

In Act III, 2, of this play the Amazonian Cleomena enters "*with a Truncheon in her Hand*", and when at the conclusion Orsames appears as King of Dacia he is "*drest gay with a Truncheon in his Hand*".

The truncheon, indeed, was very generally borne by Kings, Generals, and Heroes on the stage. In Act V of *Secret Love; or, The Maiden Queen* we have: "*Enter* Philocles *with a Commander's Staff in his Hand, attended.*" When he is about to take leave of the Queen of Syracuse, Brutus in Tate's tragedy *Brutus of Alba,* Dorset Garden, 1678, wavers and is half minded to stay. He cries :—

> Away thou foolish Utensil of War,
> [*Throws away his Truncheon.*
> I'll give my scatter'd Lawrels to the Wind . . .

Chetwood [33] tells a story of Thomas Griffith, who was of low stature, in his early days essaying the rôle of Pizarro in *The Indian*

Emperour. Betterton, who had not attended rehearsals, was at the proscenium door ready to make his entrance in the second scene when " his Ears were pierc'd with a Voice not familiar to him: He cast his Eyes upon the Stage, where he beheld the diminutive *Pizarro,* with a Truncheon as long as himself." The great man turned to Downes the prompter, " and cry'd *Zounds* Downs! *What sucking Scaramouch have you sent on there*?" When the act was over Griffith went to make his excuse to Betterton who bantered him good-humouredly but bade him stick to comedy, and cried " *After this Night, let me never see a Truncheon in thy Hand again, unless to stir the Fire* ". This would probably be at the Haymarket in 1707, when Betterton was acting Montezuma to the Almeria of Mrs. Barry.

Upon the original production of Otway's masterpiece *Venice Preserv'd,* at Dorset Garden on 9th February, 1682, William Smith who created Pierre wore a white hat as part of his costume in this rôle. Hence the custom strictly persisted throughout the eighteenth century that this character must always don a white hat, and it was very exactly observed by Verbruggen, Mills, Quin, Sheridan, Mossop, and other great actors. When The Phoenix, under my direction, gave two performances of *Venice Preserv'd* at the Lyric Theatre, Hammersmith, on the 28th and 30th November, 1920, I was careful, of course, to see that Mr. Baliol Holloway, whose fine performance as Pierre will not soon be forgotten, wore the traditional white hat. A splendid painting [34] by John Zoffany showing Garrick and Mrs. Cibber in *Venice Preserv'd,* at the conclusion of Act IV when Jaffier offers to stab Belvidera, depicts Garrick (Jaffier) in a rich contemporary costume, velvet coat and breeches, long waistcoat, cambric neckcloth, silk stockings, buckled shoes, and fashionable wig. Mrs. Cibber (Belvidera) elegantly wears a flowing modish gown. None the less the situation is supremely effective. On 15th January, 1802, *Venice Preserv'd* with Kemble as Jaffier; Barrymore, Pierre; and Mrs. Siddons, Belvidera, was revived at Drury Lane, the scenes and dresses being advertised as new. The production called forth a somewhat sharp protest in *The Monthly Mirror* for March, 1802.[35] The critic writes: " The scenes were those used in general on every occasion. " Jaffier's habit was a something of what was the fashion in Charles I's reign, as were those of many of the other characters." Over his tawdry jerkin Jaffier sported a brilliantly broidered sash. The action of the tragedy historically belongs to the year 1618, but " Pierre's dress was confessedly the modern trim of an officer, with *red coat, pantaloons, cocked hat* and *dressed hair* ". The soldiers wore fancy habits " leaning more to the Russian uniform, as now worn than to any thing else. The dresses of the females owning no authority than uncontrolled whim, are below our remark". It is true that in a portrait of 1790 of Mrs. Esten, who played Belvidera at Covent Garden to the Jaffier of Holman, this lady is wearing an entirely nondescript but extremely pleasing white satin dress, which recalls a Vandyke robe in its grace and richness of fold.

The well-known print of Quin as *Coriolanus* in Thomson's rhetorical tragedy produced at Covent Garden, 13th January, 1749, shows the full tragic equipment of plumed head-gear, full peruke, buskins, and mighty truncheon grasped in the right hand. The dress of Coriolanus is certainly most extraordinary with its ample skirt which seems to be stiffened by whalebone, of no place and no period. Quin, indeed, much affected the old traditional costumes and would abate no jot of detail. Pope's couplet (*Imitations of Horace,* I) is famous :—

> Such is the shout, the long-applauding note,
> At Quin's high plume, or Oldfield's petticoat.

An even more magnificent set of feathers than Quin wore in *Coriolanus* crowns Cyrus in the frontispiece by John Nickolls to the 1735 duodecimo edition of Banks' *Cyrus the Great ; or, The Tragedy of Love,* which was originally produced at Lincoln's Inn Fields in December, 1695. In his classical baroque with huge nodding plumes, his buskins, and wielding his truncheon Cyrus is the typical figure of grandiose tragedy. Thornhill's picture which represents the first scene of Young's *Busiris, King of Egypt,* produced at Drury Lane 7th March, 1719, represents a temple in Memphis, and Auletes prostrating himself before the King who wears a noble coronal of waving plumes. The panached pseudo-Roman helmet is worn by Diocles and Maximinian in the copperplate illustrating the libretto of the operatic *The Prophetess,* 12mo, 1716 ; by Hannibal in the frontispiece by G. Vander Gucht to Lee's *Sophonisba,* 12mo, 1726 ; by Martell in the plate of *The Tragedy of Thierry and Theodoret,* Tonson's Beaumont and Fletcher, 1711, vol. vii, p. 3697.

Addison in *The Spectator,* No. 42, Wednesday, 18th April, 1711, very agreeably rallies the traditional tragic costumes of the theatre. He says that "the Dresses and Decorations of the Stage have their place in raising the Aristotelian Terror and Pity in the Audience, hence these adjuncts must neither be neglected nor disesteemed. The ordinary Method of making an Hero, is to clap a huge Plume of Feathers upon his Head, which rises so very high, that there is often a greater Length from his Chin to

CYRUS THE GREAT: OR, THE TRAGEDY OF LOVE
Collection of the Author

[*face p.* 268

the Top of his Head, than to the sole of his Foot. One would believe, that we thought a great Man and a tall Man the same thing. This very much embarrasses the Actor, who is forced to hold his Neck extremely stiff and steady all the while he speaks; and notwithstanding any Anxieties which he pretends for his Mistress, his Country or his Friends, one may see by his Action, that his greatest Care and Concern is to keep the Plume of Feathers from falling off his Head. For my own part, when I see a Man uttering his Complaints under such a Mountain of Feathers, I am apt to look upon him rather as an unfortunate Lunatick, than a Distressed Hero. As these superfluous Ornaments upon the Head make a great Man, a Princess generally receives her Grandeur from those additional incumbrances that fall into her Tail; I mean the broad sweeping Train that follows her in all her Motions, and finds constant Employment for a Boy who stands behind her to open and spread it to Advantage. I do not know how others are affected at this Sight, but I must confess, my Eyes are wholly taken up with the Page's Part; and as for the Queen, I am not so attentive to any thing she speaks, as to the right adjusting of her Train, lest it should chance to trip up her Heels or incommode her, as she walks to and fro upon the Stage. It is, in my Opinion, a very odd Spectacle, to see a Queen venting her Passion in a disordered Motion, and a little Boy taking Care all the while that they do not ruffle the Tail of her Gown. The Parts that the two Persons act on the Stage at the same Time, are very different; the Princess is afraid lest she should incur the Displeasure of the King her Father, or lose the Hero her Lover, whilst her Attendant is only concerned lest she should entangle her Feet in her Petticoat".

When these Thespian Princes and Princesses, these Heroes and Heroines, in their soft silks and figured brocades, their ermines and gold galloons, their feathers and falbalas, came to die nightly from "*The Dagger and the Cup of Poison*" both "*alwaies in a readiness*", as Dryden remarks,[36] it was necessary to protect these gorgeous robes from being soiled and slutted in the dust and dirt of the boards, and accordingly if Melpomene topped the bills the stage was discreetly spread with "the green-baize carpet of tragedy", to speak in the words of Charles Lamb.

Indeed it is a question whether in the earlier years of the Restoration theatre the stage was not permanently covered with green cloth. Such indeed is implied in the Elegy "Upon The Most Execrable Murther of Mr. Clun, On[e] of the Comedeans of the Theator Royal",[37] who was assassinated by padders on Tuesday, 2nd August, 1664. This piece commences:—

Mourn Royal Stage, your Poets pens implore,
To cease to write, since *Clun* can be no more;
Turn all your Sceans to black, and let them be,
The Emblimes of our cares; *Cluns* Tragedy:
Go hide your Tapestry, and Clothes of green,
Act now on black, *Clun* will no more be seen.

By the end of the seventeenth century, however, it would appear that a green stage cloth definitely indicated the performance of a tragedy, and the green baize carpet of tragedy remained in evidence until at least the third quarter of the nineteenth century, when gradually it at length came to be spread no more. Thus we find Sheridan Le Fanu, writing in 1865, in his fine romance *Guy Deverell,*[38] whilst describing a domestic catastrophe in which murder may have been done, quite naturally phrases it: "Something had happened . . . Or was all right, and no one of the actors stretched on the green baize carpet before the floats?"

Throughout the eighteenth century, and later, well-nigh innumerable references to the traditional tragic carpet, which old playgoers loved to see, might be cited both from prose and poem. A couple of allusions may suffice. In the Epilogue, written by Garrick to Home's tragedy *Alfred,*[39] produced at Drury Lane, 27th February, 1773, Mrs. Barry humorously says:—

If this green cloth could speak, would it not tell,
Upon its well-worn nap how oft I fell?
To death in various forms delivered up
Steel kills me one night, and the next the Cup.

In the Epilogue, written by that great wit E. S. Barret, and spoken by Miss Booth to Sheil's tragedy *The Apostate,*[40] produced at Covent Garden, 3rd May, 1817, the actress merrily alludes to the company standing in the wings:—

Fierce *Malec* scowls at me, as if, forsooth,
He thought me Miss Florinda, not Miss Booth;
And e'en *Florinda*—ay, Ma'am, you may frown—
Who late fell poison'd on the carpet down,
Looks not at her dead Moor, but dusty gown.

There could have been no fairer embellishment than the soft radiance of the wax candles in a Restoration theatre to set off the costumes in all their bravery. "*In a Play house,*" wrote Dryden,[41] "*every thing contributes to impose upon the judgement; the Lights, the Scenes, the Habits, and, above all, the Grace of Action.*"

The main source of lighting the stage in the Restoration theatre was by pendent chandeliers, and these (at first, at any rate) were hung from the proscenium arch, well in front of the curtain, chiefly illuminating the apron, and directly over the actor's heads. To have placed chandeliers behind the curtain line among the sky borders would have been far too direct a source of danger to be risked in those days of fearful conflagrations and fatal fires. In the well-known engraving of the stage of the Duke's Theatre, Dorset Garden, as it was in 1673, illustrating the opening scene of Settle's *The Empress of Morocco,* 4to, 1673, and reproduced here, can be plainly discerned on the hither side of the floor of the projecting music-room, laying across the proscenium soffit, the six great beams to which the half-dozen chandeliers were suspended. Thus on Wednesday, 12th May, 1669, Pepys went with his wife to Lincoln's Inn Fields, " to the Duke of York's play-house, and there, in the side balcony, over against the musick, did hear, but not see, a new play, the first day acted, ' The Roman Virgin,' [42] an old play, and but ordinary, I thought; but the trouble of my eyes with the light of the candles did almost kill me." The chandeliers were obviously on a level with his line of vision.

The candles were lighted before the Prologue was spoken, that is to say before the curtain rose or was drawn, and naturally during the length of the performances the good offices of adroit candle-snuffers was required, gentry who are mocked and fleered in many a lampoon. The Introduction to Flecknoe's *The Damoiselles A La Mode,*[43] 8vo, 1667, commences: " *The Candles lighted, before the Curtains drawn, Enter one of the Actors, another* (*suppos'd no Actor*) *calling after him.*" The two actors entered by one of the proscenium doors on to the apron in front of the curtain.

Pepys more than once complains of the light of the candles affecting his eyes,[44] and Flecknoe in his *Short Discourse of the English Stage,* 1664, in reference to scenery remarks: " Of this curious Art the *Italians* (this latter age) are the greatest Masters, the *French* good proficients, and we in *England* onely Schollars and Learners yet, having proceeded no further then to bare painting, and not arriv'd to the stupendious wonders of your great Ingeniers, especially not knowing yet how to place our Lights, for the more advantage and illuminating of the Scenes." [45]

In the well-known frontispiece to *The Wits,* 1672, we see not only two branched chandeliers with eight tapers apiece hanging at the back of the stage, but also a row of six small oil lamps with double burners set in front of the stage, in fact a row of footlights.[46]

Incidentally it must once again be remarked that the long-enduring tradition which declares footlights to have been introduced by Garrick in 1765 is utterly and entirely without foundation. Yet not only is this error clung to and paraded most pertinaciously [47] and in spite of every contradiction and demonstration repeated again and again, but an attempt to establish the truth and traverse this fallacy seems to be regarded by a certain class of easy writer as something like a personal affront. None the less we have exact pictorial evidence to the contrary, the frontispiece to *The Wits,* already cited, and the frontispiece to *A Second Tale of A Tub ; Or, The History of Robert Powel the Puppet-Show-Man,* a satire by Sir W. Burnett, published in 1715. Moreover there is an allusion to early footlights in The Prologue to the Reader which introduces John Wright's translation of Seneca's *Thyestes,* 8vo, 1674, where the poet sarcastically apologizes to the wits :—

> *Nor Love, nor Honour here the Author show'd:*
> *Nay, what is worse, no Bawd'ry* A-la-mode.
> *No Amorous Song, nor a more Amorous Jigg,*
> *Where Misses Coats twirl like a Whirlegig,*
> *And such who next the Lamps themselves dispose,*
> *Think thus to recompense the stink of those,*
> *While she that Dances jilts the very eyes,*
> *Allowing only these Discoveri's*
> *A neat silk Leg, and pair of Holland thighs.*

If it be asked, what then did Garrick do the answer briefly is that Garrick removed the six chandeliers and substituted wing-lights. *The Universal Museum,*[48] September, 1765, tells us that on his return from the continent Garrick made considerable alterations in the lighting at Drury Lane : " One very considerable improvement introduced by Mr. *Garrick* on the Stage this season is the removal of the six rings that used to be suspended over the Stage, in order to illuminate the house . . . The public were agreeably surprised on the opening of *Drury-Lane* theatre, to see the Stage illuminated with a strong and clear light, and the rings removed that used to supply it, though to the great annoyance of many of the Audience, and frequently the Actors themselves.

" The Managers of *Covent-Garden* have attempted the like improvement, but not with the same success ; instead of Wax, they have given Oil, and their Lights may be said to smell too much of the *Lamp.*"

Mons. E. Despois, *Le Théâtre en France sous Louis XIV,*[49] emphasizes that in the French theatre until the middle of the seventeenth century performances were given in the afternoons, in broad day, and that it was not until the end of the reign of

Louis XIV that the play commenced towards half-past four or five o'clock, concluding before seven in the evening.[50]

It was about 1640 that the Hôtel de Bourgogne and the Théâtre au Marais were lighted by candles placed at the back of the stage, which proved so unsatisfactory that large candelabra were soon placed in front. "Ce fut le principe de la rampe," and it is significant that, "La rampe parut d'abord dans les Théâtres les moins luxueux."[51] At the Hôtel de Bourgogne about 1650, six crystal chandeliers were suspended over the stage, and moreover a row of little lamps formed the footlights. Molière at the Palais-Royal had twelve chandeliers, each holding ten candles, hanging over the stage, and forty-eight candles for his footlights.

As we know the English theatre, and Betterton in particular, kept closely in touch with the French stage, and it would have been extraordinary indeed if improvements in lighting had not been adopted at Dorset Garden, once they were established and the general rule in the Parisian playhouses.

The first English footlights were no doubt very primitive, a few separate oil lamps, but very soon there came into use footlights of the nature of "the floats", that is to say a number of cotton wicks running through large round pieces of cork and floating on a quantity of oil contained in a long, narrow tin box which fitted over a trap in front of the stage. A tin reflector screened the naked light from the spectators. These floats did not extend the whole length of the front of the stage, but only occupied a limited space, centre, and thus it was not impossible for an active member of the audience actually to clamber up on the boards at the side, as Pepys once saw during a performance of James Howard's *All Mistaken; or, The Mad Couple,* at the Theatre Royal, when "It pleased us mightily to see the natural affection of a poor woman, the mother of one of the children, brought on the stage: the child crying She by force got upon the stage, and took up her child and carried it away off the stage from Hart".[52]

"The orchestra lights at length arose, those 'fair Auroras!' Once the bell sounded . . . It rang the second time. The curtain drew up . . .—and the play was Artaxerxes!" So Charles Lamb in his delightful essay *My First Play,*[53] which he saw in the season 1781–2.

Early in the eighteenth century effects of darkness on the stage were obtained by lowering the floats,[54] and it is probable that this practice had commenced in Restoration days. Mr. Odell indeed gives it as his opinion[55] that "the stage was darkened, when necessary, by the actual removal of the lights; they came and went by the manipulation of a pulley ". That is to say the chandeliers were pulled up out of the sight of the audience. This hardly seems possible. If so, where could they have been fixed? Certainly they could not easily have been raised at will unless they were suspended behind the curtain line, when the hazard of elevating a large number of naked wax tapers among inflammable painted canvas borders, all flapping in the draught, would have been far too considerable ever to be risked, not to mention the further danger of lighted candles dropping from their sockets upon the actors' heads. It must be borne in mind that the floats were merely additional to and in no way superseded the chandeliers.

There are in Restoration plays a good many night scenes and scenes of darkness. In the first place, upon the stage scenes of absolute darkness are as unattainable as they are undesirable; a moderate gloom serves for pitchy night, and the audience therefore never fail at these moments to use a certain imagination. In Restoration days not even the quantum of realism now required in this respect was demanded, and almost certainly a general obfuscation amply sufficed for the veritable shades of Erebus and Nox. With regard to interior and domestic scenes the matter was simple enough, and the illusion of darkness was conventionally sustained by the actors taking away candles, and bringing them on again when a light effect was required. A vast number of examples might be adduced,[56] but some two or three will amply suffice. The last scene of Act IV, Wycherley's *The Plain-Dealer,* Theatre Royal, December, 1676, largely depends upon the manipulation of lights. The scene is Olivia's Lodgings. "*Enter Lord* Plausible, *and Boy with a Candle.*" When the stage is empty "*Enter* Olivia *and Boy*". A few moments later, "*Enter her Husband* Vernish, *as from a Journey.*" "Darkness every where!" he softly exclaims, and she embraces him taking him for her lover. Later Fidelia, who is disguised as a boy, visits the lady, and is just leaving when she cries: "O, Madam, we're undone! there was a Gentleman upon the stairs, coming up with a Candle." "*Enter* Vernish, *and his Man with a Light.*"

Even more essential is the business with candles in the final scene of the same play. The scene is Olivia's *Lodging.* "*Enter* Olivia *with a Candle in her hand.*" She puts out the candle, apostrophizing "Kind darkness", and Fidelia enters followed by Manly. Olivia retires; and Vernish who suspects her enters "*with a dark Lanthorn and a Sword*". He fights with Manly in the dark, and when Olivia returns she cannot even distinguish the combatants, until Freeman and others appear "*lighted by the two* Sailors *with torches*".

In D'Urfey's *The Fond Husband,* Dorset Garden, May, 1677, Act IV, Rashley and Emilia are together in a bedchamber. Ranger enters, and a good deal of confusion ensues in the dark. "*Enter* Bubble *and* Maria *with a Light. They stand amaz'd.*"

Shadwell in his *The Lancashire Witches,* Act IV, lays a scene in the gallery of a country house at night. Tegue O'Divelly enters with Mother Dickenson, whom he imagines to be a lady of the house, and is very gallant to her. But "*Enter* Susan *with a Candle*", and seeing the horrible harridan he bawls out: "O phaat have I done? Oh! de Vich! de Vich!" *Susan.* Oh! the Witch! the Witch! *The Witch sinks, she lets fall the Candle and runs away shrieking.*

Dryden in *The Assignation,* acted in the winter of 1672, has Act II, Scene 3: "*A Night-piece of a Garden,*" when a garden by night, with the moon and stars, was merely painted upon the flats.[57]

The convention of simulating darkness by the bringing on or carrying off a candle in a character's hand would not have been permissible in the more elaborate operatic dramas, and when we find scenes of sudden obscurity and gloom in such pieces as Shadwell's *The Tempest* or Charles Davenant's *Circe* with their multiple mechanical effects, it is plain that there must have been some method of producing darkness not too clumsily on occasion, and since the manipulation of chandeliers is out of the question it can only have been managed by lowering the floats. It should be remarked, moreover, that these operatic changes from light to darkness commenced with the storm scene in Shadwell's *The Tempest,* which was produced at Dorset Garden in the spring of 1674, that is to say just after Betterton had come back from Paris, full of new ideas and novel devices to be tried upon the English stage.

The Tempest; or, The Enchanted Island commences with the ship in a rough sea, "*And when the Ship is sinking, the whole House is darken'd, and a shower of Fire fall upon 'em . . . In the midst of the Shower of Fire the Scene changes . . . and when the Lights return discover that Beautiful Part of the Island, which was the Habitation of* Prospero."[58] "*When the Lights return,*" that is to say, when the floats are raised.

In Charles Davenant's *Circe,* Dorset Garden, May, 1677, at the final catastrophe, V, 9, we have: "*The Stage is wholly darken'd, and the City of a sudden is a Fire.*"[59] Dryden and Lee's *Oedipus,* Dorset Garden, December, 1678, or January, 1678–9, during the famous Incantation scene of Act III, which takes place in "*A dark Grove*", before the apparitions rise has "*The Stage wholly darken'd*".[60]

In Betterton's *The Prophetess,* Dorset Garden, 1690,[61] at the end of Act II, we have: "*Thunder and Lightning. The Stage is darkened on a sudden.*"

It is certain that such practised men of the theatre as Dryden, Betterton, and Elkanah Settle would not have required these and similar effects in their gorgeously spectacular dramas, had it not been possible to produce the desired illusion with speed and skill.

When we consider that the hour of the play, as has been noted in detail, was early in the afternoon there is no occasion for surprise to find that the auditorium of the theatre was not artificially lighted, since indeed there was no necessity for such illumination, and evening performances in the public play-houses were never contemplated either by the actors or the architects of the houses. On the other hand ample provision was made for a good supply of natural light. At the Theatre Royal the great glazed cupola, which domed the house, admitted not only light but rain, as Pepys found on more than one occasion to his cost. On Whit-Wednesday, 1st June, 1668, whilst he was at *The Silent Woman,* "before the play was done, it fell such a storm of hayle, that we in the middle of the pit were fain to rise; and all the house in a disorder." On Friday, May Day, 1668, he went "to the King's playhouse, and there saw 'The Surprizall': and a disorder in the pit by its raining in, from the cupolaat top, it being a very foul day and cold".

The engravings of Dorset Garden show us lanterns, belvederes, and an ample supply of windows. In John Strype's "Corrected, Improved, and very much Enlarged" edition of Stow's *Survey of the Cities of London and Westminster,* 2 vols, folio, 1720,[62] is given an iconographical map of the parish of S. Paul's, Covent Garden, and here some of the principal buildings are depicted in little. The Play-house, Wren's Theatre Royal of 1674, is drawn and marked by name. It is an oblong building with sloping roof, and looks not unlike a chapel or plain church, which it also resembles in carrying at each side six spacious windows of clear-paned glass. On 12th June, 1663, Pepys went to the first Theatre Royal, to see *The Committee,* and, as he writes, found himself troubled all night from "some cold I took to-day sitting sweating in the playhouse, and the wind blowing through the windows upon my head". Light was also thrown into the theatre by the windows of the tiring-rooms and scene-room at the back of the stage. Magalotti in 1669 speaks of this first Theatre Royal as "sufficiently lighted on the stage [i.e. by candles] and on the walls [i.e. by windows] to enable the spectators to see the scenes and performances".[63]

Because of the interest in detail, however caustic and even cruel the humour, it will not be impertinent to quote here from *The Play-House: A Satyr. By* T. G. *Gent., Poems on Affairs of State,* vol. ii, 1703 [64]:—

But enter in, my *Muse,* the Stage survey,
And all its Pomp and Pagentry display;
Trap-Doors and Pit-falls, from th' unfaithful Ground,
And Magick Walls, encompass it around:
On either side maim'd Temples fill our Eyes,
And intermixt with Brothel-Houses rise;
Disjointed Palaces in order stand,
And Groves obedient to the mover's Hand,
O'ershade the Stage, and flourish at Command.
A Stamp makes broken Touns and Trees entire:
So when *Amphion* struck the Vocal Lire,
He saw the Spacious Circuit all around,
With crowding Woods, and Neighbouring Cities croun'd.
  But next the Tyring Room Survey and see,
False Titles, and promiscuous Quality,
Confus'dly swarm from Heroes and from Queens,
To those that swing in Clouds and fill Machines.
Their various Characters they chose with Art,
The frouning Bully fits the Tyrant's part:
Swoln Cheeks, and Swaggering Bully makes a Host,
Pale meager Looks, and hollow Voice, a Ghost;
From careful Brows, and heavy down-cast Eyes,
Dull Cits, and thick scull'd Aldermen arise:
The Comick Tone, inspir'd by F[arquha]*r*, draws
At every Word Loud Laughter and Applause:
The Mincing Dame continues as before,
Her Character's unchang'd, and Acts a Whore.
  Above the rest, the Prince with mighty Stalks,
Magnificent in Purple Buskins walks:
The Royal Robe his Haughty Shoulders grace,
Profuse of *Spangles* and of *Copper-Lace*:
Officious Rascals to his mighty Thigh,
Guiltless of Blood, th' unpointed Weapon tye;
Then the Gay Glittering Diadem put on,
Pondrous with Brass, and Star'd with Bristol stone.
His Royal Consort next consults her Glass,
And out of twenty *Boxes* culls a *Face*.
The whit'ning first her Ghastly Looks besmears,
All Pale and Wan th' unfinish'd Form appears;
Till on her Cheeks the blushing Purple glows,
And a false *Virgin Modesty* bestows;
Her ruddy Lips the Deep Vermilion dyes;
Length to her Brows the Pencil's touch supplies,
And with black bending Arches shades her Eyes.

Well pleas'd at length the Picture she beholds,
And spots it o'er with Artificial *Molds;*
Her Countenance compleat, the Beaux she warms
With looks not hers, and spight of Nature, charms.
  Thus artfully their Persons they disguise,
Till the last flourish bids the Curtain rise.
The Prince then enters on the Stage in State;
Behind, a Guard of Candle-Snuffers wait:
There swoln with Empire, terrible and fierce,
He shakes the Dome, and tears his Lungs with Verse:
His Subjects tremble, the submissive Pit,
Wrapt up in Silence and Attention, sit;
Till freed at length, he lays aside the Weight
Of Publick Business and Affairs of State;
Forgets his Pomp, dead to Ambitious Fires,
And to some peaceful *Brandy-Shop* retires;
Where in full Gills his anxious thoughts he drowns,
And quaffs away the Care that waits on Crowns.
  The Princess next her painted Charms displays,
Where every look the Pencil's Art betrays.
The Callow Squire at distance feeds his Eyes,
And silently for *Paint* and *Patches* dies:
But if the Youth behind the Scenes retreat
He sees the blended Colours melt with heat,
And all the trickling *Beauty* run in Sweat.
The borrow'd Visage he admires no more,
And nauseates every Charm he lov'd before:
So the same Spear, for double force renown'd,
Apply'd the Remedy that gave the Wound.
  In tedious Lists 'twere endless to engage,
And draw at length the Rabble of the Stage,
Where one for twenty Years has given Alarms,
And call'd contending *Monarchs* to their Arms,
Another fills a more important post,
And rises every other Night a Ghost.
Thro' the cleft Stage his meager Face he rears,
Then stalks along, groans thrice and disappears;
Others with *Swords* and *Shields,* the *Soldiers* Pride,
More than a thousand times have chang'd their Side,
And in a thousand fatal *Battels* dy'd.

In a letter written by Mrs. Katherine Philips to Dorothy Temple on 22nd January, 1663-4, the fair Orinda criticizes the production a few weeks before at Lincoln's Inn Fields of the *Pompey,* "Translated out of the French by Certain Persons of Honour," which she had so long feared as being a serious rival to her own version from Corneille. Her heart is now at ease, for the "confederate translators" had made anything but a success of their job. "I wonder much," she observes, "what preparations for it would prejudice Will D'avenant when I heare they acted in English habits, & yt so a propos yt Cesar was sent in with a feather and a staff till he was hissed off ye stage." [65] And yet the feather and staff of Julius Caesar were but the essential accessories of any hero on the Restoration boards; the plumes which more than eighty years later Quin, as we have noted, donned as the fitting and only head-gear for Coriolanus; and the truncheon which seldom left the hero's hand. In the famous portrait by Pierre Mignard, of Molière, habited for precisely the same rôle, Jules César in *La Mort de Pompée,* the actor, wearing a huge peruke crowned with a superb wreath of laurel, wields an enormous truncheon, gilded and embossed. It was in the same year, too, as the London production that *La Mort de Pompée* was given by Molière's troupe, 1663. But Orinda was nothing if not *intransigeante* and hyper-critical on this occasion.

On Tuesday, 8th March, 1664, Pepys went to Lincoln's Inn Fields and saw *Heraclius,* "The garments like Romans very well. . . . But at the beginning at the drawing up of the curtaine, there was the finest scene of the Emperor and his people about him, standing in their fixed and different postures in their Roman habitts, above all that ever I yet saw at any of the theatres." These costumes *à la Romaine* were no doubt very similar to those in which the more classical statues of monarchs, princes, and generals are garbed, a close-fitting tunic or cuirass, buskins, gauntlets, a cloak, a flowing peruke, topped by a helmet with its waving panache. Sometimes a loose mantle might be assumed by the actor but the real toga was a thing of the far future, for although it had been introduced on to the French stage by Talma it did not appear in English theatres until the first quarter of the nineteenth century when it was adopted by Edmund Kean and Charles Young. It may be questioned whether the "sixteen scarlett robes" that proved no small attraction in the revival of *Catiline* at the Theatre Royal in November, 1668, although doubtless sufficiently striking were very correct. But it may be remembered that when Voltaire's *Brutus* was presented at the Comédie Française on 11th December, 1730, the red robes of the senators were greatly admired and the poet openly avowed that he had used this device to embellish "the coldness of tragedy". Such habits and the accompanying furniture, no doubt, were in the mode of "Cato's long Wig, flow'r'd gown, and lacquer'd chair".

Mrs. Manley's *Almyna; or, The Arabian Vow,* [66] Haymarket, 16th December, 1706, was "advantagiously Dress'd" owing to the care of "Mr. *Swiny* (who, with the like regard, may be assur'd of the Author's Respects, for venturing upon the good Opinion of the Play, to make so great an Expence ").

The dresses worn by the actresses in classical or exotic dramas made not the faintest pretence to accuracy. So long as they glistered rich and jewelled the ladies and the audience were amply content. Antony and Nero may have been garbed " like Romans very well " but Cleopatra and Poppea donned silken petticoats of the fashion that the Duchess of Cleveland or the Duchess of Portsmouth were at the moment displaying in the royal box.

Audiences of the seventeenth and eighteenth centuries expected and indeed insisted that Cleopatra in Dryden's *All for Love; Or, The World well Lost* (originally produced at the Theatre Royal, December, 1677) should be attired with especial and unusual magnificence. On the occasion of a revival at Drury Lane, 3rd December, 1718, for example, this tragedy was announced as " not acted 12 years, all the Habits being entirely new with Decorations proper to the play ", and Cibber tells us: " Upon the Revival of *Dryden's* All For Love, the Habits of that Tragedy amounted to an Expense of nearly six hundred Pounds; a Sum unheard of, for many Years before, on the like Occasions." Mrs. Oldfield appeared as Cleopatra; Mrs. Porter, Octavia; and Booth, Antony.

At Dublin, during the season 1745–6, when the beautiful George Ann Bellamy was playing Cleopatra, the manager Sheridan, being in London during the summer, " purchased a superb suit of clothes that had belonged to the Princess of *Wales*, and had only been worn by her on the birth-day." This suit was made into the robes of Cleopatra, and as though the material, the ground of which was silver tissue, were not rich enough in itself they sewed a large number of diamonds upon the lovely stuff to give it a yet more dazzling sheen. These jewels had been lent by Mrs. Butler, a leader of Irish society, and an especial patroness of the Bellamy. Unfortunately a rival actress, Mrs. Furnival, who was cast for Octavia, seeing the magnificent costume appropriated it for her own use, and in spite of argument and remonstrance walked on the boards robed in the imperial attire of Cleopatra, who was obliged to content herself with white satin and milky pearls. Behind the scenes Sheridan treated Miss Bellamy to a regular jobation, whilst in the front of the house Mrs. Butler, who was seated in a stage-box, on seeing Mrs. Furnival, cried out loud, " Good Heaven, the woman has got on my diamonds! " A vast deal of confusion ensued; Mrs. Furnival was saluted with hisses and cat-calls, whereupon she promptly fell into fits, and Mrs. Elmy who happened to be at the back was hurriedly called upon to dress for and finish the rôle.[67]

There is an engraving (*Edwards inv., B. Reading, sculpt.*) representing Anna Maria Yates as Cleopatra, a part she sustained at Drury Lane in 1766 to the Antony of Charles Holland. The moment depicted is at the commencement of Act V when, grasping her poniard, the queen exclaims: "I'll die; I will not bear it." The gesture is magnificent, and one can well discern "The brow, still fix'd in Sorrow's sullen frame". The costume, although of course by no means correct in any detail, is certainly striking, and seems intended to be neo-classical in design. A royal mantle, edged with ermine, gives an appearance of amply flowing robes. The hair, without powder, is mounted over a cushion, entwined with pearls and adorned with a small stephane from which hangs a veil. In fine it is the dress of a tragic princess, stately and proud.

On 28th April, 1773, at Covent Garden, Mrs. Hartley, a most accomplished tragedienne and a beautiful woman, played Cleopatra to the Antony of Smith. There was published an engraving of her in this rôle, sold by J. Wenman, 144 Fleet Street; 1778. She is represented in the scene which commences the Fifth Act. The Egyptian amorosa reclines in a gilt rococo chair, and is dressed in a huge hooped petticoat of brocade, flounced and furbelowed, and fairly criss-crossed with an elaborate floralia. The hair is powdered, dressed high, woven with pearls, and surmounted by a diadem all adorned with waving ostrich plumes. In fact, the costume is a very magnificent court suit of the period.

It is amusing to note that when amateurs of quality gave a performance of *All for Love* in "*the Bow-window Room*" at Blenheim before the old Duke of Marlborough, Lady Blayney in a letter written in the latter part of her life tells us that Miss Cairnes who acted Serapion "as high-priest, wore a very fine surplice, that came from Holland for the chapel (no sacrilege), for the chapel was not finished many years after. What makes me call it a fine surplice is, that all the breast was worked in what, many years after, was called Dresden work . . . I suppose we made a very grand appearance, there was profusion of brocade rolls, &c., of what was to be the window curtains at Blenheim. Jewels you may believe in plenty; and I think Mark Anthony wore the sword that the emperor gave the Duke of Marlborough."[68]

All For Love was revived under my direction by "The Phoenix" for two performances at the Shaftesbury Theatre on 19th and 20th March, 1922. The play, so excellently produced by Miss Edith Craig, was received with great applause. Miss Edith Evans sustained Cleopatra to the Antony of Mr. Ion Swinley. I well remember that Miss Craig and myself had many a long and earnest consultation concerning the dresses. The tragedy was with great care presented in costumes such as would have been worn at the *première*. Thus Antony and the men donned perukes, whilst Cleopatra was coiffured, jewelled, and attired on the model of a Lely canvas. " The whole tragedy," wrote one critic, " was given admirably in the Restoration manner, with Antony as a Restoration gallant in a Restoration periwig."

It will hardly be credited that one writer regarded this presentment as " false ". Mr. St. John Ervine characteristically delivered himself in the following heavily humorous vein: " I do not know who had the bright idea of using Restoration costumes for a play about Romans and Egyptians, but I suggest to the Council of the Phoenix Society that if this genius has any more bright ideas he should be persuaded to keep them to himself. The effect of this particular idea was to strip all the sincerity from the play and turn it into a piece of artifice. We could not believe in a Cleopatra so bedizened with petticoats that any period of residence on the banks of the Nile must have been a clammy one." [69] So might an abnormally stupid schoolboy scribble, and fondly imagine that he was penning a criticism.

In Tate's *The Ingratitude of a Commonwealth; or, The Fall of Caius Marius Coriolanus,* given at Dorset Garden in 1681, Valeria enters " Gawdily and Fantastically Drest, follow'd by Six or Seven Pages ", and her conversation which suits her attire is that of a fashionable lady of Charles' court.

Indeed there were very few female characters that wore any but modish costumes, which would have been strictly *en règle* for a jaunt to the Park or the New Exchange. It is true that as Henry VIII, Falstaff, and some few other personages were distinguished by their traditional attire, so Queen Elizabeth and perhaps one or two more were dressed more or less after existing portraits. On Saturday, 17th August, 1667, Pepys went to the Theatre Royal " where the house extraordinary full " to see the revival of Heywood's *If you Know not me, You Know no bodie; Or, the troubles of Queene Elizabeth.* He comments: " But the play is the most ridiculous that sure ever come upon the stage; and, indeed, is merely a shew, only shews the true garbe of the Queen in those days, just as we see Queen Mary and Queen Elizabeth painted; but the play is merely a puppet play, acted by living puppets. Neither the design nor language better; and one stands by and tells us the meaning of things: only I was pleased to see Knipp dance among the milkmaids, and to

WILLIAM HARRIS AS THE EMPRESS OF MOROCCO

In Duffett's farce "The Empress of Morocco"

Library of Worcester College, Oxford

[*face p.* 282

hear her sing a song to Queen Elizabeth; and to see her come out in her night-gown with no lockes on, but her bare face and hair only tied up in a knot behind; which is the comeliest dress that ever I saw her in to her advantage." Nevertheless Queen Mary of Modena presented her coronation robes to Mrs. Barry, who wore them as Queen Elizabeth in a revival of Banks' *The Unhappy Favourite; or, The Earl of Essex*. The frontispiece to *Le Comte D'Essex* in the V. Partie of the *Theatre de T. Corneille*, Amsterdam, 1701, represents both Queen Elizabeth and Le Comte de Salsbury very correctly dressed. But I have no doubt that although when Pepys saw Heywood's rather clumsy chronicle Queen Mary and Queen Elizabeth were in their native habits, the many characters who surrounded them differed little if at all in their costumes from the ordinary clothes in vogue during August, 1667. I conceive that most of the actors might have walked straight from the boards into the streets without exciting attention or remark. Flecknoe in his *The Damoiselles A La Mode*, 8vo, 1667, is careful to emphasize that the production of his comedy, which was refused, would entail no expense. "The Scænes & Cloaths being the least Considerable in it, any *Italian* Scænes with four Doors serving for the one, and for the other any *French* cloaths *A la Mode*." Thus in the illustration to *Hamlet*, Rowe's Shakespeare, 1709, which depicts the Closet scene, the ghost appears in mail wielding a truncheon, but Hamlet is clad in a peruke and a black suit such as Addison or Budgell or any member of the audience might have worn, whilst Gertrude of Denmark is simply a lady of the court of Queen Anne. Hamlet's dress is in fact "distinctly ministerial" as Mr. Lowe describes the picture of Betterton who in a painting now hanging in the Garrick Club, London, is shown with Mrs. Barry in this very scene. "The actor's face is certainly depicted pale as his neck-cloth, which, by the way, is a very clerical-looking article of costume."[70] Mrs. Barry as the Queen wears a crimson velvet robe, over a white satin underskirt.

The story may be recalled of the old critic who, in the days of the second George when the younger men were loudly praising a recent Hamlet, proved exceptious and would allow little merit to the new interpreter of the Prince of Denmark. The chorus, however, pronounced him admirable, especially in the closet scene. Could anyone deny that his elocution was just and forcible, his carriage superb, his gestures how admirable! "Pretty well, sir, pretty well," quoth our *laudator temporis acti*, "why, it was pretty well done, but then"—with a long pinch from his box—"he did not upset the chair, sir. Now Mr. Betterton always upset the chair." This bit of business was indeed a very old tradition, and in the illustration to Rowe's Shakespeare, 1709, the chair appears duly thrown to the ground.

Naturally upon the Restoration stage even if the actresses were not historically exact in their attire they at least endeavoured to dress in character. That is to say a shepherdess would be adorned with floral garlands, a nun would wear black robes with linen wimple and fillet, the puritan housewife must have sad and sober garments, the common strumpet would flaunt her dizened petticoat and flowered justacorps. The Epilogue to Settle's *Fatal Love; or, The Forced Inconstancy*, given at the Theatre Royal in 1680 was " Spoken by *Lysandra* in the Habit of a Nun ". An actress dressed as a country lass in bongrace and stuff gown could walk through the city and but be regarded as a visitor to London. On Thursday, 24th January, 1667, Pepys entertained a number of friends. " And, anon, at about seven or eight o'clock, comes Mr. Harris, of the Duke's playhouse, and brings Mrs. Pierce with him, and also one dressed like a country-mayde with a straw hat on; which, at first, I could not tell who it was, though I expected Knipp: but it was she coming off the stage just as she acted this day in The Goblins; a merry jade."

In many plays characters were, of course, required to dress in some particular manner or costume. Thus in *The Plain-Dealer,* Drury Lane, winter of 1676, Manly wears red breeches, a tucked up peruke, a broad belt with a short sword, a scarf, and a large brandenburgh. The Widow Blackacre is described as " usually cloath'd and dagled like a Bawd in Disguise ". She enters " *with a Mantle, and a green Bag, and several Papers in the other hand*: Jerry Blackacre, *her Son, in a Gown, laden with green Bags, following her* ". At Westminster Hall she appears " *in the Middle of half a dozen Lawyers, whisper'd to by a Fellow in black* ". Later when Jerry breaks free from petticoat government he sports " *an old gaudy Suit, and red Breeches of* Freeman'*s* ". In Otway's *The Souldiers Fortune,* Dorset Garden, early in 1680, Courtine, the disbanded officer, wears " a flopping Hat, pin'd up on one side, with a sandy weather-beaten Perruque, dirty Linen, and to compleat the Figure, a long scandalous Iron Sword ". In Act II we find various stage directions; " *Enter a young fellow affectedly drest, several others with him* "; " *A Clumsie Fellow marches over the Stage drest like an Officer* "; " *Enter another gravely drest.*" In Wycherley's *The Gentleman Dancing-Master,* Dorset Garden, March, 1672, Don Diego wears a Spanish habit, and Monsieur de Paris adopts the latest French fopperies. When Paris is compelled to assume the severer Spanish attire he cries: " Adieu, then, dear Pantalloon! dear Beltè! dear Sword! dear Perruque! and dear Chappeaux Retrousee, and dear Shoe." The rôle was played by Nokes, and it may be remembered that in May, 1670, when Henrietta of Orleans visited Charles II at Dover, John Caryl's *Sir Salomon; or, The Cautious Coxcomb* was given. "The *French* Court wearing their excessive short Lac'd Coats; some Scarlet, some Blew, with Broad wast Belts; Mr. *Nokes* having at that time one shorter than the *French* fashion to Act Sir *Arthur Addle* in; the Duke of *Monmouth* gave Mr. *Nokes* his Sword and Belt from his Side, and Buckled it on himself on purpose to Ape the *French*: That Mr. *Nokes* lookt more like a Drest up Ape, than a Sir *Arthur*: Which upon his first Entrance on the Stage, put the King and Court to an Excessive Laughter: at which the *French* look'd very Shaggrin, to see themselves Ap'd by such a Buffoon as Sir *Arthur*: Mr. *Nokes* kept the Dukes Sword to his Dying Day."[71] Nell Gwyn in similar fashion parodied Nokes himself when speaking the Prologue to Dryden's *The Conquest of Granada*, Part I, Theatre Royal, December, 1670, she came forward in a monstrous waist-belt and a hat of the dimensions of a huge cart-wheel. The direction before the Prologue is: "*Spoken by* Mrs. Ellen Gwyn *in a broad-brimmed hat and waist-belt*." When Wycherley's Monsieur de Paris is to be dressed in Spanish mode he first ventures half-way and is seen "*without a Perruque, with a* Spanish *Hat, a* Spanish *Doublet, Stockins, and Shooes, but in Pantalloons, a Waste-Belt, and a* Spanish *Dagger in't, and a Crevat about his Neck*". Later he is obliged to discard the pantaloons and waist-belt, and for his cravat he dons a golilla, the distinctive Spanish collar introduced by Philip IV in 1623.

The Epilogue to *The Indian Queen,* Theatre Royal, January, 1664, has a reference to "*Our naked* Indians", and in the copper-plate (4to, 1673) which illustrates the "*Moorish Dance presented by* Moors *in several Habits*" about an artificial Palm-tree in Act II of Settle's *The Empress of Morocco,* the very active performers are not burdened with too many clothes as they twirl and whirl their sooty limbs in some antic rigadoon. In Crowne's *Sir Courtly Nice; or, It Cannot Be,* produced at Drury Lane, 4th May, 1685, when Crack personates Sir Thomas Calico, he is said to have brought with him from the Indies "several *Siamites* and *Bantamers,* that serve him as his Slaves, in the ridiculous Dresses and Modes of their own Countries". "*Enter* Crack *ridiculously dress'd, attended by Men in the Habits of* Siamites *and* Bantamers."

Reference has already been made in another connection to the Fifth Act of *The Fairy-Queen,* when amongst other spectacular marvels is discovered "*a transparent Prospect of a* Chinese *Garden . . . quite different from what we have in this part of the*

World", whilst a man and a woman from Cathay, robed in elaborately figured silks sing and dance together. Nicholas Rowe in his one comedy, *The Biter,* brought on the scene an old merchant who affects Chinese attire, and who is attended by a train of Chinese servants in native costume.

In Ravenscroft's *The Careless Lovers,* Duke's House, March, 1673, Act V, the mock-spectres, "4 *Ghosts,* 2 *Men, and* 2 *Women*" were dressed "*The Women in long winding Sheets, the Men with Mufflers, Caps, white Cloaths, Wastcoats, Drawers, Breeches, Stockings & Pumps*" whilst to complete the tableau Beatrice rose "*upright in the Coffin,* in a Winding-Sheet". Toby, who was dressed as a Bearer, and the "4 Maids *in white*" promptly decamped.

In Act V of Leanerd's *The Rambling Justice; or, The Jealous Husbands,* given at the Theatre Royal in the spring of 1678, there is an exceptionally full direction: "*Enter* Twiford *drest Ridiculously, with Stockins of two severall Colours, Breeches altogether out of Fashion, and a Coat quite different from all; and over this a Carpet cut so that his Head and Arms may come through, and the rest hang like a Senator's Gown.*"

These various examples from text and stage directions which might be almost indefinitely multiplied will, I think, make it quite clear that both in the production of comedy as well as of tragedy considerable attention was paid to the details of costume in the Restoration theatre. Historically correct indeed they may not have been, but decorative and striking the dresses always were. In many cases, especially in comtemporary comedy, the habits would appear to have been meticulously accurate.

In *The Old Batchelour,* Drury Lane, January, 1693, Bellmour when he is to visit Lætitia disguises himself as Tribulation Spin-text and appears "*in Fanatick Habit, with a Patch upon one Eye, and a Book in his hand*". No doubt the "Fanatick Habit" would have been very similar to Lacy's dress as Semple. It may be observed that the velvet patch was generally esteemed as a most excellent method of disguise.

That this device so long persisted is of course due to the very practical consideration that an actor could very easily clap on a patch, and hey presto! he was in completest masquerade, unrecognizable by any other character on the stage. The audience were always ready to enter into the game. Thus in Killigrew's *Claracilla,* produced at the Cockpit in Drury Lane, 1638–9, and revived immediately after the Restoration a patch is quite sufficient to disguise her lover Melintus from Claracilla. When he *pulls a patch from his eye* she at once perceives that the stranger with whom she has been discoursing is none other than her own Melintus, and when *He puts on his patch* nobody could suspect his identity (I, 4). Chapman's *The Blind Beggar of Alexandria,*[72] originally produced at the Rose, 12th February, 1596, is a veritable whirligig of " disguised shapes ". It will be remembered that Duke Cleanthes appears as three other individuals: Irus, the blind beggar; Count Hermes; and the usurer Leon. Irus the prophetic tells Elimine that Count Hermes is her destined suitor. The lady soliloquizes:—

> When you see one clad in a velvet gown,
> And a black patch upon his eye—a patch!
> Patch that I am, why, that may be a patch
> Of cloth, of buckram, or a fustian cloth.
> Say, with a velvet patch upon his eye,
> And so my thoughts may patch up love the better.

Whereupon Count Hermes appears, dressed just as Irus described, sporting a huge black velvet patch over his eye. In the Beaumont and Fletcher *Beggars' Bush* Gerrard, who is already disguised as the beggar Clause, appears " like a blind aquavitae-man " led by a boy. In *Look about You,* 4to, 1600, a play of many disguises, Skink effects one of his many escapes by appearing as a falconer, lure in hand, and a patch on his eye. In *The Wild Goose Chase* Mirabel, who has been choused by De-Gard in the rôle of the Duke of Savoy's nephew, exclaims:—

> What a purblind was I! Now I remember him;
> All the whole cast's on's face, though it were umber'd,
> And masked with patches.

In Monk Lewis' famous romance *The Bravo of Venice,* 1804, a great feature of the impenetrable disguise of the hero Rosalvo as the hideous bandit Abellino was " his right eye covered by a large patch ".

The " *Fanatick Habit* " adopted by Bellmour was no doubt very exactly copied from those which were seen every day in the London streets. An excellent puritan costume is that worn by Cave Underhill when he was seen as Obadiah in Sir Robert Howard's *The Committee.* There exists a character portrait of the actor in this rôle by Bing. The sad-coloured suit and cloak, the falling linen collar, the broad-brimmed hat are all most effective. Underhill played Obadiah to the Teague of Anthony Leigh after the Union of the Two Companies in 1682. It should be remarked that he was not the original representative of the part for Howard's comedy was produced at Vere Street before October, 1662. Teague was created by Lacy.

In the famous triple portrait of John Lacy by Michael Wright, now at Hampton Court, the actor on one canvas is depicted in three rôles, which Aubrey[73] identifies as "Teag, Lord Vaux, the Puritan". Langbaine[74] calls the figures "*Teague* in the *Committee,* Mr. *Scruple* in *The Cheats,* and *M. Galliard,* in *The Variety*". The identification of the central figure as M. Galliard in the Duke of Newcastle's *The Varietie* is, I think, generally accepted, nor is there much doubt that the Nonconformist minister is Mr. Scruple.[75] Evelyn, 3rd October, 1662, says that Lacy was "painted in three dresses, as a gallant, a Presbyterian minister, and a Scotch highlander in his plaid". Mrs. Jameson[76] in 1842, wrote that the third figure was Sawny the Scot in Lacy's own adaptation of *The Taming of the Shrew, Sawny the Scott; or, The Taming of the Shrew.* Planché in his *Cyclopaedia of Costume,* vol. ii, 1879, gives a chromo-lithograph of the Hampton Court painting, and emphasizes in convincing detail that "the figure in this picture is that of a Scotchman, and not of an Irishman".[77] He concludes, therefore, that the figure is Sawny, since it is clearly a mistake to identify it as the Irish Teague. It has now been suggested that this highland dress, which is most exact, is that worn by Lord Wareston in Tatham's *The Rump.*[78]

It was not unusual, if it were uncivil, to introduce upon the Restoration stage contemporary figures so little disguised that the very camouflage was a sign manual. The legitimate satire upon Shaftesbury and his crew need hardly be considered. Crowne, however, in his *City Politiques,* Drury Lane, 20th January, 1683, portrayed Titus Oates as Doctor Panchy, Stephen Colledge as the Bricklayer, Shaftesbury's *crétin* son as Crafty, and old Sergeant Maynard as Bartoline. Shadwell in *The Sullen Lovers,* Lincoln's Inn Fields, May, 1668, dragged Sir Robert Howard across the boards as Sir Positive At-all (Henry Harris); Edward Howard as Ninny (Nokes); Lord St. John, as Woodcock; and Mrs. Uphill, as the pert whore Lady Vaine. Dryden in *The Kind Keeper,* Dorset Garden, 1678, drew Lauderdale to the life as Mr. Limberham. In 1669 the Duke of Buckingham and Sir Robert Howard were preparing a play called *The Country Gentleman* which was to exhibit Sir William Coventry. There can be little doubt that in all these pieces which were performed the actors exactly dressed and made up their features to represent the persons who were satirized and exposed. When Buckingham's *The Rehearsal* was produced at the Theatre Royal on 7th December, 1671, Lacy who created Bayes, the caricature of Dryden, wore black velvet as this was the favourite attire of the laureate, whose gait and manners were all most carefully mimicked in cruel detail.[79] So in 1669, at the revival of *Catiline,* Theatre Royal, the famous Mrs. Corey, at the instigation of Lady Castlemaine, whilst acting Sempronia

JOHN LACY
By Gracious permission of His Majesty the King

[*face p.* 288

gave an imitation of Lady Harvey's oddities throughout the part. Furious at the insult Lady Harvey had the actress imprisoned, but in a few hours she was released by order of the royal mistress and bidden act it over again " worse than ever, where the King himself was ", whilst the outraged lady hired people to hiss and pelt the stage with oranges.

No doubt Mrs. Corey made up to resemble Lady Harvey, for the art of the paint-box was well known to Restoration as to Elizabethan players. Red and white they laid on most plentifully. False noses, beards, mustachios were common property. When on Saturday, 5th October, 1667, Pepys went behind the scenes at the Theatre Royal to the women's shift with Mrs. Knepp he spied Nell Gwyn making herself ready. " But, Lord! to see how they were both painted would make a man mad, and did make me loath them." In noticing Ben Johnson the actor, Downes says: " He's skilful in the Art of Painting, which is a great Adjument, very Promovent to the Art of true Elocution, which is always requirable in him, that bears the Name of an Actor." Of Dogget the old prompter notes: " On the Stage he's very Aspectabund, wearing a Farce in his Face." [80] Davies quoting from *A General View of the Stage,* 1759, writes: " I have heard confirmed from one who performed with Dogget; and that he could, with great exactness, paint his face so as to represent the age of seventy, eighty, and ninety, distinctly; which occasioned Sir Godfrey Kneller to tell him one day, at Button's, that he excelled him in painting; for that he could only copy nature fom the originals before him, but that Dogget could vary them at pleasure, and yet keep a close likeness." [81]

In spite of obvious incongruities and even extravagances, conditions and presentments which to the wight of the twentieth century would perchance seem not a little ludicrous on occasion, I conceive that the productions and costumes of the Restoration theatre were far more agreeable and far more conformably decorative and elegantly striking than the effects of stage management in the mid-eighteenth century. This to some extent is due to the fact that both dramatists and actors generally were more talented, that names of great genius flourished in the days of the second Charles and his immediate successors. When Hart [82] and Mohun, Mrs. Marshall and Nell Gwyn, Betterton and Smith, Mrs. Barry and Mrs. Bracegirdle acted what Dryden, Wycherley, Otway, and Congreve wrote the theatre with all its drawbacks had reached a zenith of brilliance which was certainly not sustained in the Hanoverian era and which will probably never again be so fully compassed and achieved.

NOTES TO CHAPTER VII

[1] 1577. I have used the edition 1579. Sig. a, and p. 37.

[2] 1579. Players men, p. 22.

[3] Folio, 1623.

[4] *Designs by Inigo Jones for Masques & Plays at Court,* "A Descriptive Catalogue of Drawings for Scenery and Costumes . . .," Oxford, For the Walpole Society, 1924. The Walpole Society, vol. xii.

[5] *Henslowe Papers,* ed. by W. W. Greg, 1907; Appendix I, p. 114, 20, 21; p. 120, 142; p. 115, 29. See also F. G. Fleay, *A Chronicle History of the London Stage,* 1559–1642, 1890, pp. 114–16.

[6] Ibid., p. 114, 4; p. 115, 28; p. 121, 182.

[7] The Pope's Mitre, *Henslowe Papers,* p. 118, 88.

[8] *Henslowe Papers,* p. 114, 17; p. 119, 122; p. 117, 80. *Henslowe's Diary,* part i, ed. Greg, 1904, F 120ᵛ, F 44, F 45ᵛ.

[9] *Henslowe Papers,* p. 114, 16.

[10] Folio, 1647. *Actus Quartus, Scena Tertia.*

Amaranta. Is thy Master gone out?
Moore. Even now, the Curat fetch'd him,
About a serious businesse as it seem'd,
For he snatch'd up his Cloak, and brush'd his hat strait,
Set his Band handsomely, and out he gallop'd.

[11] *Volpone,* folio, 1615, Act I, Scene 2:—

Volpone. Fetch me my gowne,
My furres, and night-caps; say, my couch is changing: . . .
Guie me my furres . . .
My caps, my caps, good Mosca.

[12] The traditional magnificence of the costumes worn in a masque was fully sustained in post-Restoration days upon the presentment of Crowne's *Calisto; Or, The Chaste Nimph,* acted at Court in February, 1675, "By several Persons of Great Quality."

[13] "When his *Aglaura* was (acted) he bought all the cloathes himselfe, which were very rich; no tinsill, all the lace pure gold and silver, which cost him . . . I have now forgott. He had some scaenes in it, which in those dayes were only used at masques." Aubrey, *Brief Lives,* ed. Andrew Clark, 2 vols, Oxford, 1898. *Sir John Suckling,* vol. ii, p. 244.

[14] *Letters and Dispatches of Thomas, Earl of Strafforde,* 2 vols, folio, 1739; vol. ii, p. 150.

[15] Rochester's Epilogue to Fane's *Love in the Dark; or, The Man of Bus'ness,* Theatre Royal, May, 1675; 4to, 1675:—

And Doggrel takes, which Smiths in Sattin sing.

[16] *Roscius Anglicanus,* edited by Montague Summers, pp. 2–22, 27–8, 24.

[17] 12mo, 1734.

[18] "Mrs. Behn's *Oroonoko,*" *Kittridge Anniversary Papers,* 1913, p. 419. Bernbaum remarks (p. 432): "To think of Nell Gwynn in the true costume of a Carib belle is indeed ludicrous." Very true, and I do not suppose the idea would have occurred to anyone save to Mr. Bernbaum. Odell, *Shakespeare from Betterton to Irving,* 1921, i, p. 207.

[19] *The Works of Aphra Behn,* edited by Montague Summers, 1915; vol. v, *Oroonoko,* p. 130, and note, p. 520.

[20] *History of the Stage,* 1749, p. 201.

[21] See *Dryden The Dramatic Works,* edited by Montague Summers, 1932, vol. vi, pp. 106, 35, 78, 79, 81, 91, and 93. I have drawn attention to the fact that *Don Sebastian* has many echoes of Shakespeare, and perhaps in Act IV when Benducar enters and his "*Slave follows with* Muley-Moluch's *Head upon a Spear*" Dryden had in mind the original ending of *Macbeth.*

[22] Killigrew, *Comedies and Tragedies,* folio, 1664, *The Pilgrim* (1663), p. 186.

[23] *Spectator,* No. 29, Tuesday, 3rd April, 1711.

[24] *Apology,* 1740, p. 214.
[25] *Dramatic Miscellanies,* iii, pp. 81–2.
[26] *Comedies and Tragedies,* folio, with general title-page, 1664, *The First Part of Cicilia & Clorinda,* 1663, p. 217.
[27] *Dramatic Miscellanies,* iii, p. 93.
[28] *Apology,* 1740, pp. 79–80.
[29] Op. cit., iii, pp. 94–5.
[30] *Letters from Orinda to Poliarchus.* The Second Edition. 1729, p. 95.
[31] When Bell reprinted *Oedipus* in 1791, contrary to his general rule he gave no cast, and he remarks that this tragedy " but seldom makes its appearance upon the modern stage ", a circumstance, however, which in no way affects the fact that the illustration of Kemble in the title-rôle shows us how this great actor conceived Oedipus should be dressed. When Bell in his *Shakespeare* reprinted *Titus Andronicus* and *I King Henry VI,* two plays which had hardly been seen on the stage within the memory of living man he engaged a couple of actresses to pose as models for Lavinia and La Pucelle, and thus he was able to illustrate these pieces.
[32] *Dryden The Dramatic Works,* edited by Montague Summers, 1932, vol. iv, pp. 379 and 388.
[33] *General History of the Stage,* 1749, pp. 164–5. In *The Female Wits ; or, The Triumvirate of Poets at Rehearsal,* 4to, 1704, pp. 24, 27–8, Marsilia tells Powell " I have two of your stoutest Men enter with long Truncheons " for the Prologue, and a good deal of comic business results.
[34] In the Collection of His Lordship the Earl of Durham. John Zoffany born *c.* 1725, died 1810. The painting measures 40 in. by 50 in.
[35] The *Monthly Mirror,* vol. xiii, p. 197.
[36] Dedication to *The Spanish Fryar ; Dryden The Dramatic Works,* edited by Montague Summers, v, p. 122.
[37] Reprinted from the original broadside by Mr. G. Thorn-Drury in *A Little Ark,* 1921, pp. 30–2. For Walter Clun see further Downes' *Roscius Anglicanus,* edited by Montague Summers, pp. 75–6.
[38] *Guy Deverell,* 3 volumes, 1865 ; vol. iii, chapter x, pp. 104–5.
[39] 8vo, 1773.
[40] 8vo, 1817. Malec was played by Young ; Hemeya, Charles Kemble ; Pescara, Macready ; Florinda, Miss O'Neill. The last scene, V, 2, of the tragedy is *A Dungeon, of Saracenic Architecture.* Here Florinda in bridal garments visits the prisoner Hemeya. They are interrupted by the madly jealous Pescara, who is stabbed by Hemeya. Learning that Florinda has taken poison he drives the same dagger to his heart, and she expires o'er his bleeding corse.
[41] Dedication to *The Spanish Fryar ; Dryden The Dramatic Works,* edited by Montague Summers, vol. v (1932), p. 119.
[42] *The Roman Virgin ; or, Unjust Judge,* an adaptation by Betterton from Webster's *Appius and Virginia.*
[43] Licensed for printing, 15th May, 1667 ; but not produced until 14th September, 1668. See Pepys, 15th September, 1668.
[44] See 14th April, 1669.
[45] Printed with *Love's Kingdom,* 12mo, 1664.
[46] The famous frontispiece of *The Wits ; or, Sport upon Sport,* part i, 1662, which appears in both editions, although without caption and undescribed in the original, has often been reproduced as " the interior of the Red Bull playhouse ". It is now certain that this identification cannot be accepted, but it appears to me equally certain that it is by no means " purely a work of the artist's imagination " as Mr. J. J. Elson suggests in his recension of *The Wits,* 1932, pp. 424–7. To say, again, as a critic has rashly done, that " it establishes nothing definitely, and, without fear of loss, may be safely discarded from serious consideration " is going altogether too far. There are no incongruous elements, and even if we concede that the artist has depicted no one particular pre-Restoration theatre, there are many details which have great evidential value. No artist, for example, would have drawn upon his imagination for the foot-lamps, had they not been in actual use upon the stage.
[47] It is distressing to find that Mr. George Grossmith writing to the *Daily Telegraph,* Tuesday, 26th April, 1932, and giving an account of the Theatre Royal, Drury Lane, says : " Garrick was the first to introduce footlights about 1765, in place of candles hung from the flies " ! ! He also remarks that among a host of

famous names the first to be recalled by Drury Lane is Davenant, which is odd, since Davenant never had any connection with the Theatre Royal. Nor indeed has Pepys " left an account of the opening on 7th May, 1663 ". Nor was Charles Hart's grandmother, Joan, Shakespeare's sister. The actor Hart was no relation to Shakespeare.

[48] *The Universal Museum, Or Gentleman's & Ladies polite Magazine of History, Politicks, and Literature.* London.

[49] Paris, 1886, p. 144.

[50] On the day of Molière's death *Le Malade Imaginaire* began at 4.30 and finished at 6 o'clock. Boursault, *Artémise et Polianthe,* Paris, 1670, pp. 1–16, relates that the *première* of *Britannicus* was concluded by 7 o'clock.

[51] Mons. Germain Bapst, *Essai sur l'Histoire du Théâtre,* Paris, 1893, pp. 375 and 377.

[52] Pepys, Saturday, 28th December, 1667. On 27th April, 1682, " Mr. *Ch*[*arles*] *De*[*ering*], son to Sr. *Edward D.,* and Mr. *V*[*aughan*], quarrelled in the *Duke*'s Play-house, and presently mounted the Stage and fought, and Mr. *D.* was dangerously wounded, and Mr. *V.* secured lest it should prove mortal." Janeway's *Impartial Protestant Mercury,* 2nd May, 1682.

[53] *London Magazine,* December, 1821.

[54] To give one late example from Lillo's *The London Merchant,* then called *George Barnwell.* Act III, Scene 3: " *A walk at some distance from a country seat.—Lights down. Enter* Barnwell, R. *Barn.* A dismal gloom obscures the face of day . . ." Dolby's edition, " Printed from the Acting Copy," 1825, p. 30.

[55] *Shakespeare from Betterton to Irving,* i, p. 147. Mr. Odell largely bases his theory on the lantern which appears in the sculpture of Act I, Scene 1, of *The Empress of Morocco,* 4to, 1673. But it might just as fairly be argued that this lantern was a stage property, and we must not make any deductions therefrom. It is true that Mons. Bapst, *Histoire du Théâtre,* 1893, p. 375, tells us in reference to the crystal chandeliers of the French Stage: " ils descendaient et remontaient à volonté, comme on peut le voir dans la gravure de Charles Coypel représentant la scène et le rideau du Théâtre-Français de la rue de l'Ancienne Comédie vers 1726." Sabbatini in his *Practica di Fabricar Scene e Machine ne' Teatri* (ed. 1638), suggests for transition from light to darkness a device by which shades hung over the lights are lowered or easily raised. In the Restoration theatre, however, this would not have been practicable.

[56] Mrs. Behn has many of these scenes, e.g. *The Rover,* I, Act III, 2 (an important scene), and 3; IV, 1, " *Discovers* Belvile, *as by Dark alone. Enter* Antonio . . . *with a light . . . He sets the Candle on the Table.*" *The Rover,* II, Act V, 1, " *she runs away with the Candle, they are by dark.*" *The Roundheads,* Act IV, 1, and 5, when the Flat Scene draws off to a chamber with " *a Table behind with Lights* ". *The Young King,* III, 1, one of the rare examples of the curtain being dropped during the action of a play. " *The Curtain is let down—being drawn up, discovers* Orsames *seated on a Throne. . . . On either side of the stage, Courtiers ready drest, and multitude of Lights.*" Cf. Mrs. Manley's *The Royal Mischief,* 4to, 1696, Act IV, Scene 1: " *The Curtain flies up to the sound of Flutes and Hoboys, and discovers . . . a walk of Trees, the length of the House* [i.e. the stage]; *Lights fixed in Chrystal Candlesticks to the Branches.*" In Mrs. Behn's *The City Heiress,* IV, 2, a room in Lady Galliard's house, Lady Galliard to escape an awkward situation *puts out the Candles* which are on the table, murmuring " Shield me, ye Shades of Night ". " What, what all in darkness? " exclaims Sir Charles as he enters. See also *Sir Patient Fancy,* Act III, 3 and 4; and *The Younger Brother,* IV, 1, where George says: " I will obscure the Lights." *Puts away the Lights.* Presently, " *Enter* Manage *groping* " who exclaims: "—what, by dark? "

[57] The engraving by Gravelot (*G. V^{dr}. Gucht Sculp.*) in the 1735, Tonson edition of Dryden's *Dramatick Works,* vol. iii, p. 289, gives the night-scene of Act IV, 5. It is, of course, half a century too late, and *The Assignation* had not been played since 1716, but I believe it may be taken as a very fair illustration of this particular scene.

[58] *The Complete Works of Thomas Shadwell,* 1927, edited by Montague Summers, ii, pp. 199–203.

[59] 4to, 1677, p. 58.

[60] *Dryden The Dramatic Works,* 1932, edited by Montague Summers, iv, p. 389.

[61] 4to, 1690, p. 26. There are many striking effects of sudden darkness in Orrery's unpublished *The Tragedy of Zoroastes,* for which see my article in the *Modern Language Review,* vol. xii, No. 1, January, 1917, pp. 24–32; reprinted in *Essays in Petto.*

[62] Vol. ii, B 6, p. 87.

[63] *Travels of Cosmo the Third . . . Through England,* 1821, p. 347.

[64] Vol. ii, 1703, pp. 375–7. This Satire may be found in several collections, e.g. *A Pacquet from Parnassus,* 1702, as also in manuscript, British Museum, Harl. MS. 7315, f. 267.

[65] *Martha Lady Giffard Her Life and Correspondence* (1664–1722), edited by Julia G. Longe, London, 1911, pp. 38–42.

[66] 4to, 1707.

[67] *An Apology For The Life of George Anne Bellamy* (Fourth Edition, 1786, vol. i, pp. 144–150), Letter XX.

[68] Quoted by Archdeacon Coxe in his *Memoirs of John Duke of Marlborough,* Second Edition, 1820, vol. vi, chapter 117; 1716–1722.

[69] *The Observer,* 26th March, 1922. This sour flummery was included by Mr. James Agate in his anthology *The English Dramatic Critics,* 1660–1932 (London, 1932, pp. 310–14). I conceive that it owes its place in the collection as a warning how not to do the thing.

[70] Lowe, *Thomas Betterton,* 1891, p. 87, n.

[71] *Roscius Anglicanus,* edited by Montague Summers, 1927, p. 29.

[72] I quote from the edition by T. M. Parrott; *The Comedies of George Chapman,* 1914, p. 12.

[73] *Brief Lives,* Oxford, 1898, ii, p. 29.

[74] *English Dramatick Poets,* Oxford, 1691, p. 317.

[75] Mr. Charles W. Cooper, *The Triple-Portrait of John Lacy* (*Publications of the Modern Language Association of America,* 1932, xlvii, pp. 759–765, no. liii) would identify the Nonconformist minister as Ananias in *The Alchemist.* The point which turns on the exact date of the painting is small, since Mr. Scruple and Ananias wore the same costume.

[76] *Handbook of the Public Galleries of Art in and near London,* 1842, ii, p. 398.

[77] *Cyclopaedia of Costume,* 1879, ii, p. 243. The chromo-lithograph, which is of a poor quality, is by Banks & Co., Edinburgh.

[78] See Mr. Cooper's article. His arguments are interesting, but there are flaws. We do not for example certainly know that Lacy played Lord Wareston.

[79] The story goes that on the first performance of *The Rehearsal,* 7th December, 1671, the Duke of Buckingham arranged that Dryden should be seated in a prominent position in the boxes at Drury Lane, and himself occupied the next place to the poet in order that he might enjoy the confusion and chagrin of the man whom he mocked so scurvily as Bayes. The tale may or may not be true, but it very well agrees with Buckingham's notorious brutality and callous insolence.

[80] *Roscius Anglicanus,* ed. cit., p. 52.

[81] *Dramatic Miscellanies,* 1784, iii, p. 448. It is well known that in order more naturally to play Ben—perhaps his greatest rôle—in Congreve's *Love For Love,* produced at Lincoln's Inn Fields in April, 1695, Doggett for a long while frequented Wapping so that he might make a close study of the habits, gestures, and manner of speech of the sailors in their own recognized territory.

[82] In the Dedication, addressed to Sir Robert Owen, to *Fatal Love; or, The Forc'd Inconstancy,* 4to, 1680 (produced at the Theatre Royal, September, 1680), Elkanah Settle writes: "*the* Theatre Royal *was once all Harmony . . . But, oh, that their Oracle should be quite silent! . . . This I may modestly say of him,* (*nor is it my own particular Opinion, but the Sence of all Mankind*) *that the best Tragedies on the* English Stage *have received that Lustre from Mr.* Hart*'s Performance, that he has left such an Impression behind him, that no less than the Interval of an Age can make them appear agen with half their Majesty, from any second Hand. And when he leaves the Stage, the Reign of* Tragedy *expires.*"

APPENDICES

I. *The Play-House, A Satyr*, by Robert Gould.

II. Instructions for a young Gallant how to behave himself in the Play-house. (Being Chapter V of Sam Vincent's *The Young Gallant's Academy, or, Directions how he should behave himself in all Places and Company*, 1674.)

III. The Phoenix Society for the Production of Old Plays.

APPENDIX I

THE PLAY-HOUSE

A SATYR

The First Part

SInce of all things which at this Guilty Time[1]
Have felt the honest *Satyrs* wholsom *Rhime*
The Impious *Play-House* has been most forborn,
(Tho' it of all Things most deserves our Scorn)
We'll do at last what *Justice* does require;
And strip it bare of all the Gay Attire
Which *Women* love and *Fools* so much admire.

Aid me, Ye *Scorpions* with Inveterate Spite,
Instruct me how to stab with ev'ry Word I write;
Or if my *Pen*'s too weak this Tyde to stem,
Lend me Your *Stings,* and I will wound with them:
Each home-set thrust shall pierce the vitious Heart,
And draw the Poison from th' envenom'd Part;
Lash ev'ry Fop and ev'ry Drab expose,
And to the World a hideous Scene disclose:
While the Proud *Mimicks* who now Lord it so,
Become the Publick hiss where-e'er they go,
Their *Trade* decay and they unpitied Starve;
A better Fate than most of 'em deserve.

The *Middle Galle'ry* first demands our View;
The filth of Jakes, and stench of ev'ry Stew!
Here reeking Punks like Ev'ning Insects swarm;
The *Polecat*'s Perfume much the Happier Charm.
Their very Scent gives *Apoplectick* Fits,
And yet they're thought all *Civit* by the *Cits*;
Nor can we blame 'em; for the Truth to tell,
The want of *Brains* may be the want of *Smell.*
Here ev'ry Night they sit three Hours for Sale;
The *Night-rail* always cleanlier than the *Tayl.*
If any *Gudgeon* bites they have Him sure,
For nothing Angles Blockheads like a Whore.
Discreet in this, their Faces not to shew;
The *Mask* the best Complexion of the two.
Their Noses falling and their Eyes sunk in,
A wrinkl'd Forehead and a Parchment Skin:

Their Breath as hot as *Ætna's* Sulph'rous Fire;
Yet cold as Ice compar'd with their *Desire.*
The Physick each has singly swallow'd up,
Produc'd again, wou'd stock ev'n *Chase's* Shop.
Yet such as these our Modern Fops admire;
Perhaps to be Inur'd for hotter Fire.
A Woman's ne'er so Wicked, but she can
Find one as Wicked, or much worse in Man,
To satisfy her Lust, obey her Will,
And at her Nod perform the greatest Ill:
These ride not Strumpets, but are Strumpet-rid,
And *Dog-like,* fetch and carry as they're bid;

But, naming *Dogs,* did You yet ever meet
A *proud Bitch* and her Gallants in the Street?
Shock, Mastiff, Mungrel, Spaniel Blithe and Gay
With Brandish'd Tails, and panting o'er their Prey,
Have You observ'd with what Obsequious Art
They make their Court? So Am'rous at the Heart,
The more their Mistress snarls the less inclin'd to part.
This is an Emblem of our *Gall'ry Ware,*
The Scene we may see Nightly Acted here
Not but we must give *Dog* and *Bitch* their due,
As much the Chaster Creatures of the two;
Their Season past they're cool;—'tis only here
The Commerce holds, Insatiate, all the Year.
About one Jilt a Hundred *Apes* shall move,
And which is strange, at once all Chatt'ring Love:
So loud the Din, that who the Play wou'd hear
Might be as well Inform'd at Home, as there.
At last they to the * *Rose* [2] direct their Way
(It's Staple Trade such Customers as they)
To end th' Intrigue agreed on at the *Play.*
Luxurious, there they Gormandize at large,
And all at the Licentious Cully's Charge;
Till drain'd both Purse and Chine he does retire,
And within three Days finds He's all on Fire:
The total, thus, of all *Venereal* Jobs
Begin in *Whore,* and Terminate in † *Hobs.*
If he wou'd find the Nymph that caus'd his Moan,
He toils in vain,—the Bird of Night is flown:
Yet not this warning makes the *Sot* give o'er,
He must repeat the Dang'rous Bliss once more,
But still finds harder Usage than before.

Hence 'tis our *Surgeons* and our *Quacks* are grown
To make so great a Figure in the Town;
Heaping up large Estates by our Debauches;
Our keeping Strumpets makes them keep their Coaches:

* An adjacent Tavern. † A famous Surgeon.

Their *Consorts* so Extravagantly Gay,
You in their *Dress* behold their Husband's *Pay*:
But backward look, you'll find it is the *Stage*
That makes these *Locusts* swarm upon the Age:
There 'tis the fruitful *Bane* is plough'd and till'd,
But these have all the Harvest of the Field.
There's many of 'em for their single Share,
Pocket, 'tis said, some Thousands ev'ry Year:
Nor is it strange in such a spreading Crime,
Where half the Town is Fluxing at a Time:
Wide as the Grave to take its Comers in,
Their Gates stand open for the Sons of Sin:
But then the *Tales* deliver'd out again,
Just as the *Parson* has his *One* in *Ten*:
And they so pale and Meagre, you'd swear
A Ghost were Weightier, tho they're nought but Air.
So craving too are these *Pox-Emp'ricks* grown.
Live ye, or Die, they make the *Cash* their own.
Expensive Malady! where People give
More to be kill'd than many wou'd to live!
Some get Estates when others drop, but here
The very Dying does undo the Heir.
O that the custom were again Return'd,
That Bodies might on Funeral Piles be burn'd
The Pestilential Vapours which the Sun
Sucks from the Ground, and thro' the Air are thrown,
Giving all Catching Plagues and Fevers Birth,
Are only Steams Exhal'd from *Pocky Earth*:
From whence this *Town* we may conclude accurst,
For here few Die but are half Rotten first.

Nor is this *Middle Gall'ry* only found
With Drabs of Common Trading to abound;
But, to the Eternal Scandal of their *Race,*
Her *Honour* often, and as oft her *Grace*
Sail hither, Mask'd and Muffl'd in Disguise;
And with pert Carriage and their smart Replies
Set all the Men agog, who strait agree
They must of course, be Punks of Quality;
So lead 'em off to give their Longings vent,
For 'tis presum'd they came for that Intent:
At least, if not for common Use, t'employ
Some Friend assign'd, and take their Swill of Joy.
How often, *Cl——d*,[3] hast thou here been found
By a Lascivious Herd encompass'd round?
How often have you hence retir'd, and lain
A Leash of Stallions breathless on the Plain?
Then back return'd; another Leash enjoy'd;
Another after that, when those were cloy'd;
And so elsewhere, and here, has half your Life employ'd.

Till not a Drab appears in History,
So Shameless and Libidinous as Thee.
Scarce does an Ev'ning pass thro' all the Year,
But many of the highest Rank are here:
True, if discover'd, for a blind they'll say,
They only came to take a strict Survey
If Whores cou'd be so bad as some Report;—
And that they might as well have known at *Court*.
But they're but Flesh, and 'tis in vain to rail,
Since fed the higher 'tis the oftner frail.

Withold, ye *Citizens,* Your Wives from hence,
If You'd Preserve their Fame and Innocence,
You else are sure to live in *Cuckold*'s *Row;*
There is not yet one *Precedent* to show
Our Wives by coming here can Vertuous grow:
That *Plays* may make 'em Vitious, Truth assures;
Especially, so much Inclin'd as Yours.
The *London Cuckolds* [4] they all Flock to see,
And Triumph in their Infidelity:
In vain Your Counsel;—Nothing can reclaim
A *Wife* that once has shaken Hands with Shame.
If e'er they take their Ply th' Adult'rous Way,
The *Devil* may as soon recant as they:
To sure Destruction wilfully they run;
In View of Hell, and yet go daring on.

Choak't with the stench of Brimstone, 'twill be fit
To Visit next the *Boxes* and the *Pit,*
And for the *Muse* a Nobler Scene prepare,
And let Her breathe awhile in Milder Air.
But such a sudden Glare invades her Eyes,
So vast a Crowd of diffe'rent Vanities,
She knows where not to fix her Rancour first;
So very Wicked all, that all are worst!
Here painted Ladies, aiming at the Heart,
Their Graces Arm, and all their Charms exert:
Dress'd, one and all, with Nice Exactness there,
But Mobb'd like Dowdies at the House of Prayer.
How diffe'rent will the Scene at Night be shown!
When they restore to ev'ry Box it's Own,
When like themselves th' affrighting Things appear,
Divested of their Patches, Gemms and Hair:
This sight th' Obsequious Coxcombs shou'd attend;
Like a Death's Head 'twou'd warn 'em of their End:
But they, alas! for vainer things design'd,
Fix here their Hopes and Nothing Future Mind.
Between the *Acts* they to the *Boxes* throng,
With Whining Voices warbling each his *Song*:

Their Own, You may besure; for none but such
Can write what cou'd Delight that Sex so much.
Some few soft Lines (but such as well express
Their *Wit* is as much Borrow'd as their *Dress*)
Does set 'em up for *Poets*; all their Time
Supinely trifl'd off in *Love* and *Rhime*.
These are the Womens Men, their dear Delight;
For just as Ladies Chatter, Coxcombs write.

Not far from hence, another much distress'd,
At once makes *Cupid* and himself a Jest:
With a low Cringe, Her Vanity to Please,
He Drawls his Passion in such Terms as these.

MADAM! by Heav'n You have an Air so Fine,
It renders the least thing You do—Divine!
We dare not say You were Created here,
But dropt an ANGEL from th' ÆTHEREAL SPHERE
Ten Thousand CUPIDS on Your FORE-HEAD Sit,
And shoot resistless Darts thro' all the PIT.
Before Your Feet, see! Your Adorers *lie,*
Live, if You Smile; *and if You* Frown, *they die!*
Ev'n I, Your true Predestinated Slave,
Rather than meet Your Hate *wou'd meet my* Grave:
Ah! Pity then, Bright Nymph *the Wound You gave!*

Thus sighs the Sot, thus tells his Am'rous Tale,
And thinks his florid Nonsense must prevail;
Bows, and withdraws: And next to prove his Love,
Steals up, and Courts the *Fulsome Punks* above.
Mean while the *Nymph,* proud of her Conquest, looks
Big as *Wreath'd Poets* in the Front of Books;
Surveys the Pit with a Majestick Grace,
To see who falls a Victim to her Face;
Does in her Glass her self with Wonder view,
And fancies all the Coxcomb said was true.
Hence 'tis the Whiffling, Vain, Fantastick Chit
Is the Fair Ladies only Man of Wit.
With Servile Flatt'ry sleeking his Address,
Where e'er he goes, he's certain of Success.
Speak *Truth* to our fine Women, and you'll find,
Of all things, *That* the least can make 'em kind:
Nor can we blame 'em; for it calls 'em plain,
Deceitful, Idle, Foolish, Fond and Vain.
Wit in a Lover more than Death they fear;
For only *Witty Men* can tell what Trash they are.
But a pert, airy, empty, Noisy Ass,
In their Esteem does all his Sex Surpass:
Believ'd a *Hero*, tho' by Heav'n design'd
The Grin of Wit, and Scandal of his Kind.

Such Giddy Insects here for ever come,
And very little *Dare,* but much *Presume :*
Perpetually the Ladies Ears they ply,
And Whisper Slander at the Standers by :
Then laugh aloud ; which now is grown a part
Of Play-house Breeding, and of Courtly Art.
The true Sign of Your Modish *Beau Garson*
Is Chatt'ring like a Ladies lewd *Baboon,*
Shewing their Teeth to charm some pretty Creature ;
For grinning, among *Fops,* is held a Feature.
Nor is this all ; they are so oddly dress'd,
As if they'd sworn to be a standing Jest,
Ap'd into Men for Pastime to the Rest.
Observe 'em well, You'll think their Bodies made
T'attend the Empty Motions of the Head ;
If that but wags the whole Machine does move,
From top to Toe devoted all to *Love.*
Their *Whigs* and *Steinkirks* [5] to that height refin'd,
They dare not tempt their Enemy—the Wind ;
Of the least slender puff each *Sot* affraid is,
It kills the *Curls* design'd to kill the *Ladies.*
So stiff they are, in all Parts ty'd so strait,
'Tis strange to me the Blood shou'd Circulate.
But leaving these *Musk-Cats* to publick Shame,
I'll turn my Head and seek out other Game.

In the *Side-Box Moll Hinton* You may see,
Or *Howard Moll,*[6] much wickeder than she ;
That is their Throne ; for there they best Survey
All the Young *Fops* that flutter to the Play.
So known, so Courted, in an Hour, or less,
You'll see a Hundred making their Address ;
Bow, Cringe and Leer, as supple *Poets* do,
The *Patron*'s Guineas shining in their View :
While they, Promiscuous, let their Favours fall,
And give the same Incouragement to all.
Harlots of all things shou'd be most abhorr'd,
And in the *Play-house* nothing's more ador'd :
In that lewd *Mart* the rankest Trash goes off,
Tho' rotten to the Core, and Death to Cough ;
Tho' *Vlcers* on their Lungs as thick take Place
As Firey Pimples on a Drunkards Face.

Discharg'd of these, observe another way
The Fops in Scarlet swearing at the Play :
Nor yet unduly they themselves acquit,
For Fustian on the Stage, too, goes for Wit.
A Harmless Jest, or Accidental Blow,
Spilling their Snuff, or touching but the Toe,

With many other things too small to name,
Does blow these Sparks of Honour to a Flame:
For such vile Trifles, or some Viler *Drab,*
'Tis in an Instant *Damn me,* and a *Stab.*
No mild Perswasion can these Brutes reclaim;
'Tis thus to Night, to Morrow 'tis the same.
What a long List might Justice here Produce
Of Blood, of Fighting, Banning and Abuse?
What *Weekly Bill,* for Number, can compare
To those that have been basely Butcher'd here,
Within the Compass but of Twenty Year?
One Actress has at least, to name no more,
Been her own self the Slaughter of a Score.
Murder's so Rife, with like Concern we hear
Of a Man kill'd, as Baiting of a *Bear.*
All People now, the Place is grown so ill,
Before they see a *Play* shou'd make their *Will*:
For with much more Security, a Man
Might take a three Years Voyage to *Japan.*

Here others, who no doubt believe they're Witty,
Are hot at Repartee with *Orange Betty*:
Who, tho' not blest with half a Grain of *Sense*
To Leven her whole Lump of *Impudence,*
Aided by that, perpetually's too hard
For the vain Fops, and beats 'em from their Guard:
When fearing the Observing few may carp,
They laughing cry, *egad the* Jade *was Sharp*:
Who'd think with Banter *she shou'd Us outdo?*
Nay more, be found the better Punster *too?*
When, without Boasting we may safely Swear
We thought w'ad gain'd the Height of what these Arts *cou'd bear.*
Yet these true *Owphs* wou'd think it an offence
More than all Human Wit cou'd Recompence,
Not to be rank't among the *Men of Sense.*
Were selfish Coxcombs truely what they thought,
They'd first be *Gods,* and next with *Incense* sought.
But 'tis a Truth, fixt in *Apollo*'s Rules,
Your *Wou'd-be-Wits* are but the *Van of Fools*;
The very same that we in *Armies* find;
The *Apes* in *Office* worse than all behind:
Who tho' they fiercely look and loudly roar,
A *Game Cock*'s Feather wou'd outweigh a score.

Another *Set* together whispering run,
Where they may best Debauch when *Farce* is done:
Th' Agreement made, out *Pander'us* whips before
To bespeak *Musick, Supper, Wine* and *Whore*:
There they till Midnight Soak, and Cram and Drench,
The *Bumper* now in Use, and now the *Wench.*

Top-full at last, away they Scow'ring[7] run,
And leave no Mischief in their Pow'r undone.
The Cries of Martyr'd *Watchmen* now You'll hear,
As soon, Demolish'd Windows clattering there.
Whose ever Fate it is to walk the Street,
And with these *Bullies* and their *Harlots* meet,
They must avoid, or else be sure to feel
Deep in their Lungs some Villains fatal Steel;
Villain, I say, that for Cause so small
As not t' *Uncap,* or reeling to the *Wall,*
And yet much oftner for no Cause at all,
Shall those poor Innocents of Life disarm,
That neither Spoke, Design'd, or wish'd 'em harm.
Like any *Hero* these will Foam and Fight,
When they're urg'd on by Strumpet or by Spite;
But if their *King* and *Country* claim their Aid,
As none cou'd threaten more, there's none so much afraid.
Not One will move, not one his *Prowess* show,
But stand stock still, when *Honour* bids 'em go.

A Hundred Others, had they but their due,
Of such as these, we shou'd expose to view;
But, with what's past, too feelingly perplext,
We'll shew the Crimes of *Plays* and *Players* next.

The Second Part

NO longer in the Streets, my *Muse,* appear,
But back, a *Fury,* to the *Play-house* steer;
We have not yet, done half our Bus'ness there.
A Thousand Crimes, already, we've expos'd,
A Thousand more remain, not yet disclos'd.
On boldly then, nor fear to miss your Aim;
Don't want for *Rage,* and we can't want for *Theme.*

Here a Cabal of *Criticks* you may see,
Discoursing of *Dramatick Poesie.*
While one, and he the wittiest of the Gang,
(By whom you'll guess how fit they're all to hang)
Shall entertain you with this learn'd Harangue.

They talk of Ancient Plays, *that they are such,*
So Good, they ne'er can be admir'd too much:
'Tis all an Error.—In our present Days,
I grant, we've many claim Immortal Praise.
The Cheats of Scapin,[8] *One; A Noble Thing;*
What a throng'd Audience *does it always bring!*
The Emp'rour of the Moon,[9] *'twill never tire;*
The same Fate has the fam'd Alsatian Squire.[10]

Not Jevon's *Learned Piece*[11] *has more Pretence*
Than these, to Fancy, Language and Good Sense.
And here, my Friends, I'd have it understood
The Age is nice; what pleases must be Good.
Again, for Instance, that clean Piece of Wit
The City Heiress,[12] *by* chast Sappho[13] *Writ:*
Where the Lewd Widow *comes, with brazen Face,*
Just reeking from a Stallion's *rank Embrace*
T'acquaint the Audience *with her* Filthy Case.
Where can you find a Scene *for juster Praise,*
In Shakespear, Johnson, *or in* Fletcher's Plays?
The Modest Poet *always will be* Dull;
For what is Desdemona *but a Fool?*
Our Plays *shall tell you, if the* Husband's *ill,*
The more the Wife *may prosecute her* Will.
If jealous, they must date Revenge *from thence,*
And make 'em Cuckolds, *in their own Defence.*
A Hundred others we might quickly name,
Where the Success *and the* Design's *the same;*
Writ purposely th' Unwary to entice,
Enervate Goodness, *and encourage* Vice:
And that the Suffrage of both Sexes wins:
But see! The Curtains *rise, the* Play *begins.*

Thus holds the *Ideot* forth;—the other *Sparks*
Applaud, and hug him for his Wise Remarks;
Swear that such things must ev'ry Humour fit,
And Universally be Clap'd for Wit;
But most the *Ladies* please; who here are taught
That *Truth's* a Sham and *Lewdness* not a Fau't;
That *Wit,* is Infamy on Worth to fix;
And an Unblemish'd Fame, *a Coach and Six.*
But let the Flatt'rer feed their Endless Pride,
And, if he please, all their Desires beside;
Here let 'em with their Utmost Lustre Shine,
Believ'd by Coxcombs and themselves Divine;
To those that clearly see, and rightly know,
'Tis all Destructive Glare, and hideous show:
The true Renown which all the rest Exceeds,
Is that which is Deriv'd from Vert'ous Deeds.

What a fine Set of *Criticks* all the while
Are these? and what the *Audience* that can smile
At things so mean, Ridiculous and Vile?
Farce has of late almost o'erwhelm'd the Stage;
But *foolish Writers* suit a foolish Age:
Our topping *Authors* oft descend so low,
That *Hains* and *Ho—rd*[14] pass for *Poets* too!
How can *Instruction* from their Works proceed
Whom 'tis a Mortal Breach of Wit to read?

Not but we grant they yet Admirers gain—
But such as have the Rickets in the Brain;
A weakly Race who only Judge by Rote,
And have no Sense to tast a Beauteous Thought:
Thus heavy *Fops* the heaviest *Authors* prize:—
But at the *Theatre* the fair Disguise
Deceives the *Brave,* the *Witty* and the *Wise*:
Struck with the Presence of so bright a Show,
They like the *Punk,* tho' they despise the *Beau.*
'Tis hard for *Youth* and *Beauty* to escape
Destruction, dress'd in such a pleasing shape:
It gilds their Ruin with a specious Baite,
Too quickly Swallow'd and observ'd too late;
Too late their Perish'd Vertue to recall—
There is no rising from so sad a Fall!
Their Fate the worst the more they have of Sense,
For *Wit* does deepliest Rue the loss of *Innocence.*

Nor only *Farce*; our *Plays* alike are Writ
With neither *Manners, Modesty,* or *Wit,*
Rais'd with their *Authors,* to the last Excess
Of Irreligion, Smut and Beastliness.
Not that I'd have You think I'm so severe
To damn all *Plays*; that wou'd absurd appear:
Beside, of *Writers,* some adorn the *Stage,*
And *Southern* is the Credit of his Age:
In short, I court the *Good,* and loath the *Ill,*
Let the Presuming *Bard* be who he will.
Tho' a *Lord* Write, I'll not at Random Praise,
Or flatter *Dr.* ——*n* [15] tho' he wear the *Bays*:
Or court fair *Sappho* [16] in her Wanton fit,
When she'd put *Luscious Bawdry* off for *Wit*:
Or pity *B—ks* [17] in Tatters, when I know
'Twas his bad *Poetry* that Cloath'd him so:
Or Commend *Durf—y* [18] to Indulge his Curse;
Fond to write on, yet Scribble worse and worse:
Or *Cr*——*n* [19] for blaming Coxcombs, when I see
Sir Courtly's not a vainer Fop than He:
Or think that *Ra*——*ft* [20] for Wise can pass,
When *Mother Dobson* says he is an Ass;
That damn'd, ridiculous, insipid *Farce!*
Or write a *Panegyrick* to the Fame
Of *Sh—d—l,* [21] or of Starving *Set*——'s [22] Name,
Who have abus'd, unpardonable things,
The best of *Governments,* and best of *Kings.*
But Thee, my *Otway,* [23] from the Grave I'll raise,
And crown thy Mem'ry with Immortal Praise;
At least, Sweet *Bard,* it should Immortal be,
If I cou'd reach the Clouds, and Charm the Ear like thee!

Thy *Orphan* and *Venetian* Piece Sublime
Shall ever stand, and dare the Teeth of *Time*.
Th' *Ammonian* Youth and *Mithridates, LEE*[24]
In spite of thy Unhappy *Lunacy*,
Shall yield another Deathless Name to thee.
But honest *Truth* obliges me to tell,
Your other *Tragick Plays* are not so well;
Not with that ease and that Exactness writ,
With less of *Nature* too;—and *Nature* here is Wit:
Not but they may assume a decent Pride
To vye ev'n with our Noblest *Plays* beside.
The Name of *Etheridge* next renown'd we see[25]
For easy *Stile*, and Wit in *Comedy*,
Tho' not so strong as that of *Wycherley*[26]:
His Play of * *Manly* (ne'er to be out-writ)
A Prodigy of *Satyr, Sense* and *Wit!*
In all the Characters so just and true,
It will be ever fam'd, and ever New!
And justly with the rest our *Laureat* claims
To take his Place among Immortal Names:
For *Oedipus*[27] (tho' *Sophocles* and *Lee*
Share something of the Praise, but not so much as *He*)
Our *Fear* and *Pity* does advance as high
As ever yet was done in *Tragedy*.
His *All for Love*, and most Correct of all,
Of just and vast Applause can never fail,
Never! but when his *Limberham* I name
I hide my head and blush with Friendly shame,
To think the *Author* of both these the same:
So thick the *Smut* is spread in ev'ry *Page*,
'Twas Actually the *Brothel* of the *Stage*.
If (as some *Criticks* fancy) Witty 'tis,
It shou'd be fluxt for the *Obscene Disease*:
For as the *Pox* to ev'ry Part does go,
So that's with *Lewdness* tainted thro' and thro'.
Not but sometimes He to the Clouds does rise,
And sails at pleasure thro' the Boundless Skies:
Born up on Indefatigable Wings,
He greatly thinks and as Divinely Sings.—
But then his *Plays in Rhime* (with all their *Rules*)
Only chime in the *Women*, and their *Fools*,
Who see with Joy their Favourite Ebb and Flow,
Now above *Reason*, and as soon below:
This part they *Great*, and that they *Tender* call;
When first to last 'tis, oft, Unnatural all.
His *Hero*, too, outdoes all *Homer*'s *Gods;*
For 'tis a turn of State when e'er he Nodds.[28]
Thus tho' in *Time* and *Place* they boast their Skill,
For Five *good Poets* there's Five Hundred *Ill*.

* *Plain Dealer*.

Fly then the reading *Plays* so vain as these;
Such Jingling *Authors* nor *Instruct,* nor *Please.*

But if with *Profit* you wou'd reap *Delight,*
Lay *Shakespear, Ben,* and *Fletcher* in Your sight:
Where Human Actions are with Life express'd,
Vertue advanc'd, and *Vice* as much depress'd.
There the kind Lovers with such Zeal complain,
You in their Eyes behold their inmost Pain,
And pray such Truth may not be Plac'd in vain.
There *Natures* secret Springs may all be view'd,
And, when she doubles, how to be pursu'd.
There *Art,* in all her subtle Shifts display'd,
There ev'ry *Humour* You may see pourtray'd,
From *Legislative Fops* down to the *Slaves of Trade.*
There all the *Passions,* weak, you'll first espy,
Hate, Envy, Fear, Revenge and *Jealousy*;
And by what Fewel fed to flame at last so high.
While *Wit* attending You'll for ever see,
Faithful amidst this vast Variety;
Like *Proteus,* but affording Nobler Game,
She ev'ry Shape assumes, and yet Remains the same.
In short, none ever Wrote or will again
So useful things in such a Heav'nly strain!

When e'er I *Hamlet* or *Othello* read,
My Hair starts up, and my Nerves shrink with dread!
Pity and *Terrour* raise my Wonder high'r,
'Till betwixt both I'm ready to expire!
When curs'd *Iago* cruelly I see
Work up the Noble *Moor* to *Jealousy,*
How cunningly the Villain weaves his Sin,
And how the other takes the Poison in;
Or when I hear his Godlike *Romans* rage,
And by what just degrees He does Asswage
Their Angry Mood, and by a Secret Art
Return the mutual Union back to either Heart;
When these and other such like *Scenes* I scan,
'Tis then, Great Soul, I think thee more than Man!
Homer was Blind, yet cou'd all Nature see;
THOU wert unlearn'd, yet knew as much as He!
In *Timon, Lear,* the *Tempest,* we may find
Vast Images of thy Unbounded Mind:
These have been alter'd by our *Poets* now,[29]
And with Success, too, that we must allow:
Third Days they get when *Part of THEE* is shown,
Which they but Seldom do when *All's* their own.

Nor shall *Philaster, The Maids Tragedy,*
Thy *King and no King,* Fletcher, ever dye,
But reach, with like Applause, to late Posterity.

'Tis true, they're Censur'd by a Modern Wit[30];
But he shou'd not have blam'd, or not have Writ:
For after all his Scandal on 'em thrown,
'Tis certain they're Superiour to his Own.
We grant he has the *Languages* at Will;
But some have Blessings, and they use 'em ill:
The *Usurer's* Poor in spite of all his Pence,
And so your Linguists may be lean of Sense.
Let then this *Maxim* never be forgot,
An *Arrant Scholar* is an *Arrant Sot.*

Thee, Mighty *Ben,* we ever shall affect,
Thee ever Mention with profound Respect,
Thou most Judicious *Poet!* most *Correct!*
I know not on what single Piece to fall,
Sublimely Writ, and admirable all.
Yet we must give Thee but thy just Desert;
Y'ad less of *Nature,* tho' much more of *Art*:
The *Springs* that move our *Souls* thou did'st not touch:
But then thy *Judgement, Care* and *Pains* were such,
We never yet did any *Author* see
(Nor shall, perhaps, thro' all Futurity)
That wrote so many *Perfect Plays* as *Thee.*
Not one vain *Humour* thy strict view escapes,
Or *Folly,* in their Thousand Various shapes:
The *Lines* You drew did ev'ry *Blemish* hit,
Your *Dresses* ev'ry *Knave* and *Coxcomb* fit;
So vast the unbounded *Ward-robe* of Your *WIT!*

Hail Sacred *Bards!* Hail ye Immortal *Three!*
The *British Muses* Great *Triumviri!*
Secure of Fame, You on the *Stage* will live
Whilst we have *Wits* to hear, and they have *Praise* to give.
'Tis some where said our *Courtiers* speak more *Wit,*[31]
In *Conversation* than these *Poets* Writ:
Unjust Detraction! like it's *Author,* base;
And it shall here stand Branded with Disgrace.
Not but they had their Failings too;—but then
They were such Faults as only spoke 'em Men;
Errors which Human Frailty must admit,
The Wanton Rovings of Luxurious Wit.
To the Judicious plainly it appears,
Their Slips were more the Ages Fault than theirs:
Scarce had they ever struck upon the Shelves,
If not oblig'd to stoop beneath themselves:
Where *Fletcher*'s loose, 'twas Writ to serve the *Stage*;
And *Shakespear* play'd with Words to please a Quibbling Age.

If *Plays* you love let these Your thoughts employ;
When *Wit* is read by *Wit* 'twill never cloy,

No other *Poets* so sublimely tell
The useful, happy Art of *Living Well*:
All strew'd with *Morals,* thick in ev'ry *Page*
Alike Instructive both to Youth and Age.
'Tis certain on a *Mistress* and a *Friend*
The chiefest Blessings of our Lives depend;
And by their *Draughts* we may exactly find
If that be Faithful, or if this be kind.
There You may breath the Air of ev'ry Clime
And make Remarks on *Custom, Place* and *Time.*
Thro' ev'ry Stage of Life You there may View
What Ills t'avoid, what Vertues to pursue;
And so with *Pleasure* reap *Advantage* too.
Unlike the *Authors* that have lately writ,
Who in their *Plays* such *Characters* admit,
So Lewd and Impious, they shou'd Punish'd be
Almost as much as *Oates* for Perjury [32]:
With equal Scandal both supply the Age;
He has disgrac'd the *Gown,* and they the *Stage.*

Think, Ye vain Scribling *Tribe,* of *Shirley*'s [33] Fate,
You that Write *Farce,* and You that *Farce* Translate;
Shirley! the Scandal of the Ancient Stage,
Shirley! the very *Drf—y* [34] of his Age:
Think how he lies in *Duck-lane* [35] Shops forlorn,
And never mention'd but with utmost Scorn.
Think that the End of all your boasted Skill,
As I presume to Prophesy it will,
Justly—for many of You Write as ill.
Change then Your *Bias* and Write *Satyr* all;
Convert the little *Wit* You have to *Gall.*
Care not to what a Bulk Your Labours swell;
The Fame in which the Happy Few excell
Lies not in Writing *Much,* but Writing *Well.*
This Point obtain'd, attack the Impious *Stage,*
Which *You* have made the *Nusance* of the Age;
Nor fear but in th' Attempt Applause You'll get;
Their Cause is *Infamy,* and ours is *Wit.*
Lash the Lewd *Actors*—but first stop Your Nose
The Stench is strong; and much wou'd discompose
All but Your Selves—almost as bad as those.
This Thought shou'd raise You to th' Extremest Pitch.
Their Laughing at the *Want* that makes 'em *Rich*:
Not more You Labour to increase their Store,
Than they, Inhumanly, to keep You Poor;
Making You dance Attendance, Cap in Hand,
That once, like *Spaniels,* were at Your Command;
Wou'd cringe and fawn, and who so kind as They?
Exalted with the Promise of Your *Play.*

But since * *Hart*[36] dy'd, and the two Houses join'd,[37]
What get ye? what Incouragement d'ye find?
Yet still You Write, and Sacrifice your Ease,
And for no other *Gain*—but what they please;
Expell'd the *House,* unless you give 'em way
To bilk You of *Two Thirds* in ev'ry *Play.*
Let nothing then Your sense of Wrong asswage;
The *Muses Foes* shou'd feel the *Muses Rage*:
But then be just to *Truth*; for only that
Is what th' Impartial *Satyr* levels at:
Go not beyond; all base Aspersion shun;
Let *Justice* and not *Malice* lead You on.
To please, for once I'll give You an *Essay,*
And in so good a *Cause* am proud to lead the Way.

Prepare we then to go behind the *Scenes,*
There to Survey the *Copper Kings* and *Queens,*
Strutting in State, tho' Slaves by Nature meant,
As they were truely those they *Represent*:
But most the *Women* are Audacious seen,
All *Paint* their Out-sides and all *Pox* within.
Here 'tis our *Quality* are fond of such,
Which ev'n their Wiser *Footmen* scorn to Touch:
Divested of the *Robes* in which they're Cas'd,
A *Goat's* as sweet, and *Monkey's* are as Chast.
Not that they want, when they their Looks wou'd Arm,
The Art to make, or keep their *Cullies* warm.
With faint Denyals they inflame *Desire,*
Till the hot Youth burns in his Am'rous Fire,
Then wantonly into their *Shifts* retire:
Spurr'd on by Lust the *Dunce* pursues the *Dame,*
Careless of Health, and thoughtless of his Fame:
Their Nightly She Majestically rules[38];
Like *Gallick* Princes, all her Subjects, Fools.—
But talking of their *Shifts* I mourn, my Friend,
I mourn thy sudden, and disast'rous End:
Here 'twas You did Resign Your Worthy Breath,
And fell the Victim of a Cruel Death:
The Shame, the Guilt, the Horror and Disgrace,
Light on the *Punk,* the *Murderer,* and the *Place.*
What *Satyr* can enough the Villains Sting
That fight and stab for so abhor'd a Thing?
A ten times cast off *Drab,* a Hackny Whore,
Who when Sh'has ply'd the *Stews* and tir'd a Score,
Insatiate as a *Charnell,* yawns for more.
Her ev'ry Act in the Vene'real Wars
Who e'er wou'd count, as well may count the Stars.
So Insolent! there never was a Dowd
So very basely born so very Proud:

* *A Famous Tragedian.*

Yet Covetous; She'll Prostitute with any,
Rather than wave the Getting of a Penny:
For the whole Harvest of her Youthful Crimes
Most frugally she hoards for Future Times,
That then her Life may be with Lux'ury led,
The hatter'd *Carcase* with Abundance fed;
So damns the *Soul* to get the *Body* Bread.
Yet in her Morals this is thought the best,
And it is only *Hell* can Match the rest.

An *Actress* now so fine a thing is thought,
A Place at *Court* less eagerly is sought:
As soon as in that *Roll* the Punks engross'd.
Some Reverend Bawd does thus the Drab accost,
Now is the Time You may Your Fortune *raise,*
And meet at once with Pleasure, Wealth *and* Praise;
'Tis now, like Nell *you may Immortal grow,*
Fam'd for Your Impudence, *and* Issue *too;*
Posterity, if well You Play Your Part,
Will call You Prudent, and Your Rise, Desert.—
But the true Sense is this:—*'Tis now your time*
(*For only* Vertu'ous Fools *neglect their* Prime)
With open Blandishments and secret Art
To glide into some Keeping Coxcomb's *Heart,*
Who neither Sense *or* Manhood *understands;*
And Jilt *Him of his* Patrimonial Lands:
Others this Way have reach'd the top Extreams;
Think of Ned Bush—*then think of Mistress* James [39]:
Some such like Cully *to Your Share will fall;*
The Knight *has nothing and the* Punk *has All:*
Twas by this Conduct B—y *grew so Rich;*
Preferment You can't miss and be a B—.
Th' Advice is took; and she hurries on,
Fond to be kept, and in her Chariot shown;
While Vulgar Drabs must meanly Trapes the Town.
Against the Consequence she shuts her Eyes,
For none at once were ever lewd and Wise:
Thoughtless (like merry *Andrew* in his Pride)
The higher Mounted we the more deride.
In short the *Stage* (as *Dorset-Court* assures)
Is but a *Hot-Bed* raised to force up Whores:
Nor can the Soil so fast their Growth supply,
As City, Camp and Country crowd to buy.
How great a Beast is Man!—A Vertu'ous Dame,
Unblemish'd in her Fortune and her Fame,
They fly, as if she were the worst of Harms,
And think a thrice Fluxt *Actress* has more Charms.
Yet tho' so much they slight the Chast and Fair,
No other Curses may they ever share,
But only to Continue—what they Are.

Now for the Men; whom we alike shall find
As Loose, as Vile, and Brutal in their Kind:
Here one who lately, as an Author notes,
Hawk'd thro' the Town, and cry'd *Gazettes* and *Votes*,[40]
Is grown a Man of such Accomplish'd Parts,
He thinks all Praise beneath his just Deserts:
Rich as a *Jew*, yet tho' so wealthy known,
He rasps the Under-*Actors* to the Bone.
Not *Lewis* more Tyrannically Rules,
Than He among this Herd of *Knaves* and *Fools*.
Among his other Vertues, ne'er was *Elf*
So very much Enamor'd of Himself;
But let Him if he pleases think the best
Upon that Head; and we'll Supply the rest.
What if some Scribblers to his Sense submit?
He is not therefore only Judge of Wit [41]:
Approving such, betrays a Vitious Tast:
For few can tell what will for ever last,
If all cou'd Judge of *Wit* that think they can,
The Vilest Ass wou'd be the Wittiest Man.
In Company, with either Youth or Age,
H'has all the Gum and Stiffness of the *Stage*:
Dotard! and thinks his haughty Movements there,
A Rule for his Behaviour ev'ry where.
To this we'll add his Lucre, Lust and Pride,
And Knav'ry, which in vain He strives to hide,
For thro' the thin Disguise the Canker'd Heart is spy'd.
'Tis true, his *Action* Merits just Applause;
But lies the Fame most in th' *Effect* or *Cause*?
If from good Instruments fine Musick springs,
The Credit's chiefly his that tun'd the Strings:
Thus, tho' they Speak, they speak Another's Thought;
As *Monkey*'s Grin, and *Parrots* learn by Rote.

Another You may see, a *Comick* Spark,[42]
That wou'd be *Lacy*,[43] but ne'r hits the Mark,
Not but his Making Sport must be confess'd,
For where the *Author* fails, he is Himself the Jest.
To be well laught at is his whole Delight,
And there, indeed, we do the Coxcomb Right.
Tho' the *Comedian* makes the *Audience* roar,
When off the *Stage*, the *Booby* tickles more:
When such are born some easy *Planet* rules,
And *Nature*, dozing, makes a Run of Fools.

A *Third*, a punning, drolling, bant'ring Ass,[44]
Cocks up, and fain wou'd for an *Author* pass,
His Face for *Farce* Nature at first design'd,
And match it, too, with as Burlesque a Mind:
Made him, as vilely born, so careless bred,
And gave Him Heels of *Cork*, but Brains of *Lead*.

To speak 'em all were tedious to discuss;
But if You'll Lump 'em, they're exactly thus:
A Pimping, Spunging, Idle, Impious Race,
The Shame of Vertue, and Despair of *Grace*:
A Nest of *Leachers* worse than *Sodom* bore,
And justly Merit to be Punish'd more,
Diseas'd, in Debt, and ev'ry Moment dun'd;
By all Good Christians loath'd, and their own Kindred shun'd.
To say more of 'em wou'd be wasting Time;
For it with Justice may be thought a Crime
To let such *Rubbish* have a Place in *Rhime*.

Now hear a Wonder and 'twill well declare
How resolutely lewd some Women are;
For while these Men we thus severely use,
Our *Ladies* differ hugely from the *Muse*;
Supply their wants, and raise 'em from Distress,
Advanc'd ev'n for their very Wickedness.
Goodman[45] himself, an Infidel profess'd,
With *Plays* reads *Cl——d* nightly to her Rest:
Nay in Her Coach she whirls Him up and down,
And Publishes her *Passion* to the *Town*,
As if 'twere her Delight to make it known:
And known it shall be, in my Pointed *Rhimes*
Stand Infamous to all succeeding Times.

'Twere Endless Work, describing ev'ry Vice
That from the *Play-house* takes Immediate Rise,
The Devil has on Earth no *Magazin*
That opens to us such an Impious Scene,
Or where, for Store, he lays more Lewdness in.
Not in the *Inns of Court* we hardly see,
At once, a Vaster Reach of Villany;
Tho' with the *Lawyer* the Belief does reign—
No Hell but Poverty, nor God but Gain.
Here *Murder, Lust* and *Blasphemy* are found,
And all the Crimes with which the Times abound,
To wheel in Circles an Eternal Round.
As the *New-River* does from *Islington*,
Thro' several Pipes, serve half the Spacious Town,
So the Luxurious Lewdness of the Stage,
Drain'd off, feeds half the *Brothels* of the Age.
In short (nor will it bear the least Debate)
Unless these Vices we cou'd Regulate,
The *Play-house* is the Scandal of the *State*.

But here it was (with drowsy Fumes oppress'd)
I dropt my *Pen*, and nodded into Rest;
When Fancy, willing to Improve my Spleen,
Set in my View this Visionary Scene.

The Third Part

ON a Sweet Verdant Plain methought I stood,
Just by a Hill crown'd with a Spacious Wood:
One lonely Path (which now I'd enter'd in)
Led from the Lawn up thro' the *Silvan* Scene.
On Pleas'd I went directly to the Grove,
The Silent kind Retreat of Rural Love.
The Rising Sun had now its Entrance made
Ten thousand ways, and Chequer'd all the Shade.
Thick lay the Dew, and, just like *Diamonds* Bright,
Sent thro' the leafy Arch reflected Light;
High on the Boughs were pearch'd the Feather'd Choir,
Their more Ambitious Notes ascending higher:
Each Emulating each, and plac'd apart,
Try'd all the sweet Contentions of their Art:
Now I observ'd the Tuneful Challenge here
Then how in Heav'nly Strains 'twas Answer'd there;
Neither the best, yet both above Compare.
Mean while, as with Design, a Balmy Breeze,
Rising and falling Gently by degrees,
Fann'd all the Sweets of *Flora* thro' the Trees.
Nothing there wanted but the Fruit of Gold.
To vye with the *Hesperian* Grove of old.
Ah! Heav'n, I cry'd, what Happiness there dwells
In Humble Huts and unfrequented Cells!
In some low Cottage by this Copses side,
How safely does the Country Swain reside!
How undisturb'd when down to Rest he lies!
How Joyful when the Glorious Sun does rise!
This Musick in his Ears, this Scene before his Eyes!
Ah! might I once so blest a Fortune know,
How Gladly I'd the Chase of Fame forgo?
No more I wou'd the Stingy Great rehearse,
And sing their Names in Panegyrick Verse:
No more I wou'd attempt the Tragick Strain,
When (after all th' Expence of Time and Pain)
One Female Player's Breath [46] makes all my Labours vain.

With Contemplations such as these I pass'd
Thro' the Steep Glade, and reach'd the Top at last;
Then, looking down, beheld below a Scene
Of Booths and People stragg'ling on the Green [47];
A various Mixture of each Sex intent
I drinking saw, and wonder'd what it meant.
Advancing nearer, soon the Cause appear'd
That drew together the Promiscuous Herd;

'Twas Water, *Dullwych* Waters, which they quaff'd
As Porters do their Belch—a Pint a Draught:
Till gorg'd at length, in Squadrons they withdraw
T' emit their Grief,—nor Decency a Law:
So thick they under ev'ry Bush appear,
You'd verily believe the Town was clear,
And all it's filthy Rabble Purging here.
Such Min'eral Fountains other Bards may sing;
To me they're all beneath a Common Spring.
If Instinct never for the worse does chuse,
Why shou'd we drink what Birds and Beasts refuse?
With Crudities th' Internal Parts they fill,
And the bleak Poison thro' the Blood instill,
Weaken the Sick, and make the Healthy Ill;
For, after all, we must new Methods find
To purge away the Dreggs they leave behind.
The Doctors say, indeed they'll wonders do;—
But Mountebanks commend their Ratsbane too.
In short the Waters to Physicians are
The same as Rogue-Attorneys to the Bar;
These work for Law, and those for Physick raise,
And so will do to all Succeeding Days,
While there the Client, here the Patient Pays.
But grant the Doctor all he'd have, and more;
Why must those Suit the Rich and these the Poor,
When Nature, in the Structure of our Frame,
Has of one Flesh made all Mankind the same?
The Cits are bid to *Epsom* to Resort,
And *Tunbridge* is prescrib'd for those at Court;
While *Dullwych* only serves for those Degrees
That cannot rise to be Destroy'd for Fees:
For grosser Allum, being less Genteel,
Must not pretend to vye with those of Steel:
To ease the Rich, thus, Urine is the Rule,
And Poverty must be Reliev'd by Stool.
O Dotage! which no Age but ours cou'd be
So fond of, as distinctly not to see;
For whatsoe'er the Water-Mongers think
The Vertues are of this their Mine'ral Drink,
If heedfully the true Effects they'd mind
Of being at the Wells, they'd quickly find
The Ease they feel, and all the Health they share,
Is only due (while they continue there)
To Temperance, Exercise, and Country Air.

Turning my Head, and eager to be gone,
Who shou'd I see methought, but *Hains* [48] alone?
And all alone poor *Joseph* well might be
Who, (bating those of his Fraternity,)

Cou'd not on Earth find Company to suit
A Name so Vile, and Life so Dissolute.
I date thee Fool, cry'd I, this very Hour,
Of all Mankind what need hast thou to Scow'r?
Nor Sup't last Night, nor broke thy Fast to Day
What is there in thee left to Purge away?
But why on Sunday Morning dost thou come?
The Day that all thy Brethren stay at home.
Cou'd on thy friendly care not one Prevail
To fetch him Physick, and to warm him Ale?
The Church they leave to those it more does please,
Their Souls of less concern than their Disease.
In short, what all the Week they Whore and Swill,
They Rectify to Day with *Peter*'s Pill.

Faith 'tis a just Remark, quoth Honest *Joe*;
A Jest has 'twice the odds for being true.
But if you will your Luggs this way incline,
I'll let You know this Morning's whole Design.
Our Converse with our selves, I freely own,
To be, perhaps, the worst the World has known;
The Themes we Relish with the truest Gust
Is Guile, Aspersion, Blasphemy and Lust:
If such a thing on Earth as Hell there be,
The Stage is Tophet—and it's Fiends are we.
First then, in Truth, I hither did Repair
To Bleach my Brimstone off in wholsome Air.
Next I'd some Gallery Tickets to dispose,
And in this Place I ne'er my Labour lose:
Here fifteen Pence I've always down and down,
For what wou'd yield me but a Hog [49] in Town.
And last in my Return I seldom fail
To get my Swill of *Dullwych* College Ale.
These little Shifts, grown useless for the Stage,
I'm forc'd to follow to sustain my Age.
Our Sharers, now so insolent are they,
We Under-Actors must like Slaves obey;
And toil and drudge, while they divide the Pay.
Not *Busby* more Tyrannically Rules,
Than *Bet—n* [50] among his Knaves and Fools:
But most to me is his ill Nature shown,
Because my Voice is with my Palate gone:
Not that I faster than the rest decline;
Both Men and Women in my Failing joyn,
And *B—y*'s [51] Breath is grown as rank as mine.

Uneasy with my Company, I here
Wou'd have took leave, and gave a Civil Leer.
No hold, quoth *Joe,* my Tickets all are gone,
And if you please, I'll wait on you to Town:

Of if you'll take a Sermon by the Way,
(For at the College 'tis their Preaching Day)
I shall be much Oblig'd by such a Stay.
With all my Heart, cry'd I; I'm glad your Mind
Has took that Bent;—and keep it so inclin'd:
You'll find more Comfort in one Hour of Pray'r
Than all the Clappings of the Theatre,
Tho' you should yet enjoy 'em Twenty Year.
So on I pass'd, now first, and now behind,
Still giving him the Lee-ward of the Wind;
Avoiding so the Breathings of his Chest,
Which he so frankly own'd were not the best.
At last, quoth *Joe,* you by and by shall see
The Gift of one of our Society:
Nor *Greece* nor *Rome* it's Equal ever show'd,
So Nobly is it built, so Lib'rally endow'd.
The Poet may Instruct and Please the Sense,
And worthy Schemes may be deduc'd from thence,
But 'tis a Barren Good that costs him no Expence:
Our *Allen* [52] did a nobler Pattern set,
But not one Bard has imitated yet.

His Name, said I, we to the Clouds shou'd raise
The least it merits's Everlasting Praise:
But most unjustly on the Bards you fall:
Rich tho' he was, from them he rais'd it all.
Not to disgrace his Vertue, or his Wit,
What had he got, had *Shakespear* never writ?
As to our selves, had we the Players Gains,
(And more our Right it is, as more our Pains)
We had exceeded all that he has done,
And gave the World an Instance,—more than one:
Not, but 'tis Nobler yet, to form the Mind
To Vertue,—and to keep it so inclin'd,
(The Work for which we solely were design'd
Than 'tis the Loftiest Edifice to build,
Or to Endow;—and Nobler Fruit 'twill yield.
His Charity, which justly we extol,
Does but Respect the Body;—Ours the Soul:
Twit us not then that we no Fabricks raise,
When from a better Claim we hold our Praise;
Nor think the Bard that does Exhaust his Sense,
At least that culls the richest Precepts thence,
To teach Mankind, can write without Expence:
Cou'd we our Purses wide as *Allen* strain,
'Tis nobler yet to spend upon the Brain.
In Contemplation rapt above the Skies,
We look on Yellow Dirt with heedless Eyes:
What truly Christian Bard would Gold adore,
When he may teach Contentment to the Poor.

And shew the World the Rich have no Excuse
That put not Money to its Genuine Use?
Like Him w'ave mention'd, who employ'd his Store
To breed up Friendless Youth and feed the Aged Poor.
But least of all you on the Muse shou'd throw
Your Scurril Jests, that keep her Sons so low:
How can our Suffering Tribe but chuse to be
The Sons of Hardship and Necessity?
When, let our Plays be acted half an Age,
W'ave but a third Days Gleaning of the Stage?
The rest is yours:—and hence your Sharers rise,
And once above us, all our Aid despise:
Hence has your *Osmin*[53] drawn his Wealthy Lot,
And hence has *Zara* all her Thousands got:
Zara! that Proud, Opprobrious, Shameless Jilt,
Who like a Devil justifies her Guilt,
And feels no least Remorse for all the Blood sh'has spilt.
But prithee *Joe,* since so she boasts her Blood,
And few have yet her Lineage understood,
Tell me, in short, the Harlot's true Descent,
'Twill be a Favour that you shan't repent.

Truly said *Joe,* as now the Matter goes,
What I shall speak must be beneath the Rose.
Her mother was a common Strumpet known,
Her Father half the Rabble of the Town.
Begot by Casual and Promiscuous Lust,
She still retains the same Promiscuous Gust,
For Birth into a Suburb Cellar hurl'd,
The Strumpet came up Stairs into the World.
At Twelve she'd freely in Coition join,
And far surpass'd the Honours of her Line.
As her Conception was a Complication,
So its Produce, alike, did serve the Nation;
Till by a Black, Successive Course of Ills,
She reach'd the Noble Post which now she fills;
Where, *Messalina* like, she treads the Stage,
And all Enjoys, but nothing can Asswage!

Thus towards the College we went jogging on:
Arriv'd, we found the Service just begun:—
Step in quoth *Joe*;—I'll come to you anon:
The Cook and Butler I must visit first;
For Hunger one, and t'other for my Thirst.
Let not your Corps, said I, be yet your Care;
Your better Part shou'd first be treated here:
If lasting Ease you'd to the Body find,
Let there be nothing wanting to the Mind.
My Paunch, said he, knows not what Doctrine means;—
You take the Stage;—I'll go behind the Scenes.

Sighing I enter'd;—when a kind Surprise:
Did entertain at once my Ears and Eyes:
The Organs Solemn Musick sounding there,
The Singing Boys Responding Voices here,
The Master and the Wardens grave Deport,
The Strict Devoutness of the meaner Sort,
The Management of all did soon inspire
My Soul with Joy! when joining with the Quire,
In Pray'r and Praises I perform'd my Part;
Nor less, I hope, my Ardor at the Heart.
But now the Service and the Sermon done,
(Whilst I to render Thanks was kneeling down)
Methought they of a sudden all were gone:
Surpris'd at the Event, I gaz'd about;
Saw none within, nor saw no Passage out.
'Tis well, said I,—and blest! O blest be they,
That in this Sacred Court delight to stay!
O Time! how smoothly then thou glid'st away!
When nothing Anxious in the Soul is found,
But Faith and Practice take their Equal Round;
When ev'ry Word a Pious Rapture fires,
And makes it self a Heav'n, while it to Heav'n aspires!
Thus walking up and down, to thought Resign'd,
At last the founder came into my Mind;
Nor cou'd I my Conceptions then contain,
(Tho' something for the Sacred Place too vain,)
But broke out loud in this Extatick Strain.

O happy! happy and Instructive Age
When *Shakespear* Writ, and *Allen* trod the Stage!
To Emulation fir'd, 'twas hard to tell
Which of the famous two did most Excel.
But O thou Darling Poet of our Isle,
And thou th' Erecter of this Sacred Pile,
How wou'd you Blush were you but now to see,
Both Plays and Players black Impiety!
And wish y'ad never rais'd the Infant Stage,
Since grown so black and Sinful in her Age:
With Vice she wou'd Instruct, with Vice Delight;
And all she does Pervert, that hear, that Act, that Write.

'Twas here, methought, an Awful Form appear'd
In a long Gown, and Venerable Beard.
And who art Thou, he cry'd, that thus dost Praise
The Bards and Actors of the former Days?
And what are now their Follies and their Crimes,
With which they so infest the Present Times?

I am, said I, *Apollo*'s meanest Son,
Who yet the Vices of his Greatest shun;

One, that with other Bards this Good design,
Plays to reform and make the Stage Divine:
No Vitious Plots we'd on the Age obtrude,
On Morals built, they shou'd be so pursu'd:
To Truth and Sense the Audience we'd Conduct,
And first we'd Please, that we might next Instruct;
That Centre where the Drama still shou'd tend,
As first 'twas purpos'd for no other End.
But w'are oppos'd by such an impious Train
Of Players, as make all our Studies vain;
Nothing they'll Act, and nothing they esteem
That does not Vertue shame, and God Blaspheme.
Instead of such as did this Fabrick build,
The Stage does now a Set of Monsters yield;
So openly Debauch'd, So flaming Ill,
As scarce, perhaps, are to be match'd in Hell!
Nor does this Censure only touch the Young,
But does alike to those of Years belong;
Who, rich as Jews, no other Pious Use
Make of their Wealth, but Vertue to Seduce:
Not *Allen* more did on this Pile bestow
Than they on Strumpets, or to make 'em so;
Witness Mill-Bank,[54] where *Osmin* keeps his Trulls
With what, by sharing,[55] he exacts from Fools.

APPENDIX II

THE YOUNG GALLANT'S ACADEMY

Chap. V

Instructions for a young Gallant how to behave himself in the Play-house

THe *Theatre*[1] is your *Poets-Royal Exchange,* upon which their *Muses* (that are now turned to Merchants) meeting, barter away that light Commodity of words, for a lighter ware than words, *Plaudities,* and the breath of the great Beast, which (like the threatnings of two Cowards) vanish into Air.

The *Play-house* is free for entertainment, allowing Room as well to the *Farmers Son* as to a *Templer* ; yet it is not fit that he whom the most Taylors bills make room for when he comes, should be basely, like a Viol, cased up in a corner : Therefore, I say, let our Gallant (having paid his *half Crown,* and given the Door-keeper his *Ticket*) presently advance himself into the middle of the *Pit,* where having made his Honor to the rest of the Company, but especially to the Vizard-Masks, let him pull out his Comb, and manage his flaxen Wig with all the Grace he can. Having so done, the next step is to give a hum to the *China-Orange-wench,* and give her her own rate for her Oranges (for 'tis below a *Gentleman* to stand haggling like a *Citizens wife*) and then to present the fairest to the next Vizard-mask. And that I may incourage our Gallant not like the Trades-man to save a shilling, and so sit but in the Middle-Gallery, let him but consider what large comings-in are pursed up sitting in the *Pit.*

1. First, A conspicuous Eminence is gotten, by which means the best and most essential parts of a Gentleman, as his fine Cloaths and Perruke, are perfectly revealed.

2. By sitting in the *Pit,* if you be a Knight, you may happily get you a Mistress ; which if you would, I advise you never to be absent when *Epsome Wells*[2] is plaid : for,

We see the Wells *have stoln the* Vizard-masks *away.*
(*Empress of Morocco*[3] in the *Prologue.*

But if you be but a meer *Fleetstreet* Gentleman, a Wife : but assure your self, by your continual residence there, you are the first and principal man in election to begin the number of *We three.*

It shall Crown you with rich Commendation, to laugh aloud in the midst of the most serious and sudden Scene of the terriblest Tragedy, and to let the *Clapper* (your *Tongue*) be tossed so high, that all the House may *ring* of it : for by talking and laughing, you heap *Pelion* upon *Ossa,* Glory upon Glory : as first, all the eyes in the Galleries will leave walking after the Players, and only follow you :

the most Pedantick Person in the House snatches up your name; and when he meets you in the Streets, he'l say, *He is Such a Gallant*; and the people admire you.

Secondly, You publish your temperance to the world, in that you seem not to resort thither to taste vain Pleasures with an hungry Appetite; but only as a Gentleman to spend a foolish hour or two, because you can do nothing else.

Now Sir, if the Poet be a fellow that hath *Lampoon'd* or *libelled* you, or hath had a flirt at your Mistress, you shall disgrace him worse than tossing him in a Blanket, or giving him the Bastinado in a Tavern, if in the middle of the Play you arise with a skrew'd and discontented face (as if you had the griping in the Guts) and be gone; and further to vex him, mew at passionate Speeches, blare at merry, find fault with the Musick, whistle at the Songs, and above all, curse the Sharers, that whereas the very same day you had bestowed five pounds for an embroidered Belt, you encounter with the very same on the Stage, when the Belt-maker swore the impression was new but that morning.

To conclude, hoard up the finest Play-scraps you can get, upon which your lean Wit may most savourly feed for want of other stuff; for this is only Furniture for a Courtier that is but a new Beginner, and is but in his *A B C* of Complement. The next places that are filled after the *Play-houses* be emptied, are *Taverns*. Into a *Tavern* let us then march, where the Brains of one Hogshead must be beaten out to make up another.

APPENDIX III

THE PHOENIX

The Phoenix was founded one night in September, 1919, in my house at Hampstead. Rule No. 2 set forth: "The object of the Society is the adequate presentation of the plays of the older dramatists," and in the first circular which I drew up, having explained the name—"The Phoenix takes its name from one of the most celebrated of the old theatres, the Cockpit or Phoenix, constructed in the Cockpit in Drury Lane *circa* 1617"—I went on to say, "It is intended to present each play, not in a spirit of pedantic antiquarianism, but nevertheless with due regard to the actual conditions of the theatre for which it was written." In the face of almost unanimous opposition I had always maintained that the drama of the Restoration—and for that matter any other drama too—fully to be appreciated and understood must be seen upon the stage, and the plays moreover must be given as nearly the original production as modern methods and changed conditions will reasonably permit. I was told throughout a long tale of years that no living audience would endure such comedies as *Marriage A-la-Mode* or *The Country-Wife,* and I consider the notable success of Dryden and of Wycherley when revived in some sort my vindication.

The third rule of The Phoenix stated that "The Society is organized under the auspices of the Incorporated Stage Society, and the Council of the Incorporated Stage Society for the time being shall be the Council of 'The Phoenix'". Rule 4 ran: "The Council shall elect a Committee of not more than four persons who shall be entirely responsible for conducting the business of the Society." As a matter of fact these two rules meant just nothing at all. The Council of the Stage Society never had anything to do with Phoenix business, and the Committee of not more than four persons had been elected long before the Council of the Stage Society was even aware of the existence of the new body. When Mr. Clifford Bax wrote in *The London Mercury* (November, 1929, vol. xxi, No. 121), "The Council [of the Stage Society] little realized what they had done when, in 1920, they started The Phoenix," he was wholly misinformed. The Council of the Stage Society did not institute The Phoenix. The only connection between The Phoenix and the Stage Society which I could ever discover lay in the fact that we used the same offices and had the services of the same Secretary, Miss Alice Fredman. It is true that upon our first nineteen programmes appeared the legend "Under the Auspices of the Incorporated Stage Society", but so far as I am aware nobody attached the slightest meaning to the phrase, and so far from existing under any auspices, on Friday, 29th June, 1923,

The Phoenix gave at the Regent Theatre a matinée of *Volpone* in aid of the funds of the tottering and impoverished Incorporated Stage Society.

In 1915 the Stage Society had essayed a performance of Farquhar's *The Recruiting Officer,* a production upon rather heavy and inadequate lines, which excited no attention. In the spring of 1916 my aid was requisitioned for the production of Congreve's *The Double-Dealer.* I found that the book had been drastically revised and in part modestly rewritten, all was at sixes and sevens. Upon two points I showed myself at once quite firm; the original script only was to be used and no cuts were tolerated; the conventions of the period at which the play was first performed were to be adopted, which is to say among other details that the curtain rising after the Prologue did not fall until the Epilogue had been spoken. My old friend, the late Sir Edmund Gosse, generously lent us from the treasures of his library the first quarto, 1694, and *The Double-Dealer* was given at the Queen's Theatre, on 14th and 15th May, 1916.

The following year, on 15th and 16th April, 1917, *Love for Love* was produced at the Aldwych. *The Way of the World* was produced at the King's Hall, Covent Garden, on 12th and 14th May, 1918; and, also at the King's Hall, on 12th and 14th January, 1919, *The Provok'd Wife.* Where all were so uniformly excellent it may seem invidious to single out individual performances, but in *Love for Love* I cannot pass over in silence Roy Byford as Sir Sampson Legend, Ben Field as Foresight, Basil Sydney as Valentine, Ernest Thesiger as Tattle, and Alice Mansfield as the Nurse. In *The Provok'd Wife* Hubert Carter gave a masterly character sketch as Sir John Brute; Ethel Irving as Lady Fancyfull was justly admired; and Sir Edmund Gosse had the warmest praise for Margaret Halstan as Lady Brute.

It is worth remark that upon the revival of *Love for Love* in April, 1917, this was probably the first time that Congreve's comedy has been given in its entirety, since we know that at the original production the excellent scene in Act III between Foresight and Scandal was omitted, although it is difficult to see how this could have been managed without leaving a very sensible gap in the action. During the eighteenth century Congreve's comedies, as indeed nearly all the older plays, were terribly cut and mangled, for which blood-letting Jeremy Collier's diatribe must be held to be at least partially responsible. Rarely, certain excisions were not only permissible but advantageous. Even in the days of Betterton himself the opening scene, a dialogue between two servants, Paulino and Ernesto, of *The Orphan* was omitted, "for that scene has nothing to do with the rest of the play, and has many years been cut out in the representation without the least maim to the action"; *The Laws of Poetry, as laid down by the Duke of Buckinghamshire,* London, 1721. In The Preface to *Don Sebastian,* 4to, 1690, Dryden mentions that he prints *Above twelve hundred lines* which were *cut off from this Tragedy* in representation. These were *judiciously lopt* by Mr. Betterton to *whose care and excellent action* the poet expresses himself as greatly obliged. None the less, the Earl of Dorset, no mean judge, who *read the Tragedy twice over before it was Acted* sent Dryden word that the play was so admirable *that he was displeased any thing shou'd be cut away.* (See *Dryden The Dramatic Works,* edited by Montague Summers, vol. vi, 1932, pp. 21 and 24.) It may be remembered that when *The Duchess of Malfi* was issued in 1623, a decade or so after the original production, it was published " with diuerse things Printed, that the length of the Play would not beare in the Presentment ".

For another reason Southerne was obliged to cut out the scene in the Fifth Act between the Abbé and Sir Anthony, upon the production of his brilliant comedy *Sir Anthony Love ; or, The Rambling Lady,* at Drury Lane in November, 1690, although the play languished in consequence of this excision. The fact was the amorous overtures of the old Abbé to the handsome young gallant were felt to reflect more overtly than would be allowed upon the homosexuality of Dutch William and his minions.

The whole question of Restoration prompt-books and the prompter's cuts—apart from questions of politics and personalities—is a study of extreme interest, of which I will say little more now, as I am dealing with it in detail in a later chapter. In my article *A Restoration Prompt-Book,* reprinted in *Essays in Petto* from *The Times Literary Supplement,* I described in some detail how Charles Booth, the prompter of the Theatre Royal, used the pruning-knife upon Shirley's *The Sisters* for a production of *circa* 1669–1670. A few odd lines of unimportant dialogue have been struck through here and there, but the omissions actually are trifling, and obviously intended to quicken the action of the play. In Act III the song " Beauty, and the various graces " is marked for omission. An appropriate couplet has been provided to round off Act II.

In the Sion College copy of *The Cardinal* fifteen lines of dialogue between Valeria and Celinda, Act I, Scene 2, were scored through by Booth, but unfortunately he did not complete his work on this particular quarto.

The Restoration quartos of *Hamlet,* 1676, 1683, 1695, and 1703, are exceedingly interesting, as the lines left out in presentation are appropriately marked in the printed text. Mr. Hazelton Spencer has dealt with these in his study *Shakespeare Improved,* 1927, pp. 174–187, as also more recently in a paper *Seventeenth-Century Cuts in Hamlet's Soliloquies,* 1933.

In the autumn of 1919 The Phoenix put forth its first programme : *The Duchess of Malfi ; Marriage A-la-Mode ; The Fair Maid of the West* (*Part I*) *; Don Carlos* ; and *Volpone.* Mr. William Archer, umquhile a dull dramatic critic, at once arose in fierce censorial wrath, bellowing " Why revive old rubbish ? ", in effect making himself as supremely ridiculous as he was obviously unintelligent and obtuse.

The Duchess of Malfi was given at the Lyric Theatre, Hammersmith, on 23rd and 24th November, 1919, with Cathleen Nesbitt as the Duchess, and Edith Evans Julia, rôles which in Restoration days were played by Mrs. Betterton and Mrs. Gibbs (Mrs. Shadwell).

Marriage A-la-Mode, at the Lyric Theatre, Hammersmith, 8th and 9th February, 1920, proved a triumphant success. There was a revival of this play at the Birmingham Repertory Theatre on 14th April, 1928. I am privileged to give a photograph of a scene from this production.

The Fair Maid of the West, Part I, was presented at the Lyric Theatre, Hammersmith, on 11th and 12th April, 1920.

It had been decided to replace *Don Carlos* by *Venice Preserv'd,* and accordingly Otway's masterpiece was produced at the Lyric Theatre, Hammersmith, on 28th and 30th November, 1920. Ion Swinley was Jaffier; Baliol Holloway, Pierre. The scenes of the doting senator and rampant courtezan were restored in their entirety. Stanley Lathbury acted Antonio; and Edith Evans, Aquilina.

Volpone was produced at the Lyric Theatre, Hammersmith, on 30th January and 1st February, 1921. Baliol Holloway, Volpone; Ion Swinley, Mosca; Margaret Yarde, Fine Madam Would-Bee; an unforgettable performance.

Love for Love, at the Lyric Theatre, Hammersmith, 20th and 22nd March, 1921.

The Witch of Edmonton, at the Lyric Theatre, Hammersmith, 24th and 26th April, 1921. Ion Swinley, Frank; Sybil Thorndike, the Witch; Russell Thorndike, the Familiar—two very eerie and grue figures; Edith Evans, Anne Ratcliffe—in her mad scene extraordinarily fine.

Bartholomew Fair, at the New Oxford Theatre, 26th and 27th June, 1921, a panoramic host of good things.

The Maid's Tragedy, at the Lyric Theatre, Hammersmith, 13th and 15th November, 1921. Ion Swinley, Amintor; Sybil Thorndike, Evadne; Isabel Jeans, Aspatia; most excellently done.

The Chances, by His Grace the Duke of Buckingham, at the Shaftesbury Theatre, 29th and 30th January, 1922. Margaret Yarde very great as the Bawd.

All for Love, at the Shaftesbury Theatre, 19th and 20th March, 1922. Produced by Edith Craig. Ion Swinley, Marc Anthony; Edith Evans, Cleopatra. A very exquisite and striking production.

Amphitryon, at Daly's Theatre, 28th and 30th May, 1922. Ben Field, Sosia; Marda Vanne, Phaedra; an inimitable pair. Laughter holding both his sides.

The Rich Jew of Malta, at Daly's Theatre, 5th and 6th November, 1922. Baliol Holloway, the Jew; and Ernest Thesiger, Ithamore.

'Tis Pity She's a Whore, at the Shaftesbury Theatre, 28th and 29th January, 1923. Ion Swinley, Giovanni; Harold Scott, Bergetto; and Moyna Macgill, Annabella.

The Alchemist, at the Regent Theatre, 18th and 19th March, 1923. Baliol Holloway, Subtle; Margaret Yarde, Dol Common; H. R. Hignett, Tribulation; and Stanley Lathbury, Ananias. This masterpiece was masterly acted.

The generous co-operation of Sir Thomas Beecham made it possible for The Phoenix to produce at the Shaftesbury Theatre on 24th and 25th June, 1923, *The Faithful Shepherdess,* a thing of rare beauty.

Sir Thomas arranged and conducted the music; Miss Edith Craig produced the pastoral. Murray Kinnell, Thenot; Henry C. Hewitt, Alexis; Frederick Ranalow, the God of the River; Cathleen Nesbitt, Amarillis; Isabel Jeans, Cloe; and Harold Scott, the Satyr.

On 29th June, 1923, The Phoenix gave at the Regent Theatre a special matinée of *Volpone* in aid of the funds of the Incorporated Stage Society.

At the Regent Theatre, on 18th and 19th November, 1923, *Edward II*, with Duncan Yarrow as the King; Ernest Thesiger, Piers Gaveston; and Gwen Ffrangcon-Davies, Queen Isabella.

The Country-Wife, on 17th and 18th February, 1924, at the Regent Theatre. Baliol Holloway, Horner; Ernest Thesiger, Sparkish; Stanley Lathbury, Sir Jasper Fidget; Athene Seyler, My Lady Fidget; Colette O'Niel, Mrs. Squeamish; Louise Holbrooke, Old Lady Squeamish; and—a superb performance—Isabel Jeans, Mrs. Margery Pinchwife. The play was received with great and deserved applause.

At the Regent Theatre, on 30th and 31st March, 1924, *King Lear*. Hubert Carter, Lear; and Leon Quartermaine, the Fool.

In the prospectus of The Phoenix, September, 1923, *The Way of the World* had been announced, but in view of the production of this comedy at the Lyric Theatre, Hammersmith, there was substituted *The Old Bachelor*, which was given at the Regent Theatre, on 1st and 2nd June, 1924. Heartwell, W. J. Rea; Bellmour, Esmé Percy; Belinda, Laura Cowie; Silvia, Stella Arbenina; and Lætitia, Isabel Jeans.

In June, 1924, The Phoenix announced as the Programme for the following season, 1924–5, *The Silent Woman; The Assignation; The Orphan;* and *The Fatal Marriage*.

Unhappily there had for some time been stirring a spirit of domestic discontent, originated and all too actively energized by petty spite and meaner jealousies. Satisfactorily to continue work in so churlish an atmosphere was impossible. To enter into details here is needless. Suffice to say that our President, Lady Cunard, to whom The Phoenix owed so much, withdrew her patronage; we lost the valuable services of our Organizing Secretary, Miss Fredman; and for myself, I preferred in the future to take no part whatsoever in the proceedings of the Society.

At the Regent Theatre, 16th and 18th November, 1924, *The Silent Woman*.

At the Aldwych Theatre, 25th and 26th January, 1925, *The Assignation*.

At the Aldwych Theatre, 10th and 11th May, 1925, *The Orphan*.

At the Regent Theatre, 5th and 6th July, 1925, *The Rehearsal*.

The Programme for the Season 1925–6 announced *Doctor Faustus*, October, 1925; *The Gentleman Dancing-Master*, December, 1925; *The White Devil*, February, 1926; and *The Soldier's Fortune*, April, 1926.

At the New Oxford Theatre, 25th and 26th October, 1925, *Doctor Faustus*.

At the Regent Theatre, 20th December, 1925, *The Gentleman Dancing-Master*.

For a twelvemonth and more past it had been only too evident that the Society was crumbling. How cool was the reception accorded to *The Assignation* and *The Orphan* in particular may be gathered from contemporary newspapers. When, in spite of the fact that on 11th and 12th October, 1925, at the Scala Theatre, a brilliant revival of *The White Devil* had been given by The Renaissance Theatre, there was announced by The Phoenix for 11th and 12th April, 1926, at the Royal Court Theatre, *The White Devil,* to be produced by the veriest amateur, the Town declined to be so preposterously quizzed.

A matinée at the Chelsea Palace Theatre on 12th December, 1927, to provide funds for a revival of The Phoenix Society failed to achieve its object. It might not unfairly be observed that such plays as *Happy Families* and *The Admirable Bashville* seem very incongruous and not at all suited to this occasion.

The Renaissance Theatre under the directorship of Alice Fredman and J. T. Grein celebrated the Tercentenary of John Fletcher by the production at the Scala Theatre of three of his plays.

The Maid's Tragedy, 17th and 18th May, 1925. Amintor, Ion Swinley; Melantius, Baliol Holloway; Evadne Edith Evans. I am able to give as an illustration a photograph from my collection of Baliol Holloway and Edith Evans in the great scene of Act III.

Rule a Wife and Have a Wife, on 28th and 29th June, 1925. Baliol Holloway, the Copper Captain; Jeanne de Casalis, Margarita; Margaret Yarde, the Old Woman.

The Wild-Goose Chase, 19th and 20th July, 1925.

We may remind ourselves that these three plays, all of which were produced for the Renaissance Theatre by Frank Cellier, were prime favourites upon the Restoration stage. Charles Hart and Michael Mohun shone eminent in Amintor and Melantius; Mrs. Marshall was superlative as Evadne. In *Rule a Wife and Have a Wife* Hart acted the Copper Captain; Ann Marshall, Margarita.

On 11th and 12th October, 1925, at the Scala Theatre, *The White Devil* was produced for the Renaissance Theatre by Edith Craig. Esmé Percy, Brachiano; Cedric Hardwicke, Flamineo; Viola Tree, Isabella; and Laura Cowie magnificent as Vittoria Corombona.

At the Scala Theatre, 15th November, 1925, for the Renaissance Theatre, Esmé Percy produced *The Plain-Dealer.* The Widow Blackacre, Margaret Yarde.

In order to complete the full cycle of Congreve's plays the present writer independently organized under the Patronage of Lady Cunard and the late Sir Edmund Gosse a single performance of *The Mourning Bride* at the Scala Theatre on 22nd November, 1925.

NOTES TO APPENDIX I

The Play-House, A Satyr

[1] Of Robert Gould little is known save what may be gathered from his own writings. His life, indeed, seems to have been humble and poor throughout. In his younger days he was an inferior member of the household of Charles, Earl of Dorset and Middlesex, and lived in London. Later he found a patron and staunch friend in James, Earl of Abingdon, who employed the poet upon the family estate at Rycote, Oxon. He died in 1708, or early in the following year. Thereupon his widow, Martha, published his collected *Works* in two volumes, 8vo, 1709. Gould composed a large number of poems, most of which were included in *Poems, chiefly consisting of Satyrs and Satyrical Epistles,* 1689; second edition, 1697.

Gould also wrote two plays. *The Rival Sisters; Or, The Violence of Love,* a tragedy, was produced at Drury Lane in September, 1695; 4to, 1696. Publication advertised, *London Gazette,* 7th–11th November, 1695.

A second tragedy, unacted, *Innocence Distress'd; Or, The Royal Penitents,* was published, 8vo, 1737, by subscription for the benefit of the author's surviving daughter, Hannah Gould.

The Play-House "Writ in the year 1685" is to be found in the *Poems,* 1689, pp. 155–185, but the text here printed is from the edition of 1709, as being ampler and as having received the author's last corrections. Owing to this violent attack on the theatre and Thespians generally Gould found great difficulty in getting his play *The Rival Sisters* accepted for production. One is not surprised to learn that "*the two* Head Actors *of either Sex*", Betterton and Mrs. Barry, were heavily incensed, and the poet complains: "*I have descended even below my own Character (which for that Reason must needs be very low) to get my self and my Plays into their Good Graces : I put 'em in mind I was very Young when this* Satyr *was Written, and by Consequence cou'd not know the value of what I slighted.*" He even offered to omit from the new edition any couplets which offended. "*All that this cou'd obtain from the Mighty* Actress *was plainly to tell me,* She was not so good a *Christian* as to forgive; *and, indeed, I really and readily believ'd Her: For as I had not my self, so I never heard of any other Person that Accus'd Her of Vertue.*" Gould accordingly retaliated in kind, and snibbed the lady pretty sharply, bidding her "*take this along with Her, that 'tis to her own Unequall'd Pride and Inveteracy She owes the Addition of the* Third Part *of this* Satyr; *which is Calculated for Her Meridian only.*" With regard to Betterton, he somewhat naively remarks: "*As to the Man, I forgive Him his mistake for Injuring Me upon a Supposition, and expect from Him an equal Generous Usage, what Merit there is in that Place, belonging to Him only.*"

[2] The Rose Tavern was in Russell Street, Covent Garden, hard by the Theatre Royal. There are innumerable references to this famous house.

[3] Barbara Villiers, Duchess of Cleveland, born 1640, died 1709. Of this lady there is an excellent *Memoir of Barbara, Duchess of Cleveland* by G. Steinman Steinman, Esq., F.S.A., Printed for Private Circulation, 1871.

[4] By Edward Ravenscroft. This popular comedy was produced at Dorset Garden in November, 1681, and printed 4to, 1682. For the long and interesting theatrical history see *Restoration Comedies* (Introduction, pp. xxxi-xxxviii), edited by Montague Summers, 1921, in which I have reprinted the play.

[5] *The Dictionary of the Canting Crew* has: "Steenkirk, a Muslin-neckcloth carelessly put on, first, at the Battel of *Steenkirk,* afterwards a fashion for both Sexes." The French gained a victory over the English at Steenkirke, Belgium, on 3rd August, 1692. The French nobles hastily called to the field are said to have tied their cravats loosely and hurriedly, hence the new mode and its name.

[6] These two ladies, Moll Hinton and Moll Howard, are again and again very indecently handled in contemporary pasquils and lampoon.

[7] To Scower is to rampage the streets violently assaulting and assailing all honest folk decently walking and passing by; thus *The Dictionary of the Canting Crew* has: "*Scowrers,* Drunkards, beating the Watch, breaking Windows, clearing the Streets, *&c.*" Shadwell's comedy, The Scowrers, Theatre Royal, 1690; 4to, 1691; gives a very complete and realistic picture of these gentry and their blackguardly exploits. See *The Works of Thomas Shadwell,* edited by Montague Summers, 1927, vol. iv, pp. 79–150, with the notes.

[8] This popular farce by Thomas Otway was first given at Dorset Garden in December, 1676. It followed *Titus and Berenice,* and was published with that tragedy, 4to, 1677. At Covent Garden it was played as late as 1812, and could be seen for another twenty years at the minor theatres and in the provinces. See *The Works of Thomas Otway,* edited by Montague Summers, 1926, vol. i, pp. 181–212.

[9] Mrs. Behn's pantomime farce *The Emperor of the Moon* was produced at Dorset Garden, April, 1687, and published 4to, 1687. Second edition, 4to, 1688. See *The Works of Aphra Behn,* edited by Montague Summers, 1915, vol. iii, pp. 383–463, and pp. 494–498.

[10] Thomas Shadwell's *The Squire of Alsatia,* a comedy produced at Drury Lane, 4th May, 1688; 4to, 1688. See *The Works of Thomas Shadwell,* edited by Montague Summers, 1927, vol. i, Introduction, pp. cxcvi-ccv, and vol. iv, pp. 191–283 and pp. 415–427.

[11] *The Devil of a Wife; Or A Comical Transformation,* by Thomas Jevon, produced at Dorset Garden, 4th March, 1685–6; 4to, 1686. Rehandled, not without considerable loss, and made into a ballad opera of three acts by John Mottley and Charles Coffey, as *The Devil to Pay; or, The Wives Metamorphos'd,* it was produced at Drury Lane in August, 1731, with great success; 8vo, 1731 (three acts). Further curtailed and reduced to one act by Theophilus Cibber it became perhaps the most popular of all the ballad operas; 8vo, 1732 (one act).

[12] Mrs. Behn's comedy *The City-Heiress; Or Sir Timothy Treat-all* was produced at Dorset Garden, 15th May, 1682; 4to, 1682. See *The Works of Aphra Behn,* edited by Montague Summers, 1915, vol. i, Memoir of Mrs. Behn, p. xli, and vol. ii, pp. 195–300 and pp. 432–8.

[13] Aphra Behn.

[14] Joseph Haines published under his name *A Fatal Mistake; Or, The Plot Spoil'd,* 4to, 1696, a Play, which is almost certainly intended as a burlesque.

Sir Robert Howard is the author of six plays. His comedy *The Committee,* first produced at the Theatre Royal, Vere Street, in October, 1662, and published folio, 1665, in *Four New Plays,* was long deservedly popular.

It is Sir Robert who is aimed at here rather than either of his brothers, both dramatists, the Hon. Edward Howard and the Hon. James Howard.

[15] Dryden.

[16] Aphra Behn.

[17] John Banks, the author of eight tragedies, died in 1706. Two of his plays, *The Unhappy Favourite; Or, The Earl of Essex,* produced at Drury Lane in the autumn of 1681; 4to, 1682; and *Vertue Betray'd; Or, Anna Bullen,* produced at Dorset Garden, 5th April, 1682; 4to, 1682; kept the stage for many years.

[18] Thomas D'Urfey, 1653–1723.

[19] John Crowne, 1640–1712. His best play is generally esteemed to be the comedy of *Sir Courtly Nice; or, It Cannot Be,* produced at Drury Lane, 4th May, 1685; 4to, 1685. I have reprinted *Sir Courtly Nice* in my *Restoration Comedies,* 1921.

[20] Edward Ravenscroft, 1643–4—1707. His comedy *Dame Dobson; or, The Cunning Woman,* produced at Dorset Garden, 1st June, 1683; 4to, 1684; was unsuccessful, yet it is difficult to see why so excellent and amusing a piece should not have been favourably received. *Dame Dobson* is largely an adaptation of *La Devineresse* by Thomas Corneille and Donneau de Visé, which was first given at Paris on 19th November, 1679, and accorded the most enthusiastic reception, being played to thronging audiences for no less than five months. *La Devineresse* was issued in book form in February, 1680. Something of its popularity was due to the fact that in Madame Jobin (Dame Dobson) the poets plainly exhibited the notorious La Voisin, bawd and sorceress.

[21] Thomas Shadwell (Poet Laureate), 1641–1692.

[22] Elkanah Settle (City Poet), 1648–1724. Both Shadwell and Settle were notorious for their Whiggish fanaticism and furies, which very irreverently let fly at the noblest and greatest in the land.

[23] Thomas Otway was born 3rd March, 1652, and died 14th April, 1685 (Anthony Wood). *The Orphan; or, The Unhappy Marriage* was produced at Dorset Garden early in the spring of 1680; 4to, 1680. *Venice Preserv'd; or, A Plot Discover'd* was produced at Dorset Garden, 9th February, 1682.

[24] Nathaniel Lee, 1648–1692. *The Rival Queens; or, The Death of Alexander The Great* (Th'*Ammonian* youth) was produced at the Theatre Royal, January, 1677; 4to, 1677. For the reference to Alexander as son of Hammon see Quintus Curtius, *De Rebus Gestis Alexandri Magni,* iv, 31: "At tum quidem regem propius adeuntem [ad Hammonis oraculum] maximus natu e sacerdotibus filium appellat, hoc nomen illi parentem Jovem reddere affirmans." Plutarch, in his *Life of Alexander,* has a similar account. *Mithridates, King of Pontus,* was produced at the Theatre Royal, January, 1678; 4to, 1678.

Oldys in his MS. notes on Langbaine observes that Lee "was some years in bedlam by intervals". Wood tells us (iii, 112) that Lee "was put in Bedlam London, Sept. or thereabouts 1684". There are many contemporary references to and anecdotes of the poet's madness.

[25] Sir George Etherege, 1635–1691. Of his three plays, all comedies, *The Comical Revenge; or, Love in a Tub* was produced at Lincoln's Inn Fields, March, 1664; 4to, 1664. (A second edition the same year.) *She wou'd if she cou'd* was produced at Lincoln's Inn Fields, 6th February, 1668; 4to, 1668. *The Man of Mode; or, Sir Fopling Flutter* was produced at Dorset Garden, 11th March, 1676; 4to, 1676.

[26] William Wycherley, 1640–1715. *The Plain-Dealer* was produced at the Theatre Royal in December, 1676; 4to, 1677. Hart created Manly, the title-rôle.

[27] *Oedipus,* a tragedy, was produced at Dorset Garden in December, 1678; 4to, 1679. Dryden tells us: "I writ the First and Third Acts of *Oedipus,* and drew the *Scenery* of the whole *Play.*" The rest belongs to Lee. See *Dryden The Dramatic Works,* edited by Montague Summers, vol. iv (1932), pp. 343 sqq.

All For Love; or, The World well Lost was produced at the Theatre Royal during the first week of December, 1677; 4to, 1678. In his Preface Dryden points out that "The Fabrick of the Play is regular enough as to the inferior parts of it; and the Unities of Time, Place, and Action, more exactly observ'd than, perhaps, the English Theater requires". *Dryden The Dramatic Works,* ut supra, pp. 165 sqq.

The Kind Keeper; or, Mr. Limberham was produced at Dorset Garden on the 11th March, 1678; 4to, 1680. "It was permitted to be acted only thrice. The Crime for which it suffer'd, was that . . . it express'd too much of the Vice which it decry'd." Actually, the personal satire in the character of Mr. Limberham was felt to be too biting and keen-toothed. *Dryden The Dramatic Works,* ut supra, pp. 236 sqq.

[28] Almanzor in *The Conquest of Granada* is particularly intended. There is a good deal of very similar satire in *The Rehearsal* when Bayes introduces Drawcansir "a fierce *Hero,* that frights his Mistress, snubs up Kings, baffles Armies, and does what he will, without regard to numbers, good manners, or justice". See also in the same burlesque, Act II, scene 4, where Bayes exclaims: "There's now an odd surprize; the whole State's turn'd quite topsie-turvy, without any puther or stir in the whole world, I gad." See *The Rehearsal,* edited by Montague Summers, 1914.

[29] *The History of Timon of Athens, The Man-Hater,* Made into a Play by Thomas Shadwell was produced at Dorset Garden in December, 1677, or in January, 1678; 4to, 1678.

The History of King Lear, Reviv'd with Alterations by Nahum Tate, was produced at Dorset Garden in September, 1680; 4to, 1681.

The Tempest; or, The Enchanted Island, a comedy altered from Shakespeare by John Dryden and Sir William Davenant, was produced at Lincoln's Inn Fields, 7th November, 1667; 4to, 1670 (two issues). *The Tempest; or, The Enchanted Island,* Shadwell's operatic version of the Dryden and Davenant comedy, was produced at Dorset Garden, 30th April, 1674; 4to, 1674.

I have reprinted this mournival of adaptations. For *The History of Timon of Athens* see my edition of Shadwell's *Works,* vol. ii. For *The History of King Lear* see my *Shakespearean Adaptations,* 1922, which also contains *The Tempest,*

Dryden and Davenant. Shadwell's operatic *The Tempest* is given in Shadwell's *Works* (ut supra), vol. ii.

[30] Thomas Rymer, 1641–1713. In his *The Tragedies of the Last Age consider'd and examin'd*; 8vo, 1678; Licensed for printing, 17th July, 1677; this critic very sharply attacks *Rollo, A King and No King,* and *The Maid's Tragedy.* In *A Short View of Tragedy,* 1693, (but published in the winter of 1692) he gives Shakespeare the benefit of his attention. *Othello* is summed up as " a bloody farce ". To show how the thing ought to be done, Rymer obliged the world with *Edgar*; *or, The English Monarch,* An Heroick Tragedy, unacted; 4to, 1678; 4to, 1691; and as *The English Monarch*; 4to, 1693.

[31] We may compare in the Dedication of *A True Widow*; 4to, 1679; Shadwell's compliment to Sir Charles Sedley, " *whom I have heard speak more Wit at a Supper, than all my Adversaries, with their Heads joyn'd together, can write in a year.*"

[32] On 10th May, 1684, Titus Oates was laid by the heels at the instance of His Royal Highness the Duke of York in an action for *scandalum magnatum.* On 8th May, 1685, Oates was put on his trial for perjury, and an exemplary punishment followed.

[33] James Shirley, 1596–1666. For a decade after the Restoration Shirley's plays were popular, and it is impossible to devine why he became a very nayword and the pattern of the sorriest poetaster. Yet he is alluded to with scorn and contumely by Dryden, Oldham, Pope, and others. Thus in *MacFlecknoe* (published 1682) we have:

> *Heywood* and *Shirley* were but Types of thee,
> Thou last great Prophet of Tautology.

And a little later:

> From dusty shops neglected Authors come,
> Martyrs of Pies and Reliques of the Bum.
> Much *Heywood, Shirley, Ogleby* there lay,
> But loads of *Sh*—— almost choakt the way.

[34] D'Urfey, for whom see above note 18.

[35] Oldham, *A Satyr,* the Person of Spencer Dissuading the Author from the Study of Poetry, writes:—

> And so may'st thou perchance pass up and down,
> And pleasè a while th'admiring Court and Town,
> Who after shalt in *Duck-lane* Shops be thrown,
> To mould with *Silvester,* and *Shirley* there,
> And truck for pots of Ale next *Stour-bridg-Fair.*

Duck Lane, afterwards Duke Street, and then Little Britain, West Smithfield. " Duck Lane cometh up out of Little Britain, and falls into Smithfield, a place generally inhabited by Booksellers that sell second-hand books." Strype, Book III. There are many allusions, e.g. in Randolph, *Poems,* ed. 1668, p. 325; Howell's *Letters,* ed. 1737, p. 484; in Pepys, Garth, Swift, and others. Pope in his *Essay upon Criticism* has:

> Scotists and Thomists now in peace remain,
> Amid their kindred cobwebs in *Duck Lane.*

His note is: "A place where old and second-hand books were sold formerly, near Smithfield."

[36] Charles Hart upon leaving the stage at the Union of the two companies in 1682 retired to his country house at Stanmore Magna in Middlesex, and dying of the stone on 18th August, 1683, he was buried here 20th August. See *Roscius Anglicanus* by John Downes, edited by Montague Summers, pp. 16, 71, 72.

[37] The Union of the two Houses, Dorset Garden and the Theatre Royal, was effected in 1682. Thereafter the United Company played for the most part at the Theatre Royal, the more magnifical Dorset Garden being used mainly for operatic and spectacular productions.

[38] The following lines are particularly aimed at Mrs. Barry. Contemporary satires—and there are many—on this great actress display exceptional grossness and ill-nature. " That mercenary prostituting dame," so a *Satyr on the Players* sums up her character. See further *The Works of Thomas Otway,* edited by Montague Summers, 1926, vol. i, Introduction, pp. lxiii-iv.

[39] An actress of Killigrew's company. Little is known of this lady save that she was much admired for her beauty and that she was gifted with a pleasing voice.

She filled a large number of secondary but not unimportant parts. In *Tyrannick Love,* Theatre Royal, June, 1669, she sang the spirit Damilcar; in *The Conquest of Granada,* Drury Lane, Part II, January, 1671, she was Isabella, Queen of Spain; in June–July, 1671, she was Alleria in Corye's *The Generous Enemies,* Theatre Royal; at Lincoln's Inn Fields she acted in three of Dryden's plays; Amalthea, *Marriage A-la-Mode,* about Easter, 1672; the Abbess Sophronia, *The Assignation,* winter of 1672; Julia, *Amboyna,* May, 1673. At the same house she was seen as Arabella in Duffett's *The Amorous Old-woman,* spring of 1674. At the Theatre Royal, again, she was Alithea in *The Country-Wife,* January, 1675; Aurana in Fane's *Love In The Dark,* May, 1675; and Julia, daughter of Augustus, in Lee's *Gloriana,* January, 1676. She also acted Bianca in *Othello.* About 1677 she was by force of Love Erept the Stage.

[40] Thomas Betterton, 1635–1710. Betterton told Pope that he was apprenticed to John Holden the bookseller, whilst Gildon says that Rhodes was Betterton's employer. There are extant at least two volumes which bear the imprint of Thomas Betterton, *A Mixt Poem . . . upon the Happy Return of His Sacred Majesty Charles the Second,* 1660; and *The Muses Joy For the Recovery of that weeping Vine, Henrietta Maria,* 1661.

[41] The dramatists thought highly of Betterton's judgement. In the Preface to *Don Sebastian, King of Portugal,* 4to, 1690, Dryden acknowledges that his play as written was too long to be presented entire, and pays the great actor an immortal compliment: "*Above twelve hundred lines have been cut off from this Tragedy, since it was first deliver'd to the Actors. They were indeed so judiciously lopt by Mr.* Betterton, *to whose care and excellent action I am equally obliged, that the connexion of the story was not lost.*" See *Dryden The Dramatic Works,* edited by Montague Summers, vol. vi (1932), p. 21.

[42] James Nokes, the famous comedian, died 8th September, 1696. See *Roscius Anglicanus,* edited by Montague Summers, pp. 152–4.

[43] John Lacy, died 17th September, 1681. The original Bayes in Buckingham's *The Rehearsal.* Langbaine thus praises Lacy, he "perform'd all Parts that he undertook to a miracle: insomuch that I am apt to believe, that as *this* Age never had, so the *next* never will have his *Equal,* at least not his *Superiour*". See *Roscius Anglicanus,* ed. cit., p. 73.

[44] Thomas Jevon, 1652–1688. Jevon, who was a Catholic, in 1680 was living in the parish of S. Dunstan-in-the-West. Before he became an actor he was a dancing-master. On the stage he was noted for his grace of movement and agility, and was the first English Harlequin. He wrote one merry farce, *The Devil of a Wife,* to which allusion has been made above, n. 11. Langbaine, writing in 1691, mentions him as "A Person lately dead, and one sufficiently known to all that frequent the Theatre, both for his Excellencies in Dancing and Acting". See *Roscius Anglicanus,* ed. cit., pp. 216–17.

[45] The amours of Cardell Goodman, the actor, and the Duchess of Cleveland by whom he was kept, were notorious. Oldmixon very disrespectfully writes of Her Grace as follows (*History of England during the Reign of the Royal House of Stewart,* ii, f. 576): "This woman was so infamous in her amours, that she made no scruple of owning her lovers; among whom was Goodman the player, who so narrowly escaped the gallows some years after; and the fellow was so insolent upon it, that, one night when the Queen [Mary II] was at the Theatre, and the curtain as usual was immediately ordered to be drawn up, Goodman cry'd, 'Is my Duchess come?' and being answered, 'No,' he swore terribly, the curtain should not be drawn till the Duchess came, which was at the instant, and sav'd the affront to the Queen." *The Protestant Mercury,* 25th–30th June, 1697, announces: "'Tis said, Mr. *Goodman* is dead in the *Bastille* in *France.*"

[46] Mrs. Barry, who opposed the production of Gould's *The Rival Sisters.*

[47] Dulwich, of which Sir Walter Besant says: "There was, in fact, no more favourite place of resort for the better sort of citizens than Dulwich in the summer." *South London,* 1899, pp. 308–310. See also W. W. Hutchings, *London Town,* 1909, vol. ii, p. 1047, who, writing of Dulwich, remarks: "'The Green Man' was a favourite resort here in the eighteenth century [and earlier], being convenient to a saline spring which attracted a number of valetudinarians."

[48] Joseph Haines, 1648–1701, the famous comic actor and buffoon.

[49] "*Hog,* a Shilling." *Dictionary of the Canting Crew.*

[50] Betterton.

[51] Mrs. Barry.

[52] Edward Alleyn, 1566–1626, the famous Elizabethan actor and founder of the College of God's Gift at Dulwich. The Chapel was consecrated by Archbishop Abbot on 1st September, 1616. On 13th September, 1619, Alleyn read and signed the deed of foundation in the chapel with much solemnity before a stately company. Provision was made for a Master, a Warden, four Fellows, six poor brothers, six poor sisters, and twelve poor scholars.

[53] Osmin, created by Betterton, is the hero of Congreve's *The Mourning Bride,* produced at Lincoln's Inn Fields, 28th February, 1697. In this tragedy Mrs. Barry created Zara.

[54] Similar charges of immorality are brought against Betterton in the contemporary *A Satyr on the Players,* first printed in my edition of the *Roscius Anglicanus,* 1928, pp. 55–59. Millbank, Westminster, " beginneth by Lindsey House or rather by the Old Palace Yard, and runneth up into Peterborough [afterwards Grosvenor] House." Strype, Book VI.

[55] Colley Cibber, in Chapter IV of his *Apology* writes that after the Union of the Theatre Royal and Dorset Garden, " One only Theatre being now in possession of the whole Town, the United Patentees imposed their own Terms upon the Actors, For the Profits of Acting were then divided into Twenty Shares, ten of which went to the Proprietors, and the other Moiety to the principal Actors, in such Sub-divisions as their different Merit might pretend to." Betterton's share was naturally large, and there were continual jealousies and quarrels amongst the sharing actors. In September, 1691, Betterton preferred to relinquish his share and go on salary. In the following year, however, he came into share again. The contentions and rivalry before long led to a definite split in the Thespian camp.

NOTES TO APPENDIX II

The Young Gallant's Academy

[1] Chapter IV concludes : " Some are gone to one *Theatre,* some to the other. Let us take a pair of Oars for *Dorset-stairs,* and so in to the *Theatre* after them as fast as we can."

[2] Shadwell's comedy *Epsom-Wells* was produced at Dorset Garden, 2nd December, 1672, and proved immensely popular. The play was published, 4to, 1673.

[3] *The Empress of Morocco,* a tragedy by Elkanah Settle, was produced at Dorset Garden, 3rd July, 1673 ; 4to, 1673. See my edition of this piece.

GENERAL INDEX

INDEX OF PLAYS